The Social Economics
of Jean-Baptiste Say

This book is a fine piece of academic work. The focus on Say and the intellectual milieu in which he made his significant contributions is most worthy of comment. The use of archival material and the translation of *Olbie* will be fine additions to the scholarly output. The author's record is excellent. The work will unquestionably fill existing gaps in the literature.

John Wood, Notre Dame University, Australia

Jean-Baptiste Say was one of the most influential and colourful figures of classical economics, but until now there has been no book devoted to the analysis of his economics. This book uses archival and published sources to place Say in context, at the confluence of several major currents in social philosophy. Familiar with the writers of the Scottish enlightment, especially Adam Smith, he was profoundly influenced by the Revolution, the Terror and Bonaparte's Empire, and by the republican thinkers with whom he associated. His long and varied career included periods as a journalist, an editor, a tribune under Bonaparte, a cotton manufacturer and, ultimately, as the most important political economist in France.

The Say that emerges from this study is far from being the one-dimensional populariser of Smith and proponent of libertarian ideology that he is often depicted as. Rather he is an eighteenth-century republican trying to knit together support for free markets and industrial development with a profound respect for the importance of the legislator, the administrator and the educator in the creation and maintenance of civil society.

This book contains the only English translation of the full text of *Olbie*, Say's utopian novel written in the style of Rousseau for an academic competition sponsored by the Institut National and published in 1800.

Evelyn L. Forget is professor of economics at the University of Manitoba in Canada. She has published several articles on classical economics and is currently writing a study of representations of economics in utopian fantasy.

Routledge Studies in the History of Economics

The Social Economics of Jean-Baptiste Say

Markets and virtue

Evelyn L. Forget

London and New York

First published 1999
by Routledge
2 Park Square, Milton Park, Abingdon, Oxon, OX14 4RN

Simultaneously published in the USA and Canada
by Routledge
270 Madison Ave, New York NY 10016

Routledge is an imprint of the Taylor & Francis Group

Transferred to Digital Printing 2005

© 1999 Evelyn L. Forget

Typeset in Garamond by
Prepress Projects, Perth, Scotland

British Library Cataloguing in Publication Data
A catalogue record for this book is available
from the British Library

Library of Congress Cataloging in Publication Data
    Forget, Evelyn L., 1956–
    The social economics of Jean-Baptiste Say : markets and virtue /
    Evelyn L. Forget.
    p. cm. – (Routledge studies in the history of economics : 30)
    Contains the only English translation of the full text of Olbie.
    Includes bibliographical references and index.
    1. Say, Jean Baptiste, 1767–1832. 2. Markets. 3. Virtue.
    I. Title. II. Series.
    HB105.S25F67   1999
    330.15'3–dc21   98-47366
    CIP

    ISBN 0–415–20308–2

Printed and bound by Antony Rowe Ltd, Eastbourne

For Ian McDonald

They constantly try to escape
From the darkness outside and within
By dreaming of systems so perfect that no one will need to be good.
But the man that is will shadow
The man that pretends to be.

T. S. Eliot, Choruses from *The Rock*

Contents

PART II

Figures

Acknowledgements

My debts are many.

I thank those people who were generous enough to read and to comment on various parts of the manuscript: Philippe Fontaine, R. Hébert, Sam Hollander, Rick Kleer, Ian McDonald, John Ridpath, Margaret Schabas, Evert Schoorl, Andrew Skinner and Philippe Steiner are among many other colleagues at professional meetings and conferences where I rehearsed parts of the argument. Arnold Heertje has been most generous in making his knowledge and his library available to me. Robin Hoople, whose humanist sensibilities were severely tested by my economist's prose, read the entire manuscript and offered suggestions and encouragement. Richard Lobdell, whose proofreader's eye is better than mine, read the entire manuscript. My colleague Anthony Waterman has a superb critical sense, and I have benefited immensely from his knowledge and from his attempt to make me write more clearly and more persuasively.

To my family, friends and colleagues, I apologise that M. Say has appeared at many social events to which he was not invited. My daughter, Angela, has lived with his ghost for most of her life and is heartily weary of the eighteenth century. Sister Virginia Evard, who offered the hospitality of St. Benedict's Monastery and who understands better than me the difference between pride and humility, I thank for a gift of which she is unaware.

Finally, I thank the Social Sciences and Humanities Research Council of Canada and the Institute for the Humanities at the University of Manitoba for their generous support of the research upon which this book is based.

Evelyn L. Forget
May 1999

Part I

1   Introduction

In 1820, 14-year-old John Stuart Mill spent nearly a year in the south of France with the family of Samuel Bentham, brother of the philosopher Jeremy. On his way through Paris, both going and returning, John passed some time at the house of Jean-Baptiste Say, whom he had met during Say's brief stay in England after the peace.[1] The young man affectionately described Say in his journal (A. J. Mill 1960), and in his autobiography refers to 'M. Say, the eminent political economist' as 'a man of the later period of the French Revolution – a fine specimen of the best kind of French republican, one of those who had never bent the knee to Bonaparte though courted by him to do so; a truly upright, brave, and enlightened man. He lived a quiet and studious life, made happy by warm affections, public and private. He was acquainted with many of the chiefs of the Liberal party...' (J. S. Mill 1981: 61–3).

I want to tell the story of this 'best kind of French republican' by making use of one of Jean-Baptiste Say's own images. Say introduces the entrepreneur, that dynamic central figure of his economic analysis, in words seeking to describe an informational network before such an idea became commonplace:

> He is the intermediary between the capitalist and the rentier, between the scholar and the worker, between all productive classes, and between these and the consumer. He administers the work of production, he is the centre of many connections; he profits from what others know and what they do not know, and from all the accidental advantages of production. It is also among this class of producers, when events favour their skills, that are found almost all great fortunes.
>
> (Say 1803, III: 228)

Say was, himself, the central figure of a network with connections to a large family, to the major Parisian social thinkers of his period, to eminent scientists, physiologists and doctors, to publishers and writers, to entrepreneurs such as his brother Louis, who made the family fortune in sugar, to politicians of various stripes not excluding Bonaparte and to the British economists and social writers Jeremy Bentham, T. R. Malthus, James Mill and David Ricardo. He was present at the most important social gatherings of moderate republicans, wrote from the same perspective when he was an editor of *La Décade*,[2] took up a position as Tribune under Bonaparte, all before he left Paris in 1804 to establish a cotton mill and to try to put into practice his economic doctrines. All of these linkages and connections gave him a particular perspective on economic and social analysis, and they allowed him to profit intellectually 'from what others know and what they do not know'.

This book is not intended to be an exhaustive account of Jean-Baptiste Say's economics. It does not trace all of the influences upon his thought, nor does it delineate all of the implications of his analysis. I shall begin with an early period of Say's intellectual development, between Terror and Empire, that roughly encompasses two of the principal texts for which Say is known: *Olbie, ou essai sur les moyens de réformer les moeurs d'une nation* (published in 1800) and the first edition of the *Traité d'Économie Politique* (1803). My goal is to suggest the existence of a transition in Say's social thinking between this early period when he created a social analysis heavily influenced by *idéologie* and a later period of his intellectual life, beginning more or less with the publication of the second edition of the *Traité* in 1814 and continuing to develop throughout the rest of his life, during which, under the influence of the British economists and the political debates surrounding the Restoration government, he took a much more consciously liberal line.

Olbie allows us to place Jean-Baptiste Say in the context of a very prolific and politically significant intellectual and social milieu. In the period during which Jean-Baptiste Say was actively developing the first edition of his *Traité d'Économie Politique* (1803), he was affiliated with the *idéologues*, a group of writers and scientists defined by Pierre-Louis Roederer[3] as 'soldiers of the philosophical party' (see Lutfalla 1991: 16).[4] The term *idéologue* is used in this volume to refer to these individuals who coalesced around the moral philosophy of Destutt de Tracy and the physiology of P.-J.-G. Cabanis and applied the method of the Encyclopaedists to all of the human sciences. It seems axiomatic that people ought to be allowed to name themselves, but I have chosen not to use Tracy's neologism *idéologiste* because *idéologue*, the term invented by Bonaparte and used by intellectual adversaries as a term of opprobrium, has triumphed in the secondary literature.[5]

Resembling Tracy and Roederer, contemporaries who also contributed to the development and institutionalisation of economic analysis, Say developed a social analysis self-consciously based upon a sensationalist philosophy drawn from Condillac, explicitly used the method of 'analysis' that was seen as fundamental to any scientific investigation, borrowed the insights, methods and metaphors of physiology, and addressed the fundamental problem of complex organisation that all *idéologues* thought they were facing in one form or another. Ideological[6] physiologists wondered how to account for the apparent fact that the human body, which was newly seen as a complex of highly differentiated systems, managed to function as a coordinated system. Moral philosophers, including J.-B. Say, used the human body as an analogy for society, and addressed the problem of how to maintain political order in a republic comprising individuals with apparently divergent interests.

An overview of the argument

This book deals with an issue that lies at the heart of classical economics: if society functions in an orderly way, must we assume that someone or some group of people has planned matters well by constructing and imposing functional legislation and social institutions? Or did the social order come into being and does it continue to survive in spite of, rather than because of, individual intentions?

If this really is a central question of classical economics, we can see much of nineteenth-century political economy as an attempt to deal with the questions raised by the French Revolution. After the destruction of the *ancien régime*, how should social philosophers and politicians go about re-establishing and maintaining social order? One answer to that question emerged from David Hume[7] and Adam Smith and their contemporaries: individuals, they claimed, pursuing their own very distinct and often opposing interests would bring about an order that they had no intention of establishing. Moreover, as time passes, those institutions that emerge and are, in some sense, successful will remain, whereas others will gradually whither away.

This particular reading of classical economics establishes the idea of spontaneous order as a key insight. However, this raises a problem for the interpretation of Jean-Baptiste Say's work because he has often been portrayed as nothing but a continental populariser of Adam Smith (see Blaug 1986: 212); and yet, spontaneous order plays a very minor role in his social analysis. Why, one might ask, should this be so?

I claim that Say was quite aware of the idea of spontaneous order. He simply constrained its use to the marketplace, building his society instead upon the ideas that had come to him in various forms from the physiocrats and, more directly, from the revolutionary thinkers with whom he associated. These specifically French sources embody the idea that social order is a consequence of good legislation and, even more importantly, good education designed to subordinate individual self-seeking behaviour to the social good by teaching people their true interests that are, in more cases than not, harmonious.

Now, this is not an obvious case to make because Say begins his most important work in political economy, his *Cours Complet d'Économie Politique Pratique* (1828–9), with a statement that seems to support my claim that the idea of spontaneous order lies at the heart of classical economics and that he agrees with it:

> Dugald Stewart has argued forcefully, in his *Elements of the philosophy of the human mind*, that it has long been imagined that social order is entirely the effect of art; and that wherever defects are apparent in this order these are necessarily the consequence of a lack of foresight on the part of the

legislator, or by some negligence on the part of the magistrate charged with the supervision of this complicated machine. From this is born the plans for imaginary societies such as Plato's *Republic*, More's *Utopia*, Harrington's *Oceana*, etc. Each has believed it possible to replace a defective organisation with a better one, without paying attention to the fact that there exists in societies a *nature of things* that is independent of the will of man, which we cannot arbitrarily ignore.

(Say 1843: 1)

Moreover, Say is perfectly well aware of the centrality of the pursuit of individual self-interest:

...if we set aside the interior relations between the members of a family that can be considered as forming a single individual because their interests are common, and the purely personal relationship of a man with his Creator that one can hardly consider as part of the social body, all social questions reduce to the valuation of reciprocal interests.

(Say 1843: 2–3)

However, Say, I argue, does not take the next step.

Individual interests, properly understood, are, according to Say, generally harmonious, in the same way that the 'true interests' of the individual organs in a human body cannot be other than harmonious. Just as it is in the interest of the heart and the liver to keep the host body alive, it is in the interest of the individual organs of the social body to maintain the health of a society. And a healthy society is an ordered society:

Political societies...are living bodies, just like human bodies. They only exist and survive through the actions of the organs of which they are composed, just as an individual body only survives through the action of its organs. The study of the nature and functions of the human body has created a set of ideas, a science to which has been given the name *physiology*. The study of the nature and function of the different parts of the social body has similarly created a set of ideas, a science to which has been given the name *political economy*, but which might better be named *social economy*.

(Say 1843: 1)

And what of those cases in which the interests of the individual organs of the social body appear to be in opposition? That requires, according to Say, the recognition that these issues are 'the province of morality, of legislation, perhaps of speculative politics, as much as the province of political economy' (1843: 4).

Although Say recognises that the study of political economy suggests that 'in most cases, it is best to leave men to themselves because it is thus that they best develop their faculties' (1843: 16), it does not follow that they cannot benefit from understanding those laws that govern such development. In particular, 'what man has no interest in understanding the strengths and the weaknesses of the social position into which fate has cast him?' (1843: 16). More to the point, 'people and governments ignorant of their true interests persecute one another for insignificant or absurd dogmas and declare war through jealousy or in the belief that the prosperity of another is an obstacle to their own happiness' (1843: 10). The study of political economy, because it would teach people their true interests, would demonstrate to them that true interests are harmonious. It is the duty of legislators, of social philosophers and of political economists to teach individuals their true, and harmonious, interests.

Moral and intellectual education is, however, aided by industrialisation:

> Industry...renders indispensable the relationships between men; it teaches them to help one another instead of destroying one another as in the savage state that has so unreasonably been called the state of nature; it mellows morality while procuring comfort; in showing men what they have to gain from joining together, it is the cement of society.
>
> (Say 1843: 12)

Despite his apparent approval of Dugald Stewart's distinction between the made order and the grown order and despite his qualified support of *laissez faire* in economic matters, J.-B. Say is the product of a very different current of social thought. He is the true heir of the physiocrats, of the natural law philosophers and, most importantly, of the proponents of *idéologie*, all of whom recognised a central role for the learned administrator in the creation of an ordered society. If I can return for one instant to the parallel Say draws between physiology and political economy, I might remark that Say's model of the physiologist was the physician who was charged with the task of curing the body and the soul when either was disordered. Similarly, the task of Say's political economist, or his legislator trained in the truths of political economy, is to restore the health of the social body – a health not guaranteed without the intervention of the professional.

If this orientation is apparent in the *Cours Complet*, written towards the end of his life, it is even more apparent in Say's early writing, especially the first edition of the *Traité* (1803) and his own imaginary society *Olbie* (1800a). Despite the profound challenges that Bonaparte's Empire raised for an entire generation of social philosophers, challenges that are reflected in Say's later emphasis on the need to curb the power of government to reduce the threat of tyranny, there remains at the heart of Say's political economy an inescapable and essential role for an active public administration assisted by the services of an intellectual élite.

The idea that Say's own intellectual orientation may have undergone a transition between the early perspective just described and a better articulated liberalism later in his life ought not to come as a surprise. The secondary literature shows a quite noticeable split with several commentators attributing to Say a nascent liberalism [usually citing evidence from the mature work, such as the later editions of the *Traité* and the *Cours Complet* (1828–9)], and others maintaining that Say's republicanism was very distinct from what later came to be called liberalism. Philippe Steiner (1997), for example, has argued that Say's political analysis was quite different from that of the physiocrats and focused on the legitimation of government and on the need for a dynamic citizenry to control the excesses of government, and Breton and Lutfalla (1991) find in Say the roots of liberalism. Moravia (1976: 1473) has called attention to the need to study the relationships among the writing of Say, Daunou and Tracy and the beginnings of nineteenth-century liberalism, and it is this task that motivates Welch (1984: 198n3). By contrast, Donald Winch has emphasised the subtleties of political orientation, especially in Britain, at the end of the eighteenth century (see Winch 1978; 1983; 1996), as have a number of historians keen to discourage a too prompt tendency to label (Burrow 1988; Mandler 1990; Sack 1993). However, the convenience of a ready category into which to slot the emerging political orientation keen on economic freedoms lures too many of us to recognise in Say an incipient liberalism, without documenting the ways in which Say was very much of an earlier period (Welch 1984; Staum 1987 and 1996; and, alas, Forget 1993).

This investigation leads us to ask whether the notion of a congruence between economic liberalism and a political orientation in which the state alongside the family and various voluntary organisations such as 'clubs' (although not, perhaps, churches) plays an essential role in disseminating civic virtues may be a more apt characterisation of Say's outlook early in his life. However, the more important possibility is that we may find, in the body of Say's writing, evidence for this perspective alongside a more clearly articulated need to contain public authority, with both views differently emphasised at different times of his life. What we will most certainly not find is clear evidence of an abrupt transformation similar to that which befell Saul on the route to Damascus; Say always maintained evidence of his debt to *idéologie* and, even at an early stage in his life, had some recognition and concern for those issues that began to play a larger intellectual role in nineteenth-century liberalisms. The change is one of emphasis, not of kind.

To some extent, the literature has always implicitly recognised the unique and pivotal role played by Say and, indeed, by *idéologie*. Meek (1973), Hecht (1986) and Lutfalla (1991) have placed Say's economics somewhere between physiocracy and classicism. I shall argue that it is surely not coincidental that Say, in correspondence with James Mill, Ricardo and Malthus, was fleshing out the details of the law of markets at precisely the same time that the political and philosophical orientation of many of the *idéologues* was undergoing change. That a widespread change of political orientation occurred, probably during the Empire and was made manifest when the Restoration allowed the publication of many new books, seems uncontroversial. Richard Fargher (1952:

220–38), for example, has documented the fundamental impact of Bonaparte and the Empire on the changing spirit of the age, and this orientation is reflected in scathing correspondence between Andrieux and J.-B. Say (Kitchin 1966: 93). Kennedy (1978: 190) documents Tracy's similar disdain for Bonaparte after the declaration of Empire, but this change can also be seen in purely intellectual matters. It is during this period that Maine de Biran, the psychologist best known for studying consciousness and the internal life of the mind, abandoned *idéologie*. This is the period when Kaiser finds evidence of a 'growing élitism' in the writing of Tracy and Roederer (Kaiser 1980), and Welch sees a new emphasis on the belief that *industrialisme*[8] in the sphere of production and economics would provide a new set of guarantees for political liberty in the work of Tracy (Welch 1984: 157f). It is not surprising, I think, that a desire to limit the power of government might have accompanied Bonaparte. It is, perhaps, a bit surprising that Robespierre was not a sufficient inducement.

The argument in brief

This book is divided into two sections. The first section argues the case for the above perspective. I begin by providing a brief biography of Jean-Baptiste Say and also by introducing some of the formal and informal institutions that gave shape to *idéologie*, most especially its publication venues, its place in the salons, its role in the *Institut National* and the political events of the period that gave it substance and edge. Not only do these chapters provide some context for Say's preoccupations, they also help to document his personal connections with *idéologie*. Chapters 4 and 5 introduce the philosophical, psychological and physiological arguments of the leading philosophers of *idéologie*, including especially Tracy and Cabanis as well as the writers, such as Condillac, from whom they drew inspiration. Chapter 6 establishes the connection between moral philosophy and physiology in ideological thought by documenting the peculiar form that the social body metaphor took in *idéologie*. It demonstrates the link between sympathy and moral education, and illustrates the theme by reference to Say's *Olbie* and Tracy's 'Quels sont les moyens...?' (Tracy 1798c). Chapters 7 and 8 argue that Say's *Olbie* is fundamentally influenced by the preoccupations of *idéologie* by demonstrating how his proposed solutions to poverty and his analysis of gender reflect characteristic ideological concerns. In particular, Say argues that social and political stability require the active intervention of an intellectual élite charged with the dual tasks of educating the population and creating institutions appropriate to the amelioration of poverty. Chapters 9–13 examine some aspects of Say's social economics and attempt to determine how the economic analysis continues to reflect some ideological preoccupations throughout Say's life, while simultaneously developing an integrity and relevance independent of *idéologie*. Chapter 14 examines the extent to which *idéologie* is useful in a consideration of Say the economist.

The second section of the book presents four documents in translation, prefaced by an introduction that discusses the two literary traditions into which *Olbie* falls. *Olbie* was an academic work submitted to the *Institut National* with the hope (says Monsieur Say) 'of being useful', but its young author would hardly have declined the academic recognition that accrued to winners of such contests that were well-established rites of passage for aspiring intellectuals. It was also a very odd little utopian novel, written in a popular style of the period usually attributed to 'Rousseaux des ruisseaux' (gutter Rousseaus). *Olbie* was intended to be widely read.

Each submission to the morality prize competition sheds light on both the political and the intellectual environment and also upon the development of economic analysis. Roederer's address instructs contestants to consider the institutions that are most appropriate to the inculcation of public morality. Say's *Olbie, ou Essai sur les Moyens de Réformer les Moeurs d'une Nation* is accompanied by Say's handwritten reflection on *Olbie*, composed after his significant work in economic analysis had been completed, in which he reconsiders the topic and gives some indication of the way in which a mature Say would have approached the question. And, finally, Tracy's 'Quels sont les moyens...?' (Tracy 1798c) offers an alternative answer to Roederer's challenge.

Roederer's speech of 15 Vendémiaire Year 6 [6 October 1797] (after the antiroyalist coup of Fructidor) makes the claim that the *Institut* takes it for granted that, since 1789, a consensus has emerged in favour of the Revolution, individual rights, liberty and property, and that political and civil institutions therefore need not be considered by the contestants. Incidentally, Roederer offers a pious address on the virtues of industrialism, and makes very clear his own and, he claims, the *Institut*'s position that civic virtue and industrialism are intimately connected.

Say's contest entry illustrates the state of his thinking on the topics of industrialism, social class and gender, the relationship between civil society and economic progress and that between civic virtue and economic analysis before he published the first edition of his *Traité d'Économie Politique* in 1803. *Olbie* demonstrates the intellectual debt he owed to the Enlightenment[9] philosophers and, more specifically and directly, his *idéologue* contacts. Without trying to create a homogeneity that does not exist among this loose association of scholars who travelled under the label of *idéologie*, we can determine the extent to which Say shared their preoccupations. Like Roederer, Say was more concerned with the political, economic and sociological aspects of *idéologie* than with the sensationalist ideas of Tracy or with the physiology of Pierre-Jean-Georges Cabanis, who were the leading philosophers of the movement.

Say's handwritten memoir is a fascinating document for an intellectual historian because it allows the mature Say to confront the still idealistic Say and to reconsider his youthful exuberance. The document does betray the encroaching cynicism of experience, but it also demonstrates the extent to which Say maintained an allegiance to the ideas of *idéologie* throughout his life. Education he saw as one of the keys to public morality in his youth; with age, education became fundamental. The notion of human perfectibility was reined in by many more years of experience, but belief in both economic and intellectual progress was still maintained as a capstone of his philosophical orientation. One difference that does appear is the way in which education is considered. In *Olbie*, people had to be educated with respect to their true interests. Say never rejected that claim, but the emphasis in this latter piece is on the role of universal education of the citizen in constraining the power of governments and the universal threat of tyranny.

Finally, Tracy's essay was not a contest entry, but rather an attempt on his part to clarify his own ideas on the question posed. The response he creates is less optimistic about the potential effectiveness of moral education and is more committed to the need to constrain self-interested behaviour on the part of individuals through the establishment of strong institutions. Both Tracy and Say, however, share one fundamental perspective with Roederer: all three see a role for the intervention of an intellectual élite in the creation of public morality either in the form of institutions created and imposed by administrators or in the form of direct public education, or both.

2   A brief biography of Jean-Baptiste Say (1767–1832)[1]

Jean-Baptiste Say, the eldest of three sons, was born in Lyon on 5 January 1767 into a family of Protestant refugees. The family can be traced to David Say in the seventeenth century, a master tailor in Nîmes, who had six children. One of these children, Robert, who was born in 1614, had seven of his own, including Louis who became a cloth merchant. An Huguenot, Louis emigrated to Geneva. His grandson, Jean-Etienne, was born in 1739 and eventually embarked on a career as a commercial lawyer in Lyon in the employ of M. Castanet, also a Protestant of Nîmes. This business relationship soon turned more intimate when Jean-Etienne succeeded Castanet after marrying one of his daughters. Their three children, Jean-Baptiste, Horace and Louis, were destined for business careers (Lutfalla 1991: 17).

The second son, Horace,[2] was wounded in 1799 during the siege of Saint-Jean-d'Acre, where he served with distinction and died after the amputation of his right arm. The third son, Louis, died in 1840 in Paris, where he had retired after a very lucrative career as a sugar refiner in Nantes. Happy and successful in business, he began as a manufacturer of calico in Abbeville before he took over the Nantes sugar beet factory, which he transformed into a cane sugar refinery after the Napoleonic wars. Louis was the author of several books on economic matters that received considerably less attention than those of his more famous brother, in which he attempted to correct what he perceived to be the errors of Jean-Baptiste.[3] The latter was not entirely pleased with this development, and wrote to tell his brother as much. In 1822, Louis Say's *Considérations sur l'industrie et la législation sous le rapport de leur influence sur la richesse des Etats, et examen critique des principaux ouvrages qui ont paru sur l'économie politique* appeared, and Jean-Baptiste wrote to him that it was 'vexing', both from a personal and scientific perspective, that such a work might appear and confuse a badly informed public (Lutfalla 1991: 27–8). In 1827, Louis Say's *Traité Élémentaire de la Richesse* appeared, and Jean-Baptiste wrote 'I will not hide from you that I am annoyed by this new publication…you err; the nature of things perpetually contradicts you' (Say 1848: 543–5).

Say's father arranged for him a solid education. As a very young child, he excelled in a course in experimental physics offered by Lefèvre in Lyon. At the age of 9 years, Jean-Baptiste enrolled in a boarding school set up by two

Italian immigrants, Giro and Gorati, dedicated to innovative methods of education and scientific, as opposed to classical or religious, study. There, he came into contact with new ideas that were beginning to revolutionise natural science.

Financial difficulties required Say to withdraw from the school, accompany his family to Paris and take up employment. Nevertheless, as soon as the opportunity arose, his father sent Jean-Baptiste and Horace to England in 1785 to learn the English language and to study commercial affairs, as was the fashion for young men of their background. Nothing could have had a more dramatic impact on the young Say than the opportunity to observe British commercial affairs at a time when her industries were just about to reap the effects of industrial technology and to conquer the markets of the world. Industrial expansion, the full effects of which would not be apparent for some time, was imminent. Whatever setbacks and industrial crises Jean-Baptiste would witness over the course of the rest of his life, and they were many and significant, he never lost the faith in industrial development that he first acquired during his youth. This enthusiasm for industrialism characterised all of his writing in political economy. Being able to read Adam Smith in English was undoubtedly one important consequence of this visit to England, but it was of relatively small importance beside the profound impact that witnessing the benefits of economic development had on his subsequent career.

This early sojourn in England was the occasion of a striking event that reappeared in a chapter of his *Cours Complet d'Économie Politique Pratique*, thirty years later, with the odd title 'Taxes that generate no revenue for the Treasury'. During his stay, Say boarded at the small village of Croydon near London. One day, his landlord appeared and proceeded to board up one of the two small windows that allowed light into his room. Say protested and demanded to know why he should be deprived of the sun that gave him so much pleasure. The landlord responded that he had no choice in the matter because he was not about to pay the window tax; one window would simply have to go. Say did without the sunshine because of the tax, but the Treasury was no richer on account of the window that was eliminated. The tax had cost Say the window, but his sacrifice made the Treasury no better off. This experience became an often told anecdote, which Say reported on many occasions to explain his early attraction to political economy, not to mention the need for sound fiscal management on the part of the public sector.

Say returned to Paris after the death of his English employer. Despite his own desire for a literary career, he bowed to his father's wishes and continued his commercial apprenticeship. In 1787, Say found employment in an insurance company directed by Clavière, who was later to become Minister of Finance. His suppressed desire to pursue a career in the arts rather than in commerce found expression in his fondness for amateur theatrical performances. Say was never to become wealthy but never lacked the comforts of middle-class life, and he claimed not to value money beyond the freedom it gave his mind and character. From Clavière, he borrowed a copy of Adam Smith's *Wealth of*

Nations, which he found so powerfully attractive that he purchased and annotated his own copy which was ultimately presented to the Academy of Moral and Political Sciences by his grandson Léon Say on 7 January 1888. He was later to attribute his meticulous judgement to the habits of order that he learned in Clavière's austere office.

Say's first publication appeared in 1789, a pamphlet entitled *Sur la Liberté de la Presse*. In later life, he evinced a certain amount of discomfort with this early effort, condemning its rashness and poor style. Nevertheless, it did attract the attention of Mirabeau, who employed Say on the staff of his republican newspaper, the *Courrier de Provence*. Despite his claim that this position brought him nothing but the opportunity to process subscriptions (Say 1848: 556, 'letter to Dumont'), it in fact brought Say into direct contact with the ideas of the principal French writers of the period.

In 1792, the invasion of Champagne called the French to arms, and Say enlisted in a company of young intellectuals organised as the *Compagnie des arts*. Almost immediately after his return, he married Mlle Deloches, who was the daughter of a respected lawyer, on 25 May 1793. This marriage, forged in the midst of the Terror, lasted close to forty years and was, by all accounts, a happy one. Marriage had the effect of establishing the young writer definitively in Paris.

The relatively small fortunes of both the Say and the Deloches families were compromised by the depreciation of paper currency. In fact, the financial catastrophes of the period destroyed the finances of Say's father, and constrained his own ability to establish himself in business. These setbacks encouraged him to establish, with Chamfort, Ginguené, Amaury Duval and Andrieux, *La Décade philosophique* in 1794. This became the first literary review to emerge from the chaos of revolution. Say contributed a number of articles and opinion pieces to this journal dedicated to literature, morality and politics. He served as general editor for six years. By 1807, when it was suppressed, the review had filled fifty-four volumes.

The founding of *La Décade* accompanied Robespierre's execution on 28 July 1794[4] (after an unsuccessful suicide attempt), which left a political vacuum. The Convention had closed the Jacobin clubs and had repealed the Decree of 22 Prairial (10 June 1794), which would have permitted arrest on any pretext, forbidden defence counsel and significantly broadened the applicability of the death penalty. Fearing for their own lives, Robespierre's enemies had forged a temporary alliance and, when he called for them to be purged, he was arrested. Desperate food shortages and high prices provoked serious unrest in Paris, and forced the Convention to produce a new Constitution. The *jeunesse dorée* (gilded youth) fomented opposition to Terror, and battled in the streets with the sans-culottes. The gilded youth were the indulged children of the professional classes, who had avoided conscription through family ties. Tolerated by both extremes, they were responsible for the re-emergence of moderate royalists. The White Terror began when Jacobins in the west and the southeast of France were massacred by royalist supporters. A royalist attempt to seize power in the Convention was thwarted when the army, under Bonaparte, was called in to suppress it.

The Constitution of 28 October 1795 limited suffrage to property owners, and established a system of government led by an executive Directory consisting of five members with control over the *Council of Ancients* and the *Council of Five Hundred*. This lasted four years, during which Bonaparte's military successes contrasted sharply with the disorder in Paris. The Directory was threatened by Jacobins in the Babeuf plot of April 1796, and in a *coup d'état* on 18 Fructidor (4 September 1797) royalist supporters were removed from the Directory. A further coup on 18 Brumaire (9 November 1799) abolished the Directory itself. Say was named a member of the Tribunate in December 1799, just as Bonaparte's Consulate ushered in an era that would see the demise of the Tribunate.

The 18 Brumaire coup was engineered by Bonaparte's brother Lucien, who was president of the *Council of Five Hundred*, and the Abbé Sieyès. Lucien's goal was to cement Bonaparte's power, whereas Sieyès intended to reform the constitution. The fifty-member legislative commission that managed the transition that brought Bonaparte to power included Cabanis, J.-B. Say, Daunou and Chénier (Welch 1984: 38). Lucien created so much distrust between the two councils that the Ancients passed a decree constituting Sieyès, Bonaparte and Pierre-Roger Ducos as a provisional government in the role of consuls. Bonaparte manoeuvred to replace Sieyès and Ducos with figurehead consuls Charles-François Lebrun and Jean-Jacques de Cambacérès, effectively giving himself sole executive power. Sieyès's new constitution came into power on Christmas Day 1799, but it did not limit Bonaparte's authority. Ironically, Bonaparte had just been granted more absolute power than Louis XVI had enjoyed before the revolution.

It did not take long for future trends to become clear to Say. As long as he remained a Tribune, he dedicated himself to financial affairs and economic reform. Say continued to protest against Bonaparte's usurpations, but actually made only a few contributions on relatively minor matters (Steiner 1991: 189n). His past connections with Bonaparte apparently allowed him to escape the purge of 1802, but Say left the Tribunate in 1804 just after the publication of the first edition of the *Traité d'Économie Politique*.[5] Despite an offer engineered by friends, Say turned down a lucrative position in the taxation bureaucracy, in part because he was unable to overcome a repugnance toward consumption taxes and in part because he sought in business the freedom and independence of mind that public employment had not offered.

Say trained himself in the techniques of all the various trades involved in cotton manufacture, with the aid of his son Horace who served as apprentice, by reading the *Encyclopédie* in the galleries of the *Conservatoire des arts et métiers*, where he would later teach. He soon established a mill in an old abbey in the *département de l'Oise*, then in a larger monastery at Auchy in the Pas-de-Calais. Actively taking on the roles, by turn, of engineer, architect, mechanic and so on, Say practised the methods of the various trades. He became aware of the importance of location in manufacturing, the inadequacy of canals and roads, and the difficulty a manufacturer faced in finding adequate markets. These preoccupations would reappear in his *Traité* and his *Cours Complet*, as well as his lectures.

In *Olbie*, written and submitted before Say took office as a Tribune, Say had proposed the creation of a *Traité d'Économie Politique*; he furnished his own in 1803. This was the first major work of Say as an economist. The *Traité*, even before the revisions that the work would receive in four subsequent editions during his lifetime, was already an original and a considerable work. Whatever opinion one might have of the doctrines of the author, his book was remarkable for its explicit statement of method, its clarity and simplicity of exposition and its attempts to illustrate the principles of theory with examples drawn from the real world. Adam Smith's *Wealth of Nations* had made considerable advances in articulating economic principles, but it did little (according to Say) to make itself accessible to those ordinary citizens who had not undertaken a detailed study of political economy. Say believed that essential illustrations were missing, and that some very important ideas were either missing or misplaced (Hashimoto 1980). Say attempted to put it all in order, and to create a vocabulary and codify definitions in order to give the science a solid base and clear limits. Political economy was, he claimed, the exposition of the laws that regulate the production, distribution and consumption of goods and services. These goods and services are produced by three great branches of industry: agriculture, manufacturing and commerce.

Say claimed that Bonaparte was responsible for crushing political economy during his rule, and his bitterness is apparent even many years later in the *Cours Complet* [(1828–9); 1843: 5, 26, 541]. He held Bonaparte responsible for the years when he could not bring out a new edition of the *Traité* and indeed claimed that his flight from the Tribunate was a response to a demand to rework the *Traité* to make it more consistent with 'political exigencies', a demand which he would not meet. It is not a surprise that Say's *Traité* provoked the would-be emperor. Say preached about liberty of commerce in the presence of the continental system, about a reduction of taxes in the face of the crushing increase of *droits-réunis* or consumption taxes, and about the evils of public borrowing and debt in the midst of a large increase in public expenditure.

The events that obstructed Say's economic opinions also affected his position as a manufacturer. Excessive duties on primary materials and onerous taxation rendered industry perilous. He left it all to an associate in order to return to Paris near the end of 1812. The memory of this time never entirely left him and can be discerned much later in a few uncharacteristically passionate words in subsequent editions of the *Traité* and the *Cours Complet*, the only ones that depart from the careful balance and objectivity of his writings. Even age did not appease this ferocious resentment. At the end of his life, Say can still be seen applauding the end of the Empire even though he had little regard for the Restoration that, in the event, did not take long to disappoint any hope he may have held.

Indeed, Say was never naive, and very early in 1815 he sought the advice of Thomas Jefferson, who greatly admired his writing on political economy,[6] about the feasibility of relocating to America for both political and economic reasons. Say saw in nineteenth-century America the entrepreneurial energy and potential for industrial expansion he had earlier observed in England, and was eager to play a role in the new nation. Jefferson, in a letter dated 2 March 1815, welcomed Say warmly and gave him a great deal of information about the economic and social geography of Virginia, but realistically advised him that, at almost 50 years of age, he would find the transition from Paris to Charlottesville onerous (Jefferson 1903–4, 14: 258–67).

Back in Paris, Say benefited from the liberties of 1814 and brought out a second edition of his *Traité*, longer and better argued than the first and much better received. Peace opened a new career in political economy. The analysis that assured continued recognition of Say was, of course, the law of markets, which appeared in almost final form in this second edition of the *Traité* after significant debate with James Mill, David Ricardo and T. R. Malthus. Say used this analysis to argue that nations only pay for products with products, and that any laws that prevent the purchase of commodities also restrict sales. All nations share in good, as in bad, fortune, whereas wars impoverish even the victor. Say argued that peace was the source of the wealth of nations, and he urged all nations to peace through a consideration of their own true interest.

The embargo ended; England, crushed under its debt and reduced to a regime of paper money, suspended payment in specie. The war had created shortages of capital, raising the return on investment but restricting the opportunities of potential entrepreneurs who were unable to access the investment capital they thought they could profitably use. Shortages of workers raised wages. These difficulties, however, did not emerge in the first years of peace that J.-B. Say used to his advantage to return to England on a semiofficial mission to observe the industrial state of the nation. He was received with much distinction by the leading English economists David Ricardo, T. R. Malthus and Jeremy Bentham. He even reports having been invited in Glasgow to sit in the chair of Adam Smith, a significant honour that touched him deeply. Upon his return, he submitted a very detailed report to the government (which has, apparently, not survived). At the same time, he published a pamphlet entitled *De l'Angleterre et des Anglais* (1815), in which he reasserted for a broader audience his antipathy towards the wastes created by poor public administration.

This work was followed by a book of which the title is almost longer than the text: the *Catéchisme d'Économie Politique ou Instruction Familière qui Montre de Quelle Façon les Richesses sont Produites, Distribuées et Consommées dans la Société; Ouvrage Fondé sur les Faits, et Utile aux Différentes Classes d'Hommes, en ce qu'il Indique les Avantages que Chacun Peut Retirer de sa Position et de ses Talents* (1815), an elementary treatise in which the author introduces the fundamental principles of the discipline to a popular audience by means of brief dialogues. At this particular moment in his life, J.-B. Say decided to step back and to examine the world with a philosophical eye, very much in the manner of Benjamin Franklin. He had printed, under the title *Petit Volume Contenant Quelques Aperçus des Hommes et de la Société* (1817), a book of thoughts, the naive style of which masked a caustic wit. This little book says more about his personality and private life than any of his other works: he was sceptical and enjoyed teasing and puncturing the pretensions of the pompous. This man whose wit was honed in the salons clearly enjoyed debate, and he exercised that wit at the expense of unprincipled people. Needless to say, periods of political turmoil offer many targets.

In an excess of enthusiasm, the Restoration government promised the suppression of *droits-réunis*, but was forced by fiscal necessity to retain them under the name of 'indirect contributions'. A commission, upon which J.-B. Say was asked to serve, was named to examine this question, but he refused to take part in work that he considered useless and he returned to his writing.

At almost the same time, the third edition of his *Traité* (1817) appeared, and two works on the *Navigation Intérieure de la France* (1818). Say attracted a great deal of public attention. He was read widely, and his lectures were in demand; he gave his first lessons at the *Athénée royal de Paris*[7] with great success and almost immediately produced the fourth edition of the *Traité* (1819), already translated into many languages and considered a classic throughout Europe.[8]

J.-B. Say was called to be professor at the *Conservatoire des arts et métiers* in 1819 after a remarkable work presented to Monsieur le baron Thénard on the utility of industrial teaching, in which he emphasised its importance to the orderly development of industry. His experience as a manufacturer helped him as a lecturer, a task in which he may have excelled had he not chosen to read his lessons from printed scripts. However, Say preferred to enlighten rather than to seduce, and considered the quality of the listeners more important than the quantity. His students had always been limited, and Say decided to broaden his appeal by publishing his conservatory lessons under the title *Cours Complet d'Économie Politique Pratique* (1828–9), a work better received by industrial workers than his *Traité* even though it lacked the order, the precision and the method of the latter. The *Cours Complet*, which emphasised illustrations, was very successful, even after the publication of the fifth edition of the *Traité*.

The French press was inundated with Say's ideas without the editors necessarily having any very clear idea of the source of some of the doctrines. Say lived quietly, surrounded by his family and a small circle of devoted friends. He received, once a week, the most distinguished visitors from France and abroad. Say was drawn into several well-publicised debates, in the context of which the details of Say's law of markets and his ideas concerning industrialism were sharpened. His three most important adversaries were Malthus, Sismondi and Ricardo.

The July monarchy offered Say a chair in political economy at the *Collège de France*, and he devoted himself entirely to this work. Say was never elected to any academic body in France, but he was a member of the major academies in Europe: *L'académie des sciences de Saint-Pétersbourg*, and those of Madrid, Berlin and Naples. There was a place set aside for him in the *Academy des sciences morales et politiques*, but he had barely 15 days to live after that body was re-established. The death of his wife had come as a terrible blow. His health began to decline, and he suffered a series of strokes. He succumbed to a fatal stroke on 15 November 1832, at the age of 66, leaving two sons and two daughters to mourn.

3   Jean-Baptiste Say and the institutions of *idéologie*

After 1789, Paris was left scrambling to recreate and resuscitate the formal and informal institutions that gave structure to the lives of its people. It is not surprising that many of the institutions of the *ancien régime*, perhaps most notably the informal institutions of that period, were retained and made to serve similar and new roles. Other institutions, such as the Academies and the religious institutions, could not survive the Terror, and were replaced. Sometimes, the new institutions were new in name only; they functioned very much as did their predecessors. Other times, they were significantly transformed. Both formal and informal institutions, especially the salon culture and the newspapers, were fundamental to the dissemination of *idéologie*.

Jean-Baptiste Say absorbed the fundamental tenets of *idéologie* at the homes of Mme Helvétius and other hostesses of the period, and wrote about them in *La Décade*. Many commentators have devoted enormous amounts of effort to untangling the various intellectual influences on the development of *idéologie*, including most notably Gusdorf (1978), Moravia (1968; 1974), Kaiser (1976), Azouvi (1992) and many others. However, there is little evidence that Say came to advocate *idéologie* by reading Locke or Condillac, or by working carefully through the physiology of Cabanis. He was undoubtedly well read, but the impression one has is that his *idéologie* came to him in a distinctly less linear and systematic way, mediated by the conversation of the salons, the articles in newspapers and broadsheets, the popular fiction of the period and, in general, through all kinds of informal social institutions and networks. *Idéologie* came to Say by means of his imagination and sensibilities, absorbed from the atmosphere in which he was immersed. Contrast this with Say's approach to economic analysis. There does exist evidence that his economic analysis was developed in a very systematic way, by reading, understanding and criticising his predecessors, including the physiocratic writers and Adam Smith. The purpose of this chapter, then, is to give some indication of the various institutions that favoured the dissemination of *idéologie*, and to draw some very tentative conclusions about the nature of their influence.

It is no simple task to determine who ought to be included under the rubric *idéologue*. *Idéologie* published no membership list. Its doctrines, to the extent that such can be discerned, were not shared equally by everyone travelling under the label. Many of the social and political reforms associated with its adherents, and especially its estimation of the importance of the environment on human behaviour, were widely advocated by individuals not associated with *idéologie*. Yet, there certainly did exist a movement known as *idéologie*, and that movement had a core of philosophers surrounded by a much larger group of peripheral members, who were associated more or less closely with *idéologie* and who shared many of the ideals of its central philosophers.

Idéologie has generated a very large literature, much of it devoted to determining the extent to which ideological thought and practices were 'revolutionary'. Moravia (1974) argued that *idéologie* represents the last gasp of the Enlightenment, and Gusdorf (1978) appealed to its status as the 'revolutionary conscience'. Baker (1990) emphasised the continuity that links the techniques of protest of the *ancien régime* with the political theory of the Revolution. Staum (1996: 5) argued that a balanced view would have to link Enlightenment discourse and the cultural practices of the *ancien régime* with the revolutionary context. Picavet (1891) is a classic analysis of *idéologie*, which has in recent years been supplemented by a number of excellent general studies including Head (1985), Kaiser (1976), Welch (1984) and Azouvi (1992; 1995). Particular philosophers have occasioned detailed studies by others, and institutions such as the *Institut National* have been examined by J. Simon (1885) and Staum (1996) and *La Décade* has been examined by Kitchin (1966) and Régaldo (1976). All of these contributions share one fundamental problem that they solve in various ways: they must determine whom to include under the label *idéologue*.

Any movement of significance has both an identifiable intellectual content and a framework of formal and informal institutions, which give it structure and coherence. In the case of *idéologie*, four of these institutions are worth examining in some detail. First, *idéologie* took shape in the salon culture; its social organisation was perpetuated by the salons hosted by Mme Helvétius, Cabanis and later Destutt de Tracy. Second, *idéologie* was codified and institutionalised in the academic culture provided by the *Institut National*. Third, *idéologie* was founded upon the idea that social harmony and order would ensue to the extent that enlightenment was widely dispersed, especially among 'la classe mitoyenne' of the population. *La Décade philosophique* attempted to serve a role of public education at the same time that it provided a forum for communication and for debate among *idéologues*. Fourth, the central goal of *idéologie* was to promote harmony and social order, and to that end *idéologues* had a political context and role. Jean-Baptiste Say can be identified with all four of these institutions.

The informal network of salon culture

The salons of Paris created an unofficial and non-hierarchical opportunity for intellectually inclined people to meet regularly outside the confines of academic and political institutions, and for them to share conversation of a particular sort in the home of a hostess with social acumen and some financial resources. There was usually a supper, sometimes a musical performance or a literary reading, and always conversation. The style was witty, light and bantering – a far cry from academic meetings, whether these were sponsored by the old Academies or the newly created *Institut National*. To be boring was a *faux pas*, punishable by banishment. The style and atmosphere, however, does not imply that nothing of substance was discussed. Very often quite serious subjects, such as the nature of the soul or the existence of God or the role of sensation or the principles of pleasure and pain would be introduced. The only check was that the conversation did not become plodding or heavy.

The role of the hostesses was to bring together interesting people and ideas, to include everyone in the conversation and to make sure that no one became pedantic or unpleasantly disputatious. Conflicts within the salons, which often led to ruptures and the creation of new groupings, occurred when hostesses invited antagonistic guests. To choose one's guests with some care was the consummate skill of the successful hostess (Kennedy 1989: 20–2).

The political role of the salons was, generally, not direct. However, the intellectual sociability created when a number of sympathetic individuals were brought together outside the responsibilities and constraints of official organisations, by a hostess capable of nurturing an analytical spirit and with a witty irreverence for existing authorities, worked effectively to undermine official institutions. At the same time, the company of individuals who shared similar aspirations and goals helped to create morale and energy. This atmosphere, when it was successful, created a potent opportunity for individuals to imagine what society might be like if certain changes were to occur. This, of course, is the very essence of *Olbie* and, indeed, of very much Revolutionary writing.

The salon of Mme Helvétius (Guillois 1894; Stephens 1922) at Auteuil was the only important salon to survive throughout the Revolutionary period, and it underwent a growing politicisation during the period leading up to the Revolution. In the last years of the *ancien régime*, it started to attract a younger crowd of political commentators and journalists including Dominique-Joseph Garat, Pierre-Louis Roederer, Pierre-Louis Ginguené, François Andrieux and Jean-Baptiste Say, who gradually began to replace the more famous *philosophes* (Welch 1984: 6). Also present were the poet André Chénier and his brother Marie-Joseph Chénier, a political dramatist who would become famous as the writer of Revolutionary songs. Destutt de Tracy and Pierre-Jean-Georges Cabanis, the two individuals most closely aligned with the emerging philosophical and physiological foundations of *idéologie*, were both associated with this group. Tracy moved to Auteuil in 1792, and Cabanis became a protégé of Mme Helvétius as a young medical student in 1778.

The new members were often introduced by Condorcet, who, along with Sieyès, was the most important Revolutionary theorist to frequent the salon. Before the Terror, the two collaborated on the application of the analysis of ideas to political issues (specifically the analysis of political rhetoric) in order to clarify the theory of natural rights that was the primary justification for the new order.

After Mme Helvétius died in 1800, the *idéologues* continued to meet in Auteuil at the home of Cabanis to whom she had bequeathed her property. In 1808, after Cabanis's death, Tracy moved the salon to Paris. After the Restoration, it became an important meeting place for the liberal opposition.

The salon hosted by Mme Helvétius, followed by Cabanis and finally Tracy, created an informal network among individuals with similar political and philosophical orientations. Without the academic pretence, charges of political patronage and stifling hierarchy of the Academies, which were abolished in 1793 in any case, younger men could be introduced to the pervasive culture of the salon and imbibe the utilitarianism of Helvétius and the sensationalism of Condillac, the political references of Sieyès and Condorcet, and the pervasive belief in the doctrine of human perfectibility associated with the last. Although the formal academic establishments, such as the Academies and the *Institut National*, were dominated by legal and medical professionals, journalists and populists dominated at Auteuil. It is particularly important to recognise that none of the salons existed in a vacuum. These were interlocking networks of individuals who attended different salons on different evenings of the same week, each of which would have a guest list with a particular flavour. Few of the guests at Auteuil had social lives limited to the interaction in Mme Helvétius's salon. For example, Say was among the thirty-six members of the salon of the Princesse de Salm (Figure 3.1) that met from the Directory into the Empire (Kennedy 1989: 25).[1] It was, nevertheless, in the Auteuil salon that the ideas read about and picked up at different gatherings would be brought together for discussion in an atmosphere of enlightened literary humanism.

The *Institut National* and *idéologie*

In contrast to the irreverence and informality of salon culture, formal academic institutions at the end of the *ancien régime* continued to reflect the absolute control of the state and the social hierarchy that characterised the rest of society.[2] Before 1764, secondary education was provided by religious orders and primary education was generally provided by lay teachers under the authority of the local bishops. The universities were similarly of ecclesiastic origin, but state control had gradually come to dominate before 1789. The *Collège de France*, which specialised in language and history, continued to operate throughout the Revolution. The *Jardin du Roi* became the *Muséum d'histoire naturelle* in 1793 and natural history was studied there under the direction of Georges-Louis-Leclerc Buffon until 1789, and then under the direction of Antoine-François de Fourcroy. Both were appointed by the state.

The seven Royal Academies were created between 1635 (the Académie française) and 1776 (the Société royale de médecine) by the monarchy. Each was chartered and patented by the government bureaucracy, which also appointed its secretaries and regulated the election of its members. Research

Figure 3.1 Drawing from *Oeuvres Complètes de Mme la Princesse Constance de Salm*. Paris, 1841. The members of the salon of the Princesse de Salm. 1, Mme La Princesse de Salm; 2, Melle, sa fille; 3, Le Prince; 4, Vigie; 5, Martine; 6, Montelle; 7, Pinkerton; 8, Langlès; 9, Brequet; 10, Preny; 11, La Lande; 12, Thuret; 13, Clavier; 14, Gehier; 15, Andrieux; 16, Lemontey; 17, Courier; 18, La Chabeaussrière; 19, Lantier; 20, Ginguené; 21, Mme Dufreney; 22, Raboteau; 23, Grudin; 24, Millin; 25, Talma; 26, Hendon; 27, Girodet; 28, Say; 29, Naigeon; 30, Guérin; 31, Laya; 32, Pajou; 33, Vernet; 34, H. Duval; 35, A. Duval; 36, Amaury Duval; 37, De Humboldt; 38, Decandelle; 39, De Tussieu.

was often directed. Monetary and other awards and privileges granted by the state and patronage of scientific investigation reinforced direct control in the form of official regulation. The Academies themselves were charged with the responsibility of arbitrating literary merit, censoring scientific writing and patenting inventions. They were, that is, both a reflection of the hierarchy and privilege of the *ancien régime* and a tool of its extension, at the same time as they attempted to create a society of merit and equality among members. This expression of privilege had led to the growth of a number of rival societies of 'amateurs' during the years preceding the Revolution.

The Academies were abolished on 8 August 1793, a month after Robespierre's ascension, when a number of deputies spoke against privilege and exclusivity and against the egoism of academics. The universities had already been closed before the end of 1792, when the government also stopped paying the salaries of schoolteachers. The Abbé Grégoire argued that the human mind has no need of an Academy (Kennedy 1989: 188) and that distinction between academics and non-academics was identical in spirit to the distinctions made between the nobility and the bourgeoisie, differential ranks which the Revolution had attacked. A recitation of individuals unjustly excluded from the academies over the years followed. The artist Jacques-Louis David seconded the motion on similar grounds. There was consensus with the claims earlier published in Marat's *Ami du Peuple* that the academies were establishments of luxury and were useless, censorious and discriminatory (Kennedy 1989: 188). The decision succeeded in throwing the educational system into further disarray.

The *Institut National des Sciences et Arts* was created on 25 October 1795, just before the Convention yielded to the Directory, as part of the programme of the Thermidorian reaction and, at least in part, to undermine the claim of counter-revolutionaries throughout Europe who argued that France had become barbaric. After the fall of Robespierre, the desire to combat Jacobinism without giving support to royalists or the Church led to the decision to implement some of the revolutionary proposals for educational reform in the hope of encouraging a 'rational philosophy'. In October of 1795, the Convention passed the Law of Third Brumaire an IV, which created primary schools in each canton, *écoles centrales* (secondary schools) in each department, an *école normale* in Paris and the *Institut National des Sciences et des Arts*, the aim of which was to create a living *Encyclopédie* (Palmer 1985: 230f).

The institute was divided into three classes: the class of Physical and Mathematical Sciences, the class of Moral and Political Sciences, and the class of Literature and Fine Arts. The second class was divided into sections: Analysis of Sensations and Ideas; Morality; Social Science and Legislation; Political Economy; History; and Geography. This second class created a place for the discussion and dissemination of the newly emerging social sciences, and many of the *idéologues* became members. The new institution's mandate was to create a forum for intellectual debate, correspond with similar institutions abroad, conduct and publish research and advise the Directory about literary and scientific matters.

The traditional view of the *Institut National* is provided by Moravia (1968; 1974; 1976) and Gusdorf (1978: 295), who wrote of an institution dominated by *idéologues*. J. Simon (1885) and Hahn (1971) point the way towards a view with more nuance, in which dissension occurred more often than blind agreement. Staum (1996) has followed this path, examining minutes and reports to demonstrate that, in fact, *idéologues* constituted a distinct minority within the *Institut National*. The dissenting factions within the *Institut* create an opportunity to sharpen our understanding of the context and content of *idéologie* because it is in the context of debate that ideas are formulated most cogently. As we shall see, the public morality prize competition is a case in point.

The *idéologues* soon came to constitute a very vocal minority of members of the second class. Virtually all the members of the second class adopted as a fundamental principle the need to create social and political stability, but not all the members advocated the same reforms or based their analyses on the same philosophical foundations. The Roman Catholic church still had advocates, and many others saw the pragmatic role that religion could play in limiting political upheaval. Other members of the class advocated systems of morality independent of the Church and yet not based on the materialism of Helvétius or the sensationalism of Condillac. Staum (1996: 5) argues that 'there were at least three or even four routes to stability – the path of the Idéologues, the route of the chastened ex-philosophes, the reactionary nostalgia of royalist conservatives, and the practices of Bonapartist pragmatists'.

The method adopted by the second class was 'analysis', by which was meant the decomposition of all ideas into their basic elements or 'facts' verifiable by the senses and their subsequent recombination into complex ideas. Based upon the theories of Condillac, Cabanis and Tracy delivered a series of lectures to the section studying the Analysis of Sensations and Ideas on the physiological and rational aspects of analysis, which formed the theoretical core of what became known as *idéologie*. Tracy argued that the knowledge of human understanding formed the basis of the art of communication (grammar), of logic, of teaching or instruction, of forming habits in a population (education), of morality and, finally, of regulating society (Head 1985: 31f). *Idéologie* would both explain social and political organisation and transform it in such a way as to maximise human happiness.

On 20 June 1796, Destutt de Tracy introduced the term *idéologie* to his colleagues in the class of Moral and Political Sciences at the *Institut National*, thereby formalising and giving a new impetus to a movement that was already well established by personal connections. He argued that the etymology of the term made it the appropriate descriptor of 'the analysis of sensations and ideas' that preoccupied his section of the class. In fact, the clumsy title given to Tracy's section by the legislators who established the *Institut* ('*Analyse des sensations et des idées*') provoked Tracy's search for an appropriate label for a science 'so new it does not yet have a name' (Tracy 1798a: 322). The importance of nomenclature in the progress of science had been emphasised by Lavoisier and Condillac, and Tracy considered and rejected a series of alternative descriptors. Condillac had settled for the term *métaphysique*, insisting only that 'facts' should be gathered and analysed using scientific procedures. Tracy rejected this possibility because the common meaning of *métaphysique* is

> a science which treats the nature of beings, spirits (esprits), different orders of intelligence, the origin of things and their first cause. Now these are not the objects of your research...Moreover, metaphysics strictly means something other than physics: yet the knowledge of the faculties of man, as Locke believed, is certainly a part – an important part – of physics, whatever (ultimate) cause one wants to ascribe to these faculties.
>
> (Tracy 1798a: 322–3; quoted in Head 1985: 32)

Condillac had also adopted the term *psychologie*,[3] but Tracy argued that this word literally meant 'science of the soul', giving the impression that the science concerns itself with first causes and spiritual entities rather than 'the knowledge of effects and their practical consequences' (Tracy 1798a: 324). Clearly, a new word was required for 'the science of ideas that treats ideas or perceptions, and the faculty of thinking or perceiving' (Tracy 1798a: 325), and Tracy coined the term *idéologie*.

This naming process had accomplished two goals. First, Tracy had defined the content of the science in behavioural terms by focusing on effects and consequences; and second, he equated 'ideas' with 'perceptions' and 'thinking' with 'perceiving'. This sensationalist doctrine placed limits on what is, in principle, knowable. Reliable knowledge in any field must, according to Tracy, be derived from careful observation and disciplined judgement. *Idéologie* becomes the primary science (sometimes, Tracy insists that it is the only science) because it establishes the appropriate methods for attaining certainty in applications, through its analysis of the fundamental operation of the intellectual faculties of human beings. Tracy also argues that the science of ideas is fundamental to all knowledge because

> ...nothing exists for us except through the ideas we have, since our ideas are our whole being, our very existence, the examination of the manner in which we perceive and combine them is alone able to show us in what consists our knowledge, what it encompasses, what are its limits, and what method we must follow in the pursuit of truths in every field.
>
> (Tracy 1798a: 286)

La Décade philosophique

It is not insignificant that Jean-Baptiste Say's first important piece of work was a pamphlet advocating freedom of the press (Say 1789). He began his career as a journalist. On 5 July 1788, the free publication of opinion was permitted by the monarchy in preparation for the Estates General. Over 600 pamphlets appeared almost immediately. The remaining constraints on the press during the Estates General were challenged by Brissot, who published the *Patriote Français*, and by Mirabeau, who published the *Courrier de Provence* (Kennedy 1989: 320). Volney's *Sentinel du Peuple* became the official organ of the Breton club, which was later transformed into the Jacobin club. Copies of some 2,000 Revolutionary newspapers, many of which lasted for no more than a single issue, survive today (Bellanger *et al.* 1969–76;[4] Kennedy 1989: 319ff.). This writing is ephemeral. It reacts to the immediate situation, and the stories, the papers and even the presses come and go at an almost inconceivable rate matched only by the tempo of political change.

The role of the press has been a matter of significant contention. Did the press shape public opinion, or was it merely the means by which information and opinions of the cafés, the clubs, the Assembly and private gatherings was relayed to the public? From our perspective, the debate is inconsequential. What is important is that various publications and organs did serve to cement the ties of the *idéologues* and to create a space in which debates could be aired, opinions supported or challenged and particular pieces of legislation attacked or reinforced. It was also the arena in which J.-B. Say honed his skills as a writer.

Book publication slowed considerably during the Revolution, and reading focused on pamphlets, posters, newspapers and broadsheets that could remain current with the tempo of political events (Kennedy 1989: 317). Newspapers took various forms; there was the official *Le Moniteur* and the counter-revolutionary *Actes des apôtres* among many others, and various kinds of scientific periodicals appealing to different audiences. The papers themselves were rapidly issued, often only a few pages in length and occasionally published on an erratic schedule. Sometimes, they were the work of a single individual. Frequent name changes occurred. In addition, the entire industry was subject to censorship of varying degrees over the course of the decade.

Newspapers of the *ancien régime* focused on relaying information and publishing book and theatre reviews. The latter remained an important part of most revolutionary newspapers, which combined these staples with often quite aggressive political opinion pieces. Although freedom of the press had been declared in 1789, all this meant in practice was the elimination of prior censorship and not freedom from subsequent punishment for defamation, which might take the form of confiscation of copies of the paper or destruction of the presses.

In 1792, the Commune of Paris ordered the closure of all antipatriotic newspapers, and repression became more general in 1794. Article 355 of the constitution of Year III (1795) stated that there would be no limitation of the press, unless circumstances 'make it necessary'. After Fructidor (Year V), this exclusion once again permitted broad censorship that was actually more thorough and devastating to opposition than censorship during the Terror. Newspapers kept closing and reopening under new names to escape surveillance and censorship. The government attempted to assure the loyalty of some papers (such as the *Moniteur*) by subsidising them and planting articles.

The *idéologues* also had their own organs of communication and dissemination, and chief among them was the periodical *La Décade philosophique, Littéraire et Politique*,[5] which was published from 10 Floréal an II (29 April 1794) until 30 Fructidor an XII (17 September 1804) and then with a couple of name changes until 1807. Edited by Jean-Baptiste Say from 1794 until 1800 followed by Amaury Duval, *La Décade* was owned and largely written by a team of six men, all of whom were relatively young (between 27 and 46 years of age at its foundation), all of whom had impeccable credentials as *idéologues*, and all of whom were to play significant roles in the *Institut* and in public administration between the Thermidorian reaction and the accession of Bonaparte. The administration of *La Décade* was complicated by the fact that the editor had no real role except that of coordinator. All decisions were to be made by the team of six, which theoretically (but rarely in practice) met every 10 days (that is, once a décade, or revolutionary week) to decide editorial matters.

Pierre-Louis Ginguené (1748–1816) played the leading role in assembling the team. Imprisoned during the Terror, he was released and then named a member and finally director of the Committee on Public Instruction (1795–8), he was a member of the class of Moral and Political Sciences (1796), ambassador to Turin (1798), where his support for the liberation of Italy hastened his recall, and Tribune (1800). In the last position, Ginguené showed himself one of the chief opponents of Bonaparte and was purged in 1802.

François-Guillaume-Jean-Stanislas Andrieux (1759–1833) was a poet and moralist, affiliated with the *Institut* and a member of the Tribunate, and was also purged in 1802. Despite his heartfelt support for the educational reforms of the revolution, Andrieux criticised the intellectualism of the *idéologues*, protesting in the pages of the *Décade* against 'la manie d'analyser' (Kitchin 1966: 12). The naturalist Georges Toscan (1756–1826) was a librarian at the Museum of Natural History, and he occupied himself with his garden, his family and his library instead of meddling in the affairs of the day. Ginguené found for Amaury Duval (1760–1838) a position on the Committee on Public Instruction that allowed him to write and from which he resigned to devote himself full time to his literary endeavours upon his election to the *Institut* (class of Ancient History and Literature) in 1811.

Joachim Le Breton (1760–1819) was an unfrocked priest who became a member and the secretary of the class of Moral and Political Sciences, and who then became a member of the class of Ancient History and Literature and perpetual secretary of the class of Fine Arts. Le Breton was described as a superb administrator but a scholar without originality (Kitchin 1966: 15). He was simultaneously head of the Bureau of Fine Arts and Minister of the Interior. As a Tribune, his remarks were less inflammatory than those of Ginguené and Andrieux and he escaped the purge of 1802. The purge of 1815, however, deprived him of his positions in the administration and in the *Institut*. He was murdered in Rio de Janeiro, where he had fled with other French refugees intending to found an industrial enterprise and an agricultural society. Jean-Baptiste Say, of course, constituted the sixth team member.

These owner/editors were supplemented by a stable of regular contributors, including Say's brother Horace and *idéologues* such as François Thurot and, less often, Garat, Fauriel, Volney, Cabanis and Destutt de Tracy. It is in this context that Jean-Baptiste Say came to maturity as a writer and editor. His ready and quite accessible syntheses of material from many different sources in *Olbie* and in his economic writing show evidence of the consummate newswriter.

The political context of *idéologie*[6]

One of the enduring achievements of *idéologie* is that a number of individuals associated with the movement worked to establish institutions that translated some of the ideals of the Revolution into political reality. Philosophers were associated, more or less closely, with different regimes that came into and fell out of favour. *Idéologie* is far from a simple reaction to political events, but the political context was, to some extent, partly the product of *idéologie* and partly the context within which it developed. One of the more interesting issues is the extent to which individuals associated with *idéologie* helped to bring Bonaparte to power, thereby establishing a regime that would lead to the suppression of the very institutions and ideas that the movement advocated. Indeed, the history of *idéologie* can be read as the story of recurring attempts of intellectuals to bring to power sympathetic politicians, who subsequently betrayed their ideals for political expedience.

After the publication of the Constitution in 1793, the language of natural rights began to be adopted to justify not only the rights of the propertied members of the Third Estate but also the unpropertied in general (Welch 1984: 23). Fearful that unscrupulous agitators would use the weapon provided by the rhetoric of natural rights to arouse the population, moderates saw their fears confirmed. Revolutionary crowds began to use the slogans and ideas that were originally intended to garner a larger share of power for the propertied in order to support anarchy and insurrection. After the fall of the monarchy, when the Girondin and Jacobin factions fought for leadership of the Republic, the Jacobins forged a temporary working relationship with the sans-culottes. Robespierre argued that intellectuals were no more than lukewarm and opportunistic supporters of the Revolution, and that artisans were its soul:

> Petty, vain men, blush if you can. The marvels that have immortalised this epoch of human history were brought about without you and in spite of you... While the artisan proved himself an expert in knowledge of the rights of man, the scribbler of books, almost republican in 1788, was stupidly defending the cause of kings in 1793.
>
> (Robespierre 1965a: 270)

The Jacobin ascendancy saw the rhetoric of natural rights used to defend economic controls such as the *maximum* (or price controls), and the Committee of Public Safety's calculated use of revolutionary terror. The moderates, a group that included the fledgling *idéologues*, grew increasingly alarmed throughout the Terror and particularly regretted (and in some cases denounced[7]) their own earlier use of the slogans based on natural rights.

The group supported the proclamation of the Republic but played no direct role in the Convention, taking a self-consciously neutral position. Unfortunately, their political opinions and insistence on procedural justice deviated from the Jacobin position, and many suffered exile, imprisonment or death. Condorcet died while hiding from the Committee of Public Safety, Cabanis was under constant surveillance, and Volney, Daunou, Ginguené, La Roche and Destutt de Tracy were imprisoned. The Terror instilled an unshakable support for civil liberties and for the rule of law in these individuals who became *idéologues*, but forced them to question the role of political rhetoric.

The Constitution of Year III prevailed from October 1795 until November 1799, and the period was one of bloody violence and domestic disorder. Between royalist intrigue on the one side and radical agitation in the form of Babeuf's Conspiracy of Equals on the other, the relatively moderate republicans who ran the Directory panicked and enforced a series of repressive measures. Many of the earlier terrorists were imprisoned and the sans-culottes disarmed, but the ruling body never really distinguished between the new wave of democratic clubs that emerged in 1797 and 1798 and the excesses of the Terror. They tended to equate dissent with subversion, and the essential instability of the period is reflected in the *coup d'état* of 18 Fructidor, which ended the First Directory by purging royalists, and in the law of 22 Floréal (a year later) that eliminated 121 newly elected Directors who were seen as too Jacobin.

Under the Directory, *idéologie* became a distinct intellectual entity and attracted a group of individuals who shared a common political and intellectual philosophy. They were resolutely anti-Jacobin, antiroyalist and anticlerical. They favoured a republic dominated by an educated secular élite. More importantly, they shared Tracy's conviction that a science of ideas was essential for the reconstruction of society, and that this science ought to be based upon the sensationalism inherited from Condillac. The common intellectual position of this group found an outlet in political activity.

The driving motivation of the *idéologues* was to re-establish order in the Republic, and many individuals associated with the *Institut* lent their support to the Directory despite some concerns about the political organisation and the absence of procedural justice. The *Institut* was closely tied to the Ministry of the Interior, and it furnished several departmental administrators and foreign ambassadors. Ginguené, Garat, Daunou, Cabanis and Chénier served in the legislative councils. *La Décade* consistently supported Directory policies, once the Constitution was voted by the Convention (Welch 1984: 37; Kitchin 1966). Say had originally expressed some doubts about the strict division of government powers (as had Daunou) and hesitated about prefixing the Constitution with the Declaration of Rights (undoubtedly concerned about the power this afforded Jacobin insurgents), but the periodical rallied to support the Directory. Horace Say, the political editor during this period, supported measures against émigrés and refractory priests. After the Babeuf plot came to light, he supported measures enacted against the Jacobins. The Fructidor coup in 1797 against the royalists was supported as was the purge of 22 Floréal, albeit somewhat more reluctantly. An anonymous editor wrote against the preparations for this latter coup, fearing another violation of the Constitution, but after 22 Floréal J.-B. Say wrote an editorial supporting the measures taken.[8] *La Décade*, under J.-B. Say's general editorship during this period, was even prepared to acquiesce to regulation and surveillance of the press – a particularly startling event given that Say's first published piece was a vociferous defence of freedom of the press (1789).

The dictatorial extremes of the Directory, however, became less tolerable to the *idéologues* and most supported the movement coalescing around Sieyès, who was elected to the Directory in May 1799. The intention of the conspiracy was to strengthen and centralise the government while maintaining the Republic, and Sieyès hatched a complicated plot to overthrow the Directory. Sieyès sought out Bonaparte, recognising that military force was essential, and Bonaparte actively courted the *idéologues* by making a symbolic trip to visit Mme Helvétius at Auteuil (Welch 1984: 38). Volney wrote articles praising Bonaparte in the *Moniteur*, which was another outlet for *idéologie* during this period.[9] The legislative commission that managed the transition included Cabanis, J.-B. Say, Daunou and Chénier. Unfortunately, the *idéologues*, who supported the Sieyès plot because they believed that a stronger central government was essential to the maintenance of the Republic, soon discovered that Bonaparte was not as easily managed as they expected. The support of the *idéologues* for the coup of 18 Brumaire was soon enough regretted as Bonaparte came to reject their philosophy and especially their political outlook.

Bonaparte easily outmanoeuvred the *idéologues*. Sieyès accepted the gift of a wealthy estate from the General, and was widely castigated for selling out principle for personal gain. Although Bonaparte was popularly seen as a pragmatic leader with great personal charisma, the intellectuals and academics who opposed him were blamed for their previous support of the corrupt Directory. This faction, however, was a significant voice in the Tribunate, in which they tried to block many of Bonaparte's attempts to consolidate power. They protested restrictions on legislative debate, the parts of the Napoleonic Code that were regarded as regressive and the establishment of special criminal courts. Say, as a member of the Finance Committee, tried to implement the requirement of an English-styled budget before funds would be released to Bonaparte, arguing that this would stem the movement towards dictatorship, but the Committee refused to endorse his report (see Chapter 10, note 7). *La Décade* reported favourably on the various protests in the Tribunate, but found little public support. Bonaparte was angered by the opposition of 'obstructionists' and mounted a campaign against those he labelled *idéologues* in a spirit mockingly similar to that of Robespierre:

> Metaphysicians are my *bêtes noires*. I have classed all that crowd under the denomination of *idéologues*...The word has caught on, I believe, because it was my own...Yes, they are obsessed with meddling in my government, those windbags! My aversion for this race of *idéologues* amounts to disgust.
> (Leroy: 160; quoted in Welch 1984: 39–40)

With the support of the Catholics and the royalists, Bonaparte easily purged the Tribunate in 1802.

A particular blow to the *idéologues* was the abolition of the central schools in 1802. Tracy, keen to protect these institutions, wrote a series of pamphlets de-emphasising the political implications of *idéologie* and arguing that ideological reasoning was essential to the development of the moral sciences. Because Bonaparte saw the moral sciences as part of the problem, these writings garnered Tracy little favour. The *Institut* was reorganised in 1803, and the class of Moral and Political Sciences suppressed (Staum 1996: 150). Although *La Décade* continued to advocate ideology as well as some economic policies contrary to official policy, it became increasingly docile after 1802 (Kitchin 1966). It was, however, too much a tool of the *idéologues* (according to Bonaparte) to avoid suppression in 1807. Volney, Cabanis and Tracy remained in the powerless Napoleonic Senate and Daunou became the archivist of the Empire, but 1800–15 were years of cultural and political isolation as counter-revolutionary attitudes became fashionable. Say, escaping the purge of 1802, left the Tribunate in 1804 to manufacture cotton.

Jean-Baptiste Say as *idéologue*

Despite the fact that the *idéologues* never constituted anything such as an organised sect, it is not difficult to establish Say as an *idéologue*. Both his social and intellectual network and his published works attest to his sympathies. Say was never a member of the *Institut National*, but the second class was suppressed in 1803 when Say was only 35, the same year that he published his first significant work in political economy – the *Traité d'Économie Politique*. His connection with, and indeed his post as general editor of, *La Décade* has already been explored. He was a familiar face at the salons of Mme Helvétius and of the Princesse de Salm, and he served as Tribune until 1804. All of these institutional connections should establish him as an *idéologue* beyond very much doubt. But Say, in a not uncommon stance during the period, declared himself 'a man of no party'. If a more solid link is required, one need only examine two key works – *Olbie, ou Essai sur les Moyens de Réformer les Moeurs d'une Nation*, written for the public morality prize competition sponsored by the class of Moral and Political Sciences of the *Institut* in Year VIII, and the forty-six page methodological introduction to the *Traité d'Économie Politique* first published in 1803 and maintained with only minor revisions throughout all later editions. That is the task of the subsequent chapters.

Olbie was published as Sieyès was handing the government over to Bonaparte, who was still believed to be a sympathiser of *idéologie*, and is a clear statement of Say's philosophical sympathies. Because it is a portrait of an imaginary nation that has just survived a revolution and is in the process of setting up institutions to support the republic, it focuses on the educational and political goals of the *idéologues*. The methods and goals of educational reform are clearly spelled out, as is the necessity of economic reform designed to eliminate great extremes of wealth and poverty. The importance of public ceremonies and structures designed to strengthen the commitment of citizens to the needs of the republic are emphasised. The signature anticlericalism of *idéologie* is present, as are the antiroyalist sentiments; and Say's great hopes for the Napoleonic régime, so soon to be dashed, are encapsulated in an advertisement written within months of Brumaire:

> As my principal desire, in composing this work, was to be useful, I had no choice but to publish it. What could be a more favourable time for the publication of a work on the morals of a nation than this, when two men, of eminent talent and morality unquestioned even by their greatest enemies, conceived of the project of founding a stable Republic on the observation of rules of morality, and were acclaimed by their fellow citizens as First Consuls? Certainly, it is in such a period that one is permitted to engage in dreams of a philanthropic imagination.
>
> (Say 1800a: ix–x; below, p. 197)

These dreams were soon disappointed, but they sustained Say while he put the finishing touches to his first major contribution to political economy to be published three years later.

4 Towards a psychology of rational individuals

Psychology attempts to explain human consciousness and conduct. It merges with philosophy when it deals with reasoning, thinking, perceiving, feeling and remembering. When it deals with behaviour, motivation and other determinants of action, especially when these are regarded as a function of the nervous system, psychology merges with physiology. It is difficult to discuss sensing, perceiving, reasoning and learning in isolation from one another, and it is equally difficult to discuss these processes apart from the motivational aspects of behaviour. But the natural historians of the eighteenth century noticed that even the distinction between the individual and the environment, which includes the immediate situation and past experiences, is somewhat arbitrary. Because individual organisms underlie group and social phenomena, the behaviour of individuals acting in groups cannot be neglected. That is, there are no clear boundaries between psychology, philosophy and the related social and biological sciences, and the wide-ranging writings of *idéologues* such as Cabanis and Bichat reflect this idea of the unity of human knowledge. Nevertheless, this chapter deals, somewhat artificially, with the origin of ideas, and it relegates closely related physiological, behavioural and ethical considerations to subsequent chapters.

It is significant that Jean Le Rond D'Alembert wrote, in the introduction to Denis Diderot's and Jean le Rond d'Alembert's *Encyclopédie* (1751–80), that 'nothing is more indisputable than the existence of our sensations'. *Idéologie* emerged from more than a century of sensationalist thinking that saturated multiple and varied sources. The *idéologues* reached into this bouillabaisse and plucked out luscious bits that they could incorporate into 'analysis'; they were not discriminating about their sources, but they were very much more inclined to cite some sources than others.

Idéologie drew its inspiration from two distinct lineages: (1) the empirical philosophers, including Francis Bacon, John Locke, George Berkeley, and their Continental counterparts such as Pierre Bayle and Etienne-Bonnot de Condillac, whose parentage they celebrated, and (2) the rationalist philosophers, who were descendants of René Descartes and Leibniz and whose ancestry they were less pleased to claim. The *idéologues*, however, were engaged in what Bacon, and later Newton, called 'experimental philosophy'. They drew inspiration from both rationalism and empiricism, but in the end were strictly aligned with neither. More to the point, *idéologie* shared what has long been recognised as perhaps the fundamental characteristic of Enlightenment philosophy (see Coleman 1996: 208): its leading scholars constantly repeated the doctrine that the senses, through observation and experience, are the source of all true knowledge, and yet the actual method of the period was more often theoretical than empirical.

This chapter begins with an exercise in iconology. By the end of the eighteenth century, at least insofar as the *idéologues* were concerned, Bacon and Descartes were far more important as symbols of particular sets of social attitudes than they were sources of true philosophical inspiration. Descartes and Cartesian rationalism had been captured by the Church and were being used to shore up the divine rights of monarchs, the power of the Church and the defence of privilege of all sorts, whereas the empiricists who claimed allegiance to Baconian principles often saw their epistemologies as preludes to moral treatises that supported social and political reforms. Next, we take a brief detour and examine the importance of the materialist philosophers LaMettrie and Holbach for *idéologie*. Again, these philosophers had a greater symbolic than real import for Condillac and his heirs because the critics of *idéologie* often used the extreme and naive writing of LaMettrie and Holbach as straw men in their rhetoric, attacking in the same breath Condillac's 'statue' and LaMettrie's 'man-machine'. Then, we look at the sensationalist philosophy of John Locke and Etienne Bonnot de Condillac, which was the principal inspiration for Tracy's *idéologie*, the subject of the final section.

Iconology: Descartes and Bacon

Rationalism is not a simple concept composed of a single set of ideas. Following Coleman (1996: 209), it is useful to distinguish between two sets of ideas that constitute rationalism, one dealing with the nature of the world and the other with epistemology. For the great seventeenth-century rationalists Leibniz and Descartes, the world was conceived as an orderly structure. The apparent chaos was either dismissed as errors of observation or, to the extent that disorder really exists, superficial. In any case, the fundamental, although perhaps hidden, reality is one of order. Consequently, a true understanding of reality must rely on the intellect to sift out the relevant 'principles' upon which to base a 'system' that will explain particular cases.

The rationalist tradition dates from the seventeenth-century philosopher René Descartes, who engaged in anatomical investigations and physiological experiments alongside his speculative discourse. Descartes's psychological theses are contained in the *Discours de la Méthode* (1637), the second and sixth of his *Meditationes de Prima Philosophia* (1641), and *Les Passions de l'Âme* (1641). The first work sets out the four rules for the pursuit of knowledge: to accept nothing as true unless demonstrated; to solve problems systematically by decomposing them into their elements; to proceed from the simple to the complex; and to review everything thoroughly. It also sets out the metaphysical aspects of his system, further developed in the *Meditationes*. *Les Passions* outlines his ethical views. *Principia philosophia* (1644) attempts to summarise a system of mechanical principles that underlies all natural phenomena. His controversial *Treatise on Man and the Formation of the Fetus* was published posthumously in 1664, and contains the principles of his psychobiological analysis.

Applying the method of scepticism and recognising the limitations of the senses, Descartes was led to ask whether there was anything absolute. He concluded that a being whose scepticism extends to its very existence is caught in a contradiction: that which doubts, that which thinks, must be. Even if the body is an illusion, and our actions and experiences unreal, the ideas of the mind must exist or doubt itself becomes impossible. That is, the first principle of philosophy accepts as fundamental that the being itself exists, and that existence is demonstrated by reason rather than matter. In parts V and VI of the *Discours*, Descartes outlines the discoveries he has made in the biological and physical sciences using his method. He refers to the work on the circulation of the blood conducted by a 'physician of England' (William Harvey) for those who require experimental confirmation of what is demonstrable by reason. He also advises that one ought to begin with reason and the immediate facts at hand before devising elaborate experiments because these become necessary only when knowledge is already well advanced.

Descartes established the dualistic idea that mind and body are separate, that the mind is unextended substance (and therefore immaterial) and the body extended substance (and therefore in a place). Because they are of entirely different substances, mind cannot be reduced to matter. That the mind comes to affect the body means that the two must be in intimate contact. This idea is introduced in the sixth *Meditation*, and elaborated in *Les Passions* in which it constitutes the entire subject. His major problem is captured in the question: how can an unextended substance (the mind) move an extended substance (a material body)?; or, more prosaically, how can an idea cause a muscle to contract? The apparent difficulty of establishing an answer to the problem led those who followed Descartes to adopt one of two positions: either they insisted that everything ultimately reduces to matter, or they claimed that everything reduces to mind. The more subtle thinkers claimed that everything either reduces to mind, or to matter, or to some presently unknown third option. Descartes did not solve the problem, but his analysis founded what became known as the dualistic tradition.

Descartes claimed that sensitivity, motion, extension, growth and decay are inherent in the body. Thought, however, resides in the mind. Thought determines voluntary actions and feelings (*Les Passions*: Article 17). Most of our perceptions are determined by the action of external objects on the sensory nerves, and feelings such as heat, cold, pain and hunger ensue (*Les Passions*: Articles 23–4). Emotions, however, are the property of the mind that is not of the body, but is in intimate contact with every part of the body (*Les Passions*:

Article 30). When the body dies, the mind (or soul, which for Descartes was the same thing) withdraws. While it lives, however, the soul must be able to regulate the flow of animal spirits along the nerves through the brain and back to the muscles along the nerves. This process was referred to as *undulatio reflexa* because the nervous system can be regarded as reflecting the animal spirits as it redirects their course to produce action. Descartes's best guess was that the pineal gland, unique because it is not duplicated on both sides of the brain, was the site of this control (*Les Passions*: Articles 31–2). In all cases, the passions result from the flow of animal spirits through the brain (*Les Passions*: Article 37). The soul's ability to direct the animal spirits results from the action of *will* that, through God, is free (*Les Passions*: Article 41). Human beings differ because brains differ (*Les Passions*: Article 39). Because animals have no rational minds, they can be regarded as machines that behave according to their properties and the nature of the forces acting upon them.

Descartes's method appeared to offer an alternative to the radical empiricism that Bacon's *Novum Organum* seemed to advocate. But the materialist aspects of his explanation of reflex as the link between sensation and action began a tradition that remained fundamental to physiological psychology, and that reappeared in Cabanis's physiology.

Descartes's analysis mutated into an elaborate Cartesian system against which eighteenth-century *philosophes* warred. On the surface, this battle was centred on Descartes's physics that, after Newton, was judged to be simply wrong.[1] The scientific debates focused on the method in which the systems of Descartes were set against the evidence of direct observation and experience, the method attributed to Newton and Bacon. Of course, Newton framed a good many theories and Descartes engaged in experimental investigation, but one might argue that the real debate, at least from the point of view of the *idéologues*, was not about method but rather about the nature of society.

The philosophers from whom the *idéologues* claimed to draw their inspiration were battling against Cartesianism on political and social, as well as scientific, grounds (see Pranchère 1996). After all, if human beings possess an immaterial soul and human beings are distinguished from animals on the basis of something that cannot be reduced to matter, there is no a priori reason for challenging the Church. Souls imply the existence of God. If there is a God, one must work harder to justify any attempt to limit the power of His earthly representatives. Similarly, if 'all brains are not created equal', can human beings be equal? What educational implications flow from the recognition that there are inherent differences between human beings that are the result of nature? The battle between the *idéologues* and the advocates of system was about far more than physics and method; it was about human nature, social theory (because individuals make up society) and governance. And Cartesian rationalism was seen by the *idéologues* to be one of the pillars of that supreme certainty of the natural order that characterised the eighteenth century.[2] Joseph de Maistre, for example, attacked the *idéologues* and their empirical forerunners from precisely this platform (see Pranchère 1996; Lebrun 1988).

Before we examine the empirical tradition that the *idéologues* did choose to acknowledge, it is essential to note the criticism of the Cartesian system offered by Pierre Gassendi (1592–1655). Gassendi was an esteemed philosopher with a large following, whose influential works formed the basis for the anti-Cartesianism of the eighteenth century. He became the centre of a revival of interest in Epicurus and Roman Epicureans, and published *Paradoxes Against the Aristotelians* (1624). Gassendi's attack on Descartes lasted six years, and it took the form of a series of rebuttals to which Descartes responded in print.

Gassendi adopted the Epicurean division of philosophy into three parts: logic, physics and ethics. In the first, he opposed Aristotelianism at every turn, seeking to replace Cartesian systems with observational science, and to accept nature, including human nature, as matter. This antirationalist line had the ultimate effect of confusing the boundaries between theories and 'facts' (not that either Descartes or Newton had managed to keep them entirely clear), and it allowed considerable theorising under the guise of 'general facts' in the eighteenth and nineteenth centuries (see Coleman 1996).[3] Gassendi advocated a sensationalist approach to knowledge, arguing that only data derived from the human senses could be the foundation for knowledge. In the area of physics, he defended a mechanistic explanation of nature and sensation. Yet, he was an ordained priest and not an atheist. He considered metaphysics an aspect of physics, and believed that he could discern the existence of God in the harmonies of the universe, and the existence of an immortal soul in the ability of human beings to reflect and to be aware of morality. In the area of ethics, he claimed that human happiness was not to be sought in this world, but rather in the next (Collins 1967: 45ff.). Gassendi was an important precursor of French materialism and, as such, an important influence on the development of ideological thought.[4]

In the same way that Descartes was known to the *idéologues* largely through the Cartesian system with which they battled, Francis Bacon and Isaac Newton were icons more than they were inspiration. Bacon's first major work, *The Proficiency and Advancement of Learning*, appeared in 1605 and served as an outline for the project undertaken more fully in *De Augmentis Scientiarum* (1623) and in the much more important *Novum Organum* (1620). He stated five goals: to set out the causes of ignorance and disagreement; to determine the nature and role of authority in scientific discourse; to indicate those areas of science that require further investigation; to set out an appropriate method of scientific investigation; and to determine which scientific projects are worth undertaking.

The causes of ignorance and disagreement in science he attributed in the first book of *Novum* to four 'idols'. The 'idols of the tribe' refer to basic human propensities towards error, such as the tendency to see system where none exists (i.e. to oversimplify) and the tendency to overrate the importance of particularly striking, yet unrepresentative, occurrences. The 'idols of the cave' are the intellectual traits of particular individuals. Some people focus on detail and others on generalities; some fasten on differences, and others on similarities. The 'idols of the marketplace' are errors for which language is responsible.[5] 'Idols of the theatre' are mistaken systems of philosophy in the broadest sense of that term. These systems may take the form of Scholasticism, against which Bacon formulated his analysis. They may also take the form of systems of the occult, against which Bacon argued that individual reports are insufficient because human beings are prone to credit the strange and the unexpected.

As to which works ought to be undertaken, Bacon was insistent that the value of a project is determined by its potential benefit to human beings. *Usefulness* was the watchword, and if a project is unlikely to be useful to human beings in the daily affairs of life there is little reason to undertake it (Bacon 1878: 135). The primary impediments to true knowledge are 'systems' of one type or another. Too great a reverence for the accomplishments and theories of authorities is one such pernicious source of error.

Bacon delineated the regions of possible discovery in book II of the *Advancement of Learning* and books II–IX of *De Augmentis Scientiarum*. He begins with a distinction between three human faculties: memory, imagination and reason. To each faculty, he assigns an area of knowledge: history (divided between natural and civil, the latter including ecclesiastical and literary history, by which he means the history of ideas), 'poesie' (or 'feigned history') and philosophy. History serves as raw material for philosophy, or the knowledge that can be derived inductively from it. 'Poesie' is divided into the dramatic and the allusive, but because it is not really considered cognitive at all it is subsequently ignored. Knowledge is also to be divided between the secular and the divine. Divine knowledge must be based on revelation, and therefore has nothing to do with reason. A second division is drawn between the sciences and the arts, or the theoretical and the practical disciplines. He also recognises the existence of what he calls 'first philosophy', which is confined to the principles common to all the sciences. Natural science is divided into physics (or the study of observable correlations) and metaphysics (or the theoretical analysis of the structures underlying observable correlations between causes and effects). Having delineated all these areas of possible knowledge, Bacon set as a task for future generations the application of his method to these areas.

It is, of course, Bacon's stated method to which the *idéologues* drew the most attention, and this is developed most fully in the account of inductive reasoning set out in book II of *Novum Organum*. He castigated earlier systems for accepting as principles hasty and insupportable generalisations, or those simply assumed to be self-evident. He advocated a system of 'gradual ascent' – the accumulation of well-founded propositions of steadily increasing degrees of generality. He recognised that induction must work by elimination and not by mere accumulation of supporting evidence. For example, he established a system of tables to allow him to present single pieces of evidence and allow him to recognise false generalisations. Bacon developed tables of presence, absence and degree. In the first, a set of cases all containing a particular property is set out. Then, cases are examined for other properties. Any property not found in even a single case can be eliminated as a necessary cause of the property under consideration. Tables of absence contain cases as alike as possible, except for the property under consideration. Any property found in a single case cannot be a sufficient cause for the property under consideration. In tables of degree, proportionate variations of two properties are compared to see whether the proportion is maintained.[6]

The materialist philosophers: LaMettrie and Holbach

By 1700, continental rationalism had come together with the experimental science of Newton and Galileo to create the intellectual ferment out of which a thoroughly materialistic analysis of human nature would appear. Thomas Hobbes's *Leviathan* (1651), among his other writing, and Gassendi's attack on Descartes had fuelled the fires of materialism and, although it would be another century before materialism emerged as an important and developed system of analysis under the auspices of *idéologie*, its birth seems, in hindsight, to have been foreshadowed. One thread of influence, less intellectually weighty than the epistemology already discussed but no less well known to contemporaries of the *idéologues*, must not be neglected.

In 1748, Julien-Offroy de LaMettrie, the boldest of the psychological materialists, published his *L'Homme Machine*, which reduced human beings entirely to matter. This provocatively titled work became a favourite target for opponents of the *idéologues* some fifty years later. It is unfortunate that such a felicitously titled book should be so superficial, but it did have an historical importance (beyond that enjoyed by any book officially condemned) because it acted as straw man for those who disputed the claims of *idéologie*. Louis-Sébastien Mercier,[7] for example, attacked the 'materialist' analysis of Destutt de Tracy and Cabanis indirectly by mocking the 'mechanical metaphysics', the 'pulleys, springs, levers', the 'thinking automaton' of LaMettrie.[8] In February 1798, Jean-Jacques de Cambacérès, a lawyer and later partisan of Bonaparte, attacked the 'fanaticism of idolatry, the scepticism of the Academy, the man-machine of LaMettrie, the absurd man of the materialists, all of which undermine social foundations' in a broad appeal against *idéologie* (quoted in Staum 1996: 115). LaMettrie's book, like his earlier *Histoire Naturelle de l'Âme* (1745), was short, easily read and highly polemical.

In *L'Homme Machine*, the soul is reduced to an 'enlightened machine' and all psychological faculties reduced to brain physiology. Needless to say, if the targets of LaMettrie are those who argue that human beings have immortal and incorporeal souls, or even the Cartesian who claims that the will is directed by the soul that resides in a region of the brain, LaMettrie's observations of 'jumping' animal hearts, headless chickens and second-hand tales of battlefield casualties could not be expected to have been definitive. LaMettrie summarised the respects in which human beings are matter, but he went on to argue that human beings are only matter. Materialist methods were no more likely to establish that point in the eighteenth century than they are today.

Another early eighteenth-century manifestation of extreme mechanical materialism can be found in the writings of Paul-Henri Dietrich, Baron d'Holbach. Born in 1723 near Landau, Holbach became a naturalised French citizen in 1749. His inherited wealth allowed him to entertain and to sponsor many of the more important philosophers of the period, including Buffon, Rousseau and d'Alembert, until some chose to distance themselves from the extremity of his views. Holbach contributed several hundred articles to Diderot's and le Rond d'Alembert's *Encyclopédie*, mostly on chemistry. *Le Christianisme Dévoilé* (1761), published under the name of N. A. Boulanger, set the stage. *Système de la Nature* (1770), published under the name of J. B. Mirabaud, outlined an argument in which human beings, stripped of free will, were portrayed as machines, and all causality was reduced to physical laws of motion. *Système Social* (1773), an early expression of what became utilitarianism, carried the argument into the realm of politics and morality and argued that 'duty' was no more than self-interest.

The materialist philosophers form a curious bridge between empiricism and the physiological analysis of *idéologie* that we will examine in the next chapter. The *idéologues*, although less explicit about the mechanistic aspects of the analysis than their antecedents, did share this approach at some level. Even the metaphors are similar, which provided fuel for the passionate denunciations of opponents both within the class of Moral and Political Sciences and elsewhere. LaMettrie's 'man-machine', for example, is echoed in the form of Condillac's statue that, provided with a single sense, acquires through experience and associative principles the attributes of the human mind. Despite the superficial resemblance, however, the identification of *idéologie* with the materialism of Holbach and LaMettrie is an unjust caricature as we shall see. It was, nevertheless, a very useful rhetorical device.

John Locke and Etienne Bonnot de Condillac: the sources of sensationalism

By the end of the seventeenth century, the banner of empiricism was being flown by two great intellects: Pierre Bayle and John Locke. Bayle was the son of a Calvinist minister and taught philosophy at the Protestant Academy of Sedan from 1675 to 1681. In 1681, he moved to Rotterdam, where he taught philosophy and history. In 1682, he published anonymously his reflections on the comet of 1680, criticising the superstitious belief that comets forecast disaster while simultaneously attacking many Christian doctrines. His plea for religious tolerance and support for the anti-Calvinist government of Louis XIV ultimately deprived him of his professorship in 1683. From that time, he devoted himself to his *Dictionnaire Historique et Critique* (1697). The articles in this dictionary, on philosophy, history and religion, are much less significant than the numerous commentaries and quotations that were intended to undermine whatever orthodoxy the articles contained. The work was criticised for its support of radical (Pyrrhonist) scepticism, atheism and Epicureanism, and Bayle was accused of using scripture to introduce indecencies. The *Dictionnaire*'s method of oblique and subversive criticism of orthodox doctrines was adopted by the eighteenth-century *Encyclopédistes*. The intellectual link between empiricism and atheism forged by Bayle remained characteristic of empiricist philosophy, at least in the minds of its critics. Try as some might to avoid the attribution, throughout the eighteenth century rationalism remained associated with the Church and empiricism with charges of atheism, at least in France.

John Locke's *An Essay Concerning Human Understanding* (1690) specifically attempts to avoid all physiological considerations and theological disputes:

> I shall not at present meddle with the physical considerations of the mind, or trouble myself to examine wherein its essence consists or by what motion of our spirits, or alterations of our bodies, we come to have any sensation by our organs, or any *ideas* in our understanding; and whether those ideas do, in their formation, any or all of them, depend on matter or not.
>
> (Locke 1956: introduction)

Only *reflection* and *sensation* can give rise to ideas. Sensation is the apprehension of particular objects in the physical world via our sense organs. Locke claimed that we do not perceive categories such as 'species' or 'classes', but rather only particular individual entities. But *reflection* gives the human mind the ability to examine its contents and its operations. The contents of the mind derive from sensory experience, but the operations of the mind include the effects of the passions. Perception depends on the active direction of the mind towards the sensory input; it is not a passive process.

Locke's psychology is uncompromisingly sensationalist. He insists that human beings are born without innate ideas, and that everything that an individual comes to know will be the ultimate result of the interaction of sensation and reflection. That is, no one can have an understanding about that which has not been experienced. He insists, for example, that a man born blind and then caused to see will not be able to distinguish by sight a globe from a cube because his sensory experience involved only the sense of touch (1956, II, IX: section 8). He leaves open the possibility that the human fetus may have certain sensory experiences before birth, but argues that no rudimentary ideas in the mind of a newborn can be understood as innate (1956, II, IX: section 7).

Perception[9] and thinking are, according to Locke, the same process. All we know, we know from reflection upon experience. Our ideas are initially simple but, through experience, we build up knowledge by degrees. First, we simply recognise the existence of something ('identity'). Then, we form associations between two ideas in our mind that he called 'relation', which is to say that the mind becomes aware that two ideas are related. (For example, that object is 'swimming' and is 'feathered'.) At a slightly more complex stage, we form larger bodies of associations in our mind through habitual association, which he called 'coexistence' (i.e. ducks have feathers, swim, have beaks and eat breadcrumbs.) Finally, we have knowledge of 'real existence' (i.e. that object is a duck).

These concepts explain the foundations of knowledge, but say nothing about degrees of certainty. Locke distinguished between *intuitive, demonstrative* and *sensitive* knowledge. The first is knowledge of which we are immediately aware and that no one would dispute. Demonstrative knowledge allows one to deduce certain truths from intuitive knowledge. That is, it allows us to compare objects in our minds through the process of reflection. Both intuitive and demonstrative knowledge allow us to be certain. Sensitive knowledge, however, comprises the knowledge of particulars that we gain from sensory data. Sensitive knowledge can be divided into knowledge of *primary qualities* (such as size, shape, number, place and motion that can be directly perceived by our senses) and *secondary qualities* that exist only through the act of perception because human senses are not acute enough to perceive, for example, the reality of gold beyond the yellow colour our senses recognise (Locke, 1956, II, XXIII: sections 9 and 11).

Locke argues that knowledge is of three categories. We know ourselves by intuition; we know God by demonstration; everything else we know through sensation. Our faculty of *memory* allows us to derive knowledge of causes and effects through experience without endless repetition. The extent of this knowledge is enhanced if our experiences are associated with *pleasure* or *pain* (1956, IV, XI: section 6).

Etienne-Bonnot de Condillac (1715–88) was ordained a Roman Catholic priest in 1740 and, despite his naturalistic philosophy, maintained a belief in the reality of the soul and the nature of religion consistent with his vocation. He did not believe any conflict existed between such a position and his *Essai sur l'origine des Connaissances Humaines* (1746), which reflected his inherent tension between rationalism and empiricism in beginning with the sentence: 'Whether we rise to heaven, or descend to the abyss, we never get outside ourselves – it is always our own thoughts that we perceive.' The *idéologues* claimed descent from his empirical sensationalism, expounded in the *Essai*, which was based upon the principle that observations and sense perceptions are the foundation of human knowledge. One of the areas of disagreement was the extent to which Condillac's 'dualism' was compatible with the empirical sensationalism upon which *idéologie* was based.

Condillac was a lifelong friend of J.-J. Rousseau, and was well acquainted with Denis Diderot and the Encyclopaedists. His reputation was established by his first book, the *Essai* (1746) and *Traité des Systèmes* (1749). In 1752, he was elected to the Berlin Academy. *Traité des Sensations* (1754) and *Traité des Animaux* (1755) followed. In 1758, he was appointed tutor to Prince Ferdinand of Parma and, in 1768, was elected to the *Académie Française*. *Grammaire* was published in 1775. *Le Commerce et le Gouvernement Considérés Rélativement l'Un à l'Autre* (1776) outlined his economic analysis that contained the notion that value depends upon 'utility'. He moved away from the irreligious atmosphere in Paris and he spent his last years writing *La Logique* (1780) and *La Langue des Calculs* (1798), which was published posthumously.

Condillac was responsible for expounding, if not necessarily creating, three ideas upon which *idéologie* was based. His first argument was that the sciences ought to be unified by means of a common method of 'analysis', in which complex ideas would be decomposed into their simplest elements and reconstructed into more complex ideas respecting the integrity of the individual 'truths' (1947–51, I: 105–6; I: 213; I: 435; II: 374–6).

Second, he applied the method of 'analysis' to the human mind, in the modern sense of the term psychology. In his most significant work, the *Traité des Sensations*, Condillac systematically expounded the ideas of John Locke (1632–1704), who was already well known in France through the efforts of Voltaire, although he took exception to some important issues. As did Locke, he argued that observations made by sense perception are the primary foundation for human knowledge, and in fact the only knowledge we have of the world. Objects can only be perceived in terms of the sensations they generate (Condillac 1947–51, II: 381). But sensations are more than the shadows of external objects (Condillac 1947–51, II: 329), which, as Locke argued, reflection then engages.

Condillac denied Locke's claim that there was a separate faculty of 'reflection' and instead transformed sense data into all the faculties of knowledge such as memory, attention, comparison, imagination and judgement, as well as 'desire' and 'passion' (Condillac 1947–51, I: 222ff.). Condillac, in a well-known example, echoed Locke's claim that an individual blind from birth who, as an adult, is granted the opportunity to see will not make naturally correct judgements about size, distance, position and shape of objects (Condillac 1947–51, I: 57). He examined the knowledge gained by each sense, and argued that all human knowledge is simply 'transformed sensation'. Locke's separate faculty of 'reflection' was not necessary. Each sensation, through the principles of pleasure and pain, generate human passions and the will (Condillac 1947–51, I: 239ff.).

Although Condillac argued that reflection is simply a form of sensation, he did not suggest that sensation alone was sufficient to generate the complex ideas that are the end result of human processing. Just as a blind person given the opportunity to see needs to learn to understand the sensations his eyes gather, human beings need to learn to elicit ideas from all of the other sensations. This, he argued, was the fundamental error of Locke, who seemed to pass too quickly over the origin of knowledge (Condillac 1947–51, I: 5).

Condillac solved this problem by attempting to demonstrate that the 'transformation of sensation' was responsible for both the development of the ability to reason, understand and feel in human beings and for the development of knowledge based upon the faculties of the mind. For example, he argued that the simple ability to experience sensation led to attention, which generated memory, which allowed the ability to compare sensations, which allowed the development of judgement. Judgement preceded imagination, which ultimately led to recognition (Condillac 1947–51, I: 224–32). The emotional faculties developed simultaneously: the ability to feel desire led to passion, which evolved into the ability to love and hate. From love and hate came the ability to hope and fear, and, ultimately, the faculty of will (Condillac 1947–51, I: 232–3). That is, from sensation came abstract ideas, including ideas of number and particular and general truths (Condillac 1947–51, I: 233–8).

This 'transformed sensation' model had the effect of equating psychology and epistemology because, Condillac argued, as the faculties of the mind are given by nature it follows that the only appropriate method of eliciting ideas from sensation (or reasoning) will also be given (Condillac 1947–51, II: 374ff.; I: 239). The appropriate goal is to return to the methods of acquiring knowledge that came naturally in childhood, when one learned by observing and putting one's judgements to the test of observation and experiment (Condillac 1947–51, II: 374). There is no distinction, for Condillac, between the method of reasoning and the way in which the mind operates; that is, there can be no distinction between epistemology and psychology.

It is not very difficult to see how Condillac's 'transformed sensations' model set the stage for the Revolutionary attempts, adopted by many of the individuals who entered the morality prize competition, to further the moral education of the people through the use of pageants and festivals designed to stimulate the senses. These events, they hoped, would help to create, through the 'association of ideas', human beings capable of taking on the tasks of citizens in the Republic. All ideological pedagogical models, whether applied to traditional areas of study, new 'trades' courses designed for artisans, or moral education, began with Condillac's model.

Condillac's third major influence on the *idéologues* was his claim that language formed the basis for all reasoning. In his *Essai* (1746), he stressed the idea that clear linguistic 'signs' are required as the basis of scientific progress, an idea that Lavoisier explicitly acknowledged as the basis for his own work in chemical nomenclature (Lavoisier 1789: i–xxxii). In *Langue des Calculs* (1798), he raised the contentious idea, much debated and ultimately rejected by *idéologues* such as Cabanis and Tracy, that all sciences could be expressed in terms of algebraic symbols, thereby achieving the certainty of mathematical reasoning. Despite the fact that he went much further than many of his disciples were prepared to follow, Condillac's estimation of the importance of language influenced those of the *idéologues* who wanted to place 'language' at the centre of pedagogy, recognising its importance both in mastering the knowledge already amassed and generating new knowledge.

One of the sources through which the *idéologues* came into contact with the ideas of Locke and Condillac was Helvétius. Claude-Adrien Helvétius, son of the Queen's chief physician, was born in Paris in 1715. He was appointed Farmer General in 1738, but resigned his post upon his marriage in 1751 and retired to his estate at Voré. There, he published *De l'Esprit* in 1758, which was widely condemned for its attack on all forms of morality based on religion. Although the book was published openly, it was soon condemned and ordered to be burned in public. Voltaire and Rousseau both criticised the work and Helvétius was called upon to recant, which he did – three times. Despite these efforts, publication of the *Encyclopédie* was suspended, and other works, including many by Voltaire, were also burned. Helvétius fled to England in 1764 and to Berlin in 1765. Later that same year, he returned to France to find that the *philosophes* were, once again, in favour and he spent the rest of his life at Voré, where he died in 1771.

Helvétius was of importance to the *idéologues* because he purged the empirical sensationalism of Condillac of its unobservable religious remnants, and forged a psychology based upon physical sensation and a moral philosophy based upon the manipulation of self-interest. Moral judgement was to be based on 'the interest of the public, that is to say of the greatest number', and Helvétius concluded that justice involved performing 'actions useful to the greatest number' (Halévy 1955: 19). His *De l'Esprit* (1758) intended to 'treat morals like any other science and to make an experimental morality like an experimental physics' (preface, cited in Halévy 1955: 19). Bentham wrote of Helvétius: 'What Bacon was to the physical world, Helvétius was to the moral. The moral world has therefore had its Bacon; but its Newton is yet to come' (cited in Halévy 1955: 19).

Antoine-Louis-Claude Destutt de Tracy (1754–1836)

Tracy is the acknowledged philosopher and psychologist of *idéologie*, and his science of ideas is explicitly based on the work of Condillac. He acknowledges, as did Condillac, that all human faculties derive from sensation, and that human thought is transformed sensation. But Condillac, according to Tracy, erred in attempting to trace out a long path by means of which sensations are transformed into ideas by the human mind. Rather, he should have acknowledged that sense perceptions and thinking are, in fact, identical – that ideas are merely sensations of different types with different effects (Tracy 1817, 1: 24–5). This notion renders superfluous Condillac's conception of the mind as an independent entity.

Moreover, Condillac's 'statue', who is progressively endowed with each human sense and allowed to discover the world, is an inadequate representation of human reasoning, according to Tracy, because it neglects the entire realm of internal sensations captured by the science of physiology. If one were to imagine the process of sensation correctly, Tracy argued, the interaction between the human body and its physical environment would give rise to a disturbance of nerves in the body, which would give rise to sensations, and which would set in motion the internal process of sensibility (Tracy 1817, 1: 34). The mechanism through which sensibility occurred was vague, but Tracy was certain that the flow of 'nervous fluids' would be central (Tracy 1817, 1: 234). Tracy, however, was content to cede development of physiology to

Cabanis, who 'is the first to have clearly distinguished the different effects of our sensibility, and developed all their circumstances and consequences' (Tracy 1817, 3: 175n).

Tracy spent some time trying to determine how it is that we can know that there is a reality external to ourselves. Condillac had relied on touch to account for our knowledge of reality, but Tracy declared that this was insufficient (Tracy 1798a: 299). He attempted to develop the concept of *motilité*, arguing that the interaction between muscular activity and nervous sensitivity gives rise to a sensation of movement against a resistant world. This constitutes the basic communication between an interior self and the outside world and introduces, Welch argues, a dynamic element of time into his analysis (Welch 1984: 53).

However, Tracy was soon distracted from this attempt to answer Bishop Berkeley, and shifted his focus instead to the problem of ensuring correct inference and reasoning as an aspect of all experience. Tracy distinguished between four types of sensation in his mature work: simple sensations, both internal and external; memory, or the sensation of recall; judgement, or the sensing of relations between simple sensations; and sensing desires, or the faculty of will (Head 1985: 38; Welch 1984: 54).

Tracy argued that complex ideas must be generalised from simple sense impressions of many concrete examples, and that such associations must be constantly checked against the concrete reality of particular examples (Tracy 1817, 1: 81–106). Condillac had taken it for granted that data derived directly from the senses were accurate in the sense that they reflected some objective reality, and he argued that rational thinking requires merely the accurate judgement about relationships between sensations. His solution was to reduce such judgement to an algebraic formula: complex notions ought to be reduced to their constituent simple ideas, and the number of ideas in each ought to be counted and compared (Condillac 1947–51 *Oeuvres* I: 39).

Tracy rejected this mechanistic model, arguing that 'if to calculate is to reason, [it does not follow that] to reason is to calculate' (Tracy 1798a: 321). Ideas, he noted, are fundamentally heterogeneous, and there is no reason to imagine that the constituent simple ideas contained in the concept 'food' would be comparable in any sense to those ideas contained in the notion 'justice' or 'government' (Tracy 1817, 3: 54–5). Moreover, human memories, upon which such complex associations necessarily rest, are notoriously imperfect (Tracy 1817, 3: 186) and, even if an event is correctly recalled, the state of mind that entertained the initial event and that accompanied its recall may be so different as to generate quite different internal sensations (Tracy 1817, 3: 182–3).

Therefore, Tracy turned his attention to three elements that he hoped would assist memory in rendering judgements more rational and thought more correct: attention, habit and language. Human beings ought not to be perceived as statues bombarded by sensations, as Condillac would have them, but rather as beings who have the capacity to select and to turn their attention to particular sensations, while ignoring the effects of others. That is, Tracy argued that attention is not automatic, but is rather under the governance of will (Tracy 1817, 1: 219).

Second, one must not neglect the importance of habit in human judgement and thought. Habit can be seen as an impediment to learning, but it might also be a powerful tool in the hands of an educator or social engineer:

> [Sensations,] the more they are repeated, the easier and quicker they become;...the easier and quicker they are, the less they are perceptible, that is to say the perceptions they cause in us are diminished, even to the point of vanishing, though the movement itself still occurs.
>
> (Tracy 1817, 1: 266)

That is, correct judgements and the behaviour based upon them are much more likely when they are habitual because they do not require careful decoding each time a particular situation arises. This becomes useful for one who would reform society when new habits have been created, and, for example, republican behaviour has become the norm. However, habit can also stand in the way of teaching new forms of thought and behaviour because of the habits created under previous regimes. This insight is at the heart of Tracy's contribution to the morality prize competition.

Third, Tracy, like Condillac, turned his attention to the role that language (or signs) might play in helping individuals form correct judgements about the relationships between various sensations. This problem underscores the second volume of Tracy's *Elémens* entitled 'Grammaire'. His basic premise is that the purpose of a rational language is to achieve an accurate chain of ideas from the simple to the more complex (Tracy 1817, 2: 21). The more ornate language is, the more likely that it alone will introduce error into the process of reasoning and render the judgements an individual makes about the relationships between sensations inaccurate.

The foundation of Tracy's social analysis can be found in volume four of his *Elémens*, in which he considers the problem of human will. It seemed obvious to Tracy that human rights are generated by needs (1817, 4: 108). Moreover, a need is, according to Tracy, a pure sensation that gives rise to the perception of pleasure or pain in an individual, but that an individual can only conceive of needs in terms of desires, which are a matter of will (Tracy 1817, 4: 79). For example, an individual may feel hunger, which is a pure need; but the individual processes that sensation of hunger by remembering the sensation that is generated by consuming food, comparing the two sensations, which is a matter of judgement, and then formulating the desire to consume food, which is a matter of will. The desire for food is the way in which an individual perceives the need generated by hunger.

The construction of desires, however, is not instinctive or automatic. Desire or will is a social process, and individual wills can be affected through appropriate education. Human judgements, that is, might be 'corrected' through an educational programme designed to teach individuals their true interests (Tracy 1798a: 356).

There are two ideas that are fundamental to the ethical relationships among people in society: sympathy and language or signs. Tracy does not develop the idea of sympathy, referring instead to the work of Cabanis and others (see Tracy 1817, 3: 200–1; 4: 72–3, 133–4; 5: 514). Yet, he takes it as axiomatic that social morality consists in the subordination of individual desire to enlightened self-interest (Welch 1984: 215n57). And enlightened self-interest, as we shall argue in subsequent chapters, contains within it the concept of sympathy. Moreover, it is only with language that human beings can conceive and speak of what is just and what is unjust (Tracy 1817, 4: 128). Therefore, it is only in society that morality can be conceived.

Idéologie and its critics in the *Institut National*

This chapter has argued that *idéologie* emerged out of early eighteenth-century attempts to reconcile the idea that the universe is governed by general laws with the belief, simultaneously held, that sensation is the source of all knowledge about the world. Epistemological systems, however, were not isolated from ideas about human nature, social theory and governance, and by the end of the eighteenth century, notwithstanding attempts by some empiricists such as Locke to immunise their analysis against accusations of atheism and sedition, there was a tendency to equate rationalism with support for the Church and the state and empiricism with atheism and a radical and reductive materialism. People such as Bayle provided ammunition for critics of empiricism through their only very slightly veiled subversive criticism, and materialist philosophers such as LaMettrie and Holbach offered much more extreme and provocatively reductive materialist models of human nature.

Tracy became the pre-eminent philosopher of *idéologie*, building his epistemology on the writing of Locke and, more explicitly, Condillac. His position, however, was not uncritically adopted by the class of Moral and Political Sciences and, by the time the class was dissolved in 1803, Laromiguière, Degérando and Maine de Biran had openly defected from the belief in transformed sensations. The *Journal des Débats* cited with approval Mercier's critique of the 'sensualism' of Helvétius and the 'doll' of Condillac as 'desolating systems' (newspaper article published 1 Germinal VIII: 3 [22 March 1800]). In fact, Mercier's contributions to the debate within the class of Moral and Political Sciences mirrors the opposition to *idéologie* within that institution. Staum's investigations reveal that, as early as 1799, Mercier had begun to attack the 'errors' of Locke and Condillac, whom he claimed had identified ideas, sensations and sentiments as physical sensitivity. He claimed that innate ideas preceded sensation and that they were the spiritual visions of celestial truths, that free will allowed reason to overcome sensuality, and that the performance of one's duty was evidence of the triumph of virtue. Between 1800 and 1802, Mercier read four memoirs on innate ideas and the philosophies of Kant and Fichte. Kant became, for some of those members of the class most opposed to *idéologie* such as Grégoire, a defence against the materialism and atheism that they associated with Condillac, Locke and Cabanis (Staum 1996: 114).

5   Physiology, order and chaos

Medicine and social theory in eighteenth-century France developed in tandem (Rosen 1946; Ramsey 1988; E. A. Williams 1994; Vila 1997). Tracy recognised physiology as one of the primary areas of investigation of *idéologie*, relying upon the investigations of Bichat and Cabanis to furnish an analysis of the internal sensations that allow individuals to formulate ideas from their sensory impressions. However, Tracy, Say and Roederer were eager to extend the method of analysis to the study of human beings in society. Here, too, physiology would come to the rescue, providing an analysis of the natural force of sympathy that allows human beings to live together in society.

It was clear that philosophy and social theory must take into account and be consistent with the new discoveries that were emerging from the empirical and clinical investigations of *idéologues* such as Cabanis, Bichat and Pinel. But social theory was not simply to be derived from the life sciences as a subordinate application. Rather, the same rigorous observation and analysis, the same method, was expected to lead to similar progress in social science as had been observed in the natural sciences. But the most important debt of social science to physiology was the articulation of a common problem to be investigated. Under the auspices of *idéologues* such as Cabanis, the unifying problem of physiology was to explain how the various functional systems in a living body work together to ensure the health of the entire body. Social theorists transported this problem to their own realm of investigation and asked how various functional systems of the body politic work together to ensure the health of society.

In this chapter, we document the ways in which physiologists attempted to explain how the different functional systems of the human body work together. In the next, we will examine how social philosophers would attempt to explain how the different functional parts of a society, each pursuing its own distinct interests, could be harmonised. Just as the physiologists inevitably began to focus on mental and physical diseases – examples in which the harmony of the human body breaks down and requires the intervention of doctors for body or mind – social scientists would begin to examine the ways in which an intellectual élite can help to bring about the harmony that social order required. In the work of Philippe Pinel, *idéologue* and superintendent of various Parisian hospitals for the insane, we find a link between the two areas of investigation, as we document below.

The unity of knowledge

One of the points upon which there was widespread agreement among the *idéologues* is that 'beautiful and great idea that all the sciences and all the arts constitute an ensemble, an indivisible whole, or form the branches of the same single trunk, united by a common origin' (Cabanis 1956, I: 124). Similarly, Tracy argued that the arts were, in principle, inseparable from the sciences in the sense that the arts must be based upon the sciences, the principles of which they were applications (Tracy 1817–18, III: 3). But the theoretical unity of knowledge did not, for the *idéologues*, mean that all scientific investigations ought to be carried out as if there were no important distinctions between the way in which objects were considered in different areas of study (Cabanis 1956, II: 184). The proper organisation of knowledge and, in particular, the appropriate distinction between the sciences became an important area of investigation for the *idéologues*, and was approached in the same manner as all other classificatory schemes were to be approached: worthwhile as long as useful, and best derived from careful observation of the subject matter itself (see Tracy 1817–18, III: 3ff.; Cabanis 1956, II: 509ff.; see Kaiser 1976: 491–504).

François-Xavier Bichat (1771–1802), despite his premature death, was an important contributor to the physiology of the *idéologues*, to the medical history of the nineteenth century and to Tracy's psychology of human beings. He was also responsible for the neologism 'biologie' in 1801 (Bichat 1801: 11). Strongly influenced by Pinel and Cabanis, Bichat published *Traité des Membranes* and *Recherches Physiologiques sur la Vie et la Mort* in 1800, and *Anatomie Générale Appliquée à la Physiologie et à la Médecine* in 1801.[1]

If one places to one side those phenomena that are the objects of the physical sciences, Bichat argued, and to the other, those phenomena that are the subject matter of physiology, one would see an immense difference between the two sciences and between the laws that govern each set of phenomena. Physical objects are invariable, and subject to constant laws: gravity varies according to the square of the distances between objects, for example, everywhere and always. By contrast, living beings are subject to all the laws of physics, but also to laws that vary beyond anything apparent in the physical world: living beings are subject to laws relating to sensibility and movement. If one attempts to express matters of physiology in terms of the language of physics, Bichat argued, rather than clarify matters, one would muddle them beyond all measure (Bichat 1852: 310–12). Mechanical explanations and physical determinism simply do not allow one to understand the domain of life, and using the words of physics as an approximation is, Bichat claimed, not helpful. In fact, Bichat went further. If physiology rather than physics had developed first, he argued, one would expect to find physical phenomena explained in terms more appropriate to living matter: crystals would attract one another by means of the 'excitation' that they would exert on each other's sensibilities, and planets would move because they 'irritate' one another across great distances. This, he noted, is no more, and certainly no less, exact than talking about 'doses', 'quantities', 'sums', or 'gravitation', 'attraction' and 'repulsion' in physiology (Bichat 1852: 57–9).

The sciences, then, must be kept distinct even though there is a theoretical unity of knowledge, because the phenomena, studied by physics and those that are the subject of physiology are subject to different laws. This distinction provided the basis for Bichat's definition of life: all objects are subject to forces that tend to destroy them, and life is distinguished from non-life to the extent that its organisation resists disintegration. Put differently, life is that which resists death (Bichat 1852: 1).

Order and chaos in complex bodies: anatomy and physiology

As in almost every area of theory, the contributions of the *idéologues* to the life sciences exhibit both change and continuity. They adopted the method of their eighteenth-century predecessors, privileging observation and classification over preconceived systems and deduction from first principles, and yet they recognised that the fundamental quest of eighteenth-century natural history could be restated in terms of their own favourite metaphor: the problem, they decided, was 'order'. This problem found its expression in a number of different forms: what are the categories of classification that data derived from the observation of living beings suggest? How are the various functional systems to be organised interdependently within an individual human or animal body such that the body itself has an integrity greater than the sum of its individual parts? How should diseases be analysed, or symptoms categorised?

Cabanis distinguished between anatomy as the set of structural relations in a body, and physiology as a set of functional relations. The first was a descriptive analysis, in which he claimed the anatomist resembled a geographer who is satisfied to 'portray areas without tracing the physical changes they experience over the course of time, without indicating the political events of which the country might have been the theatre and the successive revolutions which might have disrupted its inhabitants' (Cabanis 1956, II: 190–1). Physiology, by contrast, was an 'historical analysis', and the physiologist must:

> Follow with attention and care the entire series of...phenomena presented by the body or object of examination: [physiology] portrays them in their order of succession with all the characteristics which distinguish them; it seeks to identify the type or degree of influence that they exercise on each other; it tries to determine the one among them to which all the others relate and which can be considered as either their source or their common tie.
>
> (Cabanis 1956, II: 190–1)

Anatomy and physiology were both, therefore, necessary for any understanding of the nature of an organism, just as history and geography were both essential to the study of societies.

Vicq d'Azyr, the most important devotee of the science of anatomy, recognised that progress in anatomy could best be achieved if detailed description were to become more selective, focusing on the basic structure of each organism and noting their similarities to one another. This, he claimed, would require a new vocabulary (Vicq d'Azyr 1805, IV: 218). The *idéologues*, despite Vicq d'Azyr's zeal, devoted relatively little effort to comparative anatomy and they turned most of their attention to physiology.

Both Cabanis and Bichat distinguished between the basic life functions of the interior (organic life) and the 'animal life' that enabled beings to move and establish relations with other beings, and 'plus souvent,...communiquer par la voix ses désirs et ses peines' (Bichat 1852: 2ff.).[2] According to Bichat, what distinguished life from non-life, and animal life from plant life, was simply the degree of organisation or 'order' present in the object under study. The more complex the being, the greater the degree of coordination required between the constituent parts, and the more complex the laws that governed its existence.

Once one can distinguish life from non-life, then one is in a position to categorise living beings along the scale put in place by Lamarck. However, categorising living beings is only one aspect of the need to bring order to this area of investigation. It was equally important to categorise and describe the organs in individual complex bodies such as those of human beings. Moreover, where anatomists had in the past limited themselves to the investigation of individual animals and individual parts of animals, now they were prepared to conduct studies on a comparative basis in an attempt to understand how the parts of an organism work together to create a unified being, and to understand the similarities and differences among the structures of different organisms. Buffon had focused on the external characteristics of animal species, but the appropriate use of a renovated anatomy would allow a better understanding of the characteristics of genera and species by discerning the 'immutable relationships of the mechanical structure' (Pinel 1792, I: 52). More importantly, however, anatomy could be used as the basis for the new science of physiology.

Order and the human body

Cabanis argued that the most important task to be completed by physiologists was the identification of various functional systems and the observation of their interaction with one another because, in his phrase that anticipates the links we shall draw between physiology and social analysis, 'everything is connected...in the animal economy' (Cabanis 1956, II: 209). And the 'animal economy', just like the social economy, was subject to disruption and disorder.

There was disagreement over the list of functional systems in a living body. Vicq d'Azyr listed nine: nutrition, circulation, secretion, generation, respiration, irritability, sensibility, digestion and ossification (Vicq d'Azyr *Table* 1774; cited in Kaiser 1976: 379). Bichat (1834, III: 10) argued that irritability and sensibility were not 'systems' but were 'properties'. Nevertheless, they all agreed that there were interdependent functional systems, at least in the higher animals such as human beings, and were therefore faced with the task of explaining how all these systems worked together to maintain the life of the organism (Cabanis 1956, I: 533).

Because they could not agree on a list of functional systems, it is not surprising that some uncertainty surrounded the process by which the various systems communicated with one another and produced coordinated effects (Cabanis 1956, I: 539). Nevertheless, there was widespread agreement that somehow the cerebral system – as the seat of 'reason' and 'will', the receptor of all internal and external sensory data, and the source of the 'nerves' that can communicate with all the organs of the body – 'governs all' (Cabanis 1956, I: 606).

The brain received, Cabanis argued, two types of impressions: external impressions, which he labelled 'sensation' when their perception is distinct, and internal impressions, which are more often vague and not experienced by the organism in terms of clear cause and effect. Sensation results from the application of external objects to the sense organs, and 'primary ideas' depend upon such external impressions. Internal impressions, by contrast, are influenced by 'habit' and 'diseases' of the various organs, and are the source of 'instinct' (Cabanis 1956, I: 197). Because the nervous system received both internal and external sensory data, it possessed the most information about the needs of the body (Cabanis 1956, I: 168). As the source of 'reason' and 'will', the brain was capable of comprehending the data, of formulating appropriate responses and of communicating the appropriate actions to the various systems via the 'nerves'. How this happened was a matter yet to be worked out by science (Cabanis 1956, I: 540), but it was clear that 'secretions' of the brain had something to do with it.

The nervous system, Cabanis concluded, 'governs all', but like any ruler it is, to some extent, subject to the will of the governed. The 'lower functions' – 'instincts', 'penchants' and 'passions' – could certainly influence the 'higher functions', such as 'reason', 'will', 'sense' and 'memory'. Sexual passion and hunger, for example, were believed to be somewhat under the control of the nervous system, but the control was fragile and, very often, the 'passions' could lead organisms to behave in ways contrary to their own best interests (Cabanis 1956, I: 353–5).

Needless to say, these uncontrolled 'passions' could also have adverse effects on other organisms with which the first lived in a community. It was, therefore, essential to the maintenance of human society to ameliorate the 'lower functions', through moral education and through anything else that might rebalance the forces within the organism such that both the individual and a society would benefit. But the disruptive effects of the passions were not the only ways in which an individual related to other individuals. A 'sympathetic force', thought to be under the control of the will yet independent of reflection and emanating from the brain, was the source of the generally coordinated and mutually beneficial behaviour characterising society when it functioned well (Cabanis 1956, I: 565ff.). In human society, sympathy was expressed through imitation, and sympathetic instincts and reason worked together to ensure that the 'passions' were sublimated to the counsels of reason, and reason was leavened by the action of 'sentiment' (Cabanis 1956, I: 576).

If one were to couple this analysis to the sensationalism of Condillac and Helvétius, one would not be surprised to see a claim that one could, through moral education and the nurturing of sympathy through external stimuli, bring about an ideal temperament – a human being fit, at last, to live peacefully in society. Cabanis, however, was less optimistic. There are, he claimed, a number of distinct temperaments and, although one could modify temperament within very narrow limits, deeply ingrained temperament does not change. Moreover, it reappears generation after generation, despite variations in education, regimen, climate and work (Cabanis 1956, I: 354–5).[3]

In the same vein, individuals such as Pierre Roussel could argue that nature had endowed women with innately different temperaments from men: women are more sensitive – more receptive to sensations from external phenomena – but less equipped to develop abstract and complex ideas from these sensations through reason, and less capable of subordinating the lower faculties (the 'passions') to the higher ('reason' and 'will'). Hence, nature itself had decreed that women and men were not identical, and he extended the analysis to argue that such naturally unequal beings could not aspire to social equality (see Steinbrügge 1995: 35–43; Staum 1996: 100–1).

Philippe Pinel: disease and the passions

Cabanis recognised that one of the ways in which an imbalance could arise between the various functional systems of the physical body is through disease. Disease can disrupt the harmony that exists between functional systems, requiring intervention if death is to be avoided and the system to become healthy and harmonious once again. Similarly, mental disease could disrupt the harmonious relationship between reason and the passions. It seemed clear enough that 'lunatics', those poor souls still chained in Bicêtre and Salpêtrière, were people with imbalances between the passions and reason. Therefore, the physiological investigations of *idéologie* find their counterpart in the study of the mentally ill pioneered by Philippe Pinel. Physical disease and disorder are mirrored in the conception of mental illness as a disorder, or a lack of coordination, between functional systems. Moreover, the role accorded the doctor, as an individual charged with restoring physical order to a diseased organism, is reflected in a new conception of the role of an individual charged with the care of the mentally ill. Success would be reflected in the restoration of order between the various components of the cerebral system and the healing (rather than the warehousing) of the individual so afflicted.

Philippe Pinel (1745–1826) pioneered the humane treatment of the mentally ill, and his medical and physiological writing contributed to the analytical foundation of *idéologie*. His *Nosographie Philosophique, ou la Méthode de l'Analyse Appliquée à la Médecine* (1813 [1798]), in which he described various psychoses on the basis of their symptoms, and *Traité Médico-Philosophique sur l'Aliénation Mentale ou la Manie* (1801), which describes his clinical treatments, remain his best-known works. Throughout his work one can see a long intellectual struggle to treat disease, including various 'manias', not as independent entities characterised by various symptoms, as Buffon had ordered the natural world in the eighteenth century, but rather as disorders of particular functional systems, and a lack of coordination between them. This intellectual undertaking coincided with a genuine effort to reform the way in which the mentally ill were housed and treated, and Pinel attempted to rationalise his proposed reforms through appeal to his scientific study. However, this is an instance in which reform was advocated by an individual associated with *idéologie* on the basis of 'analysis', and yet the scientific work, although consistent with the proposed reform, was neither necessary nor sufficient to justify the reform.

Pinel first arrived in Paris in 1778, and he supported himself for a number of years by translating medical and scientific works and teaching mathematics. He also began treating privately confined patients and publishing articles based upon his observations. Pinel was appointed chief physician of the public insane asylum for men in 1792, and he advocated substantial reform of a system already regarded as outdated and barbaric by those colleagues and philosophers with whom Pinel had begun to associate. Pariset's 'Eloge de Pinel' paints a graphic picture:

Vice, crime, misfortune, infirmity, diseases, the most varied and the most revolting, all were heaped together and treated alike. The buildings were untenable. Men crouched, covered with filth, in cells of stone that were narrow, cold, dripping, without air or light, and furnished only with a litter of straw, rarely renewed and soon infected – hideous lairs in which one would have hesitated to shut up the vilest animal. The insane, thrown into these sewers, were at the mercy of their keepers and their keepers were malefactors from the prisons. The wretched patients were loaded with chains and tied with ropes like convicts. Handed over thus to the cruelty of their guardians, they were made the butt of insulting raillery or of blind and wanton brutality. The injustice of their savage treatment transported them with rage; and despair and wrath inflaming their deranged minds, drew from them night and day cries and howlings that rendered still more dreadful the clanking of their chains. Some, more patient or more cunning, showed themselves insensible to such outrages; but they only concealed their frenzy to gratify it more surely. They watched with their eyes the movements of their tormentors until, surprising them in a helpless attitude, they struck them with blows of their chains on the head or stomach and dashed them dying at their feet. Thus, ferocity on one side and murder on the other.

(Pariset 1828; quoted in Riese 1969: 4)

Pinel is routinely given credit for 'removing the chains' at Bicêtre but, in fact, that honour ought to be accorded the supervisor, a man named M. Pussin, who succeeded in implementing the reforms both he and Pinel sought on 4 Prairial, Year VI, in the face of substantial opposition from the Central Office.

Pinel's clinical work eliminated such routine treatments as bleeding, purging and blistering, and included discussion of personal difficulties with the patient and a regime of useful activity. The reforms that he undertook were part of a larger movement towards reform throughout Europe, where the popular view of the mentally ill was changing from that of demonic possession or dangerous criminality towards the view that patients were simply victims who deserved to be treated with compassion (Gusdorf 1978: 466–71). In England, John Howard and William and Samuel Tuke campaigned for the reform of the treatment of the mentally ill. In Italy, Vincenzo Chiarugi instituted reforms at his model hospital in Florence, and in Germany Johann Gottfried Langermann and Johann Christian Reil agitated for reform (Gusdorf 1978: 470). Although one might see the clinical reforms as part of a different way of seeing human beings influenced by writers such as Rousseau, one could also argue that the clinical reforms themselves were evidence of an 'analytical' transformation of medicine, consistent with the titles of Pinel's books.

The most apparent way to define and understand disease in the eighteenth century seemed to be to apply the careful method of observation that Buffon had articulated as appropriate for natural history. One could, for example, characterise, classify and name a disease on the basis of its clinical symptoms. In fact, because one was restricted to external observation, one would seem to have little choice. But, as the body or the organism began to emerge as a system of interrelated functional systems in the work of the physiologists of *idéologie* such as Cabanis, a new view of disease seemed appropriate. Rather than imagining a particular disease as theoretically separable from whatever it infected, with an integrity of its own and characterised by a set of symptoms in the same way that an organism is characterised by anatomical features, it was now appropriate to imagine disease as a disorder in a particular functional system. It was not, even in principle, separable from its manifestation.

Pinel's *Nosographie* (1813 [1798]) is, Kaiser argues, the best example in his work of the earlier approach to classifying diseases, based upon the careful observation and data collection of the eighteenth century (Kaiser 1976: 394–5). Pinel categorised various psychoses on the basis of their symptoms, and carefully described symptoms such as hallucinations and delusions. Diseases, that is, were seen as agglomerations of symptoms. But Pinel's treatments of insanity revealed a more complex understanding of the relationship between disease, parts of the body and the entire organism than did his theoretical writing. He argued that insanity was a physiological disorder of the mental faculties, and that treatment therefore had to be applied directly to the nervous system at the same time that the general state of the body was to be regulated (Pinel 1801: 105). What is more, he recognised very clearly that 'will' and 'reason', related as they might be, seem very often to operate independently of one another and to be subject to quite distinct influences (Pinel 1801: 81). Sometimes, therapeutic intervention required that the 'will', which could clearly operate independently of rational control, be restored to its appropriate and subordinate position in cerebral function:

> One of the major principles of the psychological management of the insane is to break their will in a skilfully timed manner without causing wounds or imposing hard labour. Rather, a formidable show of terror should convince [them] that they are not free to pursue their impetuous wilfulness and that their only choice is to submit.
>
> (Pinel 1801: 48–9).

Restoring the appropriate hierarchy in cerebral function also required the recognition and enforcement of the hierarchical relationship between inmate and asylum superintendent.

In general, though, Pinel's management of the insane required the restoration of order in the disordered mind and, as Tracy acknowledges in a footnote in *Elémens d'Idéologie* (part I), 'the art of healing the demented is no different from that of handling the passions and directing the opinions of the ordinary man...The moral treatment that Pinel uses to restore confused minds is rightly the precise opposite of the procedures used by the oratorical art to excite man's imagination and enlist his acquiescence' (Tracy 1817: 299–300):

> In mania, at its highest degree of intensity, when the understanding is assailed by a rapid succession of the most incoherent and tumultuous ideas, attention is completely destroyed, as well as judgement and the inner awareness of one's own existence. The insane, incapable of all reflection about himself, is unaware of all his relations to external objects. From his gestures and his utterances we observe in him ideas other than those which could be produced by impressions upon his sense organs; and these ideas are without order, are disconnected, and seem to arise automatically, to appear and disappear instantaneously, and to follow their impetuous course like a torrent.
>
> (Pinel 1809: 78–9; quoted in Riese 1969: 150)

Pinel's clinical responsibility towards his inmates required that the minds of the insane be healed, and Tracy, at least, recognised the parallel between such clinical practice and the need to develop analogous methods to ensure that ordinary people would be less vulnerable to the seductions of those who would prey upon their ignorance and impulsiveness and who would use them for purposes not in accord with social harmony. This does require 'directing the opinions of the ordinary man' so that he is capable of discerning his own true interest.

Implications for a science of society

Pinel creates a link between physiology and social theory in two ways. We have already noted the common rationale behind his clinical techniques and the educational schemes that we will examine in the next chapter. More generally, society, as captured by the idea of the body politic, was imagined to have a moral aspect related to, but essentially distinct from, its physical aspect. Jean-Baptiste Say recognised that 'the social body is a moral as well as a physical being' (*Catéchisme* 1815: 186). Roederer, in his address to potential contestants, recognised that although a distinct set of moral institutions, such as books, festivals and monuments, existed separately from the institutions of production (below, p. 193) the two were mutually interdependent and would reinforce one another. It was, Roederer argued, the moral aspects of society that made it possible for society to 'conserve and reproduce itself' (Roederer 1853–9, 8: 139), and they included those intellectual and moral qualities of human beings that are required to maintain the harmony between the parts of society (Roederer 1853–9, 8: 131).

What is more, the body politic was imagined to have a will that, like the will exhibited by Pinel's patients, very often seemed to operate quite independently of reason. Individuals were the source of all social behaviour (Roederer 1853–9, 8: 131) but, at least some of the time, it was recognised that the behaviour of a society may differ in some significant ways from individual behaviour. Cabanis, for example, argued that leaders must study societies as well as individuals because if they try to govern on the basis of individual human nature 'without having seen men act in great masses, without having followed the development of their passions in contact with others, of their interests placed in conflict', they would be vulnerable to great error (Cabanis 1956, II: 465).

The *idéologues* realised that if the social body could, like the inmates of Bicêtre and Salpêtrière, become the victim of a will deprived of the governance of reason and subject to quite different influences, then it was incumbent upon those who would bring order to society to find a way to engage and channel the general will. The ideological solution, which we shall examine in the next chapter, is that society ought to be subjected to the firm direction of those better equipped to understand the innate harmony of their true interests. This is a position with strong antecedents. The Enlightenment, with its *Encyclopédie* and its Academies, embodied the idea that, if only the *lumières* were given the opportunity to educate and to govern, the people would freely adopt the policies and behaviours that could be shown to be the fruits of reason.

This notion was picked up by the revolutionary theorists. J. J. Rousseau's *Du Contrat Social* (1762; translated version 1978), for example, solves the fundamental social problem of conflicting individual interests by imagining society as an artificial person united by a general will (*'volonté générale'*). The social contract that brings Rousseau's republic into being is a creation of the 'general will', and society exists so long as its members voluntarily trade their natural rights for the civil rights legitimised and enforced by the entire community. Any individual who, enslaved by individual passions, violates the law of the community could justly be coerced by force into obedience to the general will because, according to Rousseau, that coercion is simply 'forcing a man to be free' by making that individual aware of his 'true interests'. Rousseau, however, recognised that the majority of the citizens in a republic are not necessarily the most intelligent members of society. Therefore, the general will, although always morally sound, is sometimes simply mistaken. Hence, the people need a legislator, a great mind like Solon or Lycurgus, to set up a constitution and a set of laws that truly reflect the needs of society.[4] This suggestion echoes Machiavelli, a theorist to whom Rousseau owed much.[5]

The complexity and tensions that characterised physiology were to reappear in very similar dress in the social analysis of the *idéologues*. However, the intellectual connection between physiology and social analysis in *idéologie* reflects a use of human bodies as analogies for social bodies that long predates *idéologie*.

Conclusion

One of the great achievements of the eighteenth century was to begin to develop an analysis that saw the human body as a natural phenomenon, subject to the laws of nature and embedded within the natural world. The *idéologues* built upon this analysis, arguing that the same scientific methods of observation and categorisation would yield data about both human bodies and the natural world. Moreover, they believed that the same philosophical problem existed in the natural world, in the world of human bodies and in society: how is it that a collection of separate and distinct, yet clearly interdependent, functional systems can be organised to the benefit of the whole? How can order rather than chaos be ensured?

Physiology seemed to provide, if not the answer, at least the most promising pathway towards an answer. Cabanis, recognising that communication between the nervous system and the various functional systems of the body was still a mystery to science, had great faith that the future would generate an answer. But he was prepared, notwithstanding his incomplete knowledge, to argue that something was already known about how different organisms within a society maintained a peaceful coexistence. He posited, as we have seen, sympathy as the natural source of the bonds between human beings, a subject we take up below as we examine the idea of the body politic. Corporeal metaphors, of course, were hardly new to social theory. But they became profoundly important to the social theory of the *idéologues*, who recognised that, once the old hierarchies were undermined, there was a fundamental problem of harmonisation between the functional parts of society that reflected the intellectual problem the physiologists addressed when they attempted to understand the operation of the human body.

The physicians, such as Cabanis, studying the relationships between the various systems of the physical body saw their roles as helping to re-establish the health of human bodies whose functional systems had become uncoordinated. Philippe Pinel, the physiologist whose clinical practice centred on the alienated inmates of the asylums, saw his role as re-establishing order between the various parts of the human mind. And the patients that Pinel observed seemed to embody within themselves precisely the same uncoordinated and self-destructive behaviour that human society exhibits when individuals within that society operate at cross purposes. Pinel's clinical responsibility was to bring about harmony within these patients; Roederer, Say and Tracy were required to bring about harmony within the social body. And none of these writers postulated that either individuals or societies could do without the assistance of professional healers charged with the duty of ensuring coordination between the various functional systems. In particular, societies had need of perceptive and wise leaders prepared to take into account the needs of the people.

It is clear that advances in physiology, anatomy and medicine on the one hand and human psychology and social theory on the other reinforced one another during this period. The articulated method of acquiring knowledge is similar, and the resulting models of the natural world, the human body and the social body bear certain similarities. It is equally clear that the models were not complete. Cabanis could not explain precisely how the various functional systems within the human body communicated with one another and coordinated their activities. Nor could the social theorists explain how the interdependent functional systems in a society related to one another. Pinel's patients and the social dislocations of Terror seemed to suggest, however, that harmony in both spheres was a problem to be solved rather than a natural attribute to be explained. And the solution to the problem of disorder in physical, moral and social bodies required the intervention of an intellectual élite who could re-establish the appropriate relationship between the various functional systems. Like the human body and the human mind, the body politic required its own set of physicians.

6 From physiology to social theory: the body politic, sympathy and moral education

The conception of disease as a lack of coordination between functional systems in a human body led to new ideas about the causes and cures for social disorder in the 'body politic'. This chapter considers first the metaphor of the body politic and its relationship to the physiological writing of the *idéologues*, then it examines the role that sympathy plays as the social cement that allows society to function as an integrated system. Sympathy is, Tracy acknowledges, a 'powerful attraction that brings us close again to our fellows at times when our individuality draws us apart' (Tracy 1817, 4: 516). And if sympathy is the foundation upon which society is based (Tracy 1817, 4: 515) then moral education[1] must have, as its fundamental goal, the cultivation of sympathy. The final section of this chapter considers to what extent a programme of public education designed to create a 'rational morality' through the inculcation of sympathy was characteristic of the writing of Roederer, Say, Cabanis and Tracy.

As we shall see, both Roederer and Say took it for granted that moral education was both desirable and effective. Tracy's 'Quels sont les moyens...' (Tracy 1798c), however, rejects such mass education, not because it was undesirable or illiberal but rather because he expected it to be far less effective than his preferred alternative method of inculcating morality: the swift and certain punishment of crimes and misdemeanours. This would best be ensured by the creation of appropriate institutions by legislators, who certainly knew the 'true interests' of the people better than any ordinary person. But, whatever the emphases of different writers, all argued that legislators and teachers must ensure the health of the body politic by creating systems that coordinate the individual members.

The body politic

The idea of the body politic was an established feature of various strains of European thought long before the *idéologues* arrived on the scene. Detailed organic images of human society were an integral feature of Greek thought, in which the body, the city and the cosmos were imagined to function according to the same principles (Haraway 1991: 7; see also Schlanger 1971[2]). Plato's

Republic (1961) compared the relationships among classes in society with the relationships among parts of the body, identifying the ruling class with the head, warriors with the breast and slaves with the abdomen. Each class was essential to the life of the whole society in the same way that each part of the body was required by the individual.

St. Paul makes use of a similar metaphor in his epistles to the Romans and the Corinthians: 'For as we have many members in one body, and all members have not the same office: so we, being many, are one body in Christ, and every one members one of another' (Romans 12: 4 and 5), and '...For as the body is one, and hath many members, and all the members of that one body, being many, are one body: so also is Christ...For the body is not one member, but many. [...] If the whole body were an eye, where were the hearing? If the whole were hearing, where were the smelling?...And if they were all one member, where were the body? But now are they many members, but one body...' (1 Corinthians: 12). For Christians, this metaphor was made concrete in the sacrament of the Eucharist (see Waterman 1996).

Although the *idéologues*, including Say, were certainly familiar with both the Bible and Plato's *Republic*, a more congenial source may have been Hobbes's *Leviathan* (1651), in which the Leviathan represents the sovereign. In this case, the metaphor is graphically illustrated on the often-copied frontispiece of the first edition, in which the 'commonweal' is represented as a king-like giant composed of many smaller individuals representing the submission of individual wills to that of the sovereign.

But the most immediate ancestor of the social body of the *idéologues* was undoubtedly the artificial person (the 'common man') of Rousseau's *Du Contrat Social* [1978 (1762)], and Rousseau made potent use of the metaphor in the context of his creation of the concept of the General Will. His expression of the concept in *The Discourse on Political Economy*, which was published in the *Encyclopédie*, is even more direct:

> The body politic, taken individually, may be considered as an organised, living body, resembling that of man. The sovereign power represents the head; the laws and customs are the brain, the source of the nerves and seat of the understanding, will, and senses, of which the Judges and Magistrates are the organs: commerce, industry and agriculture are the mouth and stomach which prepare the common subsistence; the public income is the blood, which a prudent *economy* in performing the functions of the heart causes to distribute through the whole body nutriment and life: the citizens are the body and the members, which make the machine live, move, and work; and no part of this machine can be damaged without the painful impression being at once conveyed to the brain, if the animal is in a state of health...Where this...formal unity disappears, the man is dead, or the State is dissolved.
>
> [J. J. Rousseau (*A Discourse on Political Economy*) 1973: 131–2]

Fundamental to most versions of the idea is the claim that social order requires the obedience of social inferior to superior, but also the recognition that social superiors have obligations and duties to their inferiors. That is, there must be a mutual subjection of each to all because human society (the body politic) resembles a biological organism, and without mutual subordination of the differentiated parts there must be disease, death and disorder.[3] The representation of human society in terms of the human body was justified and articulated in a number of distinct ways, and all postulated some form of necessary hierarchy between the organs of the human body in the one case and between the individuals and offices of society in the other.

One particular version of this metaphor of subordination is the 'Great Chain of Being', in which all creatures in the universe are ranked along a gradation from the perfection of angelic beings to the lowest of living organisms. According to Lovejoy, the Great Chain of Being was used in eighteenth-century Britain to justify social and economic inequality in two distinct ways. First, the concept implies that human beings occupy an intermediate position in the universe and, limited as such a creature must inevitably be, no great improvement in political behaviour or the organisation of society can be anticipated (Lovejoy 1936: 203). Second, human society is, like the very universe and an individual body, a reflection of the Great Chain of Being, composed of a finely graded ordering from absolute perfection to abject nothingness. This second proposition implies a 'natural' human inequality based on divine prescription. The Great Chain of Being, in itself, is a distinctly restrictive concept because it invariably excludes those eighteenth-century writers who shared the political pessimism of the concept but had no need for the metaphysical trappings, quite as much as it excluded writers such as the *idéologues* who were trying to deal with the problem of social disorder in a political system with aspirations of greater social equality than was characteristic of the *ancien régime*. Samuel Johnson's review of Jenyns (1790 [1787]) considerably limited the popular recitation of the idea in Britain, as did Voltaire's philosophical opposition in France (Lovejoy 1936: 251–3).

Lovejoy (1936) traced the idea of The Great Chain of Being from its source in Plato through to the beginning of the nineteenth century, finding it in Renaissance and in early modern cosmology, in the philosophies of Locke, Leibnitz, Spinoza and Kant, in eighteenth-century biology, in the theology of Hooker, in the politics of Bodin and in the poetry of Alexander Pope. From the last source, it found its way into Soame Jenyns's *Free Inquiry into the Nature and Origin of Evil* (1790 [1798]), in which it became the target for Samuel Johnson (Waterman 1994: 124). The body metaphor was pervasive. Sir William Petty began his *Political History of Ireland* (1691) by citing Bacon's 'judicious parallel...between the *Body Natural* and the *Body Politick*' (Petty 1986: 12; cited in Waterman 1994: 128). Sir Robert Filmer (1949) and Jean Bodin each made the body politic resemble the patriarchal family (Greenleaf 1964: chapters V and VII).[4]

The use of the human body and its faculties as a metaphor for society in the period surrounding the Revolution has long been recognised (see, for example, Hunt 1992). Waterman (1994) has argued that a version of the body metaphor was widely supported by both Tory and Whig sympathisers in eighteenth-century Britain. Needless to say, the rationales offered were quite different. Knud Haakonssen (1981) argues that one of the clearest expositions of the Whig version of subordination is to be found in Adam Smith, who expounds upon the 'pleasure of being governed' as a natural propensity to deference in the *Theory of Moral Sentiments* (e.g. Smith 1976: 114–25). In the *Lectures on Jurisprudence*, this is labelled the 'principle of authority' and is contrasted with the 'principle of common or general interest', which he also called the 'principle of utility':

> In all governments both these principles take place in some degree, but in a monarchy the principle of authority prevails, and in a democracy that of utility. In Brittain [sic] ...the faction's [sic] formed sometime ago under the names of Whig and Tory were influenced by these principles; the former submitted to government on account of it's [sic] utility and the advantages which they derived from it, while the latter pretended it was of divine institution,[5] and to offend against it was equally criminal as for a child to rebell against it's [sic] parent. Men in general follow these principles according to their natural dispositions. In a man of a bold, daring and bustling turn the principle of utility is predominant, and a peaceable, easy turn of mind usually is pleased with a tame submission to superiority.
>
> (Smith 1982: 402)

Whatever the intellectual justifications offered for the metaphor of the body politic, it is clear that human bodies were very widely used as analogies for social bodies. This conception was not limited to a particular political orientation, it transcended national and religious boundaries and it was used for a variety of purposes. It would, therefore, be more anomalous were the *idéologues* to do without the concept than to discover its presence in much of their writing. Nevertheless, the metaphor is uniquely appropriate to *idéologie* in a way that was not the case in other contexts. *Idéologie* is an interesting junction where the physiology of individual bodies, now free of the immaterial souls that used to be responsible for their coordination and governance, become an analogy for social bodies, now free of the governance of the Church and the King. The scientific understanding of the nature of the human body changed, just as the nature of the social body changed. But the organic metaphor remained.

As we have seen, *idéologie* drew its intellectual credibility from the advances in the life sciences, particularly physiology. It was imagined that the application of the same scientific method would yield similar advances in the social and moral sciences. Yet the congruity between physiology and the social sciences is more basic: similar intellectual problems characterised both realms. In physiology, scientists had begun to study and to understand a number of different functional systems. The question that remained was how these functional systems worked together to create a living human being.

The answers postulated in physiology all involved some hierarchical system. The sensory organs were subordinated to the spinal column that, for example, was under the governance of the cerebral organ. None of the organs operated independently; the 'governed' required the 'governor', clearly, but so too did the 'governor' or brain rely upon the data (and sustenance) fed to it by the operation of the subordinate organs. All were necessary and, perhaps more importantly, the fundamental needs of all the organs (notwithstanding their apparent divergence) were harmonious in the sense that all required the continuation of the body of which they were fundamental parts. In the case of the human body, therefore, the integrity of the whole was absolutely consistent with the true needs of the subordinate parts. Correctly understood, these needs ensured the harmonious survival of the body. The body was indeed a complex of highly differentiated systems, but the underlying harmony of needs ensured that the whole would have an integrity greater than the sum of its parts.

Bodily integrity, however, was not a foregone conclusion. Human bodies and human minds were subject to breakdown and malfunction. Indeed, the wonder that characterises the physiological and psychological writing of the period sometimes seems to suggest that physical and mental health is the exception rather than the norm. Physical breakdown, of course, takes the form of disease, and the rupture of the hierarchical bonds that characterise cerebral function takes the form of madness. In both cases, the skilled intervention and management of intellectuals – physicians who might also be physiologists such as Cabanis, or physicians who might also be trying to understand the causes and forms of madness such as Philippe Pinel – constituted the only hope for an individual so afflicted. The duty of the physician was to restore health to the organism, when possible, by restoring appropriate relations between the functional systems. Pinel, for example, sought to restore mental health to his patients in the asylums at Salpêtrière and Bicêtre, and he argued that 'an understanding of the varieties of madness teaches one to identify the almost certainly curable cases, the doubtful ones, those in which relapses are to be feared, and those without any hope of cure' (Pinel 1797).

The concept of the social body, too, seemed to some to postulate a hierarchy of one form or another, and, as one might expect, that hierarchy was also subject to breakdown and also required the attention of an intellectual élite to maintain and restore its health. The Great Chain of Being constructed such a hierarchical relationship in a peculiarly metaphysical sense that *idéologues* could not accept uncritically. But all versions of the metaphor suggest that the organs must work together for the good of the whole, and that the properly understood needs of the organs cannot differ from those of the organism. That is, the concept of a social body may indeed be used in a variety of ways and for a variety of purposes. Nevertheless, the integrity of a social body only exists to the extent that some mechanism ensures that the subordinate parts do not work at cross-purposes.

The concept of sympathy, an idea drawn from David Hume and more directly from Sophie de Condorcet's translation of Adam Smith's *Theory of Moral Sentiments* (Smith 1798), was invoked both to suggest the existence of a basic commonality of interests and to justify the various educational techniques proposed by the different *idéologues*, whether in their contributions to the public morality prize competition or elsewhere. Of the utmost importance is the implication that the integrity of the social body is not automatic. Sympathy appears instinctual to the uncritical observer but, in fact, it is a highly developed sense of judgement amenable to education of various sorts. Indeed, it is the purpose of education to develop sympathy and to teach individuals their true interests at the same time that it nurtures intellect.

The solution postulated by the *idéologues* to ensure the integrity of the social body suggests a vital role for professional educators, whether they take the form of schoolteachers, textbook writers or legislators. The social body will only survive and develop if individuals are taught their true interests, which are not necessarily apparent either to the casual observer or to the individual.

Sympathy

The basis of social life, according to the *idéologues*, is the concept of moral sympathy, which Cabanis articulates most clearly in a series of twelve lectures of which six were read at the *Institut National* in 1796 and in 1797 and which were published as *Rapports du Physique et du Morale de l'Homme* (1867 [1802]). The idea was developed into the foundation for both moral education and social analysis:

> I will add only one reflection: that is that the faculty of imitation which characterises all life, and notably human nature, is the principal method of education, both of individuals and societies; that one finds it in a way blended at its source with sympathetic tendencies, upon which the social instinct and almost all the moral sentiments are based; and that this tendency and this faculty are equally part of the essential properties of living matter combined into a system. Thus, the causes that develop all the intellectual and moral faculties are indissolubly tied to those that produce, conserve and set in motion the organisation [of the individual], and it is within the very organisation of the human race that the principle of its perfectibility is to be found.
>
> (Cabanis 1867, II: 287)

That is, sympathy is fundamental to human intellectual and moral education, and it is also fundamental to society. It is the glue that holds society together, and also the source from which a better society can be constructed. And there is a natural basis for the sympathy that the *idéologues* would cultivate in the very organisation (or physiology) of human beings.

In a section of the tenth lecture, entitled 'De la sympathie', Cabanis defines sympathy as 'the faculty of sharing the ideas and affections of others; in the desire to make them share one's own ideas and affections; in the need to act upon their will' (Cabanis 1867, II: 284). The universal human ability to imitate one another rests behind one person's ability to understand another's 'perceptions, judgements, desires' (Cabanis 1867, II: 284) without having to directly experience the precipitating event. Indeed, imitation is 'the aptitude to reproduce, without the need for the same degree of force and attention, all the movements that the different organs once executed', and 'that aptitude grows with repetition' (Cabanis 1867, II: 285). Like any 'muscle fibre', the physical correlates of moral sympathy can be strengthened with exercise: 'that which characterises muscular action occurs equally in other functions: only it is other organs and other types of movement, and as a consequence there are also other results' (Cabanis 1867, II: 286). Once one has felt the internal stimulus that excites the cerebral organ to respond in a particular way, one is in a position to understand its operation in others, or simply in one's imagination, without the need to experience the situation directly (Cabanis 1867, II: 286).

Moral sympathy, according to Cabanis, exerts its influence 'by means of glances, physiognomy, by means of exterior movements, through articulated language, by tones of voice, in a word, by all the signs: its action can be detected by all the senses' (Cabanis 1867, II: 286). But it would be an error to conclude that moral sympathy is a simple instinct because:

> The effect of glances, physiognomy and even gestures is not uniquely moral; it remains, if I can speak thus, a mixture of direct organic influences which appears to be independent of reflection. But one must not doubt that the most important part…is susceptible to cultivation; that its development is proportional to effort and to intelligence; in the end, the sympathetic moral sentiments are almost entirely a series of imperceptible judgements.
>
> (Cabanis 1867, II: 286–7)

That is, as Smith had argued (*The Theory of Moral Sentiments*, 1984, I, i, 4: 7), sympathy is less a simple instinct than an act of judgement, relying upon the cultivated imagination.

Cabanis chose not to push the analysis further in this context because at this point it 'enters the realm of ideology and morality; it is up to these sciences to complete the analysis' (Cabanis 1867, II: 287). Tracy, Say and Roederer take this notion one step further: if sympathy can be cultivated, ought it not to be one of the primary goals of the educational system to cultivate such a necessary aspect of social life? Tracy and Say both argue that the education of individual citizens requires the development of sympathy, particularly in children, who are more amenable to improvement than adults reared under the *ancien régime*. Despite Tracy's greater pessimism concerning the extent to which adults can be transformed, both he and Say share Cabanis's claim that sympathy grows stronger through exercise, and Say, as we shall see, postulates that theatre, various kinds of spectacles, parades and so on, which exercise the emotions and encourage sympathy, are more effective than the dull lectures of teachers. Similarly both, but especially Tracy (1798c: 15 and 32–3), fear the consequences of manipulation of the 'passions' by unscrupulous agitators. There is very little spontaneity about this discussion of sympathy; the people can, very often are, and probably ought to be influenced by those who understand the power of sympathy as an organising force in society. The only questions are who gets to exercise that influence, and to what ends? Clearly, there is a very real role for teachers, administrators, legislators and social theorists to play in the society imagined by the *idéologues*: individuals must be helped to understand their true interests that are in harmony with the interests of society as a whole, and they must be protected from those who would manipulate their very plastic sympathy to questionable and narrowly egoistic ends.

Moral education

It was a common feature of eighteenth-century thought that education was fundamental to improving the condition of the people through moral reform. Because people were very largely products of their environments according to the tenets of *idéologie*, it follows that superstition and ignorance will be reproduced generation after generation, unless a concerted effort is made to shape the social and cultural environment in such a way that virtue is rewarded and encouraged and vice discouraged. This, of course, requires that someone assumes the authority to change the environment and takes responsibility for the moral education of the people. The *idéologues* saw themselves as the educated élite who were best prepared to undertake this educational programme.

Before we examine the details of the plans for moral education offered by Tracy and Say, it is interesting to consider the historical context. Palmer has argued that 'of all activities of the French Revolution the hardest for a modern observer to enter into with sympathetic understanding are the measures taken for the civic indoctrination of the population as a whole' (Palmer 1985: 190). And, indeed, it is difficult not to see some of the educational efforts of the Committee of Public Safety as similar to the mass manipulation used more recently by totalitarian regimes. In Floréal of Year II (May 1794), the Committee of Public Safety attempted to bring the contributions of various artists into conformity with social needs by inviting sculptors, painters, musicians, poets and architects to submit their works to public competitions. Government committees would grant prizes, award subsidies and decide which architectural structures were to be built. There were plans for fountains, courthouses, gardens, theatres and assembly halls. Large amounts of money were awarded to music schools because of the usefulness of the art in public gatherings and in the army. There were proposals for statues of famous and virtuous men, and allegorical figures of liberty, equality, law and virtue.[6] Palmer claims that the source of these ideas is actually the Enlightenment as much as the Revolution, with the Committees of Public Safety and Public Instruction[7] simply extending forces that had already been in evidence before the Revolution (Palmer 1985: 192).

The Committee of Public Instruction had, as one of its chief concerns, the creation and celebration of national festivals. The best known of these is the festival of the Supreme Being on 20 Prairial of Year II (8 June 1794), in which Robespierre took a very active role. Palmer's description is illuminating:

> The ceremony of 20 Prairial in Paris reveals features that the planners hoped would characterise all the *fêtes nationales* and the *culte décadaire*. One was public participation, as obtained especially through mass singing and mass responses. Another was the bringing together of both sexes and all ages, with those of school age mixing with persons old enough to be their grandparents.[...] The *fêtes* were highly didactic, setting up written maxims and precepts to tell spectators what to think. They were also loquacious with many official speeches, though how such large audiences could hear a speaker in the absence of a public address system is hard to understand. There was no personality cult, no attempt to glorify a leader by name; and indeed Robespierre's prominence on this occasion was used by his enemies to denounce him as a would-be dictator.
>
> (Palmer 1985: 196)

The coincidence of timing that had this festival precede, by days, the worst of the Terror[8] ensured that nothing as elaborate occurred afterwards, but its echo can surely be seen in Say's *Olbie*.

The most profound difference between Tracy's 'Quels sont les moyens...' and Say's *Olbie* is the degree to which Tracy and Say believe that mass education would effectively create a rational morality. Both sought to strengthen the sympathetic impulses, but Tracy recognised that any attempt to achieve such a goal merely through moral education may be chimerical. Say's *Olbie*, however, demonstrates an enthusiasm for the sort of mass moral education of the Revolution. The theatre is a school for sympathy:

> They thought very highly of stage plays. Theatre gives us a more intense ability to sympathise with others; precious emotion, the opposite of selfishness, one of the most beautiful attributes of man, and which has something attractive even in its weakness! They had a theatre like the French, where in a series of engaging scenes, developed with art, there was not a guilty example nor a vicious idea, which was not presented with all the horror that it deserved and must inspire; and where models of humanity and greatness of soul were constantly offered, with the ornamentation necessary to make them enchanting.
>
> (below, p. 216)

But theatre is only one of the ways in which sympathy is encouraged among Olbians. Public festivals are potentially much more effective:

> With respect to national festivals, the Olbians sought the means to make them powerfully attractive; because one cannot direct hearts when one cannot capture them. Unless one attends a very curious spectacle, one never takes pleasure in these activities except by playing a role. The theatre is enjoyable even though the spectators are purely passive; but it requires the prestige born of the united efforts of the poet, the actor and the designer to sustain the attention of the public; as soon as one of these magicians does his trade badly, the play becomes boring and fails. But it is difficult to offer a great many people, assembled for a national ceremony, an amusement as vivid as that which results from the ensemble of talents of many artists who bring into play all the resources of their industry and all sorts of seduction. The magistrate who orders public festivals has recourse only to involving the spectators themselves in the scene, to arrange things so that each one of them sees himself as personally interested in the effectiveness of the affair; otherwise he would be arranging not a festival, but a more or less tedious stage play.
>
> (below, p. 216)

Not only are we encouraging sympathy, but 'directing hearts'.
These public festivals shape morality by rewarding virtue:

> But what gives a great character to these festivals is the distribution of honours and prizes by the Moral Guardians, to citizens who had earned them by their virtues.
>
> (below, p. 217)

But the rewards are not always so obvious and direct. Employment and positions of authority are used to reward virtue and to encourage emulation:

> The grown man is ambitious for power and prizes. This tendency, when it is unbridled, makes tyrants; well directed, it can make good citizens. Military ranks and jobs working for the festival police, were given to men who had distinguished themselves; but, at the same time, they must possess the other required talents and must be blameless of any moral weakness; and the desire to win prizes of pure skill must be accompanied by projects conducive to morals and education.
>
> (below, p. 217)

But it is not only public festivals and theatre which are used to nurture sympathy.

There are revolutionary echoes in attempts to use architecture and sculpture as tools of mass education:

The language of public monuments makes itself understood by all men because they address the heart and the imagination. Olbian monuments rarely recall purely political exercises, because political duties are abstract, founded more on reason than emotion and, in the end, because their observation necessarily follows from the observation of private and social duties which, like the strands that constitute the largest cable, form in their entirety the strongest link in the political body. The Olbians have only one Pantheon for great men and many for virtues. They do not refrain from raising a temple to Friendship, and placing over its gate a wooden sign carrying the words: To Friendship.

(below, p. 218)

Say's adoption of these methods of mass moral education is based on principles consistent with Tracy's *idéologie*. The techniques are not based on direct instruction, but rather on attempts to engage the hearts and the minds of the people.

Say, for example, accepts Tracy's claim that mass education works through imitation. Public morality is nurtured by authorities who model virtue, which the mass of the people imitate:

The fathers of the families follow, little by little, the example offered by public authority; and the example that, in the beginning, is followed a little, is that which is unfailingly imitated more over time.

(below, p. 220)

And it is destroyed by authorities who behave in ways that convince people of their own baseness:

For man to be virtuous, it is necessary that he respect himself and that he have a high opinion of the dignity of his being: one must, therefore, carefully avoid all that may tend to lower the people in their own eyes, in the fear that they will conduct themselves according to the way they are treated.

(below, p. 240)

And he recognises fully the extent to which habit can be a tool of education and also an impediment to changing the morality of the people. The most direct evidence, both of this position and of his debt to Tracy, exists as the lengthy extract of Tracy's essay that Say chooses to publish as Note F. Tracy argued, and Say quoted, that people who claim that the revolution has encouraged immorality seem unaware of the nature and the importance of habit in its creation:

They forget that morals and the sentiments of men do not change much from one day to the next, not even over a few years. It is certain, by contrast, that the present time is always the disciple of the past, and that we are governed today by the habits, the passions and the ideas contracted or acquired under the previous social order. If these are the causes of our actual evils, one must not hesitate to attribute them all to that ancien régime so foolishly yearned for...

(below, p. 228)

The mass moral education called for in *Olbie* is not merely a reflection of revolutionary practice, although it is that, but it is also a statement of accord with the principles of sensationalism. Say recognises that individuals are created by their environment, and that changing behaviour and, even more importantly, changing hearts and minds requires active intervention by intellectual and political authorities [because it is the 'magistrate' upon whom Say calls to create the festivals and to call for the election of the moral guardians (below, p. 216)]. That intervention must be designed to encourage the sympathetic tendencies.

In all of this, Say's concern was not that he might be accused of illiberal behaviour or of attempting to indoctrinate the people, but that he would be accused of romanticism:

I know well all the opposition that a similar institution would encounter among us. It would have for enemies, first the men to whom good morals are unimportant, and then all the mean spirits. But it is not these people that a government which strongly desires the public good must consult. They have, for a long time, known how to impose shackles. 'Your ideas,' says Saint Lambert who knows such people, 'will be treated as chimerical, and your schemes as romantic, by weak and narrow men who believe insane everything that they do not understand, and impossible all that they cannot do.' It is because people of this stripe are extremely numerous that one generally needs more constancy and courage than one would believe to work for good. There is no crime that will not find a defender; there is not one benefit that could not bring us to the point of a sword. Sapere audete.

(below, p. 239)

Say's *Olbie* never questions the potential or desirability of such schemes of mass moral education.

Tracy, by contrast, seems much less enamoured of the possibility that education designed to change hearts and minds would be effective. He sought to contain the 'vicious passions' through the inevitability of swift and certain punishment meted out by a well-run justice system, and to achieve desirable behaviour through the establishment of various institutions:

Set up favourable circumstances, and that which you desire will occur without your seeming to meddle.

(below, p. 258)

Although Say ultimately came to share Tracy's reticence concerning the effectiveness of mass moral education (see Say 1843: 729), in *Olbie* he lauds attempts to educate people 'as they go about their daily business' by exposing them to well-selected maxims, to statues celebrating appropriate virtues and to spectacles and games designed to act as 'a school for virtue'.

What is perhaps ironic is that although Say was prepared, in 1800, to publish an account with such a strong link to the logic of *idéologie*, Tracy and Cabanis were already beginning to question whether it was even possible to build a better world by building better human beings. Sympathy was, as Cabanis had argued, affected by the social environment, but both he and Tracy were beginning to believe that there were innate and distinct human 'temperaments' that were only somewhat amenable to rectification by a programme of moral education.

Tracy seems to have had little faith in the efficacy of education on any but very young children. In particular, those whose habits had been developed under the previous régime would be very resistant to such efforts. Tracy therefore argued that good legislation designed to curb the effects of the vicious inclinations was the first priority:

> ...the nature of men is such that they cannot come together without having distinct and opposing interests, and yet they are forced to deal with one another to help themselves and even to exist. What can they do? and, in effect, what do they do? They prescribe common rules to prevent each other from using those too frequent opportunities that they have to harm one another. These rules...are the true support of morality. They cannot destroy occasions of evil, but they limit their pernicious effects. That is the effect of good laws.
>
> (below, pp. 248–9)

The problem, as Tracy saw it, was that legislators who hoped to create a perfect society founded their mission on one of two equally impossible premises: that each individual should learn to love his neighbour as himself,[9] or that each individual should live in isolation from all others (below, p. 248). Neither is possible if people believe their interests to be innately opposed and yet human beings are forced to live in society. Legislation is the primary means by which the opposition can be contained, but it can never be complete enough or enforced well enough to eliminate all opportunities to harm one another.

Only then does Tracy turn to indirect means to influence behaviour, and to examine education in its many forms. Tracy argued forcefully against the 'very old and very absurd belief that moral principles are fixed in our minds and that they are the same for all' (below, pp. 250–1), castigating Voltaire for imagining that 'the proof...is that everywhere murder, theft have been placed in the rank of crimes, that everywhere violence and swindling are condemned. I would like as well to say that physics is a divine creation and that men have never argued about its principles because all agree that fire is hot, that the sun is bright, and that water is liquid' (below, p. 251). Morality, that is, is not innate. But even though he recognised that morality, like religion, is a human creation and differs over time and distance, he had little faith in the possibility that education would entirely eliminate the differences between individuals.

Direct instruction, Tracy argued, would be relatively ineffective. The best that one could hope to achieve was that each individual should understand well those things with which his social role placed him in direct contact. He argued that 'very few...have the time and will to follow a long course of instruction' and that 'even fewer...have the capacity to understand and retain a vast system of connected ideas' (below, p. 252). Fortunately, no one except legislators requires such systematic knowledge; most citizens need know only a little like artisans, who are content with a a few principal results of importance, 'few proven rules to follow their art, and ignore most opportunities to learn more of the advanced theories on which it is based' (below, p. 252). And for most people, Tracy argued, it is not direct instruction that would have the greatest impact on morality, but rather habit induced by observation and emulation.

Tracy acknowledged that morality is, in principle, subject to some form of moral education designed to teach individuals the 'effects of [their] inclinations':

> Morality being nothing but the knowledge of the effects of our inclinations and of our sentiments on our happiness, it is nothing but an application of the science of the generation of those sentiments and of the ideas derived from them. Its progress, therefore, cannot precede that of metaphysics: and that, as reason and experience prove, is always subordinated to the state of physics, of which it is only a part.
>
> (below, pp. 251–2)

But he held little hope that such education would eliminate all differences between human beings: 'there are...as many manners of seeing and feeling as there are individuals' and it is 'that diversity that constitutes the diversity of characters' (below, p. 252). It is this connection between 'character' and 'different manners of seeing and feeling' that allows us to link Tracy's essay on morality to Cabanis's writing on physiology that began, particularly in this period, to emphasise the innate differences between human temperaments and the demand for society to repress, and even to prevent the birth of, the 'vicious passions and habits' (Cabanis 1956, II: 449n).

Cabanis believed that the cultivation of sympathy was fundamental to the creation of social harmony. Moreover, the ability to sympathise is a natural human attribute (Cabanis 1956, II: 26). Basing his argument on the principle that there existed a hierarchy of universal forces of sympathy, from gravitational attraction to nervous sensitivity, Cabanis claimed that there was an unconscious sympathy in human beings that was the foundation for all moral education, and he claimed that the role of educators and legislators was to awaken that innate tendency towards sympathy (Cabanis 1956, I: 578; cf. Staum 1996: 127). This natural sympathy had both positive consequences, in the form of natural philanthropy for example, and negative consequences, in the form of crowd passions.

It would be easy to overestimate the degree to which Cabanis and Tracy differed, arguing as does Staum that 'Cabanis was more optimistic than Destutt de Tracy about social harmony' (Staum 1996: 127). But, in 1798 when Tracy wrote his essay on morality, the positions were quite close in terms of their implications for social organisation. Perfectibility had begun to assume second place in Cabanis's writing to a more thorough analysis of the darker side of human sympathy and the differential susceptibilities of individuals to fall under its influence, as Kaiser has claimed (Kaiser 1980: 146).

Cabanis shared Tracy's reservations concerning the power of direct instruction in moral theory to contain the passions of individuals. Whereas Tracy argued that moral instruction would do no more than 'force into a small number of heads abstract truths of moral health', Cabanis noted that 'all that which cultivates man's judgement, all that which makes a habit of continual and reflective examination, all that which gives man just notions of every object, tends at the same time to make man more moral' (Cabanis 1956, II: 449n). Nevertheless, he noted that when the imagination is invoked instead of merely the intellect 'the principles of morality enter more promptly and are engraved more profoundly in the souls of men; in this manner new habits soften by degrees and subjugate natural savage habits' (Cabanis 1956, II: 467). Both held to the idea that a pervasive system of moral instruction and social reform that had as a fundamental goal the gradual adjustment of habitual behaviour would benefit both individuals and society. However, both also accepted the notion that there were a number of distinct 'temperaments' that could be modified somewhat by the circumstances of life, but that deeply ingrained temperaments do not change and, indeed, are inherited from generation to generation 'like an ineffable mark, in the middle of the most diverse circumstances of education, climate, work, or regimen' (Cabanis 1956, I: 354–5). The perfect human being was, Cabanis claimed, 'a veritable abstraction, a purely ideal model. Has it ever really existed in nature? It seems unlikely' (Cabanis 1956, I: 354).

Tracy had claimed that repeated sense impressions leave traces in the brain or nervous system and that, therefore, intellectual operations could be improved by habit. Nevertheless, the goal of education was training individuals to make good judgements, and frequent repetitions of similar judgements might have the perverse effect of making human beings less aware. He was concerned that 'the class that has the least extended and varied communications' might be susceptible to the passions because their intellect had not been trained (1817, I: 267f). As a consequence, and unlike both Say and Roederer, Tracy and Cabanis were not prepared to endorse, enthusiastically and uncritically, the catechisms and public theatre that were the fundamental tenets of Revolutionary moral education.

If Tracy placed little faith in the efficacy of direct moral education, he offered a number of examples in which he demonstrates that 'legislators and rulers...are the true teachers of the mass of humanity' (below, p. 253). A teacher may preach that monetary matters ought not to be allowed to disrupt families, but legislation that eliminates primogeniture will eliminate this source of rivalry (below, p. 253). Similarly, the possibility of dissolution contained in a divorce law will go much further towards maintaining marital harmony than any amount of education (below, p. 255). The legal requirement that the public sector maintain a balanced budget will eliminate many opportunities for fraudulent financial dealing, and a large public debt increases the number of idle *rentiers* living off interest income (below, p. 255). Teachers may proclaim the superiority of reason, but legislation that stops the payment of priests will do more to eliminate public and private decision making based upon superstition (below, p. 254).

The cultivation of sympathy is far less important in Tracy's essay than is correct decision making by the relevant authorities, who are responsible for legislation. Even though one of the implications of *idéologie* seems to be that sympathy ought to be cultivated by mass education, the intellectual leaders of the movement were beginning to retreat from this implication as early as 1798.

None of these positions escapes from the charge of élitism at best and manipulation at worst. The implicit assumption is that an élite, composed of individuals educated in the principles of *idéologie*, would be charged with the task of determining which actions and ideas ought to be promoted as consistent with reason and virtue. Ordinary people, by contrast, would be given an education designed not to teach them the philosophical basis of social analysis, but rather to allow them to conform to the norms selected by their intellectual betters. It is this perspective that led Régaldo to describe the ideological programme as 'educational totalitarianism designed to shape minds and hearts' (Régaldo 1976: 207). Even Head, who is generally sympathetic to Tracy, is forced to acknowledge that 'Tracy left himself open to such charges by failing to provide, alongside his concern with institutional techniques of social integration and progress, a defence of a private sphere of individuality or a defence of intellectual and moral pluralism', although he argues that such criticisms are 'exaggerated'[10] (Head 1985: 104).

Conclusion

The ideological treatment of sympathy as the social force that binds together and renders harmonious the interests of the various members of the body politic finds its roots in the physiological analysis of Cabanis. The extension of the principle to moral education creates an intellectual foundation for elements of mass education similar to the enthusiasms of the Revolution and its Committee of Public Instruction. Ironically, however, the intellectual leaders of *idéologie* were already, by 1798, beginning to distance themselves from such programmes. Cabanis argued that individual temperament is only somewhat under the control of social factors, and Tracy claimed that a systematic programme of moral education for adults is bound to be less effective than a system of institutions designed to enforce conformity to a civil code through swift and certain punishment and to make behaviour more generally consistent with that desired by the intellectual élite. Say's *Olbie*, however, is consistent with the enthusiasm for mass moral education of an earlier period.

7 The amelioration of poverty in *Olbie*: the roles of educators, administrators and legislators

Profoundly new developments in the physiological investigations of the *idéologues* gave rise to a set of features that characterised ideological social analysis. One social problem that the *idéologues* confronted in 1800 was to explain how order would be established in a republic comprising individuals with apparently divergent interests. This mirrors the scientific problem faced by physiologists: how can a human body that is a complex of highly differentiated systems work together so that the human body maintains an integrity greater than the sum of its parts?

There is an element of *dirigisme* in the solutions proposed by the *idéologues*. Human bodies achieve and maintain order because physicians can re-establish appropriate hierarchies in the physical and mental system: the brain is in charge of the nervous system and, within the brain, reason has dominion over the will and the passions. If this natural hierarchy was disturbed, as it is inclined to be often enough, then Cabanis and Pinel could ply their trades and, through their expertise, re-establish order. Similarly, social bodies achieve and maintain order because social theorists and wise lawgivers can establish appropriate relations between members of a society and, most importantly, instruct individuals with respect to their true interests that are harmonious. The human body is naturally ordered but is liable to disruption, which must be cured by physicians. The social body is naturally ordered because true individual interests are harmonious but disruptions can occur when individuals are ignorant or delusional, and the re-establishment of social order requires the equivalent of physicians in the social realm.

This chapter examines the responsibilities of legislators, administrators and educators in the amelioration of poverty. Say acknowledged that the vicious inclinations of the people are due to the environment and, in particular, to the extremes of wealth and poverty that afflict many. His solution, therefore, was to make the social body harmonious by eliminating great disparity in living conditions. This he achieves through institutional reform and through education. First, I demonstrate that economic reform designed to mitigate extremes of wealth and poverty is essential to the establishment of social order and public morality in *Olbie*. Then, I claim that popular instruction is fundamental to the alleviation of poverty, and must simultaneously teach the skills that are required for basic citizenship, provide an opportunity for social mobility and teach the fundamental harmony of the true interests of all members of a society. That is, literacy and the rudiments of political economy were at least as essential an aspect of instruction, according to Say's *Olbie*, as were publicly displayed maxims an aspect of mass moral education. Finally, I suggest that the fundamental solution to poverty, according to *Olbie*, was industrialisation, which requires the active intervention of administrators and legislators as well as teachers. Individuals would come to value the 'comfort' that industrialisation brings, but industrialisation would only occur when hard work and frugality had become endemic. The encouragement of these values required not only that individuals be exposed to appropriate maxims as they went about their daily affairs, but that institutions such as savings banks be established and that other institutions that have the effect of encouraging a belief in 'fate' or 'luck' eliminated. Economic reform, popular instruction and the creation of institutions consistent with industrialisation require the active participation of educators, administrators and legislators, who play the same role of establishing order in the social body that physicians play in healing the physical body.

Administrators and the mitigation of poverty

Say notes in the *Traité* that the essential purpose of political economy is to reform the existing social order by eliminating extremes of wealth and poverty:

> [I]f one considers that in the *most prosperous* of nations, there is not one individual in one hundred thousand to whom it is given to accumulate all the pleasures [of a rich Sybarite], that one sees everywhere the exhaustion of poverty alongside the stoutness of opulence, the work forced from some to satisfy the greed of others, the hovels and the mansions, the rags of poverty mixed with the symbols of luxury, in a word, the most useless profusion in the midst of the most urgent needs, one can not regard as superfluous the researches done with the goal of knowing the causes of these evils, and the remedies to which they are susceptible. Some persons who have grasped a large enough portion in this state of things, lack not arguments to justify it to the eyes of reason. Perhaps if, from tomorrow, they were to draw again the lots that assigned to them their place in society, they would find much to criticise. There are others whose mind has never imagined a better social state, and therefore they claim that it cannot exist. They recognise these evils of the social order such as it is, and console themselves by saying that it is not possible for things to be otherwise.
>
> (Say 1803: xlii–xliii)

This spirit of idealism, of imagining a better state of society and asking how it might be achieved was the driving force behind Say's economics.

It is in this context that we must consider Say's repeated claims of the need for economic reform designed to eliminate great extremes of poverty and wealth. There are a number of instances throughout Say's work in which this preoccupation is evident, but his first detailed exposition of a progressive income or wealth[1] tax occurs in *Olbie* (1800a) before any of his substantive contributions to economics were written. It is instructive that this passage appears as a note to the claim that 'great wealth is not less harmful [than poverty that breeds desperation and crime] to good morals' (below, p. 204):

A question that appears to me worth examining carefully, is to know whether, among the methods of encouraging moderate wealth, it is useful to employ a geometric progression in the tax tables rather than an arithmetic progression. It is said that a tax which imposes more heavily on the wealthy tends to discourage industry, because the burden is greater the more successful the individual. It is also said that by following an always increasing progression, the tax must end by taking the entire revenue; this would be equivalent to expropriation. It seems to me that these two problems result solely from certain types of geometric progressions, but that there are others from which they do not follow at all. There are some that increase always in proportion to increases in revenue which never take the entire increase as tax revenue but only a part of the increase, just as certain geometric curves approach a straight line without joining it. For example, for each increase in revenue, the share of the state may take only a tenth of the increase above the last contribution; industry would not be discouraged because the industrious individual would always profit from nine tenths of the increase produced by his industry. Once this distinction is made, this seems the only equitable approach; because the needs of man do not increase in proportion to this wealth, the surplus increases progressively as wealth grows. And the tax must be in direct proportion to the surplus only; the necessary income, that is that portion without which one cannot live, must never be taxed; otherwise the tax would end in death. To achieve the same goal, it has been suggested that one should exempt a revenue that is believed to be *necessary* to live, and tax the rest without progression. But, in a state of civilisation, it is impossible to establish the level of the necessary. The necessary merges by imperceptible degrees into the surplus; and it is precisely this gradation which is equitably addressed by a well conceived progressive tax, that is, a tax which never absorbs more than a moderate portion of the increase of revenue. It is also equitable because, in a state of civilisation, increases in income are more difficult to attain at lower incomes. According to a popular saying, *the first hundred écus are harder to earn than the last hundred thousand francs*; that is, once one has achieved a certain fortune, the ease of earning is increased in the proportion of 333 to 1. I am far from desiring the progression of taxes to increase in that proportion which, if the saying is correct, would be required by equity.

(below, pp. 229–30)

It is no exaggeration to suggest that public finance was the central issue around which continental writing on economics had revolved for several centuries (see Schumpeter 1954: 199–206). In Italy, Germany, Spain and France since the fifteenth century, the question of how to pay for the rising costs of public expenditure was of paramount importance and, indeed, the *ancien régime* broke down in an attempt to secure fiscal reform. Taxation was something that Say and all of his contemporaries had thought a good deal about, and the notion of the progressive income tax was not a new one.

Graduated taxes had been applied to property from the time of Solon, through the medieval towns of France, Germany and Italy. In fourteenth-century France, the principle of *le fort portant le faible* was used to justify a graduated poll tax, although the assessors most often inverted the principle in application causing the poor to pay higher rates than the wealthy. The French tax on rental values of 1791 was progressive. Progressive income and wealth taxes had also often appeared throughout Europe. In 1742, there is evidence of a graduated income tax in Holland, and the income tax in Prussia varied from 1 to 8 per cent. In Geneva, the 1789 *taxe des grades* was slightly progressive.[2] Say could not have been unaware of the existence of progressive taxation.

The very polish and tenor of Say's argument suggests that the theoretical discussion of progressive income tax was not a new concept, and indeed it was a policy measure that had received analytical attention. Sébastien le Prestre, Seigneur de Vauban, whose treatise entitled *Projet d'une Dixme Royale* (1707) emerged at the end of the reign of Louis XIV, proposed that the existing complex system of indirect taxation be de-emphasised and replaced by an income tax in which different kinds of income would be taxed at different rates up to a maximum of 10 per cent. Similar ideas had occurred before.[3]

As early as 1758, Jean-Jacques Rousseau, whose political economy received so much criticism at the hands of Say, had very clearly argued that proportional taxation takes inadequate notice of the distinction between 'superfluities and necessities' (Rousseau 1973 [1758]: 160), that the social confederacy 'provides a powerful protection for the immense possessions of the rich, and hardly leaves the poor man in quiet possession of the cottage he builds with his own hands' (Rousseau 1973 [1758]: 160–1), and that 'the first guinea is sometimes more difficult to acquire than the second million' (Rousseau 1973 [1758]: 162):

> Putting all these considerations carefully together, we shall find that, in order to levy taxes in a truly equitable and proportionate manner, the imposition ought not to be in simple ratio to the property of the contributors, but in compound ratio to the difference of their conditions and the superfluity of their possessions. This very important and difficult operation is daily made by numbers of honest clerks, who know their arithmetic; but a Plato or a Montesquieu would not venture to undertake

it without the greatest diffidence, or without praying to Heaven for understanding and integrity.

(Rousseau 1973 [1758]: 162)

It is interesting that Say was later to find progressive taxation in Adam Smith's *Wealth of Nations*, where he notes that Smith argued that proportional taxation did not seem to go far enough and that wealthy individuals should provide somewhat more (Say 1880: 455; 1843: 495; cf. Smith 1976 [1776], book V: chapter 2). He also records Roederer's disapproval of such a measure (Say 1843: 495). Say clearly did not see this discussion of progressive taxation as a novel contribution. The mathematical tone of Say's argument, however, is interesting if one remembers that Say would, not very many years later, dispute the utility of applying mathematical reasoning to economic analysis (Say 1803: xxxix).

Say argued that wealth breeds poor morality because individuals exempted from social responsibilities can hardly be expected to do other than defend their privilege. It is unreasonable to expect them to model civic virtue. But if wealth breeds immorality, so does poverty:

> Misery exposes one to continual temptations; what can I say? to imperious needs. Not only acts of criminal violence, but also deceit, fraud, prostitution, riots, are almost always the fruit of poverty. How often men have embraced an abhorrent political party, or dangerous opinions, solely to survive! Such a man would not destroy his country, if he had the means of survival. Ah! if the wealthy, according to some people, understood well their own interests, instead of sucking the means of survival away from the poor in order to augment their own wealth, they would give charity voluntarily, and sacrifice some of their own goods in order to enjoy the rest in peace.
>
> (below, p. 204)

Economic reform and social stability are clearly linked. The elimination of the privileges and exemptions that accompanied wealth and social position before the Revolution was a necessary but not a sufficient condition for the creation of harmony between the classes. The simple existence of great extremes of wealth and poverty would, Say argued, lead to social unrest. The creation and expansion of the 'virtuous middle' would do more to bring about political stability than any amount of moral education.

Teaching individuals their true interests

If individuals believe themselves to have opposing interests, there are two fundamental ways to bring about social stability. One method accepts that individual interests are indeed opposing. If such a world is to be stable, then either a Hobbesian or a Machiavellian governor must exercise sufficient control to constrain individual pursuit of self-interest, or a spontaneous order must be posited whereby opposing interests adjust themselves and bring about a stable and ordered society. The second method, the one that I have attributed to Say and Tracy and shall extend in this chapter, asserts that notwithstanding the apparent diversity and opposition of individual self-interest, the true interests of individuals are fundamentally harmonious. Stability in such a world requires a different solution: moral and intellectual education for children and malleable adults, and prisons for deviants who are incapable of being made to understand their true interests.[4]

Before the Terror, the *idéologues* expected that economic growth in the context of the new Republic would lead to an elimination of great extremes of wealth and poverty. The social tools used to attain this goal would be greater access to education for all people and expanded opportunities for all citizens to benefit from economic advancement. This implies an acceptance of social mobility based upon individual ambition, hard work, luck and achievement. The Terror, however, demonstrated conclusively that the mass of the population could be an unruly lot even (and perhaps especially) in a republic, and that relaxing social control in order to allow individuals the freedom to benefit from education and economic opportunities could in fact lead to the very social disorder that characterised political upheaval. This fear of 'popular furies' is, perhaps, most apparent in Tracy's apparent disenchantment with the public festivals and theatre that Say still advocated as a method of shaping popular morality (below, p. 256).

Jean-Baptiste Say distinguishes between three functional classes of workers in economic production – scholars, entrepreneurs and workers (Say 1843: 47)[5] – and recognises that the social conditions and economic wellbeing of each class will differ significantly. In *Olbie*, he unwaveringly attributes the 'vicious inclinations' of the mass of the people to poverty, and he looks to both formal and informal moral education to help bring about the finer sentiments and more virtuous behaviour that economic advantage would make possible. That is, he eschews any discussion of innate differences between individuals ascribable to their disparate physical constitutions or 'temperaments'. What differs profoundly is the social environment within which individuals find themselves. As a consequence, individual behaviour is very distinct.

Educational opportunities based upon individual merit would, Say argued, allow any person to rise through the Olbian social hierarchy because hereditary honours and the rigidities of the *ancien régime* had been abolished by the Revolution and poverty would have been mitigated by good social policies (in Olbie, if not in France). Say argued that education was the principal means of social mobility for families, and it furnished the chief route out of generations of poverty. It can, however, only yield results if individuals are first relieved of extreme want:[6]

> The indigent, assailed by all his needs, looks at black symbols printed on white pages as a study in futility. He does not realise that the most sublime

knowledge, notions of political economy of the greatest utility, for example, a fertile source of prosperity and the wellbeing of nations, are hidden under the characters that he neglects. He does not know that if his ancestors had known how to lift the veil, he would not be reduced to sharing with his too-large family a morsel of black bread in the hut of a savage. Do you want him to teach his children? One must begin by assuring him of enough tranquillity and wellbeing for him to care about something which, in his eyes, can never be more than an object of secondary utility. Sufficient wellbeing for the indigent can only result from a wise sharing of general wealth which, itself, can only be the fruit of a good system of political economy.

(below, p. 200)

Economic wellbeing is both a cause and a consequence of a good system of education. Before education can be effective, individuals must realise enough of the returns to economic progress to put aside the scrabbling for survival that characterises the lives of the poorest. But once extreme want is eliminated, some individuals can climb through the social hierarchy on the basis of their own hard work and investment in the learning of their children.

It is instructive, however, that although Say believed education to be fundamental to the achievement of his social goals, he was unprepared to accept a state monopoly of the formal educational system late in his life. In the *Cours Complet* (1828–9), for example, he relied upon parents to ensure that their children were properly educated in a system that provided choice:

The propagation of enlightenment, the public good,…[requires] that there be a great number of schools which, instead of being cast in the same mould, would give different degrees such that parents may choose the best education for the future vocations of their children, and direct their work towards those studies that will be useful in the career to which their tastes and their fortune carries them.

(Say 1843: 465)

Such liberty of choice protects a nation from the 'biased and Machiavellian views of its government' (Say 1843: 465), but even more importantly protects the nation from the errors of its government. And one of the key errors that concerned Say was that a government might choose to inculcate a morality incompatible with the economic development of an industrious state. These concerns do not appear at all in *Olbie* (Say 1800a), and the general tenor, in fact, is that it is the wise administrator or legislator who would be responsible for ensuring (if not necessarily providing) basic education. But the problem of who provides the education was not seen as important enough to discuss in 1800; it clearly occupied a much more central position in Say's mind late in his life.

Education, of course, has another social consequence of great concern to

Say. Social and political stability are greatly enhanced by education. Characteristically, Say claims that it is by teaching us our true interests that education favours morality:

> Instruction civilises us by turning our ideas towards innocent and useful objects. Instructed people, in general, engage in less evil, are less destructive, than the unschooled. A man who has studied agriculture, and who knows that it requires care to grow a plant or to raise a tree, he who understands their economic uses, is less likely to destroy them than the ignorant who have no appreciation of these precious goods. Similarly, the man who has studied the bases upon which are founded the social order and the wellbeing of nations, will never destroy them without repugnance.
> (below, p. 198)

Instruction, Say implies, would include a recognition that all classes share an interest in preserving the social order. Education serves the republic both in terms of social stability and of wealth creation, and the science of political economy is an essential part of all three goals.

Both the *Traité* and the *Cours Complet* suggest that Say maintained some significant commitment to the ideals of social mobility and the improvement of human beings. Although this older and more experienced Jean-Baptiste Say was considerably less certain of the prospects for a better society or for a better human being, he nonetheless emphasised the role of education, going so far as to claim:

> If I were to rewrite my *Olbie*, I would base it on an entirely different foundation. I would demonstrate that the morality of nations depends on the degree of their instruction. Instruction consists in forming correct ideas about the nature of things...On the positive knowledge of the nature of things, depends knowledge of our true interests, and on the knowledge of our true interests the perfection of the social arts. If one wants to consider the social arts without overcoming these hurdles, one plants a tree without roots, one creates a utopia, a dream more or less chimerical.
> (below, p. 242)

Education, if anything, became an even greater concern for Say as time passed, but he no longer emphasised its role in allowing individuals to move up through the social pyramid nor did he retain his early fascination with the popular forms of moral education, such as festivals, that preoccupied him in *Olbie*. He is considerably more circumspect about the possibilities of achieving a perfect society, noting that he 'will not give men the honour of believing that they will ever see a time when there will not be tyrants among them'. Because evil and tyranny will persist, education becomes even more important a consideration because it makes the work of tyrants 'more difficult in proportion as nations become more enlightened'. But, most importantly, Say recognised that his social goals did not depend on 'a nation be[ing] composed of scholars...it is sufficient that each person have a correct idea of the things which concern him, that which is good is not absolute and, as a consequence, chimerical but gradual and, as one can see, necessary – we approach closer to the good society as each one is more certain to have correct ideas concerning those things which interest one.' Neither individuals nor society need achieve perfection through education. The gradual instruction of individuals, related to the concerns and social positions of each, is sufficient to bring about a better society. Education remains important, but now the education is focused on creating a critically aware citizenry, competent to limit the encroachments of tyranny.

Human perfectibility no longer seems realistic, but neither is it necessary. A much more pragmatic focus on the possibilities of education results, but it comes without a focus on social mobility. Paradoxically, the abandonment of human perfectibility did seem to accompany a shift away from an emphasis on education as a vehicle for self-improvement and social mobility for Jean-Baptiste Say, and towards an even greater recognition of its role in promoting social harmony through teaching individuals their true interests.

The creation of institutions consistent with industrialisation

In announcing the conditions of the morality prize competition, Roederer offered an elegy on the benefits of hard work and its impact on morality. Roederer's address directed potential contestants to consider three types of institutions that affect public morality, while removing civil, political and religious institutions from consideration because 'in 1789...liberty and property were placed under the protection of equality and under the guarantee of a republican regime' (below, p. 193). They were to consider institutions that 'enlighten the mind, like public education', those that 'warm the soul, such as monuments and national rites', and those that regulate 'the customary practice of everyday life, such as domestic institutions' (below, p. 193). But Roederer clearly believed that it would be discovered through analysis that the institution of work would be found to be 'the great regulator of private morality'.

Even more than education, Roederer relied on the work ethic motivated by hope of gain rather than fear of indigence, by the honour of work and shame of idleness rather than greed, to elevate morality (below, p. 194). The institution of labour:

> ...may make sensible and palatable the notion of the equality of rights amidst inequality in fact, by giving the rich modesty and frugality, and the poor dignity and comfort; by valuing all contributions...This institution is the most powerful guarantee of property, because it teaches everyone that benefit is acquired only through pain, and because work offers to all the opportunity to acquire. It is...the most powerful guarantee of

liberty...[and] preserves the soul from these evil, uncertain and fearful passions that boredom engenders...

(Roederer; below, p. 194)

Say, sharing Roederer's respect for the institution of labour goes further. It is, he argues, up to the legislator, the administrator and the educator to establish institutions consistent with industrialisation, and to abolish those institutions found to be inconsistent.

One of the basic requirements of industrialisation is the idea that even the poorest is not at the mercy of vague forces such as 'luck' or 'fate', but that the life one leads will, for the most part, be determined by one's own actions. This creates the idea that one can plan for the future by, for example, saving for one's old age. Conversely, this belief creates an attachment to the labour force because one is responsible for one's own life and that of one's family.

Say considers very specific institutions designed to be consistent with these values. In *Olbie*, he claims, savings banks or mutual aid societies have been established,[7] so that even the most menial worker can save for the future or for periods of want (below, pp. 206, 233). The idea of having a small annuity to support one's old age is a recurring theme. Similarly, the state would not support or condone institutions that encourage an irrational attachment to ideas of the supernatural, such as books of magic or dream interpretation, or individuals who profess to foretell the future (p. 207). Almost as dangerous, from his point of view, are institutions that seem to suggest that luck as opposed to hard work is the route by which an individual may gain his fortune. Gaming houses had been abolished, as had state lotteries (p. 207). It was clear that the state ought not to be involved in establishing or condoning institutions that were inconsistent with industrialisation.

However, Say, in fact, allows a much more active role for the state in encouraging those values consistent with industrialisation. Idleness ought to be held in low esteem, so he suggested that individuals ought to be identified by the work they undertake whenever they are called to play a role in governance or administration (p. 205). Particular posts in the administration of the state ought to be reserved and used to reward behaviour considered virtuous (p. 207). Committees ought to be established, the mandate of which would be to seek out and reward individuals demonstrating appropriate behaviour and to censure that behaviour considered inappropriate (p. 214). Among the vices to be punished would be idleness, wasteful consumption, fraud and dishonesty, and among the virtues regular attachment to hard work and the production of books deemed useful to the state would be rewarded (p. 217). Regular games and national events ought to be held, the conduct of which would reinforce the virtues of family attachment, hard work, modesty and frugality (p. 217).

Once such institutions were in place, the population would slowly start to recognise the benefits to be derived from behaving in ways consistent with the values promoted. Individuals would, for example, recognise the costs of drunken debauchery, and come to appreciate the gentle pleasures of domestic life (p. 220). And, therefore, those values recognised and promoted at the outset by the enlightened few (who would presumably be well versed in the analysis of *idéologie*) would be recognised as superior by the masses, who would voluntarily adopt them. Coercion would be unnecessary because the utility of behaving in particular ways would be obvious.

Fundamental to all of this was the idea that the science of political economy was 'the first book of morality' (p. 197). Institutions consistent with the truths of political economy ought to be encouraged, and the others ought to be discouraged. Individuals hoping to move into any administrative or elected position would demonstrate a familiarity with the science of political economy, so that any action undertaken could be expected to be consistent with 'the nature of things' because these are captured by political economy.

All of this suggests a very active role for the state in determining and inculcating a set of values consistent with industrialisation. It is clear that 'the leaders among the Olbians' first model appropriate behaviour by, for example, declaring a disgust for display and wasteful consumption (p. 209). The mass of the population would then, it is assumed, come to recognise the limitations of their previous behaviour. It was not always the case that 'the leaders' are represented by the apparatus of the state. But *Olbie* is a meritocracy, and it is clear enough that much of Say's discussion concerns the manner in which the values of this élite would be represented in the state by, for example, ensuring the election of the most worthy and learned individuals. And, often enough, the state was given a very direct role in eliminating obsolete and harmful institutions, such as the lottery, and establishing beneficial institutions, such as the system of reward and punishment captured by the proposed method of appointment to administrative positions.

Conclusion

Georges Gusdorf labelled the years between 1794 and 1800 as the 'golden age of the Idéologues', claiming that they saved the 'honour' of the Republic and assured the permanence of the Revolution of 1789 by translating the implications of their intellectual labours into the institutions of the nation (Gusdorf 1978: 305). Thomas E. Kaiser (1980) has recognised these same years as a period of transition, when the idealism that characterised ideological thought in the early years of the Revolution was challenged by Terror and began to focus increasingly on the need for social order. Kaiser quotes Roederer's plea for 'order, order…there is the object of all constitutions, the task of all governments, the principle of all prosperity'[8] as exemplifying the new cry for social stability. Martin S. Staum has adopted the slogan 'stabilising the French Revolution' to characterise the ideological programme of the *Institut National* during this period (Staum 1996). Philippe Steiner has located Jean-Baptiste Say in this intellectual endeavour, arguing that the primary focus of his writing during the period was to respond to the problem of 'how to stabilise the modern social order?' (Steiner 1990: 173).

These issues of economic reform, education and social mobility point to an underlying, and ultimately unresolved, tension in *idéologie*: how does an individual, and that individual's self-interested behaviour, relate to society and social wellbeing? Jean-Baptiste Say is clear that 'evil, uncertain and fearful passions' are the results of poverty and social ills (cf. Staum 1996: 70; Kaiser 1976: 247–8). The most direct way to reduce social discord is to reduce destitution, and that requires the active intervention of administrators, legislators and educators who are charged with three tasks: economic reform, according to the insights of political economy, designed to eliminate extremes of wealth and poverty; popular education designed to instruct individuals in such basic skills as literacy and to help shape morality; and the creation of a set of institutions compatible with industrialisation that remains, according to Say, the fundamental route out of poverty.

8   On domestic virtue[1]

One of the problematic areas of the social theory of *idéologie* is the extent to which 'natural' differences are thought to exist between individuals and to limit the effectiveness of social programmes designed to shape human attitudes and behaviour by changing the environment. We have already seen, for example, that both Cabanis and Tracy are beginning to speak of different 'characters' and different 'temperaments' as early as 1798. Say's *Olbie*, however, seems to reflect a much more consistent focus on the environment as the shaper of individual and of public morality, attributing the vicious inclinations to poverty and to maladaptive institutions and relying upon mass education to inculcate public morality. This picture changes a little bit, however, as soon as we look at the role of women in *Olbie*. Say emphasises the 'natural' differences between men and women, and argues that changing the social environment to reflect these differences would lead to social harmony. The changes he advocates are, characteristically, changes in institutions and educational reform.

One of the most striking economic and social issues of the late eighteenth and nineteenth centuries was the impoverishment of women. Wages in traditional employments were low, partly because of legislation and social constraints that kept women from entering the professions and many employments, partly because of the competition of religious communities (when these were not outlawed) that depressed women's wages because religious women whose subsistence was guaranteed would work for lower wages than independent women could contemplate, and partly because the social upheaval of the period meant that there were more women living outside families that would traditionally have provided their subsistence. This chapter attempts to place the connection between gender and political economy into a historical context by demonstrating how a patriarchal analysis of gender and a popular justification for a market economy coexisted and reinforced one another in the writing of Jean-Baptiste Say. His gender analysis is not especially unique; it was shared by his colleague Cabanis, and it represents a naturalised view of the role of women that is reminiscent of Rousseau's pre-Revolutionary Sophie.

The next section of this chapter portrays the political context of feminist[2] agitation to which Say reacted. Then, I examine Jean-Baptiste Say's analysis of the family as the fundamental unit of political economy, within which the subsistence of individuals is provided and the moral virtues inculcated. It is upon these moral virtues that a market economy and a civil society must be based, according to Say. Finally, the analogy between the firm and the family in Say's economics is documented.

Women in the French Revolution

In popular histories of the French Revolution, the representations of women range from docile 'sisters' nursing the wounded revolutionaries to 'amazons' storming the Paris Council dressed in red caps and pantaloons (Kadish 1991). The images and sympathies differ significantly, but the one point upon which all are in agreement is that women were not invisible during that conflagration. Revolutionary feminism was a significant political force, and it attracted both supporters and detractors and influenced the women's movement in France throughout the nineteenth century (Moses 1984; Rendall 1984; Bridenthal and Koonz 1977).

The 1789 *Declaration of the Rights of Man* became the preamble to the *Constitution* of 1791. Olympe de Gouges, eager to ensure that the Revolution brought women political rights in addition to the political voice they had already obtained, wrote and published a *Declaration of the Rights of Women*.[3] Drawing its inspiration and style from the earlier document, her *Declaration* demanded equal rights for women before the law and in all aspects of public and private life. This decidedly political document was a contribution to an ongoing debate, throughout the revolutionary decade, about the natural roles of women and men in society. Mary Wollstonecraft's *A Vindication of the Rights of Woman* (1792), among other works, emerged during the period and, although it may have been part of an English conversation,[4] it was certainly steeped in the drama of French circumstance. No intellectual actively involved, as was Jean-Baptiste Say, in the construction and legitimation of the social sciences could be unaware of the tumult, even if, as is much more likely, he was not aware of the many strains and details of women's activism during the decade.

The controversy wells up in distinct places: in May of 1793, Claire Lecombe (a former actress) and Pauline Léon (a former chocolate maker) founded the *Société Républicaines–Révolutionnaires*, the most notorious women's revolutionary club of the time. With Léon as president, the Club established itself in the library of the Jacobin Club and took up the battle against 'enemies of the republic'. As strong supporters of the Jacobins, these Club members took their battle to the streets where, in revolutionary bonnets and pantaloons, they harassed the Girondins and silenced them in the galleries of the National Convention.

In June, the Jacobins took over the National Convention and expelled the Girondins with the support of the *Société*. In July and August, women were accepted on the councils of the Parisian sections. But later that year, the deputies to the Convention outlawed women's political clubs with only one dissenting vote. A delegation of women was led by Claire Lecombe to protest the betrayal before the Paris Council. Pierre Chaumette, president of the Council, responded:

> It is horrible – unnatural – for a woman to want to become a man...since when has it been decent for women to abandon their pious household tasks and their children's cradles, to meet in public places yelling from the galleries? Impudent women who want to turn themselves into men, don't you have enough already? What more do you want? Your despotism is the only force we cannot resist, for it is the despotism of love, thus the work of nature. In the name of nature itself, stay as you are. Instead of envying our perilous, busy lives, you should be content to help us forget all this at home in our families, where we can rest our eyes with the enchanting sight of our children made happy through your cares.
>
> (quoted in Bessières and Niedzwiecki 1991: 8)

The rhetoric had its effect. Olympe de Gouges was already dead, a victim of the guillotine, and Lecombe effectively silenced. The Terror of Robespierre's 'virtuous republic' sent women back into their homes, except for the few chosen to personify the 'goddesses of Reason', dressed in white with blue capes and bonnets of liberty as they were carried into the transformed cathedrals to the strains of *Ça ira* and the *Marseillaise* – priestesses for the newly established 'Cult of the Supreme Being'.

The debate about gender roles was similarly the inspiration for some of the more extreme revolutionary fiction. The Marquis de Sade played the controversy out at length in several novels, and Apollinaire saw early in the twentieth century exactly how public morals were outraged by *Juliette*:

> The Marquis de Sade, that freest of spirits to have lived so far, had ideas of his own on the subject of woman: he wanted her to be as free as man. Out of these ideas – they will come through some day – grew a dual novel, *Justine* and *Juliette*. It was not by accident the Marquis chose heroines and not heroes. Justine is woman as she has been hitherto, enslaved, miserable and less than human; her opposite, Juliette represents the woman whose advent he anticipated, a figure of whom minds have as yet no conception, who is arising out of mankind, who shall have wings, and who shall renew the world.
>
> (quoted in Sade 1988: ix)

If Juliette represents 'the woman whose advent [Sade] anticipated', she also represents the woman whom many of his contemporaries dreaded.

Revolutionary tales are replete with tales of 'amazons' and 'furies', alongside heroines of unfathomable courage. It was a romantic era, and the histories of the period capture the spirit. Well-dressed gentlewomen carrying hunting knives and half-sabres along their skirts jostle for position in the old histories with Burke's 'unspeakable abominations of the furies of Hell incarnated in the fallen form of the most debased women' (quoted in Bessières and Niedzwiecki 1991: 5). It was, and we must not forget this, the women of *Les Halles* – the market district – who made up the greatest portion of the crowd that stormed Versailles, who formed the mobs in the street riots, and who challenged the revolutionaries to make sure the revolution began for women as well. No one living through the revolution or the revolutionary decade could be ignorant of either the behaviour of crowds of women, the even more colourful legends of actions allegedly perpetrated by women, or demands (reasonable and measured, alongside strident and aggressive) for political suffrage. Robespierre went far in suppressing those demands that he conceived dangerous to the Republic, and Bonaparte, coming to power in 1799, ensured that women would be effectively muzzled for much longer through the agency of the Napoleonic Code. But the period between 1789 and 1799 saw many individual women raise their voices in demands that had not been heard so clearly before, and certainly not at such insistent volume.

Idéologues, however, were not a uniform intellectual group, and the disparity of their positions on various matters related to the social sciences is well illustrated by the different analyses of women's economic and social roles that various members produced. Social and intellectual historians not primarily interested in the development of economic analysis may find, and indeed have found, the feminism of the circles surrounding Condorcet more compelling than the writing of Say and Roederer. There is no way to reconcile the two approaches represented by Say and Condorcet in order to produce a homogeneous analysis that could be attributed to *idéologie*.

Say's analysis was consistent with the physiological work of Pierre-Jean-Georges Cabanis and seems to derive intellectually from two distinct sources. The cultural presumptions fixed in the work of Rousseau, for example, were already a powerful political weapon in the 1760s, and reappeared virtually unaltered in the political and social debates of the revolutionary decade. This naturalised view of the ideal woman influenced the physiological writing of Pierre Roussel (1775), who wrote for *La Décade* and the *Mercure de France* and was elected as an associate to the Ethics section of the class of Moral and Political Sciences. His *Système Physique et Moral des Femmes* (1775) went through five editions before 1809, and was favourably reviewed in *La Décade* in 1802 and 1805.[5] His basic premise was that behavioural differences between the sexes were the result of innate differences in physiology related to the function of childbearing rather than education or social experiences. These differences produced a more flexible organic structure and a more constant temperament, and also 'briefer, finer sensations' that did not permit the concentration required by abstract thought. Rather than being imperfect men, women were beings endowed with distinct virtues: a finer sense of sympathy, natural pity and sweeter, more affectionate feelings. Roussel's work was known to Cabanis, who argued that the genital centre of sensitivity had a strong sympathy with the brain, which affected both sex drive and character (Cabanis

1956, I: 273, 278–9, 284, 291–3, 297–9). In particular, the reproductive organs at puberty begin to release substances that energise the male and reinforce female passivity. Although these natural tendencies might be modified by habit, Cabanis argues that such an attempt would undermine the 'law of nature' (Cabanis 1956, I: 291). Cabanis extends this physiological analysis to the social sphere, specifically claiming that women lack the reason, energy and character for civic and public roles and, although particularly suited to observe social relations, women are unfit for scientific or academic research (Cabanis 1956, I: 299; cf. Staum 1980a: 213–17; Welch 1984: 48–9).

These physiological works are contemporary with writing by *idéologues*, such as Tracy and Say, who were primarily interested in issues of social organisation and social order. Physiology created a scientific basis for the ideal woman they celebrated, even though Tracy was to claim that women 'do not have a different nature' (Tracy 1926: 49). Tracy argues that women have never been allowed to develop their natures fully because of the impact of social institutions and traditional law. Both men and women ought to be granted the greatest possible liberty, marital laws ought to be modified to eliminate the property considerations that might impede unions based on love, and divorce liberalised. He also argued that women should be granted access to education. But Tracy's argument remained in an unpublished document considered too radical for French public opinion.[6] Tracy considered the question of women's suffrage in his *Commentary and Review of Montesquieu's Spirit of Laws* (1819), which he was writing as early as 1806 (Welch 1984: 119), and notes that some 'respected authorities'[7] had no objection. But a much more common position among the *idéologues* is that of Roederer who, adopting the work of Cabanis and Roussel, denied women any role in public life on the basis of incapacity (Roederer 1853–9, 8: 159–63).

There is, of course, a danger involved in trying to discuss the analyses of gender offered by social commentators of earlier periods because it is difficult to answer the charge that one is implicitly holding these individuals responsible to the sensibilities of our own time.[8] These men, it is argued, are simply stating the wisdom that was the common currency of their own age; they cannot be expected to anticipate the social controversies of our own. None of these opinions are, in any sense, unusual for the period, but they are a bit unexpected coming from the advocates of *idéologie*. The personal connections of the Auteuil salon with such highly respected women as Sophie Condorcet, who translated Adam Smith's *Theory of Moral Sentiments*, and Mme de Staël, whose political acumen was well regarded, might have been expected to encourage a more egalitarian approach to gender relations, even if the logic of the political and social analyses did not. But, most importantly, the context offered by the social debate of the revolutionary decade – a debate of which no aware, conscious and thinking individual could be ignorant – might have been expected to encourage speculation about increasing the rights and the roles of women.

The structure and the role of the family in an ideal state

The primary source of Say's writing on women in society and in the economy is *Olbie*. The most striking passage concerning women in *Olbie* sounds rather unsympathetic:

> They are neither women nor men these beings in petticoats, with wild eyes and raucous voices, who, among the population of our cities, resist men, either to insult them or to lead them by the hand. This is a third sex.
>
> (below, p. 211)

The potent mixture of violence, of intellectual possibility and of social upheaval characterised by the destruction of the church and the monarchy, which ordered the *ancien régime*, may have gone just a bit too far for an economist who was really concerned with eliminating tariff barriers and reforming taxes. It is not surprising that attitudes engendered by Terror would persist, and would appear in the form of poetry extolling the feminine virtues that Say published in *La Décade* during his tenure as editor or in the guise of references to a pushy and raucous 'third sex' in *Olbie*.

Statements like this are, however, no more than an immediate reaction to the political turmoil of the period; they do not constitute an analysis. Nevertheless, Say does offer such an analysis of gender roles in *Olbie*, in which he maintained that the family is the fundamental unit of society, responsible for the maintenance of social order, and that women find their pivotal economic role in the context of household production where they share the responsibility for the maintenance of the patriarchal family.

Say argued that the family serves two purposes: it provides the nurturing and subsistence of all of its members and it is the school in which the civic virtues are learned. He observed that in Olbie, a community that had just weathered a revolution and was now in the process of setting up institutions to stabilise the republic, women play a key role in socialising other family members:

> The Olbians would have been weak moralists if they had no appreciation of the extent to which women influence morals. We owe to women our first memories and our last consolations. As children, we are the work of their hands: we are that still when we reach adulthood. Their destiny is to dominate us without cessation, by the authority of their kindness, or by that of pleasure; and where women are not virtuous, it is vain for us to aspire to virtue. It is by the education of women that we begin that of men.
>
> (below, pp. 209–10)

This sounds strikingly similar to Chaumette's earlier criticism of the women who appealed to the Paris Council and did not value the power of their 'despotism of love'. The role that the father plays in training the children in the morals of a civilisation should not be underestimated in Say's analysis. In *Olbie*, Say explicitly recognised the educational functions of the family and noted that the very principles that preserve order in the family are those that ensure social stability:

> The fathers of the families follow, little by little, the example offered by public authority; and the example that, in the beginning, is followed a little, is that which is unfailingly imitated more over time. In their houses one can read phrases applicable to order inside the family, and children nourished on these maxims, which experience shows them to be valid, regulate their conduct on the basis of them, and transmit them to their own children. One is happy because one is wise: men and nations will not be happy otherwise.
>
> (below, p. 220)

Moreover, the 'natural' attraction between men and women was to form the basis for marriage, which seems an unnecessary statement until we remember that some of the individuals writing during the revolutionary decade were imagining all kinds of alternatives to traditional (and less traditional) marriages (see Condorcet 1795):

> The Olbians do not, as is done in some sects, attack the inclination which attracts men to women. It is an instrument as powerful as it is gentle: is it necessary to break it rather than to use it? Neither do they follow the counsel of Plato who, in his imaginary Republic, wanted a lottery to determine once and for all, in an entire class of citizens, an exchange that reduces us to the level of brutes, if it is not ennobled by faithfulness and the delicate preferences of the soul. On the contrary, the Olbians blend honest love with all of their institutions that can admit it; and, one must acknowledge, they have taken some advice from our centuries of chivalry.
>
> (below, p. 210)

For Say, the family unit was not to be tampered with lightly.

Women's work and the economic role of the family

The economic role of the family in providing subsistence to its members is inseparable from the question of women's work, and Say addresses both issues in *Olbie*. The 'natural' division of labour between the sexes is economically beneficial (below, pp. 210–213); if women are not forced by poverty to work outside the home, they will receive their subsistence in exchange for household labour, which benefits the entire family 'even among the working class':

> The sexes mixed less in society, even among the working class. Good

principles of political economy having spread a little comfort in that class, the women were no longer forced by indigence to share with men those difficult and disgusting occupations which one cannot watch them undertake without shuddering. They were able to give their time and their effort to the care of their households and their families which were much better tended, and they lost those masculine aspects which, in their sex, are something hideous: Woman and gentleness are two ideas that I do not know how to separate. The power of women is that of gentleness against strength: the moment that they try to obtain something by violence, they are no more than a monstrosity.

(below, pp. 210–211)

It is, perhaps, redundant to note that Say's construction of femininity is influenced by his very sympathetic attitude towards the 'virtuous middle' classes of society. He believed that the happiness of any society, and particularly contemporary French society, would be measurably increased by expanding that part of society that lived in moderate comfort, and by eliminating great extremes of wealth and poverty.

The 'natural' career of women is to be reinforced by social institutions, including good legislation regarding marriage and divorce.[9] Say noted that in Olbie 'the law had been adjusted to the popular will insofar as the changes were compatible with social order' (below, p. 211). Say's idealisation of the patriarchal family and traditional marriage had its limits; the fundamental innovation of which he approved was the right to divorce. This argument was offered as clear support for the changes that had already occurred in France with respect to the divorce law. On 1 April 1792, a delegation of women appeared before the Legislative Assembly demanding the right to divorce by mutual consent. On 20 September 1792, a law was passed that allowed divorce not only by mutual consent but also at the request of one spouse on claims of incompatibility, and also in cases in which one spouse was abandoned for more than two years. The right to divorce persisted until the Napoleonic Code killed it in 1804. This freedom to divorce effectively gave women the right to end forced marriages and domestic slavery, and was solidly supported by the *idéologues* with whom Say identified.[10]

Nevertheless, Say did not approve of legislation supporting divorce in order to give women the opportunity to reject their 'natural' career:

[Olbians] recognise the necessity of encouraging in women the two virtues that become them more than any others, and without which the charm and the ascendancy of their sex will vanish soon enough: I mean to say gentleness and chastity. Among this people the gentleness of women is encouraged by general morality which is, itself, the fruit of all the other institutions. Domestic and private virtues are esteemed and revered because they are useful. Poor household management, the cause of both scorn and poverty, is discouraged by paying attention to those habits which

sweeten the morals and which, if I can express it thus, smooth the path of
life.

(below, p. 210)

Women still found their primary occupation within the house.

Although Say viewed household labour as a natural and valuable occupation,
he recognised that working for wages was an inevitable fate for many women.
In *Olbie*, his chief concern was to limit the mixing of the sexes in the workplace
(below, p. 213). Certain professions, having the effect 'of hardening the heart
or making bitter the character' (below, p. 210), would be closed to women,
whereas others, including dressmaking, hairdressing and cooking, would be
reserved exclusively for them (below, p. 213). Say noted that this would allow
even the poorest woman to earn an 'honest' living. He advanced a utilitarian
argument that the restriction thus imposed upon men (that is, a law preventing
them from engaging in the economic activities reserved for women) was
justified because of the social benefit derived from limiting prostitution, which
he regarded as the common result of indigence among women:

> Poverty, a cruel scourge for anyone, is frightful for the more interesting
> half of the human race. It not only deprives women of the common
> sweetness of life, it pushes them to the most shameful corruption, the
> most destitute to the attraction which sometimes disguises the ugliness
> of vice. One must be hungry to sell her favours! What other motive than
> imperious need could make so many of the unfortunate overcome the
> disgust of prostitution? the unfortunate women! without choice, without
> desire, often the victim of depression, almost always shame in their souls,
> they solicit with the gracious smile of the outcast. Who would not prefer
> to be other than this?
>
> (below, p. 211)

In any case, the cost of the policy of reserving some occupations solely for
women, Say argued, was small because men have the whole world in which to
exercise their industry, and can always count on the armed forces to provide
subsistence (below, p. 213).

This argument presented in *Olbie* was restated in a slightly more analytical
way in the first edition of the *Traité*. Say noted that wages in traditional women's
occupations were very often below subsistence because many of the labourers
who participated in the industry depended for some portion of their livelihood
on their extended families:

> The labour of workers who do not live uniquely by their labour is less
> costly than that of true labourers. They are fed; the price of their work is
> hardly regulated by the necessity to live. A typical seamstress in certain
> villages earns less than half of her expenses through labour, even though
> her needs are modest; she is mother or daughter, sister, aunt or mother-

in-law of some labourer who feeds her even when she earns absolutely nothing. If she had only her work for subsistence, it is clear that she must either double her prices or starve to death; in other words, work must pay double, or it would not be undertaken.

(Say 1803, III: 232–3)

Such is often the case for those occupations of which women are 'capable' because women workers offer their labour at rates below the level set by the needs of subsistence (Say 1803, III: 233). Excess supply of women's labour drives down its price, and the effective minimum wage below which individuals will not continue to work is not determined by the physical needs of subsistence.

The 'problem' of independent women

Say's most original suggestion to combat indigence among women also appears in *Olbie* (below, p. 212). A community of women was to be established in a house provided by the state. The work of the 'sisters' would provide for a modest but adequate lifestyle. The sole demand made by the state was that the sisters train a certain number of students to perform women's work, and that they would care for a certain number of old women. No vows were exacted, and the sisters retained the right to leave at any time. Although living in the community, sisters were required to submit to a code of behaviour (designed, apparently, to safeguard their chastity and thereby protect their value on the marriage market). They could, for example, choose their friends, but could not entertain them unless they were in the presence of two other sisters. The consequence of breaking the rules was banishment.

This quasi-convent[11] introduces several issues worth noting. The first is the very considerable restriction imposed upon individual behaviour by this institution. Say seems to have satisfied himself that the incursions upon liberty are minor ['a liberty adequate to know the pleasures of society' (below, p. 212)], and that they are in any case justified because the sisters choose to enter into a voluntary contract (below, p. 212). And the liberty would, undoubtedly, be greater than young, unmarried women had enjoyed during the *ancien régime*, although somewhat less than that which was enjoyed by the red-bonneted partisans of political debate before they were silenced. Moreover, the restrictions on liberty were necessary, Say argued, if the women were to have the possibility of leaving the institution for 'the arms of a husband' (below, p. 212). The second issue of note is that this institution reproduced the lineaments of the patriarchal family. It solved the problem of female poverty by creating an institution that recognised the 'natural dependence' of women.

It is worth remembering that one of the consequences of the revolution was the abolition of the existing religious orders. This specific proposal does not show great imagination on the part of Say, but rather an adaptation of one of the features of the *ancien régime* that he found useful: an organised way of providing social services by regimenting unmarried women. In his proposal, the state would replace the church as the authority to regiment and police the 'sisters'. The pragmatism of the approach can, perhaps, be validated by noting that industrial convents were indeed adopted in France during the nineteenth century, and by all accounts they flourished.

It is, perhaps, ironic to recognise that one of the causes of low market wages for women workers, acknowledged by a number of economic commentators including Say (Say 1803, III: 233–4), was the competition afforded by the religious orders. Because convents provided subsistence to sisters, these orders could supply labour at wages below subsistence, and this drove down wages in traditional women's occupations such as needlework. The solution Say proposed in the *Traité* was to restrict members of religious orders to the production of luxury goods. Such legislation would, he hoped, remove at least some of the downward pressure on wages in the needle trades (Say 1803, III: 234).

Economic theory and gender analysis

That economic theory is not independent of the assumptions one makes about the roles of men and women in the private and public spheres is very clear from Say's analysis. Women were poor, he argued, because they were unfortunate enough to live outside families, and not because seamstresses (the occupation by means of which most independent women tried to support themselves) earn a wage below subsistence. They turned to prostitution because they were poor. This increased social instability, and more women found themselves alone and impoverished. Therefore, the solution to female poverty was to eliminate prostitution, strengthen 'natural' families and to recreate the social role of the family in the guise of his women's establishments for those women who would otherwise live independently. These reforms would strengthen efforts to reduce the mixing of the sexes in the workplace, thereby encouraging virtue, social stability and strong families in which women were supported. Because Say defined the problem to be solved as the poverty of independent women rather than the low wages earned by women who were restricted by social and institutional barriers to particular employments, he derived a rather different solution to that problem of female poverty than one might expect. Moreover, his solution was 'natural'. Say always argued that he opposed building elaborate systems of thought; he found that understanding economics simply involves the art of asking good questions and deducing those responses that flow, as a consequence, from the 'nature of things' (Say 1803: xxxv).

An obvious question is whether Say maintained this analysis of women and the family all his life, or whether *Olbie*, and in particular the analysis of gender it contains, was simply a reaction to the red bonnets and pantaloons and raucous voices in the galleries – a temporary phenomenon. In fact, the concerns that preoccupied Say about the sexual division of labour and the related issue of impoverished women in *Olbie* are consistent with his economic analyses in the *Traité d'Économie Politique* (1803) and the *Cours Complet d'Économie Politique Pratique* (1828–9). In the *Traité*, Say claimed that women's wages were lower than men's because a man's salary must be sufficient to provide subsistence at the socially required level for himself and his wife and to raise and educate two children to working age, whereas a woman's wage need provide no more than what was necessary to keep one woman in working order. If there were too many unattached women without access to employment, even this minimum would be bid down (Say 1803, II: chapter 7, section 4). And, although wages could not permanently remain below subsistence in the case of male workers because of the Malthusian population mechanism, the fact that many women were subsidised either by religious orders or by their families implies that there was no such natural tendency for wages to rise to the level of even a physical subsistence.

In the *Cours Complet*, Say does suggest that a partial solution to the problem of women's poverty may be to increase access to alternative employment, as long as the alternatives are 'appropriate'. He castigates government regulations that exclude women from trades such as embroidery and lace making: 'a portion of humanity that already has so little is owed this resource; and they are given instead seduction and debauchery' (Say 1843: 257). The desire to separate the sexes in employment is, however, a strong undercurrent throughout all of Say's work. The solution, as he saw it, was to create separate spheres rather than to let men and women work alongside one another; given the natural laws that determine the different wages for men and women, it would seem that separation would not solve the problem by bidding wages up. But it would, Say believed, strengthen the family, which was the best solution for poor women.

How representative was Say's gender analysis?

The positions Say adopted on the role of the family and on women's work were shared by many, but not all, people both inside and outside his intellectual milieu. Some commentators, not all *idéologues*, saw the aggressive demands made by very organised and vocal groups of women as both dangerous to the stability of the Republic and unnatural. But Say's position, in fact, resulted from a much more fundamental aspect of his analysis. His social theory was based upon the idea that human beings are very largely the products of their environments, so that he could argue, for example, that a programme of moral education would effectively encourage the sympathetic tendencies. Moreover, both poverty and great wealth create environments that nurture the worst aspects of human nature, so eliminating extremes of income distribution would similarly reduce vicious inclinations. And yet, Say's gender analysis is unapologetically based on the idea that women and men have fundamentally different natures. And recognising the different natures of the two genders, and creating very different social roles for each, would in fact lead to the social stability Say desired because the true interests of men and women were fundamentally harmonious. Men and women are not identical; they do not have the same human nature. But the true interests of both are not in opposition to one another.

Gender analysis is an arena in which we can see the underlying similarities and differences of the social thought of various *idéologues*. Say, Cabanis and Roussel all argued that the natures of men and women are quite distinct, and yet the interests of men and women are harmonious. Therefore, appropriate gender relationships are created when both men and women recognise that their true interests are in accord. And, in fact, the social stability each desires would occur because men and women have been given quite distinct yet complementary roles. Tracy, interestingly enough because he was beginning to recognise unchanging 'temperaments' and 'characters' as we saw above, did not acknowledge that men and women are necessarily distinct. In the case of gender relations, he took a line much closer to Condorcet, and he argued that contemporary women seemed to be fundamentally different from men only because they had never had the same educational opportunities as men. Education would, that is, make the two genders much more similar than they have been historically.

In an era that offered many alternative versions of the way in which families and societies ought to be organised, Jean-Baptiste Say opted wholeheartedly for a 'natural' family-based system. Families were the most effective way of inculcating civic virtue, and they were the most efficient way of providing subsistence for women and children. The only modification he was prepared to make was that a divorce law seemed to him an improvement in social organisation 'insofar as the change is compatible with social order'. The family, dominated by the father, was to be the fundamental unit of civil society because social stability required well-regulated families. This was not a self-evident position in the revolutionary decade.

Families and firms as units of economic analysis

If there was no self-evident way to treat the appropriate roles of women in the private and public spheres in 1800, there was similarly no self-evident way to model the operation of firms. Say intentionally adopted the analogy between firms and families, and between captains of industry (*chefs d'entreprise*) and fathers. He explicitly developed the notion that it is the family (directed by the father) and firms (directed by the entrepreneur) that were the fundamental units of economic analysis.

In the *Cours Complet*, Say discusses the family in a manner reminiscent of the economic organisation of the firm:

> In the family, all the means of subsistence come from the father; it is in his head that all useful thoughts are born; it is he that procures capital; it

is he that works and directs the work of his children, who raises them, who sees to their establishment.

(Say 1843: 561)

Say saw an analogy between the family and the firm, in which individual workers relate to the entrepreneur as do children to their father (Say 1843: 328). But he condemned as false and pernicious widespread notions to the effect that the economy needed to be directed by a central authority just as the family needed to be directed by the father (Say 1843: 561). Rather, individual entrepreneurs require exactly the same freedom as do the governed in a civil society:

> In the state [as opposed to the family] it is an entirely different matter: the ideas that procure the support of the social body, the capital, the direction, are found among the governed. It is there that thought and action rest; it is there that the laws of nature are studied and productive enterprises are born from which are derived the revenues of society. Closer to all sorts of truths, it is the governed who analyse most successfully the moral and physical constitution of man, as well as the social economy.

(Say 1843: 561)

And it was, of course, the case that individual workers employed within a firm recognised that their own interests were served by a division of labour in which the entrepreneur directed and they obeyed, just as it was in the interests of all members of the family to recognise that the direction and financial support of the father served their own interests.

Conclusion

I have argued that the gender analysis that Jean-Baptiste Say developed in the revolutionary decade was not unique to his *idéologue* colleagues. Nevertheless, these analyses were consciously constructed in a period when a journalist, as was Say, and a scholar could not help but be aware of many suggested alternatives. The analysis of gender that Say articulated in *Olbie* persisted as the foundation of the nineteenth-century analyses that argued, for example, that the 'natural wage' of women is lower than that of men because men must support a family, whereas women need only support themselves. Similarly, this analysis allowed economic theory to be used to support the 'separate spheres' argument that justified the impoverishment of so many independent women by closing the professions to them. And because women were so resolutely relegated to the private sphere, it allowed economic theory to develop without explicitly considering the roles of men and women in society, or the role that unpaid household production played in allowing the market economy to function.

9 Natural order and spontaneous order

The picture that has emerged from Say's *Olbie* over the last three chapters affords the administrator, the legislator and the educator very active roles. These individuals are, in fact, the physicians to the social body, charged with the task of correcting and eliminating institutions inconsistent with social wellbeing, creating and nurturing institutions favourable to industrialisation, and providing a moral and intellectual education for the population consistent with social stability and economic progress.

These tasks greatly exceed those given to the legislator by Adam Smith, and yet Say has often been portrayed as little more than a reasonably competent populariser of Adam Smith (see Gide and Rist 1947, 7th edn: 112). This reading of Say as a populariser of Smith emerged as early as the first review of Say's *Traité* (1803) in England, in which James Mill claimed that:

> In the execution of this work very little is to be found which can be considered as original. Not only are all the general principles copied from Smith, but almost the whole of the facts and illustrations.
>
> (J. Mill 1805: 418)

James Mill's evaluation has become increasingly rare, although it is echoed by Blaug:

> All in all, throughout a number of works, the quality of Say's theorising is inferior to Smith in historical sweep, to Ricardo in analytical rigour and to Malthus in perceptive criticisms. His importance, particularly for French economics, was to popularise the ideas of Adam Smith, to disseminate English classical political economy on the Continent and to keep alive an emphasis on utility and demand in contrast to the English overemphasis on costs and supply.
>
> (Blaug 1986: 212)

And, as Lutfalla reminds us, it would be absurd to deny that Say did indeed play the role of Smith's continental commentator (Lutfalla 1991: 13–14).

Say's rehabilitation as a serious economic scholar began, perhaps, with Schumpeter, who noted wryly that:

Say...illustrate[s] two important though slightly paradoxical truths: first, that, in order to appraise a man properly and to put him into the right place, it is sometimes necessary to defend him not only against his enemies but also against his friends and even against himself; second that there is a fundamental difference between superficiality of exposition and superficiality of thought.

(Schumpeter 1954: 491)

Lutfalla (1991: 13), Ménard (1978: 88–9), Roll (1978: 320–32), Drucker (1985), Pribram (1983: 219–220) and Steiner (see 1996b), among others, have also argued that Say's contributions are more original and distinct from Smith's than has commonly been recognised.

A reading midway between these two positions would suggest that the first edition of Say's *Traité d'Économie Politique* (1803) was offered as a more cogent presentation of the ideas contained in Smith's *Wealth of Nations* (1776), but that Say began to develop a more independent voice with the second edition of his work (Forget 1993). But, there is little doubt that Smith was an important influence on Say, particularly early in his intellectual career.

Central to Adam Smith's *Wealth of Nations* is the argument that all systems that attempt to encourage or discourage particular branches of industry 'retard the progress of society towards real wealth and greatness'. If such unnatural intervention is removed, the 'obvious and simple system of natural liberty establishes itself of its own accord' (Smith 1976, ii [1776]: 208). This sets Smith's work in opposition to mercantilist policies, and establishes the idea of spontaneous order[1] as a key component of economic liberalism in the form of the invisible hand, and as an important limitation on the legitimate role of the state. However, this raises a problem for the interpretation of Jean-Baptiste Say's work because spontaneous order plays a very constrained role in his social analysis, especially in the first edition of his *Traité d'Économie Politique* (1803).

This chapter addresses three questions. First, what textual evidence exists for my claim that Say did not fully incorporate Smith's concept of spontaneous order into the first edition of the *Traité*? Second, what are the implications for Say's economic and social analysis? And third, is there any evidence that Say's thought underwent any transition over his lifetime such that spontaneous order plays a greater role in his more mature thought than it does in 1803?

My argument, in brief, is that Say was quite aware of the idea of spontaneous order, canonically represented by Smith's invisible hand. He simply constrained its use to the marketplace, building his society instead upon the ideas that had come to him in various forms from the physiocrats and, more directly, from *idéologie*.[2]. These specifically French sources embody the idea that social order is a consequence of good legislation and, even more importantly, good education designed to subordinate individual self-seeking behaviour to the social good by teaching people their true interests, which are in more cases than not harmonious. The key difference between Smith's and Say's economic analyses, then, turns on the much more expansive role afforded to the legislator by Say. And although there is some evidence that Say was more sympathetic to Smith's system of natural liberty at the end of his life than he was in 1803, the transition is a very subtle one. He never fully adopts Smith's analysis.

This chapter challenges the idea that Say's *Traité* is no more than a Smithian primer. His work is, I argue, a complex amalgamation of ideas drawn from British and French sources, and he maintained throughout his life some ideas that are entirely inconsistent with Smithian analysis.

Did J.-B. Say adopt Smithian notions of spontaneous order?

Although spontaneous order was a widely disseminated idea by the end of the eighteenth century,[3] it was understood in very different ways by its advocates. Some, like Say and Turgot before him, recognised that there are inherent self-ordering aspects of the marketplace, but had little regard for a more broadly applicable notion of spontaneous order through which social institutions themselves evolve from the self-seeking actions of individuals. By contrast, Haakonssen has long argued that David Hume built his system on a much more expansive idea of spontaneous order, claiming, for example, that the system of justice emerged as an unintended consequence of the actions of self-interested individuals each separately pursuing his or her own ends (Hume 1978: 528–9; see Haakonssen 1981).[4]

The distinction between Say and Smith becomes clear when one considers the duties of the legislator. As is well known, Smith introduces his system of natural liberty as an attack on mercantilist policies, which give the legislator the power to determine which industries to encourage and which to suppress. His system, by contrast, allows the legislator, at least theoretically, 'only three duties: (1) the defence of the country; (2) the administration of justice; and (3) the maintenance of certain public works' (Smith 1976, II [1776]: 208).

But controversy has governed the secondary literature on Adam Smith. Commentators who claim that Smith offered little room for the wise legislator as a shaper of social outcomes are surveyed by Donald Winch (1978: chapters 1 and 8). Recently, Stimson (1989: 91–112) and Minowitz (1993) have argued that Smith adopted a relatively strong version of the theory of spontaneous order and, consequently, narrowed the role of the legislator. Winch rejects this claim, arguing that: 'If the main lesson of Smith's science is that human affairs are best left to "the natural course of things", what positive part is there for *any* legislator to play? The only virtues he is being advised to cultivate seem to be those of the contemplative philosopher, observing natural historical and economic processes and issuing pious warnings about the harmfulness of artificial expedients' (Winch 1996: 94).

There is, in fact, evidence that Smith allows the legislator important duties in adjusting institutions and laws to new economic circumstances (cf. Winch 1996: 88; Haakonssen 1981: 90; Hollander 1973: 256–8), mitigating the detrimental effects of progress (Winch 1996: 88), establishing public works and providing public education (Haakonssen 1981: 92; Hollander 1973: 273), justice and security (Haakonssen 1981: 93; Hollander 1973: 264–5). Smith does not contemplate ongoing direct intervention in the economic activities of each citizen, or efforts on the part of the lawgiver to spread political insight through direct political education. Nevertheless, he does allow a significantly broader scope for the legislator to mould society, even in addition to his somewhat unexpected defence of usury laws, than the abstractly presented theory of spontaneous order would seem to permit (see Hollander 1973: 257–8).

Say, in a manner consistent with the analysis of *Olbie*, goes considerably further. Even in largely economic matters, the legislator (or more properly the enlightened administrator who was clearly distinguished from the self-interested politician[5]) has a significant role to play. The first edition of the *Traité* makes many references to the potentially beneficial intervention of an enlightened administration in helping to bring about a prosperous and industrious state. For example, the administration might aid in the diffusion of machines in manufacturing (Say 1803, I: 48) and government might ease the disruption machines cause for the working classes (Say 1803, I: 53). Government should take special care to encourage the improvement and diffusion of commodities destined for the consumption of the most numerous class (Say 1803, I: 140). Industrial experiments might be encouraged by a wise government, especially in agriculture in which the risk often dissuades individuals from undertaking them independently (Say 1803, I: 141, 146). Purely speculative sciences ought to be encouraged, and libraries and museums maintained (Say 1803, I: 343–4). Voyages to the far reaches of the globe ought to be undertaken at public expense (Say 1803, I: 343). And, of course, government must guarantee the security of property and help to diffuse the knowledge without which prosperity cannot occur (Say 1803, I: 340–3).

In addition to these specific tasks, Say's legislator has two very significant roles. First, citizens need help to discern their true interests, most especially outside the marketplace; individuals cannot be expected to correctly determine their own. Second, Say argues that the social and moral attitudes consistent with the growth of an industrious culture will only emerge with the help of legislation and education, and the wise statesman is integral to the system (Say 1803, I: chapters 13 and 19). Chapter 13 of book I is entitled 'The inconveniences that accompany a too great subdivision of labour', and Say argues that education is required to vitiate the intellectual effects of routine labour. That education can be encouraged in two ways: first, if laws favour an equitable distribution of income, workers will have the leisure to undertake study and to occupy themselves in ways foreign to their usual occupations (Say 1803, I: 81) and, second, noting that ordinary workers in better establishments may have personal libraries of ten or twelve books, Say speculates that if a way could be found to replace one or two of the less useful books with a few good treatises that have been created on the subjects of immediate concern, such as family health and the education of children, the morality of the nation would be greatly improved (Say 1803, I: 82n).

Similarly, chapter 19 is entitled 'A certain spirit favourable to industry' and Say contrasts England and France, recognising the beneficial impact of English institutions and habits. He notes that instead of catering to the caprices of the wealthy, English manufacturing is marked by a conformity in small details (Say 1803, I: 136), and argues that:

> The real improvement of industry tends, not to extreme refinement in detail, but rather to those aspects which tend to expand the usage of products to a larger number, to perfect these products and to make them more available through their low price. It is also these improvements which have the greatest need of encouragement by public authority.
>
> (Say 1803, I: 138)

Say recognises that ignorance and habit tend to govern the consumption of the largest class, noting, for example, that straw hats, which have become fashionable in the cities, would be of great use to village and rural women who may not know of their existence or potential usefulness (Say 1803, I: 139). Nevertheless, he argues that it is the responsibility of a wise government to encourage the creation and use of such products (Say 1803, I: 140).

Both of these tasks of the legislator promote the public interest, and neither the comprehension of true interests nor those habits and attitudes that characterise an industrious culture will emerge spontaneously through the attempts of individuals to pursue their own interests.

One persistent puzzle is why Say believed that administrators and teachers would know better an individual's true interests than the individual herself. In his 1796 article 'Boniface Veridick...', he suggests that contemporary French society was complex enough, and the general population ignorant enough, that the best one could hope for was that the population might be trained to select individuals of good intellectual and moral character to represent their interests. These benevolent individuals would, because of their innate character and superior learning, be better able to understand that the fundamental interest of all individuals is the maintenance of the society in which they live. Moreover, they would recognise, in a way that less able and less educated people may not, that the pursuit of narrow sectarian interests is destructive of society and, hence, not in their 'true interests'. The same kind of analysis runs through *Olbie* (Say 1800a). People need to be educated about the nature of the society in which they live, and that education could best be provided in the form of architecture and statues that recall the virtues, and publicly displayed maxims that recall to individuals their true interests and that help to shape behaviour gradually as individuals develop new habits without conscious decision and thought (below, pp. 218–220). This education would be supplemented by the active recognition and reward of individuals who behave in accord with their 'true interests', and the public denunciation of individuals who display narrow, egoistic interests (below, pp. 214–16), and the development of festivals and spectacles that encourage the development of appropriate values and attitudes (below, pp. 217–18). In a well-run society, the administrators and legislators are those people who know better than ordinary people what is in the true interests of all the people because it is in the general interest.

Within the context of the marketplace, narrowly defined, Say was much more inclined to allow that individuals could very often determine what was to their advantage with a high degree of accuracy. In the case of the allocation of capital by individual entrepreneurs, for example, individuals could be expected to discern their own interests with little assistance. And yet, individuals may well need the help of the enlightened administrator to understand that a progressive income tax system that reduces the degree of economic inequality, because it is consistent with peace and security and the maintenance of society, is in the true interests of the rich as it is of the poor (below, pp. 229–30). So the distinction that Say was prepared to draw was not between economic institutions *per se* and the rest of society, but rather between the narrowly defined marketplace and the rest of society. And, indeed, the market only works if individuals do know their true interests; education is (for Say as for Smith) an instance in which individual self-interest could not be trusted to generate the socially optimal investment (Say 1803, I: 340–2).

What implications does this have for Say's analysis?

Jean-Baptiste Say faced a more complex problem than did those of his ideological colleagues not particularly interested in economic matters. He shared the ideological concept of sympathy as a social organising principle that requires nurturing by an intellectual élite, and Adam Smith's reliance on a self-regulating market order based upon mutual self-interest. Therefore, one would expect him to deny that social organisation outside the market would be characterised by a tendency towards spontaneous order through the self-interested actions of individuals, while maintaining the importance of the invisible hand in the organisation of the marketplace.

This is not a position totally without precedent. In 1767, Mercier de la Rivière published *L'Ordre Naturel et Essentiel des Sociétés Politiques*, and on the basis of his argument 'property', 'liberty' and 'security' were united into a '*formule sacramentalle*' that captured the political orientation of physiocracy (Welch 1984: 200n15).[6] The physiocrats essentially argued that human beings are governed by natural law, but that natural law can only be discovered through empirical evidence rather than theoretical speculation. And the evidence seemed to show that human beings are motivated by self-interest, and that they sought happiness that was identified with material consumption. But the natural laws that governed this human behaviour also imposed moral obligations, which increased with the complexity of social organisation. Rights, therefore, were based on individual interests, which were consistent with a system of natural justice (Welch 1984: 10).

This analysis had been used to advocate economic reform in France of a type similar to that advocated by Smith: 'natural' (economic) order ought to be freed from 'unnatural' systems of encouragement and constraint. But politically, and unlike Smith, the physiocrats advocated absolute monarchy. With Revolution, however, this physiocratic doctrine was adapted by various people identified with *idéologie*[7] as justification for the Declaration of the Rights of Man and Citizen, and was used to implement political reform by abolishing absolute monarchy and replacing it with the sovereign authority of the National Assembly.

A similar division between the market and the rest of society is directly confirmed in the body of Say's writing.[8] Say introduces the first edition of his *Traité* with great praise for Adam Smith's *Wealth of Nations* and, despite Smith's claim that political economy is a branch of the 'science of the statesman or legislator', Say claims that 'until the moment Smith wrote, Politics, properly called the science of government, was confused with Political economy, which demonstrates how wealth is created, distributed and consumed' (Say 1803: i). But 'since Smith, these two bodies of doctrine have been forever distinguished: the name Political economy has been reserved for the science that treats the wealth of nations, and that of Politics alone designates the relationships that exist between the government and the people, and those between governments' (Say 1803: iii).

Say distinguished his own political economy from that of the physiocrats, from James Steuart and, significantly, from Rousseau's article in the *Encyclopédie*, all of whom he accused of confusing purely political considerations with political economy (Say 1803: iii). But:

> Wealth is independent of the nature of government. Under any form of government, a state may prosper if it is well administered. Absolute monarchs have enriched their countries, and popular councils ruined theirs. Even the forms of public administration only influence the formation of wealth, which is almost entirely the work of individuals, indirectly and accidentally.
>
> (Say 1803: ii)

Say, then, argued that the science of political economy was not a branch of the science of the legislator.

The intellectual distinction Say was prepared to emphasise between politics and political economy allowed him to separate the two senses in which the theory of spontaneous order appeared in the writings of Hume and Smith. He believed that it then became possible to advocate individual initiative in market transactions and to imagine that the institution of the market somehow reconciles individual self-interested behaviour, without advocating a passive role for a legislator in a society that also develops incrementally through the self-interested actions of individuals. Because these are two separable analyses, Say could advocate a very active role for an enlightened administrator or legislator to shape institutions in the public interest, including economic institutions, and even to shape individual morality, as he does in *Olbie*, while simultaneously arguing that the invisible hand of the marketplace must be allowed the liberty to reconcile individual economic activities driven by self-interest.

Say's attempt to distinguish between 'economics' and 'politics', however, is not entirely satisfactory. Say may have believed that 'wealth is independent of the nature of government', but it seems apparent that if the nature of government differs, then there will certainly be economic repercussions. For example, it would seem that the simplicity of republican manners coupled with a more egalitarian distribution of income would entail an entirely different pattern of consumption than would the *ancien régime*. It does not take a great deal of imagination to contemplate differing patterns of investment and savings, public expenditure and so on. Say's intellectual separation of the two spheres rests upon his distinction between 'public administration' and the 'nature of government'. Public morality, he believed, and therefore economic behaviour, was influenced by the former. And good administration was, in principle if not historically, consistent with any political organisation. That is, the analysis returns to Say's very typically ideological notion that administrators and technicians have a significant responsibility for shaping human behaviour, and that their success is dependent upon science rather than political considerations. Say, then, constructs a social analysis that protects the political analysis of *idéologie* against inroads from the theory of spontaneous order, while allowing Smith's invisible hand significant freedom to order the marketplace.

Say's conception of the role of the administrator is entirely consistent with two articles on political matters which he published in *La Décade* in Years IV and VIII [1796 and 1800].[9] In Year IV ('Boniface Veridick...'; Say 1796), Say reflected upon the role of the citizen in the modern French state and contrasted it with the role that citizens were expected to play in ancient Rome and Greece. He recognised that although the Assembly may have been composed of men of common sense and enlightenment at the outset of the Revolution, it had deteriorated through the effects of intrigues and parties. The people must learn, he claimed, to choose good representatives. But because the modern state was a system of representative democracy, Say argued that 'if they could but choose from among themselves men of common sense, probity and supportive of republican government, I would demand nothing more of them' (10 Germinal an IV: 40). Citizens could allow the government, and in particular the well-educated administrators of the civil service, to see to the establishment of those institutions necessary to the creation of a 'comfortable' State in which economic activity flourishes:

> I would desire that peace characterise [such a state], that a general confidence unite all citizens; I would wish that a firm government would guarantee from the outset their independence,[10] and their internal security. I would wish that agriculture and all species of industry would

be characterised by brilliant activity; that the seaports full of ships, the canals and rivers covered with boats, the markets tidy and well provisioned, offer the appearance of abundance. I would desire that each farm labourer, each city artisan have, if not an independent property, at least the prospect of procuring one for his old age, even if it is no more than a little life annuity. I would wish that each household, its utensils clean and well cared for, its clothes of good fabric and its linen clean, would indicate, not opulence, but ease everywhere; that each would know how to read and have in his cupboard at least a few volumes to learn of the progress of the arts and also a few newspapers, so that he would not be ignorant of the interests of the state. I would wish that public theatres, stamped with the mark of utility would inspire in those who attend not the sadness of a suffering humanity, but the contentment that comes from the spectacle of succoured humanity. I desire, in a word, that in this great republic there would be not a single idler whose unproductive existence is a burden for society, not a single pauper who, with work and good conduct, could not earn an easy subsistence, and lead a life that the English call *comfortable*.

(10 Germinal an IV: 42–3; translated from Steiner 1997: n14)

The role of the administrator and legislator in bringing about such a state of affairs is twofold. Economic wellbeing must be assured by guaranteeing peace, property and order. And the enlightened encouragement of public morality, which would be the product of a campaign of public education, must be established.

Is there evidence of an intellectual transition?

Say's early writing, then, is characterised by a recognition that education, and in particular education designed to teach people their true interests, and the creation and implementation of institutions and laws consistent with social wellbeing are essential. Moreover, both education and institutional adjustment require the intervention of an educated élite, whom Say tends to identify with 'public authority'. But Say's experience and reaction to Bonaparte and the Empire might lead us to suspect that his faith in the good will of public authority might have changed over his lifetime. Richard Fargher has documented a very widespread and fundamental shift in political orientation, amounting almost to a loss of faith in the ability of government to preserve itself from a tendency towards tyranny (Fargher 1952: 220–38). This attitudinal shift characterised many of the *idéologues* as well (Kennedy 1978: 190; Welch 1984: 157f.), and Kitchin notes that Say's own correspondence demonstrates an encroaching cynicism (Kitchin 1966: 93). Is there any reason to believe that Say's attitude towards the roles afforded public authority changed significantly? Say never abandoned the claim that society requires the intervention of an intellectual élite to educate the people, and he never abandoned the idea that institutions and laws must be adjusted in such a way that they support rather than destroy public morality. What he is much less certain of is that public authority will undertake these tasks appropriately without the constraints imposed by a well-educated citizenry, whose knowledge renders the public relatively immune to the Machiavellian tendencies of government.

The transition in Say's thought between an optimistic faith in the ability of experts, whether teachers or legislators, to bring about the utopian vision Say articulated in 1796 and again in 1800 and a much less optimistic vision of his mature reflection on *Olbie* seems quite clear. If the legislators and administrators could be trusted in 1800, a few years of Bonaparte and the debates surrounding the growth of liberalism during the Restoration ensured the greater reliance that the older Say placed on active and well-informed citizens to constrain inherent threats of despotism:

> I will not give men the honour of believing that they will ever see a time when there will not be tyrants among them; but I see that their work becomes more difficult in proportion as nations become more enlightened, and note that it is not necessary for a nation to be composed of scholars to be what I call enlightened...
>
> (below, p. 242)[11]

Say thought his change of heart so significant that it required *Olbie* to be reconstructed 'on an entirely different foundation', emphasising the importance of general education in constraining tyranny. If the optimistic voice of *Olbie* sounds in the first edition of the *Traité*, it is this sombre tone that finds its place in the *Cours Complet*, in which Say castigates the physiocrats for their 'legal despotism' (Say 1843: 569) and argues for publicly funded private schooling to protect citizens from the 'sinister interests' of authority (Say 1843: 468).

But, it is important not to overstate the extent of Say's change of heart. Consider Say's 'Essay on the Principle of Utility', which was written after the experience of Empire. The essay was originally intended to be included in his *Cours Complet*, and was written in response to the charge of unrestrained egoism that emanated from such writers as Benjamin Constant and Mme de Staël. In it, Say distinguishes very clearly between unrestrained egoism, which he identifies as the pursuit of apparent but perhaps poorly understood interests and immediate interests, and self-interest, which is based on well-understood and true interests. The true interests of an individual may diverge from apparent interests for three reasons: 'insanity, ignorance and passion' (Say 1848: 719). Insanity means that one might desire that which one knows is harmful to one. Ignorance means that one might be unaware of the harmful qualities of that which one desires, or attribute beneficial qualities to something that it does not, in fact, possess. And passion is 'a weakness which makes them sacrifice a future good to the satisfaction of a present appetite, or a present and incontestable good to a future and uncertain good, like the Trappists' (Say 1848: 719). Say is again clear about the merits of education:

> Whoever works to enlighten ignorance, to battle against insanity, and to submit the passions to the empire of reason, is a benefactor of humanity and works effectively for the happiness of men
>
> (Say 1848: 719)

Teaching people their true interests involves precisely this battle.

Say, however, was by now quite certain that the press was an important method of education, and he argued that education involves the public debate of all sides of every issue. It involves, that is, the cultivation of the intellect – the ability to correctly discern one's own interests – in addition to the inculcation of correct opinion. A tyrant with the will to deceive is virtually indestructible, Say claims, when a free press does not exist (Say 1848: 731). This is quite a movement from *Olbie*, in which Say was content to foster republican virtues, and even from 'Boniface Veridick...' (Say 1796), in which he argued that it is sufficient for the people to choose representatives wisely. Public education was no less necessary, but now what was required was intellectual education so that the public was not at the mercy of the educator.

This essay also makes clear how utilitarianism is related to individual psychology in Say's social analysis. Say notes that welfare requires the pursuit of 'true interests', 'well understood' (Say 1848: 727), but asks whose interests ought to be pursued? Obviously (he says), it ought not to be the interests of the governor at the expense of the people, or the few at the expense of the many (Say 1848: 726). But Say insists that well-understood interests are very often harmonious:

> The faithfulness to fulfil an onerous engagement is nothing but the obedience to an interest that one rightly sees as superior to the passing and dangerous benefits that one gains from not fulfilling that obligation. One fulfils it through the sentiment of general utility, of the faithfulness to promises; one fulfils it so as not to authorise the violation of obligations from others towards oneself; one fulfils it to be seen as a man of honour, and to enjoy the advantages attached to probity and esteem
>
> (Say 1848: 726)

Clearly, enlightened people are those who recognise that their true interests include the preservation of the contractual basis of the society in which they live.

If anyone is so unenlightened that he cannot see the gains from fulfilling his obligations, then the civil code exists to force him to do so. The civil code came about, according to Say, because it was created in advance by 'objective men, who were justly convinced of the advantages that men would generally enjoy as long as they are faithful to their obligations' (Say 1848: 729):

> Well-made laws are the best guides that one can give to those who are too little enlightened to know their true interests; the more advanced one is

in this knowledge, the less one has need of laws; but, at the same time, well-made laws all conform to the principle of utility, because who would dare defend a law demonstrated to be harmful?

(Say 1848: 729)

Say notes that people who understand well their own true interests have little need of law. Such people recognise the underlying harmony of interests, which stems from the recognition that one lives in society, and that the maintenance of that society is beneficial to oneself as well as others. All of these ideas are entirely consistent with Say's earliest claims about the need of the public for education and the appropriate role of institutions. All that changed was Say's willingness to believe that public authority could be trusted to act in the public interest.

Adam Smith had similarly recognised the limitations of narrow self-interest, arguing that landlords may simply be too indolent and 'incapable of that application of mind' to understand, let alone pursue, their own interests (Smith 1976 [1776], I: 276–7), that workers, lacking leisure and education, may be ignorant of their own interests (1976 [1776], I: 277) and that capitalists may, through their own unequal access to economic and political power, be able to impose their own interests on the other orders of society by arguing that particular policies are in the public interests (1976 [1776], I: 277–8). But neither in *The Theory of Moral Sentiments* nor in *The Wealth of Nations* does Smith give any authority the responsibility of either actively cultivating sympathy or teaching individuals their true interests. There is no advocacy for a campaign of public *moral* education.

Conclusion

The theory of spontaneous order was one intellectual justification for the stability of social organisations. The body politic, according to this theory, comprises many individuals with quite distinct interests, and yet does not collapse in chaos because the self-interested actions of individuals 'adjust themselves'. Through a sort of evolution, formal and informal institutions that prove successful, in some sense, survive while those that do not help to bring about order are eliminated.

This is a very distinct social theory from that advocated by the *idéologues* and the physiocrats, for example, in which a strong legislator is required to teach people their true interests, which would include an appreciation for the underlying harmony of interests. No such harmony is postulated by the theory of spontaneous order. Interests are genuinely conflicting, and the order in the larger system comes about because the unintended consequence of several individuals, each pursuing his own interest, is that the system as a whole generates an order. That is, order is a consequence of social interaction between individuals in conflict; it is not an assumption based upon some notion of sympathy naturally overpowering self-interest, nor is it ensured at the outset because administrators or legislators successfully instil the idea that true interests cannot be at odds with the 'general will'. Jean-Baptiste Say's intellectual commitment to the notion of spontaneous order in the marketplace, and his simultaneous commitment to the ideological conception of an underlying harmony of true interests based on the cultivation of sympathy and an active role for a legislator, led him to emphasise the distinction between politics and what, for want of a better name, he labelled political economy.

10 Say's social economics as a contribution to the pedagogical programme of *idéologie*

Of all the economists associated with *idéologie*, Jean-Baptiste Say was clearly the most influential in terms of his impact on future practitioners of political economy. Who now reads Destutt de Tracy's *Traité d'Économie Politique* (1817), or remembers that Pierre-Louis Roederer was an established member of the Political Economy section of the class of Moral and Political Sciences, delivering lectures on political economy and editing the *Journal d'Économie Publique* [years V–VII (1797–9)] and *Mémoires d'Économie Publique* [years VIII–IX (1800–1)] when the younger Say was still struggling for recognition? Who, indeed, now remembers that there were other economists attached to the *Institut National*, besides Roederer, Tracy and, possibly, Du Pont de Nemours?[1]

The link between 'morality' and 'political economy' in an abstract sense is made concrete in the link between Say's *Olbie* and his *Traité d'Économie Politique* (1803). In the first, he called for the widespread dissemination of the fundamental 'truths' of political economy, and the creation of a readily available basic treatise on the subject. Political economy, well understood, would govern the art of administration, including government finance, would enhance the process of industrialism and would nurture the work ethic, which was one of the fundamental institutions of morality.

In the next section of this chapter, we consider how representative Say's *Traité* (1803) was of French political economy of the period. Then, we attempt to determine what exactly was meant by the method of analysis and, more importantly, how one would recognise a treatise as a contribution to *idéologie* if one were to examine it. Next, we examine Say's statements on the appropriate method of economics from two primary sources during the period of our investigation: his notes on Adam Smith's *Wealth of Nations* (Hashimoto 1980; 1982) and the methodological introduction to the first edition of the *Traité d'Économie Politique* (1803). Then, we consider one example of the way in which the dissemination of the insights of political economy would contribute to the ideological goal of social stabilisation. Finally, we conclude that the *Traité* (1803) was Say's first attempt to be the 'saviour of his nation' (see below, p. 200) by creating a fundamental treatise on political economy designed specifically to further public understanding of the science.

Was there a social economy of *idéologie*?

Idéologie did not generate any single form of economic analysis. It was not a necessary condition for the creation of the *Traité* because *idéologie* itself grew out of more than a century of sensationalist thinking and that tradition, independently of the *idéologue* cast, could culminate in such contributions as Adam Smith's *Wealth of Nations* (1976 [1776]), which has been traditionally seen as so similar to Say's economics that Say was characterised as a continental populariser of Adam Smith (cf. Schumpeter 1954: 491–2, who knew better). Indeed, Say acknowledged, in a letter to Malthus, that Adam Smith showed him the correct path in economic reasoning when, jostled by the mercantilists on one side and the physiocrats on the other, he took his first hesitant steps in the discipline (Say 1843 [1822]: 622). He ended his *Cours Complet* with an abridged history of political economy in which he praised the *Wealth of Nations* for elevating political economy to the level of a positive science (Say 1843: 572). If Say criticised Smith, and he did, it was only because Smith was worthy of the effort; it was, Say claimed, a type of success that evaded most books that merited neither much praise nor much criticism (Say 1843: 572). There is no reason to believe that Say's *Traité* could not have been written, either by Say or by someone else, if Say had never come into contact with *idéologie*.

Say's economic analysis was not common to the Political Economy section of the class of Moral and Political Sciences of the *Institut National*, which included among its members *idéologues* such as Sieyès and Roederer and among its associates others such as Jean-Antoine-Cauvin Gallois (Staum 1996: 233). Their contributions (excluding to some extent those of Roederer) more often than not continued in the physiocratic tradition (Perrot 1992a; Faccarello and Steiner 1991a). Germain Garnier, a member of the class and remembered chiefly because he translated Smith's *Wealth of Nations*, was considered by Say to be 'the last eighteenth-century French economist', and by Marx to be the consummate economist of the Directory and the Consulate (not to mention a 'Bonapartist senator' and a 'Français insipide', who learned and understood nothing while translating the *Wealth of Nations*). Although Breton takes issue with these judgements (Breton 1990: 141–50), there is much evidence that Garnier remained closer to Turgot than to Say and to Smith. Staum argues that Garnier represented a midpoint between the 'liberal' economics of Say and Destutt de Tracy and the physiocracy of Turgot (Staum 1987). Garnier was not identified with *idéologie*, but his analysis was more representative of the class before it was suppressed in 1803 than were the contributions of Roederer and Say.

Individuals who clearly influenced the development of *idéologie* often approached political economy from the perspective of physiocracy. Say argued that the physiocrats dominated French political economy from 1760 until almost 1780, and included among those influenced by physiocracy 'Raynal, Condorcet, and many others. One might even count among these Condillac' (Say 1803: xviii–xix), to the extent, Say allowed, that a system exists at all in the political economy of the last. He exempted only Turgot who 'had his own ideas'.

Moreover, there did not seem to be any consistent 'economics' of *idéologie*. Nicolas-François Canard, for example, who was awarded a prize in Year IX for a contest sponsored by the Political Economy section of the class, occasioned a vigorous debate between Lakanal and Roederer. The latter had expressed some reservations about Canard's essay. The debate continued in *La Décade*, in which LeBreton defended Canard's contribution, and the *Journal de Paris*, which criticised the notion of 'work' it contained. LeBreton and Roederer, both *idéologues*, had very different estimations of the worth of the piece.

It would, therefore, be very difficult to suggest that there was a single economic analysis that was consistent with *idéologie* because adherents proclaimed different systems and non-*idéologues*, such as Smith, wrote treatises largely consistent with Say's *Traité* (1803). Rather, what I argue is that Say's *Traité*, although clearly not the only possible expression of an economic analysis consistent with *idéologie*, was self-consciously constructed to be a contribution to that tradition.

Say's economics in the literature

Aside from general histories of economics, much of the secondary literature on Say's economics deals, more or less directly, with the genesis, dissemination and interpretation of Say's law of markets. If we move beyond the notorious law, we must recognise the classic pieces by Liesse (1901) and Levasseur (1905–6), which examine the teaching of political economy at the *Conservatoire des Arts et Métiers* under the Restoration, and the dissemination of political economy in the nineteenth century is treated by Levan-Lemesle (1980). The Say 'dynasty' is examined by Michel (1898) and Lutfalla (1979), among others.

Specific aspects of the economics, such as the role of the entrepreneur, find analysis in Koolman (1971) and the method in Allix (1911), Hirsch (1975), Klein (1985), Liggio (1985) and Salerno (1985). Industrialism is examined in Allix (1910), Hill (1973) and especially James (1977), and the relationship between Say and the *idéologues* in Kaiser (1980) and Staum (1987). Ménard examines Say's resistance to social arithmetic (Ménard 1980), as does Breton (1986).

Our understanding of Say's economics moved to a new plane with Arnold Heertje's discovery of a trove of family papers now divided between his collection and the *Bibliothèque national*. Evert Schoorl completed a thesis on the archival contents at the University of Amsterdam entitled *J. B. Say* (Schoorl 1980),[2] under Heertje's direction. Philippe Steiner, who must be regarded as among the most perceptive and prolific of current Say scholars, has published a series of papers dealing with various aspects of Say's economics and, especially, Say's attitude towards the social concerns of the *idéologues* (1989, 1990, 1991, 1996a, 1997).

This chapter does not address a topic that has been explicitly dealt with in the secondary literature, but rather asks whether there is any direct textual evidence that the first edition of the *Traité* (1803) was consciously written as a contribution to the programme of *idéologie*. As such, it does not examine the economic analysis directly but looks at the stated goals of the *Traité,* which are found in the preliminary discourse and in Say's marginal notes on Adam Smith's *Wealth of Nations.* Before we can determine whether the *Traité* was consistent with *idéologie*, we must tackle a problem we have avoided this far. What, exactly, did *idéologie* or, more precisely, 'analysis' mean in practice? What characteristics does a piece of 'analysis' always exhibit?

How would you recognise *idéologie*?

It is no simple task to determine who, exactly, ought to be considered an *idéologue.* Traditionally, Say and many others have been included in this group, but the grounds upon which their inclusion was determined have often been less than specific (cf. Kaiser 1976; Kitchin 1966; Kennedy 1978; Head 1985). Part of the problem has been the comparatively recent attempts to salvage *idéologues* from the 'garbage cans of history', in Gusdorf's colourful phrase (1978: 7). Staum (1996) attempts to codify the selection decision, by including as *idéologues* 'authors of a major work in medical or philosophical Ideology or in elements of ethics, politics, economics, and having at least two of the following attributes: (1) attendance at the salons of Mme Helvétius, Destutt de Tracy, or Mme de Condorcet in the period 1794–1809; (2) on the staff of or a contributor to *La Décade philosophique*; (3) and moderate republican after 1794 and in opposition to Bonaparte after 1801' (Staum 1996: 233). Using this categorisation, Say belongs in the group on the basis of all three attributes.

Staum's classification follows the usual practice of determining membership in a 'school' without a membership roster, by looking for clues of personal or institutional connection. When we are attempting to paste labels on individuals, this method is the only one conceivable. When we are examining particular works, however, we can be more specific and, indeed, must be more specific if we are attempting to argue that a book was consciously constructed as a contribution to *idéologie.*

It is uncontroversial to claim that a book can be considered a contribution to *idéologie* only if it advocates the method of 'analysis'. But this only places the fundamental problem at a single remove. How, exactly, would you know if a book advocated the method of 'analysis' if the author did not state as much? Fortunately for us, few of the *idéologues* were shy about telling us what method they intended to adopt. Indeed, one of the marks of a contribution to *idéologie* is that the work is invariably prefaced by a very long methodological statement, which often claims explicitly to apply the method of 'analysis' (see Pinel 1792).

The methodological statements prefacing these various books have a number of common features. First, Bacon and Newton, and very often Locke, are icons displayed for admiration. Second, they always attack 'system'. The particular 'system' criticised depends on the field of endeavour. In philosophy, it may be Kant (see Tracy 1803), in natural history it is often Buffon (see Pinel 1792), and in political economy the physiocrats turn out to be the target (Say 1803: xvj–xvij). Third, these methodological introductions advocate the careful observation of 'the nature of things' and trust in the evidence of our senses, so that first principles may be derived inductively. Fourth, argument is said to proceed from 'particular' to 'general' truths.[3] Fifth, the author invariably makes clear a desire to use simple and unadorned language, free of the excesses of rhetoric and obfuscation. Sixth, the author spends a good deal of effort on matters of organisation and presentation of the 'truths' in the work, so that pedagogy (always a fundamental goal) is enhanced.

None of these features is unique to *idéologie*, but virtually all contributions to *idéologie* display all of them. Every one of these characteristic features is unequivocally present in the introduction to the first edition of the *Traité*, and most can be discerned in the notes Say constructed on Smith's *Wealth of Nations*.

Say on method in 1800–3: the stated principles

Between 1800 and 1803, Say annotated his own copy of the fifth edition of Adam Smith's *Wealth of Nations*, which he had purchased in 1789 and still possessed in 1827. This copy was given to his son Horace Say (1794–1860) and then to his grandson Léon Say (1826–96), who donated it to the library of the *Institut de France*. These notes were carefully transcribed and published by Hitoshi Hashimoto (1980; 1982),[4] who provides an introduction containing a brief biographical note and a statement of the editorial principles used to update obsolete spelling and to date the annotation. In 1803, the first edition of Say's *Traité* appeared, with a forty-six page preliminary discourse on method. All of the traits listed above appear in the *Traité*, and most are already present in the marginal notes in the *Wealth of Nations*. The *Traité* was, indeed, intended to be a contribution to *idéologie*.

The first attribute of analytical writing is an explicit or implicit appearance by William Blake's 'unholy trinity' – Bacon, Newton and Locke. The implied similarity between the natural sciences and the science of political economy appears several times in the introduction to the *Traité*, not least when Say reminds us that developments in the natural sciences have occurred only recently and that political economy has simply been a little slower off the mark. The appropriate method, however, is identical in all areas of science:

> [The principles of political economy] are not the work of men; they are a consequence of the nature of things; one does not establish them: one discovers them. They govern legislators and princes who can never violate them with impunity. Analysis and observation will discover them. If they are only lately being discovered, if they are yet disputed daily, it is a prerogative that they share with the fundamental principles of almost all

the sciences. It is not twenty years since we have begun to analyse the water that sustains our life, the air in which we are immersed daily; and still the experiments upon which these theories are founded are questioned every day, even though they have been repeated a thousand times, in different countries and by the most educated men in Europe.

(Say 1803: ii)

And modern physics, Say reminds us, did not achieve universal acceptance immediately. After being unanimously rejected for close to fifty years in France, it had just recently begun to be taught in all the schools (Say 1803: xliv).[5]

The second attribute of ideological writing is an attack on 'system'. The introduction to the *Traité* obliges us with a general attack on 'system' in the context of an exhortation to adopt Baconian methods:

In political economy, as in physics, as in everything, systems have been constructed before truths have been established, because a system is more easily built than a fact discovered. But this science has profited from the excellent methods that have contributed so much to the progress of other sciences. It no longer accepts anything but *the consequences rigorously established from facts well observed*, and has rejected all those prejudices, those authorities, which, in science as in morality, in literature as in administration, always used to come between man and facts.

(Say 1803: iii–iv)

The specific system he chooses to set up as an adversary to be overcome is physiocracy, of which he likens the 'enthusiasm' of the disciples to a religious mania:

The enthusiasm of [the Économistes] for their founder, the care with which they forever after followed the same dogmas, their passion for defending them, caused them to be regarded as a sect...Instead of first observing the nature of things, of classifying their observations, and deducing from them general facts, they began by posing generalities, they tried to cause all particular facts to conform, and they derived from them consequences; which engaged them in the defence of maxims evidently contrary to good sense and the experience of centuries, as one can see in many places in this work. But their antagonists did not form clearer ideas of the things over which they disputed.

(Say 1803: xvj–xvij)

Clearly, in Say's mind, the physiocrats suffered from all the excess of system builders, including a vulnerability to metaphysical speculation.

The passages from the *Traité* cited above show Say's concern that first principles be derived inductively from 'the nature of things' because they demonstrate a desire to move from 'particular facts' to 'general facts'. This latter distinction, reaching back through Condorcet (1795) to Scotland,[6] is fundamental to establishing political economy on a scientific basis (see Coleman 1996). Say distinguishes clearly between 'particular facts' and 'general facts', using physical analogies:

> There are *general* or *constant facts*, and *particular* or *variable facts*. *General facts* are the result of the action of the laws of nature which are identical in all cases; *particular facts* are also the result of natural laws because these are never violated, but they are the result of one or more actions that modify each other in a particular case. One is not less certain than the others, even when they seem to contradict one another: in physics it is a general fact that solid bodies fall towards the earth; nevertheless, our fountains spray upwards. The particular fact of a fountain is an effect where the laws of equilibrium modify those of weight without destroying them.
>
> (Say 1803: iv–v)

This distinction between general and particular facts is vital to the progress of political economy because 'political economy…is established on certain foundations the moment when its first principles are rigorous deductions from incontestable general facts' (Say 1803: vii). It is, of course, 'particular facts' that are observed, but sufficient observation and analysis will allow one to derive the underlying 'general facts', claimed Say.

Say's fascination with science, and his Baconian rhetoric, are very apparent in almost everything he wrote. But Say's rhetorical attachment to the inductive method should not be overstated. Say was quite aware that 'there is not an absurd theory, or an extravagant opinion that has not been supported by an appeal to facts; and it is by facts also that public authorities have been so often misled' (Say 1803: ix). In a later edition of the *Traité* (Say 1880: xxiii), he elaborated the appropriate method to bring to political economy:

> [T]o obtain a knowledge of the truth, it is not then so necessary to be acquainted with a great number of facts, as with such as are essential, and have a direct and immediate influence; and, above all, to examine them under all their aspects, to be enabled to deduce from them just conclusions and be assured that the consequences ascribed to them do not in reality proceed from other causes. Every other knowledge of facts, like the erudition of an almanac, is a mere compilation from which nothing results. And it may be remarked, that this sort of information is peculiar to men of clear memories and clouded judgements.
>
> (Say 1880: xxiii)

Say's crusade was not against 'system building' per se; systems are useful and, indeed, essential. His real concern was no more than to ensure that the initial premises upon which the systems were built did not deviate far from actual experience, which, he believed, could be recognised as such by anyone.

One direction in which Say was not prepared to push the deductive method was in the application of mathematics to political economy because he believed the 'facts' too numerous and too imprecise for the method to be of any value. He illustrated his concern by demonstrating the absurdity of mathematical reasoning:

> Values can be characterised as *more* or *less*, are in the mathematical domain, but as subject to the action of the faculties, the needs and the will of men, they remain in the moral domain. And this, to note in passing, demonstrates that it is superfluous to apply algebraic formulae to demonstrations of political economy. Not a single quantity is susceptible of a rigorous appreciation.
>
> (Say 1803: xxxix)

Say's concern with the language of presentation echoes the ideological concern with clear and unadorned expression. This preoccupation persisted throughout Say's life, so that we can find it as readily in the *Cours Complet* as in the *Traité*. One of the compliments Say affords Turgot is that he was sensitive to issues of rhetoric – that he knew the necessity of managing well the instrument by means of which thoughts are communicated (Say 1843: 570). Charles Comte says of Say himself that his clear, simple and elegant style can be read with pleasure because the author had studied the great writers of the seventeenth and eighteenth centuries and had concluded that 'an obscure phrase only seemed necessary to hide a false thought' (Say 1843: 7). This facility of style has led to the charge that Say was nothing but a populariser. But Say was not a simple propagandist. Although he took issues of pedagogy seriously, as we shall see, he emphasised throughout his work the distinction between the science of positive economics and the art of administration (see Say 1843: 569), and he believed that the former could not be moulded to suit political expediency.

Finally, an ideological text always exhibits a preoccupation with 'order' of presentation, just as *idéologues* pursue social and political order. Say's great quarrel with Smith's *Wealth of Nations* was the alleged lack of order in the presentation of Smith's ideas. It is worth noting at the outset that this accusation reflected Say's concerns more than an objective consideration of Smith's work. He constantly berates Smith for poor textual organisation, although most of his contemporaries were enamoured of Smith's methodical presentation and at least some accused the hapless Smith of 'system building', defined as too great a fondness for long and abstract chains of reasoning (Stewart 1858: 65–6 and 68–9; J. Mill 1806: 231–2; Buchanan 1814, IV: viii and xi; Horner 1853, I: 126–7).

Say claimed to be surprised that such an excellent thinker could put so little order into the presentation of his ideas as Smith, in this case allowing a discussion of related but peripheral ideas to intrude upon an analysis of wages (Hashimoto 1980, I: 119). A few pages earlier, Say notes (with some exasperation) that it takes Smith eight pages to prove that salaries in England are higher than would be necessary to purchase the physical means of subsistence (Hashimoto 1980, I: 111). Similarly, he remarks that chapter 10 of volume I contains many developments of material belonging in chapters 8 and 9, and 'chapter 11 is swollen beyond measure by digressions which merit *chapters* and even *books* to themselves' (Hashimoto 1980, I: 96).

The most important points that Say made in his notes on Smith concerned the alleged lack of order in the presentation, and Smith's definition of political economy. Both reflect a preoccupation with classification. Say declared that he would prefer to define political economy as a study of the means by which wealth is created, distributed and destroyed (or consumed). The government enters this system only as an accessory, to encourage or to inhibit production, or to lay a claim to a share of the produce (Hashimoto 1980, II: 138). This is an important issue because it is one that Say carried with him throughout his life. In the *Cours Complet*, for example, he blames the physiocrats for confusing the independent investigations of the science of human wants (economic analysis) and the art of political administration. Adam Smith, he claims, without sharing the error perpetuates it by using the name 'political economy' to refer to the science of economic analysis instead of 'social economy', which Say would have preferred on the grounds that careless readers would be less likely to confuse economics and politics (Say 1843: 569).

It seems clear enough that Say was identifying himself with *idéologie* in his first major contribution to economics, the *Traité d'Économie Politique* (1803). Moreover, he did not distinguish himself from Adam Smith primarily on the basis of the substance of his contribution, although he did condemn what he saw as Smith's apparent approval of a labour theory of value, which Say attempted to replace with a 'utility' analysis drawn from Cantillon (Forget 1993: 128–31). Rather, Say distinguished his contribution from Smith's by aligning political economy more directly with the 'analysis' of Condillac and the *idéologues*. Jean-Baptiste Say was not simply an *idéologue* who wrote about political economy; he was an *idéologue* who consciously struggled to bring the developments in political economy associated with Adam Smith into accord with the scientific principles of *idéologie*.

The method in practice

Say was never so simple minded as to suggest that pure observation or pure induction was either possible or helpful. Pure observation allows us only to gather data on 'particular facts', which are no more than the basis for deriving the first principles and higher order truths of political economy (Say 1803: vi). Pure induction gives us an almanac, rather than a science. Moreover, Say was fully aware as he penned his comments on Adam Smith's *Wealth of Nations* that illustrative examples alone are unconvincing. Smith, for example, had argued that only profitable industries such as sugar and tobacco could afford the luxury of using slave labour, which, he maintained, was less productive than free labour. Say responded that he could use the same 'fact' to prove, equally well, the opposite point: that is, that profits are large in sugar and tobacco production because the maintenance of slaves is less costly and they are worked harder than would be possible with a voluntary labour force (Hashimoto 1980, II: 90). It is, however, interesting to contrast the statements on method in the *Traité* with the slightly more nuanced version in the *Cours Complet*. There is no evidence that Say's fundamental approach to the nature and method of science changed over his lifetime, but the words did adjust over time because a statement of sympathy with *idéologie* was no longer a basic goal of his work.

A passage in the *Cours Complet* is representative of his later style, when he was much less concerned with differentiating his own method from that of Adam Smith:

> Men little accustomed to reflection have disdained reason; they have said: *I want nothing but facts and figures.* They have not realised that facts and figures have no value except when they prove something, and they cannot prove anything without the aid of reason. Reason alone can show how they result from a certain given, or demonstrate a certain effect.
>
> (Say 1843: 8; his italics)

Say seems intent only on ensuring that the first axioms of the science are reasonably realistic, or at least do not violate daily observation, and that the results of chains of deduction actually occur sometimes (Say 1843: 6–9). Perhaps Say realised how little separated his own work from Smith's with respect to method in application because in the *Cours Complet* he remarked of Smith: 'If he states a general truth, that abstract proposition is nothing but the common expression of many real facts' (Say 1843: 572).

When it comes to method, Say, like most economists, is a good deal more consistent in word than in deed. As much as he condemns 'system', he shows a definite taste for abstract deduction. Reynaud, for example, divided what he labels Say's primary contributions to the science into two categories. Induction, or what Reynaud calls 'la méthode réaliste', predominates in the first, which includes Say's theory of value and his discussion of the entrepreneur and of industrialism. The deductive method, however, he claims surges to the fore in Say's discussions of free trade, the law(s) of markets, money, distribution and the analyses of crises (Reynaud 1953: 17–49).

The theory of value, the role of the entrepreneur and the analysis of industrialism are matters most closely related to ideological concerns, and they appear in detail in the first edition of the *Traité* and, in the case of industrialism, even in *Olbie*. The law of markets did not appear in developed form until the second edition of the *Traité* more than a decade later, after the *idéologues* had dispersed and their institutions had crumbled. So, one might be tempted to argue that Say became more abstract as he aged. Yet, if one compares the *Traité* with the *Cours Complet*, it becomes clear that Say's illustrative examples multiplied as time passed. His earliest work is the simplest and is the most 'systematic'. His later work shows the effects of his experiences and his study; at base, it may be as deductive as anything else he wrote, but the *Cours Complet* has a richer anecdotal content. On balance, it would seem reasonable to argue that Say's actual method did not change significantly over time. This consistency also seems to be characteristic of his stated method. The preliminary discourse of the *Traité*, although modified between editions, did not change substantively.

The implications of teaching political economy

Say was a populariser. Popularisation is often spoken of with a bit of a sneer in an age when innovation is valued, and when every doctoral dissertation at every minor university is supposed to have made a significant contribution to the development of knowledge in the discipline before a degree is awarded. But the *idéologues* were drawn by matters of popular education rather than innovation; they valued the influence a social theory might have on the administration of policy more than its potential effect on the evolution of some brand of esoteric knowledge. It is in this context that one must read Say's claim that:

> The highest branches of knowledge are far from having procured for society all the advantages that one could expect from them, and without which they are nothing but idle curiosities; and perhaps it remains for the nineteenth century to perfect applications. One would see superior intellects who, after having extended the limitations of their theories, discover methods which would demonstrate important truths to less elevated minds. Then in the ordinary occurrences of life, in the most usual undertakings, one would be guided not by the lights of transcendental philosophies, but by common sense...
>
> (Say 1803: xlv)

Popularisation, in this context, is hardly to be denigrated.

One could draw attention to the need for an elementary text in political economy, articulated as one of Say's principal suggestions in *Olbie*. Such a text would be taught in public schools so that all citizens would be aware of the principles that governed their economic welfare. Anybody running for office would be publicly interrogated on the principles of the science. This early articulation of the need for education in the principles of political economy reflects the grandiose idea of the promise of political economy that characterised the social theory of the *idéologues*; it is re-emphasised in the *Cours Complet* (Say 1843: 4–10) and accords well with Say's much later recollection that 'under Napoleon's government, political economy was criticised for making men too reasonable and not submissive enough to the decrees of authority' (1843: 26).

The primary political goal of the *idéologues* was the stabilisation of the republic, and the desire for social stability permeated all of the applications of *idéologie*. Say's economic analysis was no exception. But Say does more than consider the implications of his economic analysis for social stability; he actively promotes political economy as a tool useful for the stabilisation of society.

Say believed dissemination of the principles of political economy through various channels of public education would limit social chaos, both by lowering the frequency of poor policy decisions taken through simple ignorance and by restricting the ability of governments to exploit the mistaken expectations of individuals for personal gain. This latter concern drove Say throughout his life, and appears in various guises in all his work. For example, as a member of the Finance Committee of the *Tribunat*, one of his more important contributions was to write an impassioned plea for the submission of a government budget before the committee would authorise the transfer of funds to Bonaparte. Say, quite explicitly, linked the requirement of a detailed budget with the discouragement of the rise of dictatorship. Not surprisingly, the Finance Committee feared the political consequences of suggesting that Bonaparte submit to such a requirement, and thought better of accepting Say's unaltered report; what went forward instead of the twelve-page missive that Say preserved among his papers (annotated with a good deal of self-satisfaction) was a page-long approval of the transfer of funds.[7]

It seems apparent that Say linked general knowledge of political economy with social stability, but we can make the link even more explicit by considering a specific application of political economy in Say's *Traité*. Say considers the extent to which a government's ability to borrow is related to its ability to disrupt society:

> Public credit affords such facilities to public prodigality, that many political writers have regarded it as fatal to national prosperity. For, say they, when governments feel themselves strong in the ability to borrow, they are too apt to intermeddle in every political arrangement, and to conceive gigantic projects, that lead sometimes to disgrace, sometimes to glory, but always to a state of financial exhaustion; to make war themselves, and stir up others to do the like; to subsidise every mercenary agent, and deal in the blood and the consciences of mankind; making capital, which should be the fruit of industry and virtue, the prize of ambition, pride, and wickedness.[...]These are by no means hypothetical cases: but the reader is left to make the application himself.
>
> (Say 1880: 483; 1803, II: 528–9)

By the second edition, Say explicitly links the ability of governments to create mischief through their ability to borrow with the gullibility of creditors, whose expectations are not informed by experience:

> Moreover, it is observable that the sentiments of lenders and indeed of

mankind upon all occasions, are more powerfully operated upon by the impressions of the moment, than by any other motive; experience of the past must be very recent, and the prospect of the future very near, to have any sensible effect. The monstrous breach of faith on the part of the French government in 1721, in regard to its paper-money and the Mississippi share-holders, did not prevent the ready negotiation of a loan of 200,000,000 *liv.* in 1759; nor did the bankrupt measures of the Abbé Terrai in 1772 prevent the negotiation of fresh loans in 1778 and every subsequent year.

(Say 1880: 483; 1814, II: 367–8)

Say believed that it was imperative to limit the ability of governments to cause social disorder by borrowing because 'the command of a large sum is a dangerous temptation to a national administration. Though accumulated at their expense, the people rarely, if ever profit by it: yet in point of fact, all value, and consequently, all wealth, originates with the people' (Say 1880: 487).

Even more important, however, was the role that political economy could play in containing the social disruption exacerbated by the errors of a public ignorant of how the economy functions when the government cannot be trusted to act in the best interests of the people:

I here suppose the higher orders of society to be actuated by a sincere desire to promote the public good. When this feeling, however, does not exist, when the government is faithless and corrupt, it is of still greater importance that the people should become acquainted with the real state of things, and comprehend their true interests. Otherwise, they suffer without knowing to what causes their distresses ought to be attributed, or indeed, by attributing them to erroneous causes, the views of the public are distracted, their efforts disunited, and individuals, thus deprived of general support, fail in resolution, and despotism is strengthened; or what is still worse, where the people are so badly governed as to become desperate, they listen to pernicious counsels, and exchange a vicious order of things for one still worse.

(Say 1880: lv)

This statement, significantly, does not appear in the first or the second editions of the *Traité*. Say's significant concerns about the Machiavellian tendencies of government appeared later.

It is clear enough that social disruption, Say believed, was an evil to be avoided and that political economy must play an important role and teach all economic agents 'the real state of things', including the truth about how the economy functions. This would constrain the damage caused by simple policy errors. But education could effectively limit the ability of the government to manipulate the economy for personal or group interests. Because economic decisions would be based upon an accurate knowledge of how the economy functions, they would be less volatile and less open to manipulation by interested parties. Both social and economic stability would ensue.

Conclusion

The *Traité* (1803) was Say's first major attempt to fulfil the pedagogical goals he articulated in *Olbie*, which are consistent with the ideological programme of education aimed at the enlightenment of the people. The moral education that was so much an aspect of *Olbie* and much less a feature of Say's mature writing was intended to teach people their true interests. By contrast, Say's *Traité d'Économie Politique* was self-consciously offered as a contribution to the ideological programme of instruction that also tried to combat the effects of misinformation and superstition on the decision making of ordinary people by helping them to understand their true interests.

Say's *Traité* went through several editions over his lifetime. He clearly addressed this volume to 'la classe mitoyenne' because this class, far from 'the cares and pleasures of wealth and the anguish of poverty', has the relative leisure to travel, read and reflect. Good sense taught here would gradually extend to the great and to the people, particularly as the middle classes furnish the bureaucrats behind the legislators (Say 1803: xxvii–xxix). Neither 'les grands' nor 'le peuple',[8] he claimed, were prepared to spend the time in reflection that such reading requires, and would not adopt 'truths' until they were reduced to the form of axioms. These individuals required no proofs. Say's *Catéchisme* was a simplified version of the principles of the discipline, aimed at these more elementary readers. His *Cours Complet* was designed to teach political economy to statesmen, merchants, landlords, and capitalists, scholars, farmers, manufacturers, lawyers and 'in general…all citizens'.

The *Traité* was consistent with *idéologie* in other ways as well. It self-consciously stated that the method to be used was the analytical method of Condillac, which, Say enthused, had generated progress in the natural sciences. The preliminary discourse of the *Traité* suggests that the *Traité* was intended to be an application of *idéologie* – that is, that *idéologie* is both a necessary and a sufficient foundation for the *Traité*. In fact, it seems likely that it is neither. Confirmed *idéologues* published different kinds of economic analysis, most of which seemed to be more consistent with physiocracy than with the *Wealth of Nations*. The economic reforms that Say supported were consistent with *idéologie* and they were also consistent with a broader movement towards reform supported by individuals not associated with *idéologie*, as was the case with Pinel's proposed reform for the treatment of the mentally ill. Although recognising that Say was an *idéologue* will allow us to understand his goals better, his philosophical and perhaps political orientation and, to some extent, his implicit social presuppositions, it will not allow us to better understand the economic analysis itself. The last is distinct, and fits into an intellectual tradition much broader than *idéologie*.

11 *Idéologie* and Say's theory of value

We have seen that Say constructed his *Traité* as a contribution to *idéologie*, borrowing from Adam Smith's *Wealth of Nations* to the extent that Smith's ideas were compatible with his own larger concerns. This chapter asks to what extent Say's *idéologie* might have influenced something as central to his economics as his theory of value. Unlike many aspects of Say's economics, including his law of markets and his analysis of income distribution, Say's value theory appears very early in his work in a form that he would retain without a major change of emphasis.[1]

The first section of this chapter introduces Say's theory of value. Next, we document the relationship Say posits between disequilibrium trade and social disorder. Then, we look specifically at the way in which prices work to clear a market under *laissez faire*, and contrast it with the analysis offered when prices are administered. When Say considers the implications of trade under administered prices, and the social chaos resulting from such intervention, his analytical language wanders into the realm of a 'social body', dominated by the 'lower passions' as opposed to reason. *Idéologie*, it seems, influenced Say's metaphorical language[2] and, even more importantly, characterised the manner in which Say introduced his analytical concepts. The determination of price is intimately connected to the problem of social stability, with ill-advised intervention by authorities responsible for chaotic markets and the social instability that accompanies disequilibrium in trade. Social stability, by contrast, requires that the truths of political economy be widely disseminated.

The theory of value

One of the most important early contributions Say made to economic analysis was his utility theory of value, and yet the merit and the influence of his contribution is somewhat ambiguous. Even though he can hardly be credited with the *creation* of a mature utility theory of value, both because his theory lacks any real conception of the margin and because there is a very old continental tradition of finding the source of value in utility, Jean-Baptiste Say certainly made ample use of a utility theory of value that allowed him to develop the analysis of 'immaterial products' or services. Nevertheless, Say's analysis is rejected by Walras (1952) as a true precursor because, Walras claims, Say neglected the important role that scarcity plays in valuation.

We must, however, examine the persistent claim that Say, although using the language of later contributions to economic analysis, was not an important source for Walras (1952). Schumpeter, for example, writes that:

> J. B. Say…following the French tradition (Condillac, in particular), made exchange value dependent upon utility but, failing (like Condillac) to add scarcity, stumbled over the fact, so often explained before him, that such 'useful' things as air or water normally have no exchange value at all. He said that actually they do have value; only this value is so great, infinite in fact, that nobody could pay for them and hence they go for nothing. It is true that he did not stop at this ineptitude. He did rise to the imperfect (yet so significant) statement that price is the measure of the value of things and value the measure of their utility, a statement that heralds Walras': *les valeurs d'échange sont proportionnelles aux raretés* [marginal utility, J. A. S.]. Mostly, however, he merely used a rather primitive supply-and-demand analysis.
>
> (Schumpeter 1954: 600)

This still represents the standard evaluation of Say's value theory.

Say's 'rather primitive' demand and supply analysis is adopted by John Stuart Mill, who notes that:

> Undoubtedly the true solution must have been frequently given, though I cannot call to mind anyone who had given it before myself, except the eminently clear thinker and skilful expositor, J. B. Say. I should have imagined, however, that it must be familiar to all political economists, if the writings of several did not give evidence of some want of clearness on the point…
>
> (J. S. Mill 1923 [1848]: 446)

And, in fact, the applications of J. S. Mill and Say are quite similar, and are a 'primitive' demand and supply analysis because, as Schumpeter long ago recognised, 'the concepts of supply and demand apply to a mechanism that is compatible with any theory of value and indeed is required by all' (Schumpeter 1954: 601).[3]

Schumpeter's take on Say's value theory goes all the way back to Léon Walras, who writes:

> The science of economics offers three major solutions to the problem of the origin of value. The first, that of Adam Smith, Ricardo and McCulloch, is the English solution, which traces the origin of value to *labour*. This solution is too narrow, because it fails to attribute value to things which, in fact, do have value. The second solution, that of Condillac and Jean-

Baptiste Say, is the French solution, which traces the origin of value to *utility*. This solution is too broad, because it attributes value to things which, in fact, have no value. Finally, the third, that of Burlamaqui and of my father, A. A. Walras, traces the origin of value to scarcity. This is the correct solution.

(Walras 1952: 201)

Is Say guilty of neglecting the role played by scarcity in valuation?

One can say without very much discomfort that Say did not emphasise the role of scarcity in his analysis, despite the fact that J. S. Mill found it there (1923 [1848]: 446–8). As Schumpeter notes, there are very many instances, throughout the entire corpus of Say's work, in which he claims that price is the measure of value, and value the measure of utility. For example, in a letter to his brother Louis, concerning the latter's criticism of his value theory, Jean-Baptiste clarifies at length:

> Even if one pays for products in money, one buys them only with other products; in other words, one exchanges the thing that one sells for that which one buys. One sacrifices one utility to acquire another. And since it is supposed that men give that which for them has less utility to acquire that which has more, I conclude from this that the utility that they consent to receive in exchange for a product is the measure of the utility that they find in that product.
>
> (Say 'letter to Louis Say of 21 April 1822', in 1848: 542–3)

From this he concludes that the exchange value of a commodity, or the money price of a commodity when money is the medium of exchange, is the measure of utility.[4] This exchange with Louis Say is not unique. In the first edition of the *Traité*, for example, he writes:

> To measure production exactly, it is necessary to have an exact measure of the degree of utility of each thing.[5] But how can one measure utility? That which seems necessary to one person, appears superfluous to another. Nevertheless, whatever variety we find in the needs and tastes of men, they collectively make a general estimate of the utility of each object, of which we can obtain an idea by the quantity of other objects they are prepared to give in exchange for it. [...] I ask that it be noted that the money price of objects is here used only as an imperfect measure of the exchangeable value of things, and that exchangeable value gives only an estimate, the least vague that we can find, of the degree of their utility; but that it is the degree of utility alone that truly constitutes production.
>
> (Say 1803, I: 24–7)

Say goes on to note that this is so because otherwise one could increase 'production' by raising prices through such interventionist measures as taxes.

He emphasises that prices only serve as a measure of the degree of utility when they are left to themselves, just as barometers only measure air pressure when the mercury is not interfered with (Say 1803, I: 27–8). This same argument is rehearsed from the very first edition of the *Traité* all the way to the *Cours Complet*. But it is not quite a recognition of the role of scarcity.

Is there, in fact, any explicit recognition of scarcity in the body of Say's work? Lutfalla notes that Jean-Baptiste Say, annotating the twenty-seventh chapter of Ricardo's *Principles*, writes:

> The basis of all value is, not the quantity of labour necessary to make a commodity, but the need for it that one has, balanced by its scarcity.
>
> (Lutfalla 1991: 28)

This is clear enough, but it is a rather shaky foundation upon which to build a case for a more sophisticated anticipation of Walrasian value theory.

But, perhaps Mill was correct after all, in that an awareness of scarcity was so fundamental to Say's analysis that it did not need to be emphasised. Even the first edition of the *Traité* seems to take the importance of scarcity in affecting value as obvious:

> [Current] Price is established by the relationship between the quantity of merchandise available for exchange or sale, and the quantity of that same merchandise that is wanted for sale. The more abundant is the merchandise relative to the demand for it, the more the price falls; the stronger the demand relative to the quantity of merchandise in circulation, the more price rises. These truths are trivial.
>
> (Say 1803, III: 58)

He goes on in the same context to distinguish between goods for which supply exceeds demand at all prices, such as water, and which consequently have a zero price, and goods for which demand exceeds supply at all prices, for which any market price established is no particular guide to utility because there would be no continuing and established market:

> When the quantity of a thing exceeds the demand that may exist for it, however extensive that may be, the thing has no price. This is the case of water, necessary to everyone and of value to no one. But on a ship where the need for fresh water may greatly exceed the quantity of it that one has, its price may rise very high. When the extent of demand exceeds all possibility of production [as in the case of a unique artistic production, for example], there is no basis upon which to reason about the price of a commodity.
>
> (Say 1803, III: 58–9)

Note that this analysis is not quite as ludicrous as Schumpeter suggested, and that he undoubtedly drew from Walras's contention:

> J. B. Say…tells us that air, sunlight and the waters of streams and rivers are useful and therefore have value. They are, indeed, so useful, so necessary and so indispensable that their value is immense – in fact, infinite. And that is exactly why we get them for nothing. We do not pay for them, because we could never pay the price. The explanation is ingenious, but unfortunately for the argument, there are times when we do pay for air, light and water – when, for example, they are scarce.
>
> (Walras 1952: 203)

It would seem that Say's explanations, when not distorted, demonstrate that he is quite aware of the role of scarcity in the determination of price.

The extent of demand, according to Say, is determined by price (Say 1803, III: 70–3). Current price is determined by the quantity offered for sale and the extent of demand (Say 1803, III: 58). If current price exceeds natural price, which Say defines as the price just required to hire the quantity of inputs necessary to produce a quantity of output sufficient to meet effectual demand, factors of production will be drawn to that industry by higher prices offered to their owners. Therefore, the supply will increase and price will fall (Say 1803, III: 60).[6] Similarly, if current price falls below natural price, the earnings of those who supply factors of production will fall and they will seek better employments. Supply of the commodity in question will decline, and price will increase (Say 1803, III: 60–1). All of this seems to recognise the role that scarcity plays in determining current price. Moreover, it makes clear Say's efforts to derive the returns to factors from the prices of the final products. But there is no real recognition of the role of scarcity in the determination of natural price in the first edition of the *Traité* nor is there any real recognition of a concept of the margin, despite Say's intriguing use of the phrase the 'degree of utility'.

The idea that value stems from utility can be found in Galiani, Quesnay, Beccaria, Turgot (whose value theory was popularised after his death by Du Pont de Nemours), Verri and, especially, Condillac (who cited Cantillon as an important source), as well as many minor writers (Schumpeter 1954: 302). In Germany, a similar tradition had developed (Schumpeter 1954: 600).[7] *Idéologie* cannot, therefore, be seen as necessary to the development of Say's utility theory of value, even though Say confronted the utilitarianism of Helvétius long before he was in contact with Bentham (Schoorl 1982). Both Roll (1978: 320) and Pribram (1983: 148–9) wonder whether Say's unwillingness to adopt Smith's value theory[8] might not stem from his desire to eradicate French physiocracy, with its excessive estimation of the importance of material output in agriculture.[9] Again, to the extent that such an explanation is tenable, this would undermine the importance attributed to *idéologie* in enticing Say to adopt a utility theory of value.

Disequilibrium trade as a metaphor for social disorder[10]

On the day that the Bastille fell, the price of bread was at its highest level for sixty years. The vicissitudes of climate in a largely primitive agricultural economy (Le Roy Ladurie and Goy 1981), perhaps exacerbated by the court intrigue that was certainly suspected by the population (Kaplan 1982), generated periodic crises. Poor harvests led to annual price variations, but even more onerous a burden for the poor were the seasonal variations in the prices of grain and bread. The public, ignorant of the social role that speculation can play in helping to stabilise prices, demanded strict prohibitions against hoarding and agitated for price ceilings on grain and bread. The inevitable shortages led to hunger riots, and the alarmed authorities set up a complex system of supply management for Paris, where the situation was particularly explosive, and banned exports, intervened extensively in the markets and attempted to build stockpiles of grain. Nevertheless, this was not sufficient to supply Paris in the event of poor harvests, and the hardship was extreme.

One can imagine the impact of bread shortages and the rising price of grain on the poor if one remembers that half the income of the Parisian worker was spent on bread in non-crisis periods. Rudé estimates that a Parisian worker in 1789 earned 20–30 sous per day, a mason 40, and a joiner or locksmith 50. A family of two adults and two children consumed eight pounds of bread a day (Rudé 1959: 83). When the price of a four-pound loaf rose suddenly from 8 sous to 15 or 20 sous, starvation was imminent. The demand for a *maximum*, or price ceiling, is easy to understand, as are the hunger riots as a response to the inevitable shortages.

It is in this context that one should read Jean-Baptiste Say on *current price*, demand and supply, and disequilibrium trade. Most of the classical economists, from Hume and Smith to John Stuart Mill and William Thornton, conceived of disequilibrium trade as a process during which information is made available to the actors and potential actors in a market, and the debates centred around whether or not the information and the behavioural responses it generated would drive the economy toward some market-clearing equilibrium position. Even Adam Smith, Say's ultimate authority in matters economic, conceived of out-of-equilibrium trade as a process of equilibration by means of which prices gravitated towards their 'natural' levels. In the work of Say, this process of equilibration is so attenuated as to be negligible. The matter of finding and realising a market price that brings the quantities supplied and demanded into equilibrium under conditions of perfect economic liberty, according to Say, is almost instantaneous. Individual markets and, by analogy, the entire economy are rarely out of equilibrium when *laissez faire* rules.

This is not, however, to suggest that Say never described or discussed markets that did not costlessly and quickly clear. Ill-advised attempts on the part of political authorities to intervene in the market inevitably generated such situations. For Say, disequilibrium trade always signified social upheaval, which he described in dramatic terms. Higgling was not, under these circumstances, the means of discovering an equilibrium price, but rather a process by means of which individual buyers and sellers attempted to gain differential advantages when the social ideal implicit in competitive equilibrium was not realised. Higgling would persist until the system of natural liberty was restored.

Say believed that prices, if left alone, would reflect allocative efficiency, with its associated pattern of incentives and constraints. Intervention, however, was necessarily misguided and invariably associated with social disorder. Say emphasises the political and social consequences of ill-advised tampering with market signals.

The next section of this chapter outlines Say's analysis of market price without government intervention. It demonstrates the minor role that a process of equilibration plays in such circumstances, and highlights the mechanical analogies and scientific language in terms of which Say casts the story. He even borrows a tool from Germain Garnier and develops demand in structural terms, which simply emphasises the absence of economic agents as people engaged in trade in a real marketplace. That is, the social machine dominates the story. Then, I demonstrate the contrast in the language in terms of which Say articulates out-of-equilibrium trade in a market burdened with government intervention. Well-functioning markets in a free economy characterise a stable society; disequilibrium trade is the mark of riot and revolution – crowds out of control and the 'general will' influenced predominantly by passion rather than reason, rather like Pinel's patients in the asylums.

Market price under *laissez faire*[11]

Whenever Say discusses market price determination under *laissez faire*, three things are clear. First, there are no real people cluttering up the narrative; everything is cast in terms of scientific necessity. Individual trading behaviour, in all of its potential irrationality and subjectivity, makes no appearance. Second, 'demand' and 'supply' are treated almost as physical entities. Say is aware that messy institutions and human psychology are the ultimate determinants of demand and supply and, ultimately, market price, but the story proceeds by means of mechanical analogies that suggest certainty and scientific precision. Finally, the normal state of the economy is one in which all markets clear very quickly. That is, there is little recognition of disequilibrium as a protracted process, or of 'false trading' as a usual state of affairs.

In later editions of the *Traité*, Say used the case of market price determination[12] in a manner that makes the method of 'analysis' particularly clear:

> We may, for example, know that for any given year the price of wine will infallibly depend upon the quantity to be sold, compared with the extent of the demand. But if we are desirous of submitting these two data to mathematical calculations, their ultimate elements must be decomposed

before we can become thoroughly acquainted with them, or can, with any degree of precision, distinguish the separate influence of each.

(Say 1880: xxvi–xxvii)

He went on to list the factors that would determine the quantity supplied: the quantity and quality of the vintage estimated *before* it is harvested, the stock on hand, the financial circumstances of the dealers, expectations of export opportunities that depend upon political factors, 'and probably many other besides' (Say 1880: xxvii). Quantity demanded, he noted, would depend upon price, 'as the demand for it will increase in proportion to its cheapness' (Say 1880: xxvii), stock on hand, tastes, incomes, the 'condition of industry in general, and of their own in particular' (Say 1880: xxvii), and the possibilities for substitution in consumption ('beer, cider, &c.'). In both cases, he was aware that he 'suppress[ed] an infinite number of less important considerations'.

The mathematical method, he claimed, was inappropriate because of the complexity of the problem and the uncertainty surrounding any numerical estimates of the data required. The only appropriate method for a political economist is:

...the same which would be pursued by him, under circumstances equally difficult, which decide the greater part of the actions of his life. He will examine the immediate elements of the proposed problem, and after having ascertained them with certainty, (which in political economy can be effected) will approximately value their mutual influences with the intuitive quickness of an enlightened understanding, itself only an instrument by means of which the mean result of a crowd of probabilities can be estimated, but never calculated with exactness.

(Say 1880: xxvii)

That is, mathematics is not useful because of the complexity of the data requirements, and not because the system itself is not determinate.

This discussion appears to recognise the complexity inherent in individual market behaviour. There are other places, throughout the body of his work, where similar insights are articulated: for example, 'The want or desire of any particular object depends upon the physical and moral constitution of man, the climate he may live in, the laws, customs, and manners of the particular society, in which he may happen to be enrolled' (Say 1880: 285; 1843: 168; cf. 1803, I: chapter 36; 1803, III: 73). But Say never implies that such complexity might impede the market price of any commodity from being established very quickly at a level at which markets clear. The uncertainty that he recognises might prevent the political economist from forecasting market prices correctly, but it will not prevent markets from working nor will it lead to protracted disequilibria. This distinction is responsible for allowing Say to recognise the complexity of human systems and to point to uncertainty and individual irrationality in a discussion of *method*, and, simultaneously, to de-emphasise the role of individual market behaviour (indeed, of people in general) in his *theoretical* discussion of supply and demand as the determinants of market price.

In his theoretical analysis of demand in the *Traité*, Say suppresses all discussion of expectations and uncertainty and notes only that the 'demand for all objects of pleasure, or utility, would be unlimited, did not the difficulty of attainment, or price, limit and circumscribe the supply' (Say 1880: 290; 1803, III: 72). Interestingly, as price increases, quantity demanded falls, both because the number of consumers is diminished and because the consumption of each consumer is reduced also (Say 1803, III: 70–3). Similarly, all discussion of the financial constraints faced by dealers and the uncertainty of political situations or climate is suppressed in his discussion of supply, which 'would be infinite, were it not restricted by the same circumstance, the price, or difficulty of attainment: for there can be no doubt that whatever is producible would then be produced in unlimited quantity, so long as it could find purchasers at any price at all' (Say 1880: 290). Demand and supply determine market price, and he explains the process by means of a very clear mechanical analogy: 'Demand and supply are the opposite extremes of the beam, whence depend the scales of dearness and cheapness; the price is the point of equilibrium, where the momentum of the one ceases, and that of the other begins' (Say 1880: 290). The moral of the story is that there is an equilibrium market price, which ensures that quantity demanded is just equal to quantity supplied, and that the laws of political economy (just like the laws of physics) will ensure that the equilibrium is established, but Say articulates no disequilibrium adjustment process that would generate a stable equilibrium.

The mechanical analogy of Say's *Traité* – the beam – gives way to a structural representation of demand in his *Cours Complet d'Économie Politique Pratique* (see Figure 11.1). Say's explanation of the diagram is as follows:

> The scale in this picture shows the height of the market price of different commodities, whatever the causes of the price. Beside the scale is a pyramid, which should be imagined as constructed of a multitude of vertical lines, the length of each representing someone's 'fortune' [sic]. Now, imagine the pyramid cut horizontally at different heights, according to the price of the product we want to consider; the horizontal section of the pyramid corresponding to the price represents the number of fortunes that can afford the product. The number of potential consumers declines as the price increases. In this example, a number of fortunes represented by vertical lines which do not exceed AA can afford a price represented by the 4th degree on the scale. Those whose wealth reaches the line BB can afford the price represented by the 19th degree. The 24th degree represents a price no one can afford. The area of the pyramid represents, even more precisely, the total expenditure that consumers are able *and want to* allocate to a particular product. A country where individual fortunes are, in general,

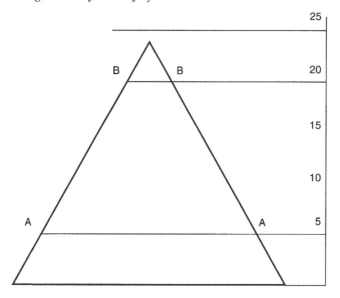

Figure 11.1 Say's pyramid.

very limited can be represented by a low, wide pyramid. One where there are many small fortunes and a few large can be represented by a pyramid with concave sides. One where wealth is fairly evenly distributed, and extremes of fortune rare, will generate a pyramid with convex sides. Such countries are the happiest.

(Say 1843: 169; author's emphasis)

Before we consider the significance of this metaphor, it is worthwhile to underline some of its features. Say casts this explanation in terms of 'fortunes', which represent (presumably) some measure of ability to pay on the part of each potential consumer; he does not consistently consider quantity desired at each price, despite the phrase italicised above, making this diagram quite different from a demand curve. Say has drawn his diagram as if each individual had a perfectly price-inelastic demand curve for each commodity, and the height of each vertical line represents the extent of that individual's resources that he is prepared to devote to the commodity in question. Similarly, the units in terms of which the commodities are to be measured (four-pound loaves per day, or 20 sous' worth?) are not specified. These represent limitations of Say's diagram rather than his understanding of demand, as is clear from an example he gives in the text, in which he must torture this diagram a little bit to represent his meaning:

When a commodity increases in price, either because of a tax or for some other reason, a certain number of consumers stop buying it, but others reduce their consumption. Consider a consumer of coffee who, when coffee increases in price, might not be forced to give it up completely. He simply reduces his usual consumption. We must imagine him as two individuals, one disposed to pay the price demanded, and the other (not so disposed) who stops drinking coffee.

(Say 1843: 169)

How useful it might be to estimate potential consumption of coffee on the basis of how many people can afford to buy it if they spent their entire fortunes on coffee remains an open question. For the Parisian labourer who did spend virtually his entire income on bread, however, this is a reasonable way to conceptualise demand. This is clearly an instance in which Say is in command of the concept of price elasticity of demand for individual consumers (he does, after all, consider the possibility of commodity substitution), but cannot capture the concept diagrammatically.

This diagram was not created by Jean-Baptiste Say. It was a feature of French economics from at least 1796, when Germain Garnier included it in his *Abrégé Élémentaire des Principes de l'Économie Politique* (cf. Theocharis 1983; Ekelund and Thornton 1991). Nevertheless, it entered mainstream French economics largely by way of Say and subsequently Dupuit. Say reproduces the diagram in the first edition of his *Cours Complet* (1828–9). Ekelund and Thornton claim that the demand analysis in the *Traité* of 1803 is written as though he had such a conception in mind, even though he chose not to reproduce the diagram.[13]

Say's use of this diagram betrays his tendency to conceive of economic questions in terms of concrete images. This picture is not a geometrical representation of demand, as is a contemporary demand curve; it is not an abstract line in Cartesian space, but rather a picture that represents some very solid and three-dimensional body. The pyramid represents the distribution of wealth in society. It is conceived in terms of a volume measurable, in principle, on a cardinal scale. Garnier had claimed (boldly) that 'these figures are arbitrary; but they can be easily replaced by actual data' (Theocharis 1983: 82–3). This is not a metaphor that brings to mind the uncertainty and subjectivity of Say's discussion of demand and supply in the methodological introduction, in which real people with unique (and possibly incorrect) expectations engage in trades in a real marketplace; it is a metaphor that, by contrast, conjures images of measurement and precision and equilibrium.

If these extracts are representative of Say's conception of market price determination, one would expect that his equilibrium focus would drive the process of equilibration from centre stage. There is, in fact, very little 'friction' in an economy without government intervention:

A law, that simply fixes the price of commodities at the rate they would naturally obtain, is merely nugatory, or serves only to alarm producers and consumers, and consequently to derange the natural proportions between the production and the demand; which proportion, if left to itself, is invariably established in the manner most favourable to both.

(Say 1880: 291; 1803, III: 100)

In fact, the market works so well that anticipated demand and supply drive market prices, and there is no indication that expectations do anything other than clear markets more rapidly:

> The prospect of an abundant vintage will lower the price of all the wine on hand, even before a single pipe of the expected vintage has been brought to market; for the supply is brisker, and the sale duller, in consequence of the anticipation. The dealers are anxious to dispose of their stock in hand, in fear of the competition of the new vintage; while the consumers, on the other hand, retard their fresh purchases, in the expectation of gaining in price by the delay. A large arrival and immediate sale of foreign articles all at once, lowers their price, by the relative excess of supply above demand. On the contrary, the expectation of a bad vintage, or the loss of many cargoes on the voyage, will raise prices above the cost of production.
>
> (Say 1880: 290)[14]

The role of the professional trader, the well-calculating and well-connected entrepreneur, is manifest.

The analysis of the *Cours Complet* is similarly frictionless; Say, for example, extends the analysis of market price to explain how supply accommodates itself to demand in cases of constant and increasing cost industries (Say 1843: 170–1). As in all the previous examples, there is no indication that this process takes any significant period of time, or that there is any risk of protracted disequilibrium. Indeed, Say downplays the importance of the adjustment process and assures us that equilibration will occur rapidly after any disturbance:

> Accidental causes, the fear of a poor harvest, the hope of a good one, fashion, often influence for some time the quantities of some commodity that one is prepared to demand or supply; and, as a consequence, the price which represents the mutual influence of these two quantities. But the costs of production on one side, and the usual needs on the other, tend always to draw the price to a level we might call 'natural', and at which producers are induced to produce and consumers to consume.
>
> (Say 1843: 172)

That is, even in the *Cours Complet*, the process of equilibration is frictionless; there is no disequilibrium in this description.

To summarise, then, Say's world is one in which the market, if left to itself, clears quickly and costlessly. Market price adjusts frictionlessly to ensure that quantity demanded is made equal to quantity supplied. The entire process is conceived in terms of mechanical and structural analogies. There are no people in Say's stories.

Administered prices and social disorder

The market, when left to itself, operates as a well-lubricated machine. Contrast the language in which Say describes the operation of the economy under the weight of administered prices. In both the *Traité* and the *Cours Complet*, Say organises his story of market price determination in very much the same way as a twentieth-century *Principles* text. First, he discusses demand and quantity demanded, and he emphasises that the latter depends upon price. Then, he defines supply. Next, he tells us how demand and supply influence market price. And, finally, he illustrates how price adjustment clears markets, by considering the impact of price ceilings and price floors. He parts company with Samuelson only in the extent to which his language becomes more and more passionate as the story of ill-advised government intervention unfolds. Not only are there people in this story but there are evil people and starving people and cunning people and dishonest people, all engaging in trickery and false trading in an attempt to profit at the expense of others. Administered prices, Say claimed, prevent the market from clearing. He could not but be aware that they might have other effects, including starvation, riot and bloody revolution.

In the *Traité*, the corn market is selected for illustration. Notice the detail of the story, and the clear recognition of considerable social 'frictions':

> When the price of any object is legally fixed below the charges of its production, the production of it is discontinued, because nobody is willing to labour for a loss; those who before earned their livelihood by this branch of production, must die of hunger, if they find no other employment...Even the produce already existing is not so properly consumed as it should be. For, in the first place, the proprietor withholds it as much as possible from the market. In the next, it passes into the hands, not of those who want it most, but of those who have the most avidity, cunning, and dishonesty; and often with the most flagrant disregard of natural equity and humanity. A scarcity of corn occurs; the price rises in consequence; yet still it is possible, that the labourer, by redoubling his exertions, or by an increase of wages, may earn wherewithal to buy it at the market price. In the meantime, the magistrate fixes corn at half its natural price: what is the consequence? Another consumer, who has already provided himself, and consequently would have bought no more corn had it remained at its natural price, gets the start of the labourer, and now, from mere superfluous precaution, and to take advantage of the forced cheapness, adds to his own store that portion, which should have gone to the labourer.
>
> (Say 1880: 291; 1803, III: 99–100; cf. 1803, 1: chapter 36).

Finally, we have evidence of real people trading in the marketplace, and it is clear that Say does not regard this activity as equilibrating. It occurs only when there is an artificial impediment to the establishment of equilibrium, and the most heinous impediment Say can imagine is the establishment of the *maximum*.

Say's real preoccupation in the discussion appears even more clearly in the next paragraph, in which he compares the activity of the national government to that of a producer with a monopoly:

> Neither need we advert to the operation of the causes of a nature purely political, that may operate to raise the price of a product above the degree of its real utility. For these are of the same class with actual robbery and spoliation, which come under the department of criminal jurisprudence, although they may intrude themselves into the business of the distribution of wealth. The functions of national government, which is a class of industry, whose result or product is consumed by the governed as fast as it is produced, may be too dearly paid for, when they get into the hands of usurpation and tyranny, and the people be compelled to contribute a larger sum than is necessary for the maintenance of good government. This is a parallel case to that of a producer without competition.
>
> (Say 1880: 290–1; 1803, III: 99–100)

Perhaps aware of the mounting passion apparent in his discussion, Say ends the chapter by attempting to regain perspective, noting that 'it is impossible to avoid sometimes touching upon the confines of policy and morality, were it only for the purpose of marking out their points of contact' (1880: 292; 1803, III: 101).

The *Cours Complet* tells the same story in terms of 'an abusive authority'; precisely the same vehement language occurs in this volume and the *Traité*, in which Say recognises that a shortage of grain ensures that 'the merchandise passes, not where there is most need, but where there is most avidity, cunning and dishonesty; often cruelly wounding the most common rights of natural justice and humanity':

> There are frequent examples [of fixed prices] in the market for bread, especially in large cities. Parisian bakers, when wheat was dear, were forced to sell for 14 sous bread that cost them 16 sous to make, and for 16 sous that which cost 18. They submitted to this onerous situation, either because they were forced to by the government, or because their licence, gained by privilege, was still worth more than this enforced loss. At other times, they were authorised to charge 12 sous for bread that cost them 10 sous. It is as if the government had authorised the bakers to charge consumers a tax of 2 sous per loaf. This would never have occurred, except through the agency of a law, and the law is evil, because it disturbs the interests of buyers and sellers which would be harmonised by the market. Under such circumstances, the unjust profits of the baker would quickly multiply their numbers, had not another abuse ensured that the number of bakers was

fixed because bakers required a licence from the police to exercise a profession which, by rights, should be open to all.

(Say 1843: 171)

Government intervention in the market leads to disequilibria, to higgling, and to social disorder. Unlike the smoothly functioning market mechanism that, when left to itself, ensures that all markets virtually always clear, and usually clear at a price just equal to cost of production, intervention (especially in the form of the dreaded *maximum*) ensured prolonged periods of social and economic chaos.

The chaos, caused by real people acting in real markets, is evidence of a disordered social body, in the same way that human behaviour becomes chaotic and disorganised when the 'will' is driven by the 'lower passions' rather than the 'light of reason'. Such cases 'are those where private interests are directly opposed to the interests of society', and that which 'wounds or favours a limb of the social body can never be a matter of indifference to society' (Say 1843: 4). That is, disorder in the social body occurs when the coordination of the various functional systems breaks down. But, unlike the breakdown of the physical body, in which disease requires the intervention of a healer, the disorder in the social body associated with economic affairs is more often *caused* by the intervention of administrators.

The appropriate role for an administrator

Say's defence of unregulated markets, and his unvarying claim that intervention in markets has at best no effect and at worst causes significant social disorder, may seem on the surface quite at odds with our earlier claim that Say allowed considerable scope for the intervention of authorities to ameliorate physical, and even social, disorder. If doctors can assist human bodies to regain health, and psychologists can help the mentally ill to return to society, then why should we not expect legislators and administrators to be able to assist the operation of markets? Is it not inconsistent to attribute the disorder of managed markets to intervention, while allowing administrators so much scope in other areas?

In fact, this apparent inconsistency is characteristic of Say's economics. Perfect liberty in the marketplace will, Say claims, lead to material wellbeing and social order. And yet, if individuals pursue a too narrowly defined self-interest, they may benefit at the expense of society. Say argues that the appropriate response is to educate these individuals about their true interests, which include an appreciation of the underlying harmony of interests (Say 1843: 10), because such a narrow calculation of self-interest can never satisfy any truly public-spirited individual nor 'any man endowed with some elevation in his soul' (Say 1843: 9).

This is, of course, just another manifestation of the intellectual puzzle Say faced when he attempted to graft Adam Smith's invisible hand onto an eighteenth-century republicanism that admitted considerable intervention in social affairs. The intervention he admits takes the form of education, and the education involves teaching people that their true interests are not nearly so opposed as, in their ignorance, they imagine.

For example, Say is clear that 'it follows, in general, from the study of political economy that it is appropriate, in most cases, to leave people to themselves because that is how they best develop their resources, but it does not follow that they may not benefit greatly from a knowledge of the laws that govern this development' (Say 1843: 16). It is not enough to teach people about the knowledge required in the exercise of their own profession because much industry is mere routine (Say 1843: 16). For instruction to be complete, individuals must learn about the elements of which society is composed and how they act in combination because 'the state of society develops interests which blend and other interests which cross, just as in chemistry, some substances combine and others neutralise one another' (Say 1843: 16). Political economy, by teaching people their true interests, is not only consistent with their narrow personal interest by helping them recognise the laws that govern the accumulation of wealth but also informs individuals of the benefits of social cooperation:

> One might represent a people ignorant of the truths proven by political economy by the image of a population obliged to live in a great cavern which encloses everything necessary to the maintenance of life. Only darkness prevents its discovery. Each one, excited by need, searches for that which he requires, passes by the object that he desires the most, or perhaps crushes it underfoot without noticing. [...] all is confusion, violence, devastation..., then all of a sudden a luminous ray penetrates the enclosure; one blushes at the harm one has caused; one notices that each can obtain that which he desires; one recognises that these goods multiply more quickly when everyone helps one another. A thousand motives to love one another, a thousand means of honourable pleasure, appear from all sides: a single ray of light has done all this. Such is the image of a people plunged in barbarism; such it becomes when it is enlightened.
>
> (Say 1843: 16)

Because individual interests, well understood, are fundamentally harmonious, instruction that aims to inculcate the truth of this idea can only be beneficial. The role of the administrator, then, is limited to instruction concerning the nature of things. This instruction can only assist the operation of 'cette machine compliquée', which is society.

Administered prices and disordered social bodies

The argument of this chapter is a simple one: Say was quite aware of how markets ought to work under perfect economic liberty, and his exposition of the demand–supply mechanism was so clear and so much superior to those of other early nineteenth-century writers that it was called up by John Stuart Mill in his *Principles* as the authoritative account. Say underplayed the role of the equilibration process in a competitive situation, implying that the economy moved instantaneously to a position of market-clearing equilibrium by means of market price adjustment and very quickly to an equilibrium at which demand just equalled supply at a price equal to cost of production. There was no higgling to speak of. By contrast, disequilibrium in the form of shortages, surpluses, parallel markets and (if allowed) wide fluctuations of price characterised an economy burdened by government intervention. Say emphasises these two distinct portraits of how markets operate by articulating the analysis in quite different language. The competitive situation is explained in terms of mechanical metaphors and demand diagrams and eliminates people, irrational behaviour and disequilibrium from the story. The economy with government intervention, by contrast, is characterised by persistent disequilibria, cunning and avaricious dealers, stupid bureaucrats, and the clear threat of social upheaval. Social disorder, I have argued, is a consequence of persistent disequilibrium at which price adjustments are not permitted to clear all markets.

Say was not simply observing and reporting on how markets worked in the real world because his story (which is overwhelmingly illustrated by reference to the grain market) is not consistent with what we know to be the case in the French grain trade. The grain market was heavily regulated in France and had been for some two centuries, excluding a very brief and unstable interlude in the 1760s. Kaplan (1984) recounts the history of the 'grain police' during the seventeenth and the eighteenth centuries. During most of that period, when prices were regulated, administered prices were, in fact, market-clearing prices. In Paris, for example, during the early eighteenth century, grain not sold by the third day could not be withdrawn, but was forcibly sold in one way or another by officials. Ironically, then, the administered price in this semiregulated market was probably not very different from Say's market-clearing price. When the market was freed during the 1760s, the grain market was anything but orderly. If he were observing 'the nature of things' in France, Say would not have developed an analysis that characterised free markets as orderly and administered markets as necessarily chaotic. The English experience, with which he was familiar, was no more likely than the French to model free markets behaving like well-regulated machines; disequilibrium trade, and the price fluctuations that accompany it, always exists in reality.

It seems clear enough that Say was doing something more than objectively observing how markets worked in the real world. Say's criticism of administered prices seems drawn almost entirely from the very recent French experiences of the hunger riots and the *maximum* under Robespierre – a period of out-of-control passions if ever there were one. Say portrayed the free market operating without the instability and irrationality that disequilibrium trade represented, whereas the regulated market necessarily exhibited irrationality and instability. Higgling, in this context, is not about discovering an equilibrium price; it is indicative of social disorder caused by the attempts of some individuals to gain at the expense of others, and a legacy of misguided intervention in the marketplace that creates opportunities for such differential gains.

12 Class analysis and the distribution of income

This chapter examines first Say's class analysis. Then, it considers the role of the entrepreneur who is given the task, among others, of coordinating the actions of the various factors of production. Next, Say's analysis of the factoral distribution of income is considered. We note that the returns to the various factors of production are determined as an application of Say's value theory; that is, the return to each factor is determined by supply and demand. The difficulty emerges when we attempt to discern what determines the demand for factors, and that is considered in some detail. Say's analysis of rent is particularly problematic, shifting in some ways over time as he engages in debate with Ricardo. The final section of this chapter examines instances of class conflict in Say's economic analysis.

Class interests, when they are properly understood, are generally harmonious in Say's economics because each class requires the cooperation of the others, and all will benefit from industrialisation. But there are examples of conflict in Say's writing, particularly between entrepreneurs and workers. This conflict, however, does not stem from the nature of capitalism itself as it does in the writing of Ricardo and Marx, but rather from the greed of entrepreneurs who are permitted to exercise what they believe to be their interests because institutions create an imbalance of power between workers and entrepreneurs. Say's solution is characteristic: the enlightened must fix the institutions that create an imbalance of power and allow entrepreneurs to exercise their untrammelled greed, which is not in their true interests, and educate the working class so that the standards embodied in the subsistence wage are elevated proportionately.

Say's conception of social classes

One of the differences between the economic writing of Adam Smith and that of Jean-Baptiste Say is the nature of the class analysis. Writing forty years before the publication of the *Wealth of Nations*, Cantillon had conceived of wages, profits and interest as the incomes of three distinct social classes, and had emphasised the role of the entrepreneur as an individual who earns his profit by buying at certain spot prices and selling at uncertain future prices

(Blaug 1986: 38). Smith similarly adopted a tripartite division of society, this time distinguishing between capitalists, workers and landlords, but eliminated an explicit consideration of the role of the entrepreneur as distinct from the capitalist.

Say criticised Smith's division, arguing that it consistently confused capitalists, or people who live exclusively off the interest generated by their property, and entrepreneurs who earn their return through their active organisation of enterprise (Hashimoto 1980: 71; cf. Forget 1993). In place of Smith's tripartite division, he recognised five functional classes in society. Capitalists sell the services of capital and receive the profits of stock, or interest. Landlords sell the services of land and receive the profits of land stock, or rent. And three groups of 'industrials', including scholars, entrepreneurs and workers (the last of which could be further subdivided into various skill levels), sell their labour and earn the profits of industry for their active role in production.[1] Capitalists might trade their profits of stock to entrepreneurs in exchange for interest income, and landowners might trade their profits of land stock to entrepreneurs for rent. Similarly, scholars and workers might trade their profits of industry to entrepreneurs in exchange for salaries. That is, everyone except the entrepreneur might receive a certain contractual income from the entrepreneur who hopes to earn an additional return by creating a product that sells for more than he was obliged to pay for the requisite services (see Say 1843: 55ff.).

Say's analysis is purely functional. He recognises that individuals may belong to several classes at the same time as their economic roles change:

> A man may belong to several classes. When a farmer experiments with grafting or pruning trees in order to obtain better fruit, he undertakes research which augments his knowledge, his science; he tries to apply this to human industry; and he undertakes his ideas himself. He is, truly, for this product in particular, scholar, entrepreneur and worker.
>
> (Say 1843: 47; cf. Say 1803: 33)

Social classes, then, are not rigidly defined social categories, but rather convenient analytical devices designed to allow him to talk about the returns to the various productive services.

This is highlighted by Say's recognition that individuals are free to move out of the classes into which they were born, and that their identification with a particular class would be determined by their various economic activities:

> The intelligent worker frequently elevates himself, and the scholar descends sometimes to take on the functions of the entrepreneur; they add to their ordinary occupations new applications. But, whether industrial operations are undertaken by the same person or whether they are shared between many individuals, one can distinguish between three types: the research

of the scholar; the applications of the entrepreneur; the execution of the worker.

(Say 1843: 46)

It is, however, important not to overestimate the degree of social mobility that Say expected to see in the real world. Workers are certainly free to become entrepreneurs, and some do so, but Say recognised that most workers will remain workers because they lack the intelligence and inventiveness – 'the personal qualities' (Say 1843: 48) – of entrepreneurs. In *Olbie*, those personal qualities depended on ambition, education and economic wellbeing rather than inherited characteristics and were at least to some extent under the influence of an intellectual élite, who undertook the important task of educating individuals and creating institutions.

It would be convenient if we could trace Say's class analysis to *idéologie*, but in fact *idéologie* provides no firm basis for any particular class analysis. Tracy recognised two classes, based on a common distinction between the 'industrious classes' and the 'idle classes' (Welch 1984: 86–7). Roederer is on record as having recognised four social classes: workers without education, who were dominated by sensation and deficient in their ability to reflect; 'the class of men of sense', made up of artisans and shopkeepers with a primary school education; 'the class of men of good sense', made up of larger property holders who were 'educated' if not necessarily 'enlightened'; and the class of wealthy 'enlightened spirits', graced with education, imagination, sensitivity and 'a certain decency' (Roederer 1853–9, 6: 378–9; cf. Kaiser 1980: 147). The four classes of Roederer combine educational attainment and economic function. Despite its recognition of the role of environment in creating individuals, sensationalist psychology focused ultimately on the individual rather than the social class. Therefore, because social classes are ultimately artefacts of the aggregation of individuals, it is conceivable that different theorists could construct quite distinct class analyses.

The entrepreneur

As in the case of value theory and the law of markets, Say was not the first economist to locate the entrepreneur in a central economic role (Hébert and Link 1982). Cantillon has a greater right to priority (Murphy 1987), and Turgot and the physiocrats similarly emphasised the significant organising role of the entrepreneur. But Say made great use of this character. The entrepreneur has traditionally been cast in four roles, with different analysts focusing on different aspects. Schumpeter came to emphasise the entrepreneur as an innovator who introduces new products and new processes of production (Hébert and Link 1982). Cantillon emphasised the role of the entrepreneur as a risk taker, buying at certain current prices and selling at uncertain future prices (Cantillon 1755; cf. Koolman 1971). Although Koolman (1971) and Steiner (1998a) correctly attribute such a conception to Say, Say's entrepreneur is primarily charged with two different tasks: he is the coordinator who brings together productive services to create a product and the consumers of that product, and he is the individual actively engaged in the creation of new markets.

The entrepreneur appears throughout Say's work, virtually unchanged, and has been attributed to Say's particular knowledge derived from his time as a cotton manufacturer (see Lutfalla 1991: 23). But the entrepreneur was fully present in 1803, so Say's knowledge, if derived inductively, had to have come from more general sources. It is much more likely that Cantillon is his source, despite the differences in emphasis between the two traditions. Great praise for the active and essential strategic position of the entrepreneur, who mediates between consumers on the one side and labour in all its forms on the other, appears throughout Say's work:

> He is the intermediary between the capitalist and the rentier, between the scholar and the worker, between all productive classes, and between these and the consumer. He administers the work of production, he is the centre of many connections; he profits from what others know and what they do not know, and from all the accidental advantages of production. It is also among this class of producers, when events favour their skills, that are found almost all great fortunes.
>
> (Say 1803, III: 228)

Say recognises the rarity of the required talents of entrepreneurs, which include moral and intellectual skills required to obtain capital, organise production, undertake risk, determine markets by assessing the needs and whims of consumers, find new and better methods of production, and so on (Say 1803, III: 223–4). The inherent scarcity of entrepreneurship limits the quantity offered at any time, and ensures a higher compensation than might otherwise be expected for this genre of work.

Say's notion of the entrepreneur, like his value theory and theory of distribution, appears early and, in fact, is intimately connected to both of these. It is not clear whether it was a fundamental appreciation of the productive role of the entrepreneur that led Say to emphasise the role of 'immaterial' services in production or whether the causation flowed from the value theory to the role of the entrepreneur. It is clear that a recognition of the active role of the entrepreneur led Say to distinguish carefully between profits of capital and the remuneration earned by the entrepreneur, even if he was wont to call the latter profit as well.

One of the more interesting aspects of entrepreneurship is that it is the entrepreneur who takes the active role in creating markets, and who undertakes the risk involved in hazardous speculation.[2] As we shall see in the next chapter, this particular aspect of entrepreneurship accounts not only for the fact that, when the entrepreneur has calculated well or been visited by unexpected good luck, great fortunes are to be made among this class. It is also a crucial link in Say's law of markets, which differentiates his own understanding of the mechanism from that of the classical economists.

The prices of productive services at the industry level

Say's theory of distribution stems from his theory of value, and it too appears in the first edition of the *Traité*. As in the case of his value theory, Say makes a number of prescient and intriguing statements.

How are factors of production paid? The returns to the productive services of each factor are determined by demand and supply, as are the prices of all goods and services (Say 1803, III: 180–1). But, the difficulty arises when one attempts to determine what constitutes the demand for any one of the productive services. Say carefully distinguishes between the demand and supply for a productive service from a particular industry and the demand and supply for that service in the aggregate:

> A multitude of motives can influence the quantity of each of these services offered relative to each particular employment, such that one finds for one employment much more industry or capital offered than for some other, and similarly one finds much more demand for one service from some industry than from another. We must consider the influence of these motives in subsequent chapters. This one is dedicated only to determining the causes of the total [i.e. economy-wide] offer and total demand of each of these services.
>
> (Say 1803, III: 174–5)

At the industry level, Say attempts to derive the value of factors of production from the values of products, of which we have already seen some evidence.

Say claims that as commodities are produced they typically go through a number of hands before they reach the final consumer. A producer such as a seamstress purchases her raw materials and the food required for her subsistence from savings. As she sells her product to the shirt manufacturer, she receives her share as an advance from the sale of the final product. Similarly, the shirt manufacturer receives his portion, which covers his expenses plus his own return, from the merchant to whom he sells his product as an advance from the final sale. The consumer who purchases a shirt from the merchant pays all of the costs of the advances, plus the return to the final seller. Hence, all factors receive their returns from the sale of the final product (Say 1803, III: 168–9). This seems obvious enough so far.

Moreover, the price of the final product is determined, as we saw in the last chapter, by the demand and supply for that product. Therefore, the price of the final product cannot be determined by merely adding up the costs of production, but rather the total payment to all of the factors is limited by the price of the final product. And the payment to each of the factors in this particular employment is determined by the unique market for each factor: that is, the return to capital in this industry depends upon the demand from this industry and the quantity of capital offered to this particular industry. And because Say tends to emphasise factor immobility rather than costless mobility,[3] microeconomic considerations do matter, at least in the short run.

The prices of productive services in the aggregate

Say wants, however, to determine the returns to productive services in the aggregate. These, too, depend on the extent of demand and the quantity offered in the market for each productive service. Because of the way Say chooses to present the analysis, however, there is a certain lack of clarity, especially in the earliest editions of the *Traité*. Generally, he argues that the prices of productive services are determined by the prices of the final commodities, but occasionally claims that the prices of final commodities can be determined by adding up the costs of production in a Smithian fashion. By the time he gets to the fifth edition of the *Traité* (1826) and the *Cours Complet* (1828–9), he is consistently arguing that the prices of productive services depend upon the prices generated by the demand and supply for final commodities. The case of rent illustrates this transition, and it is the subject of the next section.

In his earliest work, Say begins by noting that the prices of productive services, as in the case of all other products, are determined by demand and supply. The extent of demand cannot be determined by aggregate demand for commodities because the law of markets ensures that 'a nation always has the means to buy all that it produces' (Say 1803, III: 180):

> The extent of demand for the means of production in general does not depend, as too many people have imagined, on the extent of consumption. Consumption is not a cause: it is an effect.
>
> (Say 1803, III: 175)

The demand for productive services, then, is not limited by the demand for final commodities.

Therefore, what determines the demand for the means of production in general? Say argues that:

> It depends on the extent of production, and since the extent of production depends on the availability of the means of production, the demand for the means of production extends in the same proportion as the means of production themselves.
>
> (Say 1803, III: 179–80)

That is, the law of markets itself implies that the only limitation on the demand for the means of production must be found in production itself rather than in consumption.

Say clarifies matters somewhat by recognising that the demand for each separate productive service is determined by the availability of the other services with which it must be combined in production. That is, the price of any one of the factors of production depends on the quantity in circulation in combination with the demand for that factor (not demand for final commodities). The demand for workers (both labour and entrepreneurship) depends on the amount of capital and land. The demand for capital depends on the quantity of labour and land available, and the demand for land depends on the availability of capital, labour and entrepreneurship (Say 1803, III: 180–1). As an economy grows, capital becomes more readily available, thereby pushing down its price. But the ready availability of capital increases the demand for productive services, which increases the return to entrepreneurship (Say 1803, III: 183). The distinction between the return to capital and that to entrepreneurship is clear from Say's earliest economic writing, and confusing the two was one of the chief criticisms he offered against Smith (Hashimoto 1980: 67–8).

The return to the most unskilled forms of labour can never be expected to increase much above the socially determined subsistence level because, as Say notes, giving birth is never as much a problem as keeping children alive until they are 15 years old (Say 1803, III: 236); and, when the wage is high enough to keep children alive, the supply of unskilled labour will rapidly increase (Say 1803, III: 229–30 and 239). But the subsistence wage is, for Say as it was for Smith, not a physical limit:

> This measure is quite variable...It does not appear obvious to me that workers in some cantons of France can live without drinking even a single glass of wine. In London, they cannot do without beer. That beverage is there such a fundamental necessity that the poor will ask for alms to go drink a pot of beer, as they ask for a morsel of bread here; and perhaps this last scene which appears so natural to us would seem impertinent to a foreigner who arrives for the first time from a country where the indigent class can live on potatoes, manioc or other foods even more vile.
>
> (Say 1803, III: 237–8)

Subsistence, then, is determined by the habits of the unskilled workers, and elevating these tastes and habits would push up the minimum required wage for these least skilled and most numerous workers (Say 1803, III: 238). And any reasonable person, Say claimed, could only desire that the households of the poorest be more commodious, airier, better heated and lit, the clothing more appropriate for the seasons, the food more nourishing and better prepared, and the children healthier (Say 1803, III: 239).

Economic growth furnishes an opportunity for the children of the least skilled to move into the classes immediately above, in which the returns are greater, at least in part because the practitioners are less numerous (Say 1803, III: 231–2). A country that enjoys the benefits of economic growth and industrialisation will see the common living standards of its poorest citizens elevated .

The return to the scholar, who is never well enough appreciated as Say is always at pains to note whenever the opportunity presents itself, similarly depends on the extent of the other means of production, which creates an opportunity for the productive employment of such labour (Say 1803, III: 217–20). Say is particularly concerned about the limitations of contemporary property law with respect to intellectual property, noting that literary workers might see their creations pirated and their incomes destroyed before their eyes with little recourse to the law (Say 1803, III: 157–9). Nothing, of course, requires that individuals cannot earn the returns of several different occupations simultaneously, be it as scholar, entrepreneur, labourer, capitalist and even rentier if one owns a factory (Say 1803, III: 220).

The active channelling of land, labour and capital in productive enterprise, the primary function of the entrepreneur, is rewarded by the profit of industry. The actual income of the entrepreneur is determined by the difference between what he can earn by selling the output and what he has to pay for productive services. Because his return is determined as a residual after all contractual obligations have been met, his actual income may be less than the value of his labour used to bring the product or service to market if he has guessed incorrectly, or it may well exceed the value of his labour if he has been particularly clever or lucky. If the entrepreneur is forced to rent land and to borrow money, his own income will be reduced (Say 1803, III: 293). In the *Cours Complet*, Say is even more specific about the determination of the rewards to the entrepreneur. Their return, he claims, tends to be very high because the supply of entrepreneurial expertise is always tight in an industrialising nation and, in particular, will always be limited because of the difficulty of uniting in a single individual the three essential features of entrepreneurial ability: the moral and intellectual capacity required to undertake the arduous and difficult tasks of making markets; the necessity of being able to supply personally at least some of the capital required for any significant project; and the willingness to undertake projects from which the return is necessarily uncertain (Say 1843: 329). These three characteristics are responsible for the inherent limitation on the supply of entrepreneurs.[4]

The rate of interest on borrowed money is determined as a 'convention' between lenders and borrowers, and it emerges in much the same way as any other convention (Say 1803, III: 278): it is influenced by demand and supply and by the risk of the transaction, also by the general state of legislation including usury laws, and by custom. Say shared Smith's notion that interest rates, that is the 'simple' interest on invested capital, would ultimately decline because of the 'competition of capitals', arguing consistently that as growth occurred the supply of capital would increase more quickly than productive opportunities for investment thus driving down the rate of interest (Say 1803, II: 183, 189).

This presentation in terms of demand and supply, which nevertheless sees returns to factors determined by the value of the final product, seems quite consistent until we recognise that there are many instances, particularly in the earliest editions of the *Traité*, in which the prices of final commodities seem to be determined by adding up the costs of production. For example:

> The lower the ordinary rate of the wage, the lower will be the price of the commodities which embody it. If the worker wants to better his lot and

elevate his salary, the product to which he contributes must become more expensive, or the shares [parts] of the other producers must decline.

(Say 1803, III: 238)

This passage is only one example of a certain lack of clarity in the presentation and, perhaps, the thought. If this were a single instance, we could ignore it as a simple error, but Say's treatment of rent suggests that he recognised a confusion in the presentation of his earliest writing on distribution, which he claimed to have eliminated in the fifth edition of the *Traité* (1826) and the *Cours Complet* (1828–9).

The example of rent

Rent is the most problematic of productive services for Say. He recognises that land rents are very much dependent on the general state of legislation in a nation (Say 1803, III: 317). He acknowledges that it is important to distinguish between the profits of the entrepreneurial farmer and pure land rents (Say 1803, III: 304). But rental property is productive, as are the other factors of production, and its rent depends on such factors as fertility and location (Say 1803, III: 305ff.).

Superficially, little changes in Say's treatment of rent between editions of his work. Pure land rents are determined, in the same way as the returns to all productive services, by the extent of demand and the quantity offered, and demand and supply are influenced by such things as the legislative framework of the nation and the system of customs that may give authority or social influence to the landed classes. But over time, Say's position does change dramatically in such a way that, by the fifth edition of the *Traité*, he explicitly rejects any suggestion that land rents help to determine prices of final commodities in a Smithian sense, while adamantly maintaining his independence from the Ricardian suggestion that land rent depends upon the extension of cultivation to marginal lands.

On his own telling, Say did not explicitly reject the idea that higher rents lead to higher prices of agricultural output until the fifth edition of the *Traité*, according to a letter from J.-B. Say to Mme Grote dated 11 May 1827:

I have, in effect, said in my previous editions that rent raises the price of wheat; but I corrected myself, and I do not say this in this fifth edition. I say only that it is not poor land that ensures that good land furnishes a rent, but that it is the needs and the faculties of society that raises the price of grain to a level such that it allows, in addition to the costs of production, the payment of rent to the proprietor. But, Ricardo says the same thing...

(Say 1848: 571)

The analysis is clear in the *Cours Complet*, in which Say notes that Smith, contrary to Ricardo's claim, also recognised that rent is a consequence of the price of wheat:

> Adam Smith said a long time before Ricardo, that *rent is the effect and not the cause of the value of wheat*. (Book I, chapter 2.) It is true that he said at the same time that this is not the case for the profits of work and of capital, which are a cause of price and not the effect. I believe that, in this last case, Smith is himself wrong; it is, just as in the case of wheat, the needs of society which determine the price of products whatever they are, and that permit an entrepreneur to pay the profits of work and of capital, and sometimes even a profit for monopoly, when monopoly is necessary for the creation of the product, as is the case for the products of the earth.
>
> (Say 1843: 363)

Say, then, explicitly recognised by the final edition of the *Traité* published during his lifetime and the *Cours Complet*, that rent depends upon the value of the commodity produced, and he acknowledged that his previous presentation was, at best, misleading.

Say, however, should have rejected the idea that high rents can raise the price of wheat on the basis of his own analysis as it appeared in the first edition of the *Traité*, in which he notes clearly that rent emerges as a consequence of the value of the final product, which depends on the demand for that product. When writing of the influence of location on land rents, for example, he claims:

> When produce has a great value, despite being from a far-off corner of the earth, it can pay the costs of transport and a rent many thousands of leagues from the place where it is harvested. Such are the ores of Brazil and Peru, spices...and even sugar from the Antilles.
>
> (Say 1803, III: 309)

This is contrasted to the soils of poor location, which cannot generate a product that commands a high enough price to pay rent in addition to the costs of transport and the returns to capital and labour (Say 1803, III: 307–8).

Nevertheless, Say's clear recognition that demand for the services of land is a derived demand and that, therefore, land rent is a consequence of the price of the final commodity is a very long way from Ricardian analysis.[5] In particular, Say does not ever reject the idea that demand and supply are the fundamental determinants of land rent.[6] He never develops anything like a Ricardian distributional scheme, in which increasing population forces the cultivation of marginal lands that yield no rents, driving down the rate of return on capital until a stationary state emerges when the return on capital disappears and all of the produce of society is used either to maintain the population at a subsistence level or to pay rent on intramarginal land. There is nothing like a corn model in Say's analysis.

In all of this, Say was remarkably prescient, but he did not push his perspective very far because, ultimately, he lacked any method by which the contributions of the various factors might be disentangled from the price of the final product.[7] There are, without any doubt, a number of very intriguing statements in which Say seems close to recognising the significance of the marginal concept. He refers consistently to 'the degree of utility'. More importantly, by the fourth edition Prinsep translates:

> The truth is, that, in whatever class of industry a person is engaged, he subsists upon the profit he derives from the additional value, or portion of value, no matter in what ration, which his agency attaches to the product he is at work upon.
>
> (Say 1880, I: 68–9)[8]

And land, he claimed as early as 1803, yields a return 'proportional to its contribution to production' (1803, III: 307). But these remain teasing statements not integrated into the analysis.

One rather interesting aspect of Say's distribution theory lies in his very odd usage of the word 'profits'. Because, he claimed, the revenue of all the industrial workers – scholars, entrepreneurs and labourers – is of the same origin and comes from the same source, it is useful to use the same term, profits of industry, to refer to their portions. Similarly, landowners earn the profits of land stock, and capitalists earn the profits of stock. This usage is particularly noticeable in the case of the chapter entitled 'The profits of the slave' (1803, III: 247–9).[9] But the general harmony of interests that Say made so much of in 1800 comes across very clearly when the same word is used to refer to the respective shares of national output going to productive classes, which might be seen by some to have very different and opposing interests.

Class conflict

It is usual to contrast Say's analysis of industrialism with Ricardo's, recognising that there is a fundamental harmony between social classes in the former but that class interests are inextricably opposed in the latter (Scott 1988: 113–38; Kaiser 1980). Steiner has challenged this reading, noting that 'it is quite incorrect to contrast [Say's] perception of modern society with Ricardo's on the grounds that one is blissfully pacific and the other is not' (Steiner 1998a: 224n54). Steiner's reading follows that of James, who argues that Say 'in identifying areas of conflict' arrived 'at a class analysis of society' (James 1977: 470).

It is Say's analysis of rent relative to Ricardo's that allows us to see the essential distinction between class conflict as it appears in Say and in Ricardo. In Ricardo's model, class conflict is an inevitable and unavoidable aspect of growth. According to Say, by contrast, conflict between landlords and entrepreneurs on the one side and between workers and entrepreneurs on the other stems from harmful institutions that allow particular actors motivated by greed to take advantage of others. The solution to Say's conflict is to correct the institutions, abolishing those that give power to some groups relative to others, and to educate individuals so that they recognise that industrialism benefits all classes and that they have a mutual need of one another. The solution to Ricardo's dilemma is much less easily conceived.

Say does indeed recognise that there is potential conflict between classes. As James long ago noted, 'the main perceived conflict was between land and *industrie*' (James 1977: 470). Similarly, Steiner recognises that in all editions of the *Traité* and, especially in the *Cours Complet*, Say acknowledges that the entrepreneurial farmer rents land from a landowner 'whose social power is solidly rooted' (Steiner 1998a: 212). The economic consequences of this are that landowners can exploit political and social power to ensure that any contractual arrangement is to their benefit (Steiner 1998a: 213). This, indeed, is among the factors Say considers when he acknowledges that rents depend not only on fertility, location and so forth but also on the general state of legislation in a nation, which fixes property rights and contractual obligations (Say 1803, III: 317).

A more significant conflict, however, emerges between the worker and the entrepreneur, and it is much more explicit in the *Cours Complet*, in the context of Say's remarks on Sismondi, than in the *Traité*. Workers can be exploited by entrepreneurs, according to Say, because entrepreneurs are in a position to exercise market power:

> We have seen how limited in general is the number of entrepreneurs who, in each branch of industry, offer to supply the needs of society; and we are about to see how the number of workers, by contrast, does not stop growing as long as the salary of each allows him and his family to live above the level of subsistence, according to the mores of the country. It follows from this that entrepreneurs always exercise a monopoly over their workers.
>
> (Say 1843: 343)

Market power, however, results from the nature of the market forces of demand and supply for the various factors. In addition to this factor, which stems from 'the nature of things', Say allows that the entrepreneur realises other advantages over his workers, which result from 'his fortune and his situation in society' (Say 1843: 343). In particular, combinations of masters may well conspire to reduce wages, but legislation prevents similar combinations among workers (Say 1843: 343).

According to Say, 'the amelioration of the lot of the workers and the method of allowing them a more or less equitable share of the riches to which they contribute, has been rightly labelled...the most important problem of practical political economy of our day' (Say 1843: 335n1). And, more to the point, 'good institutions may well lessen the suffering without totally eliminating it'

(Say 1843: 334). Perhaps most revealing is Say's agreement with Sismondi that, despite the damage that usually results from the intervention of authority in private contracts, the law ought to intervene on behalf of the individual who is in such a precarious and powerless situation that he is forced to accept onerous conditions of employment (Say 1843: 335). Say does, however, condemn Sismondi's 'coercive measures to limit the supply of workers', and to force proprietors to employ them even when work is lacking (Say 1843: 335).

This is a very different kind of class conflict than that which emerges in Ricardo's system. Once one has adopted a Ricardian rent theory, which necessarily drives the model towards a stationary state, the conflict between the three classes becomes an unavoidable aspect of growth. Rent necessarily grows and profit necessarily shrinks as the economy grows, and no amount of education or of social intervention can eliminate or significantly reduce the resulting conflict, short of destroying the entire system and replacing it with something else. In a Ricardian system, workers are necessarily ultimately driven to subsistence wages by the population mechanism.

In Say's system, by contrast, conflict emerges because institutions are such that entrepreneurs can exploit their market advantage to the detriment of workers. The solution, therefore, is to fix the institutions. That will not change the fact that workers wages will be driven down as long as the supply of unskilled workers increases unabated. But, as early as the first edition of the *Traité*, Say recognised that education designed to elevate the standards demanded by workers would raise the subsistence wage (Say 1803, III: 238).

The distinction, then, rests upon the inevitability of class conflict in the two systems. For Ricardo, it is unavoidable if often unacknowledged. For Say, by contrast, 'all poorly considered legislation and all vice intrude upon the social organisation' (Say 1843: 335). Therefore, good legislation and good education can go far to relieve the difficulties faced by the working class. Such measures will not eliminate the 'natural' differences in market power between workers and their masters (Say 1843: 334), but they will indeed reinforce the fundamental insight of Say's system, which is that all classes benefit from growth and industrialisation and that 'the master and the worker have, in truth, much need for one another because the one can make no profit without the assistance of the other' (Say 1843: 334). In fact, in the same context, Say is concerned to point out explicitly that:

> It is not civilisation which ought to be blamed for the misery of the working class. Even with the most detestable administration, their lot is not beneath that of savage peoples. Among civilised people, perhaps three in ten will suffer: there are nine such among the savages.
>
> (Say 1843: 335)

If anything, economic development ameliorates the position of the working classes for Say. The evils in the form of poverty that attend poor administration are not caused by development, as they are according to Ricardo, but are rather the result of inept or inadequate legislation. As such, they can be reduced, if not eliminated, and in this way Say retains the optimism that characterised Adam Smith's *Wealth of Nations*, rather than submitting to the pessimism of Ricardo's analysis.

Conclusion

Idéologie, founded as it is in individual psychology and physiology, furnishes no firm foundation upon which to base a class analysis of society. Say, however, does develop a factoral distribution of income based on social classes, which reflect economic activity. These classes are not immutable; in the real world, individuals move between classes as their economic activity changes. In theory, however, the classes reflect different contributions to production.

Say's income distribution is a straightforward application of his value theory. The returns to the productive factors depend on demand and supply. The difficulty, however, emerges when one attempts to discern those factors that determine demand. In general, Say claims that the demand for any one of the productive factors is determined by the supplies of the others, which are required as complements in production.

Rent, however, emerges as a pivotal aspect of Say's analysis. Say engaged in a lengthy debate with Ricardo, but never adopted the Ricardian analysis of rent and its accompanying distributional mechanism. There is nothing resembling a corn model in Say's analysis. He did, however, clear up some of the ambiguity that accompanied his earlier writing in the fifth edition of the *Traité* (1826), in which he stated unequivocally what his theory had always suggested: rent, like all returns to productive services, is not a cause of the price of the final commodity, but the consequence.

The different analyses of rent contained in the writing of Say and Ricardo contribute to very different considerations of class conflict. In a Ricardian system, conflict is an inevitable aspect of growth. By contrast, Say constructed his system to demonstrate, like Smith, that all classes would gain from growth and industrialisation. Over time, however, and very largely in response to the challenges offered by Sismondi, Say came to accept that class conflict, particularly that between masters and workers, was a profound social problem that required address. His solutions, which are not panaceas, are characteristically ideological: institutions that produce undesirable outcomes ought to be corrected insofar as such correction is compatible with social welfare, and people, especially workers, ought to be taught their true interests.

13 The ubiquitous law of markets

The law of markets is the most notorious instance in the history of economic thought in which an analytical device escaped so thoroughly from the intentions and uses of its creator and became a template upon which various people have projected all kinds of fantasies. This chapter demonstrates how different Say's own law was from the variations of what became the law of markets.

The law of markets, as it has matured and changed over the past two hundred years, has nothing to do with *idéologie*, and it has very little to do with Say's own preoccupations. Say used the law in the context of the active creation of new markets, very often overseas markets, by entrepreneurs. His law demonstrates that the system will eventually equilibrate in such a way that everything that is produced will find a market *if* entrepreneurs know what they are doing, and they have the skills to do it adequately. That is, the law does not rule out the possibility of a misallocation of resources that causes the wrong goods to be produced. Entrepreneurs must know enough to produce and to market the specific goods for which a demand exists. Moreover, the law does not rule out the possibility of short run frictions; the law of markets, in Say's usage, is no more than a guarantee that productive capacity will not permanently outrun purchasing power; there will be no long run glut. But there is nothing mechanical about Say's use of the law or the equilibration process itself; it depends on the active will of the entrepreneur.

The evolution of the law of markets in Say's economics

Establishing the priority of what has become known, after Keynes (1973 [1936]: 26), as Say's Law has not been a simple task, at least in part because of significant controversy concerning how exactly that law ought to be formulated. Schumpeter claimed:

> So it gets down to this. A man of the name of J. B. Say had discovered a theorem of considerable interest from a theoretical point of view that, though rooted in the tradition of Cantillon and Turgot, was novel in the sense that it had never been stated in so many words. He hardly understood his discovery himself and not only expressed it faultily but also misused it

for the things that really mattered to him. Another man of the name of Ricardo understood it because it tallied with considerations that had occurred to him in his analysis of international trade, but he also put it to illegitimate use. Most people misunderstood it, some of them liking, others disliking what it was they made of it. And a discussion that reflects little credit on all parties concerned dragged on to this day when people, armed with superior technique, still keep chewing the same old cud, each of them opposing his own misunderstanding of the 'law' to the misunderstanding of the other fellow, all of them contributing to make a bogey of it.

(Schumpeter 1954: 624–5)

Let us see how far we have come.

Spengler (1945) and Lambert (1952: 5–26) traced early versions of the law of markets in the writings of the physiocrats, and Thweatt (1979: 87–8) notes an early articulation in the writing of Francis Hutcheson. Lutfalla notes that physiocrats Tucker and Le Trosne recognise early versions of the Law (Lutfalla 1991: 18–19). *The Wealth of Nations* has been cited as a source by Sowell (1972: 15–17), Spengler (1945: 182–4) and Baumol (1977: 157–9) who find some, but not all, of the law there, whereas Mirowski (1989: 169) claims to find in *The Wealth of Nations* 'the first statement of that law, which John Maynard Keynes later erroneously attributed to Jean-Baptiste Say'. Others, such as J. Hollander and T. E. Gregory (1928: lxxx), Chipman (1965) and Stigler (1965), argue that James Mill published something closer to the version of Say's Law now commonly accepted in his 1807 *Commerce Defended*, thereby anticipating Say's 1814 mature articulation of the idea in the second edition of his *Traité*, but Spengler (1945: 342–3) and Sowell (1972) argue that this claim rests on a too great focus on the chapter 'Des débouchés' and a downplaying of other relevant passages in the 1803 edition of Say's *Traité*. Winch (1966: 34) notes that Mill had already read Say's *Traité* (1803) when he wrote *Commerce Defended* (1807), and, in fact, cites Say in that work. Baumol argued (1977) that a mature articulation of the law did not appear until the second edition of Say's *Traité* (1814), but Thweatt notes that both Chipman and Baumol later accepted, in private correspondence, the priority of James Mill in articulating the mature version by 1808 (Thweatt 1979: 94n).

It should, perhaps, be noted that neither Ricardo nor Malthus ever attributed the origin of the law of markets to J.-B. Say. All of their correspondence refers to 'Mr. Mill's theory', 'proposition', 'idea' or 'error', and, shortly after meeting Say in 1814, Ricardo wrote to Malthus that Say did not appear 'to be ready in conversation on the subject on which he has very ably written' (see Thweatt 1979: 90). Complicated indeed, but the very difficulty of establishing priority is precisely what is relevant to our analysis.

Even without articulating the various versions of the law of markets [and Baumol, remember, finds 'at least eight' (1977: 145)],[1] the one idea that comes across very clearly is that Say did not articulate *de novo* a fully formed theorem all at once in 1803. This was a concept that he drew from earlier, and probably multiple, sources, developed in the context of his own analysis, debated in correspondence with at least three of the leading British economists of the day, used in a variety of ways and for a variety of purposes, and changed his mind about so often that, in 1820, he could write that 'many savings are not invested [and therefore Ricardo and, more importantly, the law of markets is] completely refuted by our present circumstances, when capitals are quietly sleeping in the coffers of their proprietors' (Say 1820: 49n). In fact, Lambert argued (1952: 25) and Thweatt agreed (1979: 92) that Say effectively admitted defeat, by arguing that if a product was created and could not be sold on the market at a cost-covering price it would be 'an expense made thoughtlessly without producing anything'; that is, the law of markets would not be violated because such an event would not be production by definition (letter to Malthus dated July 1827, reprinted Say 1843: 649). Needless to say, Ricardo was 'by no means pleased' by this development (Ricardo *Works*, 8: 301). But the important point is that Say did not develop the law of markets in the same way that he came by his *idéologie*. This was not imbibed casually with the salon suppers during the revolutionary decade, but was developed painstakingly and at length and, perhaps, the implications never understood thoroughly until, if ever, quite late in his intellectual development.

The second issue to be clarified is the role played by the law in the 1803 edition of the *Traité*. Setting aside the question of when, precisely, the change occurred between 1803 and 1814 and whether it occurred in correspondence or in Mill's *Commerce Defended* or in the 1814 edition of Say's *Traité*, most commentators agree that there are significant differences between the versions of the law of markets that appear in the 1803 and 1814 editions of the *Traité*. Most writers also acknowledge that the 1803 chapter 'Des débouchés', which is only three pages long, does not contain all of the material relating to the law of markets in the 1803 edition, a point made by James Mill in his 1805 review (Thweatt 1979: 83). In the second and subsequent editions, much of the material was collected together into that very much enlarged chapter, but the discussion itself in 1814, it is claimed, is much superior. Ricardo, for example, noted that 'Mr. Say in the *new* [1814] edition of his book…supports, I think, very ably the doctrine that demand is regulated by production' (Ricardo *Works*, 6: 163–4, emphasis added).

Most of the secondary literature makes use of the distinction by Becker and Baumol (1952) between Say's Identity – the claim that no one wants to hold money for any significant period of time, and therefore every offer of goods necessarily constitutes a demand for other goods of the same market value rendering general overproduction of goods logically impossible – and Say's Equality, which is a weaker version of the Law and admits that brief periods of disequilibrium may exist in which total demand falls short of total supply but that equilibrating forces exist that quickly eliminate such gluts. Baumol, however, unlike Sowell (1972), notes that many of Say's propositions have nothing to do with these short run variants of the law and that it is not until the 1814 edition of the *Traité* that either the Identity or the Equality is fully specified (Baumol 1977: 146).

So, what exactly did Say write where and when? Baumol finds in the chapter 'Des débouchés' of the 1803 *Traité*:

> A community's purchasing *power* (effective demand) is limited by and is equal to its output, because production provides *the means* by which outputs can be purchased. Furthermore...expenditure increases when output rises.
>
> (Baumol 1977: 147)

Say's 1803 chapter entitled 'Is the wealth of a state increased by its consumption?' (Say 1803, II) yields:

> A given investment expenditure is a far more effective stimulant to the wealth of an economy than an equal amount of consumption.
>
> (Baumol 1977: 149)

This material was moved to the chapter 'Des débouchés' in the 1814 and the subsequent editions.

Baumol also recognises that a contention that appeared in the first edition (Say 1803, II: 180) was moved to the chapter 'Des débouchés' in the second and the subsequent editions, and gives rise to:

> Over the centuries the community will always find demands for increased outputs, even for increases that are enormous.
>
> (Baumol 1977: 153)

From the first edition onward, Say makes much of the claim that money has no real effect on output, but that it merely facilitates the exchange process. This is apparent both in the chapter 'Des débouchés' and throughout, and Baumol articulates it as:

> Production of goods rather than the supply of money is the primary determinant of demand. Money facilitates commerce but does not determine the amounts of goods that are exchanged.
>
> (Baumol 1977: 154)

Baumol emphasises that Say does not claim that no one wants to hold money for its own sake and that therefore all cash would immediately be respent, but rather that the unimportance of money is derived from the fact that production of goods is the stimulus of demand and that money merely lubricates the process.

Baumol finds only one proposition directly related to modern versions of Say's Law in the first edition of the *Traité*:

Any glut in the market for a good must involve relative underproduction of some other commodity, or commodities, and the mobility of capital out of the area with excess supply and into industries whose products are insufficient to meet demand will tend rapidly to eliminate the overproduction.

(Baumol 1977: 154)

As evidence for this proposition, Baumol refers to a passage that Spengler (1945) and Sowell (1972) make much of, and in which they find sufficient evidence for attributing priority in the development of Say's Law to Jean-Baptiste Say (1803, II: 175–80):

> *But*, it may be said, *if there are goods that cannot be sold, there are necessarily more productive factors employed than there are opportunities for the consumption of their outputs*. Not at all. No glut ever occurs except when too large a quantity of factors of production is devoted to one type of production and not enough to another. In effect, what is the cause for the inability to carry out a sale? It is the difficulty of obtaining some other good (either an output or money) in exchange for the one that is offered. Means of production are consequently lacking for the former to the extent that they are superabundant for the latter. A region deep in the interior of a land finds no sale for its wheat, but if some factory is established there and part of the capital and the labour that formerly was devoted to the land is redirected to another type of production, the products of the one and the other can be exchanged without difficulty, even though these outputs have expanded rather than diminished. ...I realise that trade can be obstructed by the overabundance of particular products. It is an evil that can never be anything but temporary, for participation in the production of goods whose outputs exceed the need for them and whose value is debased will rapidly cease and it will instead be devoted to the production of the goods that are sought after. But I cannot conceive that the products of the labour of an entire nation can ever be overabundant since one good provides the means to purchase the other.
>
> (Say 1803, II: 177–9, Baumol's translation)

The full citation does indeed capture all of the propositions with which Baumol credits Say.

All that Baumol finds missing from the 1803 *Traité* is any rationale for the law, and he argues that Say, in the end, claims no more than was embodied in the first proposition: production of goods creates the means to purchase other goods or, in Baumol's words, 'the community *can afford* to purchase the goods *if it wishes to do so*' (Baumol 1977: 157). In the 1814 edition, Baumol finds the missing link, and argues that Say's eighth proposition is, indeed, Say's Law itself:

> Supply and demand are always equated by a rapid and powerful equilibration mechanism.
>
> (Baumol 1977: 159)

As evidence, he translates a passage from the 1814 edition that appears in somewhat modified form in subsequent editions:

> It is worthwhile to remark, that a product is no sooner *created* than it *from that instant* offers a market for other products to the full extent of its own value. For every product is created only to be consumed, whether productively or unproductively, and indeed to be consumed as quickly as possible, since every value whose realisation is delayed causes a loss to the individual who is currently its possessor of the interest earning corresponding to that delay...A product is therefore, so far as everyone can arrange, destined to the most rapid consumption. From the moment it exists, it consequently seeks another product with which it can be exchanged. Gold and silver are no exception since no sooner has the merchant made a sale than he seeks to employ the product of his sale [Say, 1814: 147–8, his emphasis. A somewhat modified version of this passage is found in later editions. See the 1821 English translation of the fourth edition, pp. 134–5. The translation here follows that one so far as possible.]
>
> (Baumol 1977: 158)[2]

It might seem that this adds little to the extract immediately above; the only apparent difference is that the speed of an adjustment process already recognised is well articulated. But, in fact, another difference does exist as Baumol recognises. In 1803, the *ability* to purchase all of the products of industry is stressed. In 1814, Say claims that there also exists the *will* to do so.

In any case, in both 1803 and 1814, Say expressed some version of what Becker and Baumol were later to call Say's Equality, never once using Keynes's famous phrase 'supply creates its own demand'. In terms of establishing priority for the law of markets, it seems to me that the secondary literature has demonstrated amply the point Schumpeter recognised in 1954.

The law of markets and secular gluts

The law of markets was primarily used by Say to demonstrate the impossibility of a system-wide secular glut, and was wielded in opposition to a popular view that industrial progress itself would increase output beyond the capacity of the economy to purchase or even to consume the commodities produced. The alternative position, that a secular glut was possible or even inevitable, has appeared in many forms. During Say's lifetime, the two most credible proponents were Malthus and Sismondi, both of whom Say engaged in debate.

Malthus, for example, argued that 'it was a most important error to take for granted that mankind will produce and consume all they have the power to produce and consume, and will never prefer indolence to the rewards of industry' (Malthus 1986 [1836]: 321):

> It has also been said, that there is never an indisposition to consume, that the indisposition is to produce. Yet, what is the disposition of those master manufacturers, and merchants who produce very largely and consume sparingly? Is their will to purchase commodities for their consumption proportioned to their power? Does not the use which they make of their capital clearly show that their will is to produce, not to consume? And in fact, if there were not in every country some who were indisposed to consume to the value of what they produced, how could the national capital ever be increased?
>
> (Malthus 1986 [1836]: 322)

Sismondi made a similar argument in many forms, the most important of which was his examination of the relationship between consumption and production published in 1824, which occasioned Say's 1824 response. The most felicitous of Sismondi's contributions, however, comes from a work published in *Études sur l'Économie Politique* (Sismondi 1837). He uses the fable of the sorcerer's apprentice, named Gandalin in French tradition, who becomes the industrialist who can no longer control the growth in output for which he is responsible. Gandalin one day watches the sorcerer who has boarded at his home, and hears the words the sorcerer uses each morning to charm a broomstick and turn it into a 'man-machine' to fetch water. Gandalin, however, does not hear the words to reverse the spell, and is in danger of drowning in all the water the man-machine brings for his use. Desperate, he grabs an axe and tries to chop down the broomstick only to find each piece regenerating and turning into yet another water-carrying man-machine until he is rescued by the sorcerer, who recognises that too much of a good thing is dangerous. Sismondi tells us the moral of the story:

> Water...is a good thing. It is no less necessary to life than money and capital. But one can have too much of a good thing. Magic words spoken by philosophers almost sixty years ago have brought new honours to labour. Political conditions even more mighty than these magic words have transformed all men into industrialists. They pile up products on the markets far more quickly than the broomsticks transport water, without worrying if the container is full. Each new practical application of science strikes down the man-machine set in motion by the magic words, like the axe of the sorcerer's apprentice, only for him to rise up immediately two, four-, eight-, and sixteenfold, etc. Production continues to grow at an incalculable speed. Has the moment not yet come, or is it not imminent, when we will have to say: this is too much?
>
> (Sismondi 1837: 60ff.)

The worry is very clearly about a secular glut, caused by the process of industrial expansion itself. And, as we have seen, it is this worry about the potential unsustainability that motivates Say's use of the law of markets.

Say always allowed the possibility of the overproduction of particular goods, if entrepreneurs guess incorrectly and produce goods for which there is an insufficient market instead of the goods for which an adequate demand exists (Say 1803, II: 177–9). Moreover, from the first edition of the *Traité*, he recognised the possibility that uncertain political times may cause entrepreneurs and capitalists to hoard money rather than to invest it, either because the uncertainty surrounding production was too great or because producers anticipate price increases as a result of political disturbances:

> The greatest encouragement for circulation is the desire everyone has, especially producers, to lose as little interest as possible on the funds engaged in the exercise of their industry. Circulation slows more due to the obstructions it faces than due to an absence of encouragements it might have received. Wars, embargos, onerous fees to discharge, the danger or difficulty of communication obstruct it. It is also slow in periods of fear and uncertainty, when public order is threatened and all types of enterprise hazardous. It is slow when one expects arbitrary taxation, and is forced to hide one's resources. It is slow in periods of speculation when sudden variations caused by wagering on commodities causes some people to hope for a sudden windfall caused by a simple variation in prices. Consequently, merchandise awaits a rise in price and money a fall; and both reflect idle capital, useless to production.
>
> (Say 1803, II: 136–7)

In the second edition, he illustrated the possibility of general overproduction by referring to the French recession in 1813, which he attributed to poor decision making on the part of the administration (Say 1814, II: 159n).

It is important in this case to revisit what Baumol and Sowell saw as an important innovation in the second edition of the *Traité*. The addition of the words 'dès cet instant' in the second edition was seen to imply the existence of a rapid equilibration mechanism[3] that virtually eliminated the possibility of even cyclical recessions and depressions. But the extract above suggests that poor administration was still seen as a potential impediment to equilibration. In fact, Say even contemplated the possibility that such events may persist for some time, causing unhappiness, stagnation and even depopulation (Say 1814, II: 159n). And, in his correspondence with Malthus, he continued to acknowledge the possibility of both gluts of particular commodities, occasioned by poor planning on the part of entrepreneurs, and of general gluts caused by poor administration.[4]

Samuel Hollander has suggested that Say's often cited July 1827 letter to Malthus ought to be read not as mere verbal sleight of hand, or as an implicit rejection of the applicability of the law of markets to cyclical adjustments (cf. Lambert 1952: 20; Sowell 1972: 47f), but rather as a recognition that there might indeed be secular limits to expansion (Hollander 1979: 94f). This is, in fact, the only reading that rescues Say from the charge of mere verbal jousting. According to Hollander, Say essentially argues that if there are secular limits to expansion imposed by, for example, an increasing taste for leisure rather than the products of industry, then 'commodities whose costs are therefore not covered will simply not be produced and the law of markets remains intact' (Hollander 1979: 95n). But, if this is indeed the argument Say is making, he is making it awkwardly because, although he claims that 'there is no complete production unless all the services necessary for the work are paid by the value of the product', he also says:

> I believe, therefore, that I am entitled to say that all that is truly produced will find a market; that all which is not sold was an expense made thoughtlessly without producing anything...
>
> (Say 1843: 649)

That is, it is perfectly possible that badly considered production will be undertaken and will result in output that cannot be sold at cost-covering prices. Now, it is unlikely that such output would continue to be produced indefinitely in the context of permanent limits to demand. So if, as Hollander suggests, we read this letter in a secular context, Say is probably entitled to claim that his law of markets is not violated because all output ultimately produced would find a market. But, if this is indeed his claim, it does seem that there is merit in Say's observation to Malthus that 'our discussion ...begins to be nothing but a dispute about words' (Say 1968: 649).

From his earliest writing on economics, then, Say was quite prepared to allow for misallocation of capital in the form of a glut of particular commodities accompanied by an underproduction of others. Moreover, he did recognise the possibility of general cyclical overproduction, and attributed this state of affairs to extraordinary circumstances brought about, usually, by inept public administrations that disrupt normal markets and trade channels and are reflected in unsustainable price expectations and speculation. In Say's usage, the law of markets was generally wielded to demonstrate that the growth of the economy is not ultimately constrained by the unsustainability of consumption demand. There is nothing inherent in the model that generates an inadequate purchasing power or limits to growth. If these features occur, and Say acknowledged that they did, they were undoubtedly the result of ill-advised intervention in the markets or general political instability; in the absence of such exogenous factors, the law of markets would ensure that growth is not limited and that the long-term wellbeing of the population is best served by continued industrial expansion.

The law of markets and the role of the entrepreneur

We have already noted that the law of markets was not adopted entire from previously existing sources in 1803, but developed gradually over a number of years in consultation with Ricardo, Mill and Malthus. Say's amalgamation of the law with his analysis of entrepreneurship allows us to distinguish his own use of the concept from that of the classical school. Moreover, his discussion of political upheaval as a, or perhaps the, significant reason why periods of disequilibrium may persist for some period of time reflects his characteristic concern with social and political stability.

Let us look more carefully at the process of self-adjustment that Say attributes to the economy. It turns out that Say sees a very active role in economic adjustment for the entrepreneur. Baumol recognises the significance of translating 'Des débouchés' as 'On Markets', and notes that Say refers not to a marketplace but rather to the active creation of markets or outlets for goods (Baumol 1977: 147). The individual responsible for the creation of markets is, of course, the entrepreneur with his complex of skills and attributes, including the ability to discern market opportunities. Among his many necessary qualities are 'good judgement' (Say 1843: 140–1) and a 'judicious boldness' (Say 1843: 141), a willingness to undertake necessary risk (Say 1843: 141) and to persevere (Say 1843: 141), to do the necessary research and calculate well (Say 1843: 141). All of these are necessary, of course, because the entrepreneur is, in essence, the brain of industry responsible for its direction and motivation (Say 1843: 52). This active process of market creation highlights both the entrepreneur's role as the coordinator of production, who brings together all of the various productive services required to manufacture a particular product the existence of which fulfils a desire on the part of consumers or potential consumers, and the entrepreneur's role as the calculator and bearer of risk. He cannot know with certainty that the product he brings to market will find consumers willing to purchase it at a price adequate to pay the owners of the productive services what he has contracted to pay them. The entrepreneur will profit from the difference between what he pays to bring a product to market and what he can sell it for. In those cases in which he has calculated incorrectly, this profit may well be negative. But in those cases in which he calculates well, there are fortunes to be made.

The entrepreneur is explicitly seen by Say as the active force driving the adjustment mechanism assumed by the law of markets: 'the interest of the entrepreneur guarantees that quantities created cannot permanently and continuously exceed what is required' ('Sur la balance des consommations avec les productions', Say 1848: 256–8). In his third letter to Malthus, Say attributes the existing glut, in part, to the ignorance of producers and sellers:

> This superabundance...is also due to the ignorance of producers and traders concerning the nature and extent of needs in those places where they send their merchandise. During these last years, there have been a great number of risky speculations, because there have been many new links between different nations. Everywhere there has been a lack of data required for good calculation; but because much business has been badly managed, does it follow that it is impossible, with better instruction, to

manage well? I venture to predict that as new relations become old, and reciprocal needs are better understood, gluts will disappear everywhere, and lasting mutually profitable relations will be established.

(Say 1843: 636)[5]

The adjustment mechanism, although it may occur quickly, does not occur independently of the will and the decisions of the entrepreneur.

Similarly, the partial overproduction of grain in an internal region of the country could be alleviated by the decision to build a factory, a decision taken by an individual endowed with special and by no means common powers to discern a potential market. If that individual does not appear and does not take the correct decision, the region will languish. Similarly, if entrepreneurs lack appropriate data, the economy will suffer disruption as bad decisions are taken. If a country lacks an industrial climate and does not foster the development of entrepreneurs, that nation will lag behind its neighbours in industrial development, and sometimes languish with economic opportunities not seized (Say 1843: 141). Suddenly, the law of markets seems a whole lot more contingent and a little less spontaneous.

If the actions of the entrepreneur are the gears that run the equilibration mechanism, the actions of politicians may well disrupt the smooth operation of that mechanism. As always, Say is very aware that political decisions taken may have economic consequences, and this is especially true in periods of political turmoil:

During the violence of political convulsions, there is always a sensible contraction of capital, a stagnation of industry, a disappearance of profit, and a general depression while the alarm continues: and, on the contrary, an instantaneous energy and activity highly favourable to public prosperity, upon the re-establishment of confidence.

(Say 1880: 118)

Again, even Say's most abstract contribution to economic analysis, the law of markets, bears witness through every edition of the *Traité*, through the *Cours Complet*, the correspondence and, indeed, all his writing to the fundamental concern of the *idéologues* with social stability.

Idéologie and the law of markets

Of all the aspects of the economic writing of Jean-Baptiste Say, the law of markets, as this concept developed through debate with Malthus, Mill and Ricardo, is the most independent of any social considerations and, consequently, the most independent of any influence from *idéologie*. Only the most innocuous traces appear: Say is characteristically concerned with social and political stability, and is aware of the role that instruction can play in bettering the decisions of entrepreneurs. But, neither of these two considerations dominates the uses to which the law of markets has been put by others, nor is *idéologie* an essential component of these concerns. Why, then, consider it in this study of the influence of *idéologie* on Say?

Long ago, Reynaud (1953: 1–62) attempted to distinguish between two different types of economic writing in the corpus of Say's work, which he called 'the realistic method' and 'the deductive method'; identifying the former with a concern for social factors and applied economics, and the latter with long strings of abstract reasoning. This is consistent with a much earlier discussion in Michaud's *Biographie Universelle* (1847, 81: 224ff.). Reynaud attributed Say's value theory, his analysis of the entrepreneur, immaterial products and industrialism to the realistic method, but claimed that topics such as the law of markets followed the deductive method and were no more than a polemic in favour of economic liberalism.

Say is adamant that the 'natural difficulty' of political economy 'not be augmented by useless abstraction' (Say 1843: 636), and what becomes very clear, as we follow the story of the law of markets through the classical school to Keynes and beyond, is how increasingly abstract the theory becomes. When the entrepreneur disappears from the story, the abstract becomes much more apparent.

That which distinguishes Say's own use of the law of markets from that of Ricardo and Malthus is his consistent attempt to make the speculation concrete by emphasising the role that the entrepreneur plays in the story of adjustment, and focusing on the practical difficulty of creating markets in an uncertain world. Indeed, it is Say's characteristically ideological focus on social and political stability as an overriding goal of social analysis that links institutional and analytical thought in Say's economics, and allows him to develop a mature and coherent analysis rather than a simple collection of unconnected pieces of economic journalism.

Of perhaps greater interest, though, is the manner in which the law of markets escaped from Say's world-view and became an analytical device to be used by others with very different preoccupations and living in very different economic environments. The law of markets is, in fact, an extreme case of the tendency of Say's economic writing to transcend its origins. Born out of the economic analysis bequeathed to him by the physiocrats and by Adam Smith, created in the context of *idéologie* and bearing evidence of very specific social and political concerns, Say's economics anticipates later concerns. In this case of the law of markets, as in other cases, Say created a language and an analytical apparatus to express and contain his own preoccupations, but that language was open to animation by quite different agendas. Thus, the law of markets could be used in the context of economic development and international trade, as Say used it, or it could be called upon to express a twentieth-century concern with short run fiscal stabilisation. Similarly, Say's value theory based on 'the degree of utility' and his distribution theory in which factor payments reflect 'the additional contribution of each productive service to the value of the output' were created in the context of social instability and of the ideological response to that instability, but they were created in a language that allowed the expression of the much later and very different concerns of marginal analysis.

14 *Idéologie* and the economics of J.-B. Say

Jean-Baptiste Say's early sympathy with *idéologie* marked his economics in subtle but distinct ways. In particular, Say's focus on education and instruction as helping to bring about social stability by teaching people their true interests was a hallmark of *idéologie*. And, even at its most abstract, Say's economic analysis never lost sight of the important role played by institutions that, in ideological fashion, he saw as designed and imposed by legislators and an intellectual élite rather than evolving spontaneously, as Hume would have it, through the actions of individuals, each independently pursuing self-interested ends and simultaneously helping to bring about an unintended social order. These institutions, in Say's economics, were first and foremost designed to nurture social and political order, and consequently to allow trade and industrial development to unfold and to contribute to the economic wellbeing of all the people.

These two features – education and the role of institutions – gave rise to a particular feature at the core of Say's economics that distinguishes his contributions from those of Adam Smith and from the classical school more generally. Say never quite accepted the all pervasive role of spontaneous order. Although he argued, as did the physiocrats, that economic liberalism was desirable, Say maintained, as did the physiocrats, the notion that *laissez faire* is only appropriate within the context of a well-defined institutional structure imposed from without. Moreover, individuals must be made aware of their own 'true' interests if the benefits of the market and of industrialism are to be realised. This aspect of Say's thought is most apparent in the roles afforded the public administration. Say argued that the administration must take an active role in both moral and intellectual education and in designing and imposing institutions consistent with the welfare of the people. Say's economic liberalism, that is, required the firm intervention of an enlightened élite, not in the markets themselves but in the society within which the markets unfold.

It is quite apparent that *idéologie* is not the only source of ideas such as those that characterise Say's economics. I have already acknowledged their similarity to physiocratic notions. But, in fact, *idéologie* was the dominant way in which ideas such as those of Mercier de la Rivière reached Say, as it was the route by which he came into contact with the ideas of Condillac, Condorcet,

Helvétius and others. These ideas coalesced into a particular form under the intellectual leadership of the sensationalist philosopher Destutt de Tracy and the physiologist Cabanis, a form most congenially represented by the metaphor of the social body.

The *idéologues*, like many other eighteenth-century intellectuals, imagined society as a body made up of individuals, in which the will of each separate person must be in accord with the social will if society is to flourish. Individual interests, if they are truly understood, cannot be at odds with the social will because no member of society can be indifferent to the health of the social body. In the minds of the *idéologues*, this metaphor took a particular form. Cabanis, the physiologist, argued that the human body, to remain healthy, required the intervention of physicians whose duty was to re-establish order among the separate functional systems of the physical body. Similarly, the ideological psychologist Pinel argued that the role of the psychologist was to be physician to the human soul by re-establishing order among the separate functions of the mind and, in particular, between the will and reason. And the philosopher Tracy and the economist Say conceived of the social scientist as physician to the social body. Where physicians restored order to physical bodies, and psychologists to mental states, social scientists were charged with restoring order to the body politic. This they did by means of a pervasive pedagogical programme designed to teach people their true interests, and by establishing institutions consistent with social order.

It is, I think, clear that Say's economic analysis is consistent with the preconceptions and priorities of *idéologie*. What is not at all clear is that *idéologie* is necessary to our understanding of Say's economics. In particular, we have surveyed Say's theory of value, his distribution theory and his law of markets. Although the ideological preoccupation with stabilising institutions and education is present in each case, it is certainly true that these aspects of Say's economic analysis stand alone in the sense that we can understand them quite adequately without the baggage of *idéologie*. And because it would be difficult to argue that *idéologie* is necessary to an understanding of the details of Say's economics, would not Occam's razor suggest that, as economists, we ignore the *idéologie* as, at best, unnecessary?

If I wanted to be facetious, I could argue that we can understand Say's economics quite adequately, not only without *idéologie* but without Say. And, in fact, two hundred years of the development of Say's law of markets has done precisely that. Sowell has no more need of Say than he does of *idéologie*, or any other branch of metaphysics. The history of economic thought has always stood in an odd relationship to its masters. We argue that what is essential to a working economist is the history of economic analysis – that toolbox of ideas and theorems and principles that are totally separable from individual writers and historical context. If all that matters is analysis, it is entirely irrelevant that Keynes misrepresented Say's law, or that most commentators are ignorant of the variations that the law took over the course of Say's many publications. And if we accept the notion that only economic analysis matters, then the kind of history of economic thought we ought to undertake is precisely that of Sowell. Authors, 'great masters', personalities, errors and quirks of individual contributors are irrelevant. And this kind of history is particularly pleasing because it is concrete and we can hope to have complete knowledge about that subset of questions for which evidence exists. Only the text matters and that, barring variant editions, is at least tangible.[1]

A second type of historical analysis focuses on individuals, but abstracts from everything that makes these individuals human beings. We begin with a mannequin, or a statue in Condillac's honour, and systematically strip away as unnecessary all but the economic analysis. Then, we clean up the analysis and paste it back on the statue. And we end up not with a study of Say's economic analysis nor with a study of the historical figure Jean-Baptiste Say. We have a 'man-machine' – a statue with a set of highly abstract economic ideas in a form that no human being of that time could ever have created. This man-machine, this statue, is undoubtedly more consistent than any real human being has ever been and undoubtedly more relevant to contemporary economic questions, but it is, nonetheless, an artificial creation and almost certainly a creature who would have been unrecognisable to his contemporaries. If our goal is modern relevance, we ought to focus on the ideas alone. If, by contrast, we are intrigued by how it is that ideas are created and how they change over time in response to multiple influences, then we have to undertake the far more difficult task of actually attempting to reconstruct those forces acting on a particular person at a particular time.

Here, the questions are quite different, as is the nature of the evidence and the certainty with which we can draw conclusions. This is a study of human creativity. How did political economy gel at a particular time and place? Which of the multiple and largely undefinable influences ought we to examine? What is persuasive evidence? And how can we know, with certainty, anything at all about a time and a place that requires us to set aside our unacknowledged cultural preconceptions and to try to understand the preoccupations of people living in circumstances we can never experience directly and can only document and reconstruct to the limits of the very incomplete evidence available to us? We must acknowledge that we always leave ourselves open to the charge of having ignored some influences and emphasised others out of all proportion to their actual impact. Such is life in the realm of the history of ideas, in which almost everything is overdetermined.

Part II

15 An introduction to the translations: the public morality contest of Year VIII

Olbie, the title of which can be traced to the Greek word 'olbios' meaning 'happiness',[1] derives from two distinct literary traditions: the prize essay contests of the *Institut National*, and philosophy aimed at the people and disguised as utopian fantasy. The role of the prize contests in instructing the people and in advancing academic careers is considered first. Then, I consider the role of popular philosophy and utopian fantasy in the years leading up to the Revolution.

The morality prize competition

In a fascinating study, Martin S. Staum (1996) has explored the roles played by the *Institut National* and, more specifically, the public policy roles played by the prize essay competitions sponsored by the *Institut*. Staum explores the ways in which this institution, established to promote Enlightenment social science culture, was gradually transformed very largely through the efforts of the various *idéologues* into an institution, the primary goals of which were to end political chaos and establish social order.[2]

On 15 Messidor Year 5, a prize competition was announced by the second class of the *Institut National* on the question: 'After political revolutions, what are the most appropriate means to restore a people to the principles of ethics?', subsequently revised to 'What are the best means to establish the morality of a people?', and revised on 15 Vendémiaire Year 6 to 'What are the best institutions on which to base the morality of a people?' This first competition ran until 15 Germinal Year 6, and attracted sixteen entrants. The judges did not award the prize, but they gave honourable mentions to Villaume, Silvestre and Louis-Germain Petitain.

The competition drew fire from critics within the *Institut*. Jacques-Henri Bernardin de Saint-Pierre was a member of the Ethics section of the class of Moral and Political Sciences, but was not one of the *idéologues* who were a force within the class. He criticised this first round of the contest on the grounds that it promoted a secular morality based on strict legislation and well-run police forces alongside the natural inclinations of self-love and sympathy (Bernardin de Saint-Pierre 1818). These he considered an inadequate foundation on which to base social order and harmony. As a deist, he advocated a morality explicitly based on Christianity. He identified self-love with greed and ambition, and argued that any system of ethics based on 'natural morality' would encourage repressive social control in the name of social order. Duty, and particularly the human duty to please God, rather than human inclination would provide a more certain foundation for civic virtue.

On 15 Vendémiaire Year 7, the question was revised again, at least partially in response to Bernardin de Saint-Pierre's criticism of the first round of the competition, to 'What are the most suitable institutions to give man in society habits capable of making him happy? Discuss the nature of habit.' A second round of the contest ran from 15 Vendémiaire Year 7 to 15 Vendémiaire Year 8 and attracted eight entrants. The prize was again not awarded, and three men received honourable mentions: Louis-Germain Petitain, Jean-Baptiste Say and Canolle.[3]

This particular competition, one of four topics set by the second section of the class of Moral and Political Sciences between its creation in 1795 and its suppression in 1803, casts light on the intellectual life of France in the period after the reign of Terror. It documents the demands placed upon the social sciences, including economic analysis, to help establish political and social order in the context of political uncertainty, and establishes public morality as an important area of application for *idéologie*. This competition allows the reconstruction of the broader intellectual context within which the specifically economic writing of three significant economists of the period – Jean-Baptiste Say, Pierre-Louis Roederer and Antoine-Louis-Claude Destutt de Tracy – developed. All three identified with the principles and preoccupations of *idéologie*, as these essays document, and all three contributed significantly to the development and institutionalisation of nineteenth-century economic analysis in France.

Prizes and the scholarly career

Say became a more important economist than Roederer and Tracy in the sense that his contributions to economic theory influenced European, American and English economic thought long after the period under consideration, whereas Tracy is best remembered for contributions to areas other than political economy and Roederer is generally remembered, if at all, as an editor and journalist. But when *Olbie* was published in 1800, both Tracy and Roederer were established scholars. Roederer was attached to the Political Economy section of the class of Moral and Political Sciences, and Tracy to the section concerned with the 'Analysis of sensations and ideas'. Say, by contrast, was a typical contestant – young, not yet established as a leading scholar, ambitious and eager for recognition. The prize itself was substantial: the prize medal in the form of a half kilogram of gold was the equivalent of the annual income of a minor official or schoolteacher (Staum 1996: 65). But monetary gain was of far less concern to most contestants than the opportunity for recognition.

The old Academies were suppressed during the Terror of 1793, and the *Institut National* was established in 1795 to play some of the same roles that these Academies had previously played in creating a forum for scholarly discussion and debate. The prize competitions were a well-established feature of French intellectual life before the Revolution, and the *Institut* adopted the practice for the same purposes: to guide public discourse and to encourage young scholars and rising members of the legal establishment. Many of the members of the class of Moral and Political Sciences began their careers by entering prize competitions run by the former Academies, and five out of seven prize winners of the competitions sponsored by the class later became associates, correspondents or members-at-large (Staum 1996: appendix 6). Entering a prize competition was a traditional first step in establishing a scholarly career. It was, of course, not the only point of entry to such a career. Particularly after the Revolution, political allegiance was an alternative test; Roederer, for example, was a patronage appointment sponsored by Sieyès because of his Bonaparte connections.

Staum demonstrates that the usual contestants in the competitions sponsored by the *Institut* were similar to those who had been recognised before the Revolution, although clergy and the former nobility constituted a much smaller proportion of total entrants, and small numbers of bankers, merchants (and even women) had begun to make themselves heard. Competitions were still dominated, however, by legal and medical professionals. These competitors were similar to the judges who awarded the prizes, and they had similar goals: to establish their credentials as intellectuals and, if possible, to help shape public opinion at the same time.

The topics for the prize competitions are almost embarrassingly earnest and seem naive to a more cynical age. But this tone was not lost on the wits of the period. Staum documents the satire:

> An anonymous author suggested in the summer of 1796 that the Second Class should ask, 'Who should be saved first by the father of a drowning family – his wife, mother, or ten-year-old child?'; the discussion would include the value of filial gratitude, parental responsibility, humanity, and service to the fatherland.
>
> (Staum 1996: 65)

But, these topics were designed to appeal to the public, as well as to the very young and very idealistic intellectual. The public was no longer limited to a well-educated intellectual élite, but included many more merchants and skilled craftsmen and literate workers than had previously paid attention to the entries to such contests (Staum 1996: 65). And youth was the hallmark of the entire period. The people with significant public roles in the political upheaval of the Revolution were very young, and the social sciences themselves wore the arrogance of callow youth. One need only compare the Say of *Olbie* with the Say who wrote *Cours d'Économie Politiaue*: the younger Say is much more certain of his pronouncements on human perfectibility than his older and more experienced incarnation.

Olbie and popular utopian fantasy

Olbie, however, was more than a contest entry. It was the work of a prolific journalist, who perceived his goal to be that of public education. Say published *Olbie* in Year VIII, in order 'to be useful', and took the opportunity offered by publication to articulate an argument he believed that the judges had overlooked. In doing so, he responded to the sole criticism that the panel addressed to his submission 'which would otherwise,' he believed, 'have been treated far more favourably in their report' (see below: 196). According to the judges, Say's *Olbie* 'present[ed], instead of an analysis, tableaux which show in action what others addressed by means of theory and system: but it was precisely theory and system that the competition required'.

Although accepting the judgement of the panel that, Say allowed, was perfectly consistent with the rules that the judges adopted, he defended his method:

> In the first place, I believe that I accompanied my tableaux with enough analysis for one to understand the argument; let the reader judge. In the second place, I believe that a work submitted to a competition set by a learned body is not destined solely for that institution; that its members did not set the question to enlighten themselves, but rather to encourage work which could influence general opinion, produce useful truths, and destroy dangerous errors. It is not with abstractions that one can realise this goal, but rather, if I am not mistaken, by clothing reason in the grace of elocution and the charm of sentiment. Without doubt, I am far from having achieved this goal, but should the panel blame me for trying?
>
> (below, pp. 196–7)

With these words, Jean-Baptiste Say introduces *Olbie* and establishes this work in a tradition with a revolutionary significance.

Olbie is very explicitly modelled on a literary style introduced by Rousseau. The most well-known contemporary example of the genre was a little book by Louis-Sébastien Mercier, a member of the Ethics section of the class of Moral and Political Sciences of the *Institut National*, entitled *L'An 2440, Rêve s'il en Fût Jamais* (The Year 2440, a dream if ever there were one). It was, in the words of Robert Darnton, 'the supreme best-seller' of pre-Revolutionary France, where it went through at least twenty-five editions (Darnton 1996: 115), notwithstanding a humourless[4] and didactic style that would strike most modern readers as unattractive if not entirely unreadable. *L'An 2440* became something of a revolutionary classic, spurring Mercier to claim in the preface of the 1799 edition that he had anticipated all of the important doctrines of the Revolution (Mercier 1799: ii).

Olbie, like *L'An 2440*, is a utopia. Living in a nation that had just survived the storms of revolution, the Olbians were in the process of creating institutions that support civic virtue. Writing utopias[5] was a popular pastime long before Sir Thomas More coined the word that first appeared in *Lebellus...de optimo reipublicae statu, deque nova insula Utopia* ('Concerning the highest state of the republic and the new island utopia'; 1516). Plato's *Republic* was the model for More, as it was for Say. A utopian island occurs in the *Sacred History* of Euhemerus. Plutarch's life of Lycurgus, who makes several appearances in *Olbie*, describes a utopian Sparta. Francis Bacon's *New Atlantis* (1627) is not explicitly cited by Say. Although there are important parallels between *New Atlantis* and *Olbie*, particularly in the ways in which science in Bensalem and political economy in *Olbie* are modelled as cooperative enterprises generating growing bodies of 'truths' that will benefit ordinary people, it is likely that the influence on Say, if indeed there was any, came by less systematic routes, including possibly Mercier whose *L'An 2440* was modelled more directly on Bacon's utopia. There was a very strong utopian tradition in France, particularly in the years leading up to revolution. Gabriel de Foigny's *Terre Australe Connue* (1676) emphasised liberty, whereas François Fénelon's *Télémaque* (1699) advocated simplicity. The most important of these pre-Revolutionary French utopias, however, was Mercier's *L'An 2440*. Say's *Olbie* falls into this category of practical utopias, in the sense that it advocates certain principles and speculates about their consequences.[6]

Written in 1768, *Mémoires de l'An 2440: Rêve s'il en Fût Jamais* appeared anonymously in 1771 from an Amsterdam publisher. It was placed on the Index and banned in Spain. It went through nine editions in French during its first decade of publication and, with slight variations in the title, it was translated into English by William Hooper and called *Memoirs of the Year Two Thousand Five Hundred*[7] (Hooper 1772). Mercier published four main versions of this text: in one volume in 1771, in a slightly expanded form in 1774, in three volumes in 1786 prefaced by a disclaimer of its imitators, and a signed reprint with an expanded preface in 1799 (L'An VII).[8] The English edition was similarly popular. A second English translation, by Harriot Augusta Freeman, appeared under the title *Astraea's Return; or, The Halcyon Days of France in the Year 2440: A Dream* (Freeman 1787). There were American editions of both English translations.

Mercier's utopia is seen as an innovation in the literature because *L'An 2440* was the first example of a utopia distanced from contemporary society by time rather than space. The narrator finds his way to the future Paris by falling asleep and travelling in a dream,[9] rather than voyaging by ship. One might have expected that the natural setting for a utopia in late eighteenth-century Paris would be the islands of the South Pacific; travellers' reports of idyllic societies, characterised by happy 'natural' people unconstrained by the conventions of the *ancien régime*, were a staple of popular reportage and fuelled the hack writers of sentimental fiction. To set a utopia in the future was an innovation founded on a notion that had not always been in existence – that of linear and monotonic human progress,[10] based on ideas such as those offered by Condorcet. The Greeks had no such notion, but rather envisioned history in the form of cycles of birth, growth and decay. In a sense, Mercier's time travel only became possible when ideas of human progress had become widespread. *L'An 2440* offers a blueprint for change.

The similarities between *Olbie* and *L'An 2440* consist in both style and, to a lesser extent, substance. There is no evidence at all that *Olbie* was influenced in any substantive way by *L'An 2440*, although it would have been inconceivable for Say, the journalist, to have been unaware of a popular novel so widely circulated. But, both Say and Mercier are reacting to contemporary events using a style that was by no means rare during the period. The purpose of comparing the two works is to demonstrate, first, some common features of the genre and, second, the pervasiveness of the spirit of reform. Say and Mercier do not share a common intellectual background; particularly towards the end of his life, Mercier criticised *idéologie* vehemently. And yet, both of these books are written for the same purpose: to bring the 'truths' of philosophy to the people. The styles of the two books are almost identical: concrete description of various tableaux in the main text is supplemented by very extensive footnotes, in which the narrator engages the reader directly in philosophical commentary and criticism of contemporary life. This forces a reader to constantly move back and forth between the footnotes and the main text, switching perspective with each shift. Moreover, the texts are written in a direct and clear language in the manner of Rousseau, which eliminates much of the veiled allusion, pun and wit that characterise earlier fiction. In fact, Darnton characterises Mercier as one of the many 'Rousseaus de ruisseau' (Rousseaus of the gutter) of the period (Darnton 1996: 117). Mercier was nicknamed the 'singe de Jean-Jacques [Rousseau]' by unsympathetic contemporaries, who declared him 'the mortal enemy of the blank page' (Bowen 1977: xx), and claimed that he, Réstif de la Bretonne and Cubières formed a 'triumvirate of bad taste'. Whatever its literary limitations, it sold a lot of copies and it was read widely enough to spur imitators – including, possibly, *Olbie*.

The content of the two books is similar in the way in which social relations are modelled. Both Say and Mercier follow Rousseau in sending women back into the family where, at the hearth, the mother and wife can train the next generation in natural virtue, although Say expands the analysis a little beyond Mercier by recognising that (whatever their natures) many women will be part of the workforce. *Olbie* addresses this issue by attempting to reinvent the convents of the *ancien régime*, and to remake industry so that some appropriate forms of 'honest' employment are opened to women while ensuring that men and women are confined to separate spheres. Both Say and Mercier imagine a world in which divorce is possible, in which marriage based on property no longer exists, and in which the classes can mix in marriage because love alone will be the inspiration of marriage. Both books advocate a simplicity in personal dress and a moderate lifestyle characterised by domestic harmony.

Olbie and *L'An 2440* portray a scientific establishment based upon Baconian principles. Both advocate the elimination of what they see as superstition masquerading as religion in contemporary Paris, but Mercier at least was no atheist. His detailed description of the 'communion of the two infinities', in which young men are initiated into adulthood through an introduction to the worlds revealed by the telescope and the microscope, and his portrait of the Pope, reduced to a bishopric in Rome and publishing a 'catechism of human reason', are delights that do not appear in *Olbie*. Mercier would cure atheists by putting them through a course in experimental physics, and inspire awe in the presence of the works of the Creator by creating glass domes above his cathedrals. In Mercier's *L'An 2440*, however, God is very much a 'central planner' who sees into the darkest hearts and intervenes directly to manage the moral order. This is not a portrait of a divine watchmaker, and is a far cry from the icy deism of Voltaire. The 'absolute eye' will penetrate everywhere (very much like the secret police Mercier sees as maintaining the social order with the help of censors) and will ensure that the sinful are reincarnated as snakes and toads while the good float off into space among the planets and stars until they are absorbed by the Creator.

There is little detail about the way in which the Supreme Being is expected to operate in *Olbie*. In fact, Say's anticlericalism is always a bit of a puzzle. There is no question that he opposed entrenched privilege in an established Church, and there is little to suggest that he found the religious pageantry of the *ancien régime* personally satisfying. He left among the papers now preserved in the *Bibliothèque national* an outline for a volume on 'practical politics', in which he hoped to demonstrate (among other things) that religion has historically caused more trouble than it was worth, and he acknowledged during his final illness a gift of a Bible from a relative by appreciating the sentiment but noting that his own (unspecified) beliefs differed from those of the donor. But he never publicly advocated or admitted atheism, and *Olbie* and the *Cours Complet* do, very occasionally, use expressions that suggest a vague and general acknowledgement of a Supreme Being. In any case, Say's *Olbie* has little to say about the absolute eye, and a great deal to say about the role of the censors and the secular morality police who would, with presumably less divine power, accomplish the same stability in the moral order.

Both Mercier and Say imagined a world in which there was no idle class and in which everyone worked willingly, recognising the personal benefits derived from labour and the corruption that stems from idleness. Paris, in the utopias of both Say and Mercier, became a city of moderate plenty for the many. Great extremes of luxury and poverty were eliminated and, with them, the ostentatious carriages of the wealthy and the slums of the poor. The theatre, for both, became a school for virtue rather than vice, and the patron was no longer accosted by prostitutes when leaving a performance. Education was reformed for both, emphasising science rather than the classics. Popular education was enhanced by statues and monuments commemorating virtuous leaders and important events, which educated the people as they went about their daily errands.

Olbie and *L'An 2440* could not differ more, however, in terms of their economics. Both Mercier and Say would reform public finance by eliminating lotteries and other such schemes, which they believed would corrupt public morality both by creating a widespread reliance on luck rather than hard work and foresight and by encouraging all kinds of sharp dealing. Mercier suggested that taxation would no longer be a problem in the Paris of the future because all inhabitants (except those who would be exempt because they earned no more than is required to support their families) would willingly part with a fiftieth of their income as a tribute to the (constitutional) King and many would willingly supplement these taxes with free gifts. This seems a bit naive next to Say's detailed suggestion of a progressive income tax. Similarly, Mercier would reform commerce so that the state intervenes in every interaction between buyers and sellers to ensure that prices are set to mediate the interests of the two. This is far from the spirit of Say's economics, and does not appear in *Olbie*. Mercier would limit commerce to interior trade, mostly in agricultural products, and abolish three great evils: coffee, tea and snuff, which he claimed destroyed one's memory. Say had his own concerns about coffee (or, at least, about cafés, which furnished a place for the idle to meet and cause trouble),[11] but he was unprepared to share Mercier's readiness to restrict commerce in order to banish self-love and corruption. Mercier believed that the economy would be best run if the heart rather than the head dominated decision making; Say, apparently, did not agree.

The similarity of some of the elements of *L'An 2440* and *Olbie*, the one written by a sympathiser of *idéologie* and the other by someone who saw his purpose in the *Institut National* between 1799 and 1802 as offering a constant critique of atheism and *idéologie*,[12] suggests how widespread were the reformist sympathies of the age. The fact that some aspects, including significantly the role of the markets and the legitimacy of government intervention in trade, differ so profoundly indicates that the reformist sympathies did not necessarily include a good grounding in the *Wealth of Nations*.

Mercier represents one of the tragic figures of the Revolution. After he was released from prison after Robespierre's death, he became increasingly antagonistic towards the reforms he had advocated in *L'An 2440* and the *Tableau de Paris* (2 vols 1781; 12 vols 1782–9). He published *Paris Pendant la Révolution; ou, le Nouveau Paris* (1789–98), and one of his tableaux is chilling: on a wall, someone has written 'Fraternité ou la mort' ('fraternity or death'); beneath this phrase is added 'Sois mon frère ou je te tue' ('be my brother or I will kill you') (Bowen 1977: xx). The slogans of the Revolution lose moral authority in the context of Terror. Mercier's sympathy for Rousseau disappeared and he ended his life writing a diatribe against the theories of Copernicus and Newton,[13] which, he believed, had led humanity astray with their faith in progress.

Despite the limitations of the economic analysis of *L'An 2440*, this book along with Mercier's *Tableau de Paris* is important for our analysis. The *Tableau de Paris* is the best single source from which to gain an appreciation of the mud and the smells of Paris at the end of the *ancien régime*. *L'An 2440* reminds us, again, that what people read in 1799 is not necessarily what we remember of the literature of the period. Say adopted a style similar to Mercier's, not because he admired Mercier's economics, or even necessarily his literary accomplishments, but rather because it was an extraordinarily effective tool of public discourse. As an *idéologue*, he recognised that the highest goal to which he could aim was the instruction of the public, and successful moral education depends upon a willingness to address the public in popular forms.

It hardly seems necessary to comment on the proliferation of 'censors' and 'spies' and of 'secret police' and 'morality police' in *Olbie* and *L'An 2440*. The 're-education' schemes that both Mercier and Say seem to have advocated are a bit chilling when we read them today. We can hardly help being haunted by their support for censorship, and their advocation of dogmatic instruction by means of 'catechisms'. And, when we read these things in the context provided by the constant refrain of the *idéologues*, that is the need for social order, a bit of caution seems appropriate. But, it is only fair to offer both Say and Mercier the same courtesy that Say was prepared to extend to Adam Smith when he noted that the last could hardly have been expected to foresee the disastrous mismanagement of public borrowing that would characterise France some decades after the publication of the *Wealth of Nations* (Say 1843: 575). At the end of the eighteenth century, France could produce important seers, but even the vision of prophets is shrouded by the mists of the future.

It was a different age, one well captured by Mercier's *Tableau de Paris*. And the emblem of that age may have been captured equally well by Mercier's 'Introduction' to *L'An 2440*:

> That all should be well is the wish of the philosopher [–] that sagacious and virtuous being, who desires the general happiness, in consequence of those determinate ideas of order and harmony that he entertains....he knows that evil abounds on the earth; but, at the same time, he has constantly present to his mind that beautiful and striking perfection, which might and ought to result from the conduct of a rational being ....what should prevent us from hoping that, after running round the wide extended circle of their follies, guided by their passions, men, jaded and disgusted, may not return to the pure lights of reason? Why may not the human race resemble an individual? Touchy, hasty, thoughtless, in youth; gentle, patient, prudent, in age. The man who argues thus imposes on himself the duty of being just.
>
> (Mercier 1977: 1–2)

16 Pierre-Louis Roederer: observations

On the question proposed by the *Institut National* as subject of the first prize of the class of Moral and Political Sciences, read during the meeting of 15 Vendémiaire an VI (6 October 1797).

The *Institut National*, in its last public meeting, announced that the subject of the first prize that would be awarded this year by the Class of moral and political sciences was the following question: *What are the best means by which to establish the morality of a people?* It was through an error of transcription that the question was phrased thus. The intention of the class was to ask, not *what are the best means*, but rather *what are the best INSTITUTIONS upon which to base the morality of a people*. Already a correction of this error has been announced in the public papers; but it was thought necessary to announce the correction during this meeting and to bring it to the attention of writers who may enter the competition. The object that the Class proposed is to obtain not only general principles, but also positive and practical suggestions, the execution of which would test these principles in concrete situations. To get precise and positive responses, the question must itself be precise and positive, because it is natural that whoever responds to it will not believe himself obligated to go beyond the question. It is for this reason that it is important to replace in the programme the word *means*, which is vague and may encourage abstract discussion, with the word *institutions*, which directs thought towards positive and practical ends.

Although the meaning of the word *institutions* is clear enough, the Class would like to emphasise again that it does not extend to too many objects, if that is not already clear.

All social institutions, without exception, influence the morality of peoples: the rules that concern the relations among citizens, which are called *civil institutions*; the rules that concern the relationship between citizens and the State, which we call *political institution;* the rules that concern the relationship of citizens to a Being superior to nature, which are called *religious institutions* – all contribute, more or less directly, to public morality. In fact, public morality is essentially dependent on these institutions. From the institution of government, which watches over all these tasks, to that of the public clocks which measure the time and announce the moment when we can set aside these tasks, nothing is irrelevant to the morality of a people.

But, in addition to these institutions, there are *moral institutions* narrowly described, which are a subdivision of all the others, and are distinct from these only because civil, political and religious institutions may have as objects, besides morality, safety, prosperity, general and particular wellbeing, and *moral institutions* have as a special object, and often a sole object, the morality of citizens.

It is obvious that the *Institut National*, in demanding 'what are the institutions upon which to base *the morality* of a people', intends only these moral institutions.

The question thus reduced offers yet an immense field; extended to all social institutions, it would be manifestly disproportionate to the time given for its treatment, with the brevity that habit has prescribed for works presented to literary contests, and perhaps also with the power of a single man. Furthermore, that question has been resolved with respect to civil, political and religious institutions; it was in 1789, when liberty and property were proclaimed the objects of all duties as of all rights; it was in 1792 that liberty and property were placed under the protection of equality and under the guarantee of a republican regime. It is not the *Institut National* of France, it is not an association composed of members who have long shared a republic more ancient than the French republic, and which had the immortal honour of giving it birth, I speak of the republic of letters; it is not the *Institut*, we say, which would ever ask if there are better institutions upon which to base the morality of a people than property, liberty, equality and the republican government, each of which serves as a guarantee for the others.

The system of moral institutions best for founding the morality of a people, the sole object of the proposed research, seems to embrace three particular types of institutions: those which enlighten the mind, like public education; those which warm the soul, such as monuments and national rites; those which conduct all the faculties of a man by *custom*, such as domestic institutions. In effect, morality is not really established in us except insofar as it rests upon our knowledge, it enters into our needs, and it shares our habits.

Public teaching comprises schools, societies of instruction, the sale of books and newspapers, the public libraries, spectacles.

Monuments comprise not only edifices dedicated to virtue and talent, but also all the tributes to the fine arts, such as tombs, obelisks, statues, etc.

National rites comprise not only public celebrations of some happy and honourable event, but also public *mourning* on the occasion of general unhappiness; such was the funeral celebration of an illustrious warrior or of a peacemaker even more illustrious since la Vendée [1793: a royalist uprising in the provinces of the west]; such also could be an annual penance for some great fault from which a nation desired to preserve itself in future.

The domestic institutions preoccupied the ancient legislators; the long history of the Chinese people, that of the Jewish people, prove perhaps that a nation survives as much by its domestic habits as by its laws and magistrates.

Lycurgus, Moses, Confucius submitted to law all the details of private life:

the habits, the furnishings, the clothing, the nutrition, getting up in the morning, going to sleep at night, the language, the relations between the sexes and the generations, the visits, the meetings, in a word the morals and the manners, these were all regulated, all ordained.

It is more than a little difficult to determine with precision to what extent public authority can carry the law into the details of domestic life, to bring morality into harmony with public interest, and the point where it must cease in order not to violate natural liberty, not to constrain the development of the mind, not to stop the progress of human perfectibility.

Perhaps it will be discovered, through the analysis of the subject, that the great regulator of domestic morality, that the great preceptor of private morality, is, plainly and simply, the institution of *work* through the division of labour between all the classes of society; an institution which requires nothing to establish itself in France beyond a great public respect for liberty and property.

Under the monarchy, we hardly regarded work as anything but that of which misery imposes the necessity. But any country where the comfortable man is idle does not merit the honourable title of a labouring country. Where the comfortable man is idle, the poor themselves do less than they might. For the work of a nation to be energetic, it is necessary that it be the habit of the wealthy as well as the indigent; it is necessary that the one be attracted to it by the hope of wellbeing more than by the dishonourable fear of extreme want; the other by the shame or the fear of idleness, not by greed for an evergrowing abundance. The abolition of privileges, titles and distinctions in France has already encouraged great progress in the human mind in this regard.

It is, plainly and simply, this institution of work that, developing all its talents, multiplying all its wealth, expanding the common inheritance, may alone ennoble and strengthen the relations between men. It alone may make sensible and palatable the notion of the equality of rights amidst inequality in fact, by giving the rich modesty and frugality, and the poor dignity and joy; by valuing all contributions and making everyone, recognising their mutual dependence, acknowledge and respect one another. This institution is the most powerful guarantee of property, because it teaches everyone that benefit is acquired only through pain, and because work offers to all the opportunity to acquire. It is this institution that is the most powerful guarantee of liberty, because it doubles the need the rich have of the poor, and it liberates the poor of the degradation of dependence. It is this institution that bonds the father to his children, the children to their fathers, and the spouses to each other. It is this institution, finally, that, ensuring a durable and proper happiness, placing hope beside need for the poor, reawakening desire among the rich and setting it alongside satiation, providing for all the resources necessary for enjoyment, preserves the mind from these evil, uncertain and fearful passions that boredom creates to soothe or to stimulate unoccupied minds?

Of course, this recognition of the omnipotence of work in the establishment of morality remains to be verified, and I have no wish here except to submit it to those writers who take up the question as an idea that preoccupies me. The desire of the Class of which I am the spokesman is the rectification of its programme, and the limitation of the meaning that it attaches to the word *institution*, and I add: the civic desire to see the number of contestants correspond to the importance of the subject.

Roederer, P.-L. [1797] *Journal d'Économie Politique*, du 20 Vendémiaire an VI, reprinted in: (Roederer 1857: 156–8)

17 Jean-Baptiste Say: *Olbie*, or an essay on the means of reforming the morals of a nation

Advertisement

The *Institut National*, in year 5, proposed as a subject for a prize competition this question: 'What are the means upon which to found the morality of a people?' This is one of the best questions that a learned society has ever proposed. It had a degree of utility, especially for France, which has no one to run the Republic except for men raised under the monarchy. Unfortunately, this question did not produce a single response that the Institute judged worthy of the prize.

Subsequently, the Institute rephrased the question with a restriction that made it even more difficult to deal with. It asked, not 'what are the means', but 'what are the institutions,' etc. If it was not possible to deal with the assigned problem when all means are at one's disposition, one must be even less successful when forbidden to consider 'means' which are not 'institutions'.

Finally, another revision once again reduced the resources left to the contestants, and went so far as to trace out a scheme from which they were not permitted to stray. Consequently, the Institute, on the report of a panel of adjudicators, judged that none of the submissions fulfilled the requirements of the competition, and retired the question.

Even though the essay that you are about to read was entered in this last competition, I am one of the first to applaud the decision taken by the Institute, which conformed fully with the rules they adopted. But I will take the liberty of articulating a motivation that I do not believe they considered. This, in fact, will respond to the sole criticism that the panel addressed to my submission which would otherwise, without any doubt, have been treated far more favourably in their report.

According to the panel, my method 'presents, instead of an analysis, tableaux which show in action what others addressed by means of theory and system: but it was precisely theory and system that the competition required'.

In the first place, I believe that I accompanied my tableaux with enough analysis for one to understand the argument; let the reader judge. In the second place, I believed that a work submitted to an open competition set by a learned body was not destined solely for that institution; that its members did not set the question merely to enlighten themselves, but rather to encourage work which could influence general opinion, produce useful truths, and destroy dangerous errors. One cannot attain this goal with abstractions, but rather, if I am not mistaken, by clothing reason in the grace of elocution and the charm of sentiment. Without doubt, I am far from having achieved this goal, but should the panel blame me for trying?

As my principal desire, in composing this work, was to be useful, I had no choice but to publish it. What could be a more favourable time for the publication of a work on the morals of a nation than this, when two men, of eminent talent and morality unquestioned even by their greatest enemies, conceived of the project of founding a stable Republic on the observation of rules of morality, and were acclaimed by their fellow citizens as First Consuls? Certainly, it is in such a period that one is permitted to engage in dreams of a philanthropic imagination. My only regret is that I have reduced to the length of an academic discourse, a work that, based upon the importance of its subject and the extensions to which it is susceptible, deserves a book.

Notes which are too long to go at the bottom of the page, are placed at the end. The places in the text where they belong are marked with an upper-case letter. Most involve digressions and citations that, while related to the subject, would interrupt the flow of ideas.

Summary

Definition of the words morals, moral science and morality. Goal of morality. Two types of institutions are necessary for reforming morals: those which affect new people, or children, and those which affect grown people. The nature of the first type, the second type. The people of Olbie, an imaginary people, provide examples of the application of these principles. The details of each principle are developed along with the example. A good treatise on political economy must be the first book of morality, and why. The power of money. The example of authority. The effects of instruction. The influence of women. Festivals, monuments. Guardians of Morality. Happiness considered as a 'means'. Results.

OLBIE, or essay on the means of reforming the morals of a nation

The word 'morals' [Moeurs], applied to human beings, does not refer only to honest and regular relations between the two sexes, but to the habitual behaviour of a person, or a nation, in the conduct of life.

'Moral science' [la Morale] is the science of conduct. I say science because, in the state of society, the rules of conduct are not all the result of nature; they are learned. It is true that they are learned from childhood and are routine, but must not language, which is also a science, be learned just the same?

'Morality' [La Moralité] is the habit of considering the rules of this science in all one's actions. Of all beings, man alone appears to have this faculty.

The goal of all rules of morality is to gain for human beings all the happiness compatible with their nature. In effect, rules of conduct can only be of two types (A): those which have for an object our own safety and welfare; the advantage of these is immediate and direct, and (B): those which affect the wellbeing of others. These are reciprocal. If they are faithfully followed, each person will enjoy the virtues of all others. This is a case of a mutually advantageous contract. If a nation were to recognise and generally follow rules of morality, it would be what we call 'a favourable exchange'. It would be the happiest of nations.

The Moralist is given the task of making precise and arranging these rules. Here, I am forced to assume that these are known, that one knows with certainty the needs of men, boys, brothers, citizens, magistrates, spouses and fathers. My task is to determine by what means one might encourage a people, raised on vicious habits and outmoded prejudices, to follow these rules, the observation of which would be more than compensated by an increase in its general happiness.

When the leaders of a nation turn their minds to the excellent idea of reforming national morals, there are two sorts of institutions that they must consider: those which generate good morals among human beings yet to come, that is, those which relate to education,[1] and those which are intended to reform grown people.

Education has two objects: the shaping of the physical and moral faculties of children and, in second place, the instruction of children.

Rousseau believes the first of these two goals the most important. In effect, good morals are no more than good habits, and primary education has the goal of forming good habits, both physical and moral. 'Most Republics,' says Bacon, 'would not need to create so many laws to direct men, if they took care to raise their children well.'

Nevertheless, however important moral education may be, one would make a grave error to underestimate the influence of instruction itself on morals. Instruction has, with respect to morals, two important benefits: first of all, it civilises us, and, second, it teaches us our true interests.

Instruction civilises us by turning our ideas towards innocent or useful tasks. Instructed people, in general, engage in less evil and are less destructive than the unschooled. A man who has studied agriculture and who knows that it requires care to grow a plant or to raise a tree, he who understands their economic uses, is less likely to destroy them than the ignorant man who has no appreciation of these precious goods. Similarly, the man who has studied the bases upon which are founded the social order and the wellbeing of nations, will never destroy them without repugnance.

---

1 Anyone who doubts the power of education should read the history of Sparta. I am not saying that we should imitate the institutions of Lycurgus; I am saying only that human beings are what one has made of them, without sharing the opinion of Helvétius who believes that their natural abilities are equal from birth.

But it is mainly by means of teaching us our real interests, that instruction favours morality. The manufacturer who drinks his weekly profits in a few hours, who returns to his home full of wine, beats his wife, corrupts by his example the children who could have become the support of his old age, and who, in the end, ruins his health and dies in the hospital, calculates less well than the diligent worker who, far from dissipating his small earnings, saves them and the interest they yield for his old age and spends his twilight years at the heart of an active and loving family that he has made happy.

It is, above all, in a free state that the people must be enlightened. It is from them that authority arises, and virtue or corruption spring from the summit of power. These leaders are responsible for all nominations, all social institutions, and for the example they set. If they are inept, evil or corrupt, ineptitude, perversity and corruption will inundate the entire social pyramid.

This is, I believe, the influence that both aspects of education exercise on morality.

Not having the pretension of giving in this work a treatise on education as well as a treatise on morality, I must assume that the principles of a good education are understood. They have been discussed and established by the great masters, chief of whom, among the moderns, are Montaigne, Locke and Rousseau. Montaigne, who was a just mind and a learned philosopher but an unmethodical writer, has sown in his admirable discourses the seeds of the ideas brought to fruition by the other two. Locke has assembled and polished this doctrine and extended it to all cases: but his book is dry and detailed; he does not attack all types of prejudice, and one would search in vain for any of the charm and style which makes Rousseau's *Emile* readable, not to mention that eloquence of sentiment which is reason for weak minds and which, joined to reason, enchants enlightened minds. That book of Jean-Jacques [Rousseau], despite a small number of paradoxes for which he shows perhaps a little too much predilection, and despite the fact that some of his precepts (including the principal ones) cannot be applied, produced a revolution in the way children are raised; and if never more than half the inhabitants of France learn to read, and they were to understand only half of this important book, its influence would be prodigious. In that case, an essay like this one would be the most useless thing in the world.

Even though it is not my task to enquire into the principles of a good education, I must at least determine how to encourage the mass of a still very backward nation to adopt them, because one aspect of the morality to be founded is to encourage people to sow good seed for the future.

But how can a nation that has only bad habits engender good ones in its young citizens? One must not abandon hope. Fathers may be interested in doing evil; never in teaching it. They may wish to communicate their own prejudices; but if the institutions that nourished old ideas were to no longer exist, these ideas would not germinate in their children. The fathers are ignorant – one may count on paternal pride to enjoy the merit and success of their sons. Finally, if excellent teachers exist and the future breathes in the writing of a few great men, no nation should despair. I call great men those who, in the general progress of humanity towards perfection, are ahead of their age.

A nation that has bad morals and good books, must use all of its power to encourage literacy.

The indigent, assailed by all his needs, looks at black symbols printed on white paper, as a study in futility. He does not realise that the most sublime knowledge, notions of political economy of the greatest utility, for example, a fertile source of prosperity and the wellbeing of nations, are hidden under the characters that he neglects. He does not know that if his ancestors had known how to lift the veil, he would not be reduced to share with his too-large family a morsel of black bread in the hut of a savage.

Do you want him to teach his children? One must begin by assuring him of enough tranquillity and wellbeing, for him to care about something which, in his eyes, can never be more than an object of secondary utility.

Sufficient wellbeing for the indigent can only result from a wise sharing of general wealth which, itself, can only be the fruit of a good system of political economy. This science is important, the most important of all, if morality and the happiness of human beings deserve to be regarded as the most worthy object of research.[2]

It is vain to yearn to force the natural progress of things. Good education, instruction, of which comfort will be the source and good morals the consequence, will never germinate except with the comfort of the people. And it is upon this which we must first concentrate. If one refuses to begin at the beginning, one will never create more than formal institutions, which may well have at their birth the appearance and the sound of solid institutions, but which will before long resemble those foliage garlands, those pretend trees, cut in the forests to embellish our festivals: superb plants without roots, which play for a time at rural splendour, but which, incapable of producing either flowers or fruits, offer nothing to onlookers except a pompous arrangement of dried branches.

Once established, good educational institutions are only seeds for the future. The people that they produce will have learned the good habit of virtue; their morals may exist with no other foundation. But must a nation renounce all hope of giving good morals to those already here? It would be too distressing to think so. Man has been compared to a shrub which, when still young and supple, may be bent in any direction, but, when grown, resists all efforts. Happily, the resemblance is not complete: a tree vegetates; man has a will, needs, passions, and many powerful levers may be brought to bear against his evil inclinations; but using these levers requires the will to do so and people capable of operating them.

---

2 Whoever writes an elementary treatise on political economy, capable of being taught in public schools and understood by all public bureaucrats even of the lowest level, by country men and by artisans, would be the saviour of the country.

We want people to conduct themselves well. Is it sufficient to command them? The first of our teachers, experience, tells us that it is not. If the best intentions, applied with the authority of law, the use of force, the sanction of religion, sufficed to make human beings virtuous, there would not be a nation that was not a model of virtue; because there is not one in which the laws do not command people to behave themselves; there is not a religion that does not threaten the sinner with frightful punishment and promise magnificent compensation to the good. What, nevertheless, of these nations so well indoctrinated? Is there a single one where an ambitious man has not crushed his rivals where vengeance has not unleashed its furies; where the love of money has not inspired the most shameful frauds and the most vile prostitutions (C)?

One should not delude oneself and believe that many countries offer only a few examples of such crimes. Striking examples are rare, because great occasions are always rare; but the causes which produce them on momentous occasions, exist and work perpetually in the circumstances of common life. If one does not see every day a brother dethroning his brother, every day one does see an elder brother disputing with the younger or with an illegitimate child innocent of the error of his birth, over the smallest portions of an immense inheritance.

Human justice, poor and unequal justice, deals well enough with some of the crimes that shock society, but it never addresses or destroys the causes of such crimes; from this it follows that justice punishes in effect, not the crime, but the lack of finesse of the criminal who does not know how to hide his sword. Justice does not teach morality: it teaches prudence and astuteness.

If both divine and human law have so little power to teach good morals, where should one look for help? In the heart of human beings. 'Whoever meddles in the instruction of a people,' says Rousseau, 'must know how to govern by winning over opinions.' If one wants some manner of being, some habit of life established, the last thing to do is to order that everyone obey. Do you want to be obeyed? It is not enough to want people to do something; you must get them to want to do it.[3]

I do not claim that, to make people adopt an institution, one must give in to the prejudices of those for whom it is made. It must have been true that Lycurgus attacked in some way the opinions of his era, since he incited a riot and was pelted with stones when he tried to implement his laws; but his laws survived. That one is angered by new institutions, I recognise; but if one were led by his own self-interest to protect them and if one were attracted by the nature of things rather than the orders of the legislator, then the general taste

---

3 One has made poor republicans every time that one has tried to win converts with a pistol at the throat. The appearance changed, at the very most. It would be the same with virtue: violence would do nothing but strip away all its grace and charm. The stupid prudishness that everyone was forced to adopt during the last years of Louis XIV produced the disorder of the Regency.

could be overcome. Why is this consideration, the first that one should think of when proposing a law or founding an institution, usually the last that comes to mind?

I repeat: one must look into the heart of man, and there alone, for the guarantee of his conduct.

Man aspires without cessation after happiness, and principally after the closest and most obvious happiness (D): if there is no path before him to attain happiness except that of crime, he will pursue it. If the path of virtue can lead him to wellbeing, he prefers it. This disposition, placed in our souls by nature, and which all the orators in the world can only try in vain to change, must always guide the moralist. Instead of trying to overcome the desires of men, he must use them.

It has been said that one must make virtue attractive: I dare to add that one must make it beneficial. Vice is hideous; let us make it painful.

If we have seen institutions operate on the morals of extraordinary people, let us not fool ourselves, it is because the legislators who established them were aware of this motive and used it. Three hundred Spartans died at Thermopylae for their country; this is one of the greatest examples of devotion that history has preserved. How did Lycurgus inspire this heroic courage? We could guess; but Xenophon tells us with certainty: 'This great legislator appealed to the happiness of brave men, and sacrificed the coward to unhappiness and disgrace.'[4] To flee and to be perpetually miserable were, for the companions of Leonidas, the same thing. What ordinary man, in the face of all this, could abandon his post and reappear on the banks of the Eurotas! These brave men did not have two roles to play: they had but to die; that is what they did.[5]

Let us do for virtue what Lycurgus did for courage and, in the words of J. J. Rousseau, *it may open all the doors that fate was pleased to shut.*[6] Many modern colonies that established their institutions following these principles achieved great success. The majority of Europeans who founded settlements on the coasts of North America carried with them neither the regrets nor the esteem of their former countrymen. Many were insolvent or even fraudulent debtors, and some had even greater faults to regret. Having arrived on the American continent, and needing good relations among themselves, they honoured those qualities alone which could preserve the newborn society. Work, power, credit, fortune would seek out those who were recommended by their good faith, their intelligent conduct, their love of work. Men without probity in business, without sensitivity towards women, without goodwill towards their brothers

---

4   Xén. Rép. de Sparte.

5   If anyone reproaches me for calling *brave* men who could not behave otherwise, I would respond that I call them brave because they could not tolerate shame. That is the foundation of all types of bravery; and if Lycurgus made of his Lacedemonians [Spartans] the bravest of men, it is because he knew how to establish a shame impossible to bear.

6   Gov. of Poland.

could not survive. They had to change their character or leave. And the morals of this people have generally, even during the storms of revolution, offered the nations of Europe examples of virtues unknown among themselves; and the refuse of these nations has deserved to become the model.[7]

These are, I believe, the principles that must guide the research and adoption of institutions capable of supporting the morals of a people. I will now show these same principles in practice in a society which established its political liberty on the ruins of an absolute monarchy, and which could not consolidate its liberty except by totally changing its morals or, if you wish, its habits (E). These people, who inhabit a country called *Olbios* [en français *Olbie*], have enjoyed a liberty founded upon good laws for about fifty years and are well advanced on the path of wisdom, so the reproach that might be elicited by the memory of their former corruption would not offend them. One only blushes for the faults that one might yet commit.

I can only give a few examples from Olbie within the limits I have imposed upon myself. But these examples will suffice, I hope, to give birth to more extensive and well-formulated, and perhaps more just, ideas; and then my work, however imperfect, will not have been useless.

I believed it was necessary to establish principles before offering examples, because some may be well and others badly chosen. It shall be left to people more enlightened and more powerful than I, to draw from the first all the consequences that they may yield, and to deploy their genius and their strength of character in the application of these principles; this is, without doubt, the most difficult task when it comes to creating social institutions.

It shall be seen that I assume throughout that the leaders of a nation, those upon whom the institutions depend, are firmly committed to regenerate the morals of their fellow citizens; otherwise, it is pointless to try.[8] Lycurgus changed the morals of Sparta; but he was strongly motivated.[9] If the Spartans had preferred to remain corrupt, and Lycurgus shared their opinion, I do not know of any method by which that reform could have taken place.

It is therefore up to the legislators of the nation, the most influential magistrates, the orators and writers, to work with me in this task. If only those of my fellow citizens who are in a position to influence national morals,

---

7 I know that the inhabitants of the United States have not avoided other dangers, as I will soon enough discuss; but they do not offer any less an example of the effectiveness of personal interest directed towards good. The criminals that England has transported to Botany Bay have there all become honest men.

8 They have a greater interest than anyone, because one never sees a revolution in political institutions consolidated without at the same time a revolution in moral habits. It is true that the former makes the latter easy; the Republic is a wonderful institution to reform the morals of a people (F).

9 Regarding as a first condition for reform a strong will, I would assign second place to the requirement that this will be neither hard nor intolerant. Strong will allows one to use all means at one's disposal, even patience and more patience; even though an intolerant will may succeed in bending obstacles, it will never destroy them.

by their positions in society or by their talents, would commit themselves to the accomplishment of this important and praiseworthy work. May they realise how it will result in solid glory for themselves, and true happiness for everyone!

After the revolution that allowed the Olbians to live according to the light of reason rather than according to old habits, the leaders of the nation focused on diminishing the great inequality of wealth; they realised that, in order to cultivate good morals, the most favourable situation for a nation to find itself is that where the majority of families which constitute the nation live in an honest comfort, and where excessive opulence is as rare as extreme poverty.

Misery exposes one to continual temptations; what can I say? to imperious needs. Not only acts of criminal violence, but also deceit, fraud, prostitution,[10] riots, are almost always the fruit of poverty. How often men have embraced an abhorrent political party, or dangerous opinions, solely to survive! Such a man would not destroy his country if he had the means of survival. Ah! if the wealthy, according to some people, understood well their own interests, instead of sucking the means of survival away from the poor in order to augment their own wealth, they would give charity voluntarily, and sacrifice some of their own goods, in order to enjoy the rest in peace.

Great fortunes are not less fatal to good morals (G). The ease with which men can buy produces as much evil as the temptation to sell oneself. Opulence hardens the soul: one does not appreciate the needs that one never feels or the want from which one believes oneself forever secure. The wealthy are surrounded by a crowd of admirers who, to make themselves agreeable, protect them from hideous sights and suggest diversions that they might share, rather than charities of which they are envious.

It is not regulations and sumptuary laws that protect a nation from excesses of wealth and poverty; it is the complete system of its legislation and administration. The first book of morality was, for the Olbians, a good treatise on political economy. They set up a sort of academy which they used to stock that book. All citizens who aspired to positions as first ministers were publicly interrogated on the principles of that science; principles that they might defend or attack as they chose. It was sufficient that they knew them for the academy to give them a diploma, without which the path to important positions was closed to them (H).

Before long these positions were all occupied, if not by superior minds, at least by men sufficiently enlightened to be in a position to play a fit role in important questions. Most opinions rallied around the best principles, and the result was a system in accord with political economy according to which

---

10 We must ensure that one is not forced to prostitute one's talents any more than one's person in order to live. If it is distressing to see courtesans selling, at the first opportunity, those favours which ought to be exchanged with the most tender sentiments, it is not less distressing to see the man of letters selling his approval to powerful and corrupt persons in power, and the artist lending the magic of his colours to the obscene commissions of the contemptuous wealthy.

all the authorities of the state regulated their conduct; as much as men have changed for the better, the 'maxims' remained unchanged on all important points: and because an irresistible force never fails to produce its effect, it happened that, without injustice, without tearing apart, without shock, honest comfort became very common and excesses of wealth and poverty became very rare.

The majority of citizens, not wealthy enough to spend their lives in continual pleasure but comfortable enough to resist despair or the anguish of need, dedicated themselves at that moderate work which leaves the soul all of its energy: little by little they became accustomed to finding their dearest pleasures in the society of their family and a small number of friends; they ceased to know idleness, boredom, and the parade of vices that accompany them: living more soberly, their temperaments became more even, their souls more predisposed to justice and to that kindness and charity which are the mothers of all other virtues.

In order to protect themselves even more from the evils that follow idleness (I), they revived, with a minor modification, that law of Athens which obliged each citizen to declare his means of subsistence; and if some had legitimate means of subsistence without work, they were obliged to make known their habitual occupations. This designation accompanied a man's name and signature on all public records, which could not be produced without this formality. Therefore, instead of a lucrative profession, one often saw the name of a man who occupied himself with research in physics, or perhaps agricultural experiments, or giving a liberal education to the orphan children of his brother. When there was a striking disparity between conduct and the declared occupation, it would be a source of ridicule or even more serious reproach for anyone who made a false declaration, which anyone would be at great pains to avoid. If some matter or unforeseen circumstance drew attention to a citizen, and he had neglected to make his declaration, his name was never recalled without being followed by the qualifier *useless man*.

By this method, Olbians ensured that the love of gain never became the only stimulant that induced men to work. The Olbians knew that the love of gain is a danger almost as hazardous as idleness. When that characteristic is very evident, it becomes exclusive like all others; it suffocates a host of noble and unselfish sentiments that must enter into the perfected human soul. Among certain people, or even among the inhabitants of certain cities too dedicated to commerce, any idea other than that of making money, is seen as folly; any sacrifice of money, time or talent, as foolishness. Such a people sometimes pay men of ability because they have a need for them, but these men of talent are hardly ever born amongst them. Like money given to disloyal servants, and not to faithful friends and capable citizens, nations of this type end up, sometimes very quickly, by having tribute exacted, being dominated and finally defeated by those that follow other principles. What has become of the Phoenicians, and their successors the Carthaginians? We know very little of their internal affairs, other than that they existed and abandoned themselves almost exclusively to commerce.

Our Europe offers us many similar examples.

Venice, to whom an immense trade gave the means of paying a large navy and an enormous army, commanded always by a foreign general who was little more than the head shop-assistant of these merchants; Venice sustained at one time wars against Turkey, the Empire, the Pope and France; and at the end a battalion was enough to defeat it.

Has not Holland, the richest and most densely populated country in the world, been the eternal victim of all the belligerent powers of Europe who each, in their turn, exacted tribute from the state and then disposed of its independence at their will? United States of America, beware the general tendency of mind in your beautiful republic. If what is said of you is correct, you will become wealthy, but you will not remain virtuous, and you will not long remain independent and free (K).

It is therefore necessary that the love of work be not constantly excited by the desire for gain; the happiness and even survival of society demands that a certain number of people in each nation pursue the sciences, the fine arts and letters;[11] noble wisdom that engenders elevated sentiments combined with useful talents. Some writer, in his modest office, works more effectively at establishing the glory, power and happiness of his country, than the general who wins the battles (L).

If I were no longer within the limitations imposed by this discourse, it is here that I would show what morals stand to gain from the development of the more noble faculties of the mind and the soul; I would argue incidentally against the eloquent riddles of the philosopher of Geneva (M); I would defend the only nobility that is capable of recognising political equality; that of the enlightened [les lumières], the only one that could not be dangerous and would never be the companion of mediocrity; I would note the good sense of the Chinese, who make 'mandarin' and 'lettered' synonyms, not being able to conceive that one elevated by his wisdom may be base in his rank, or that foolishness and immorality may command genius and virtue.

The Olbians encourage by other means, in the working class, that love of industry which is more useful for it than for others; they established mutual aid societies [caisses de prévoyance] (N). Everyone who managed to put aside a small sum was permitted to make a deposit to one of these banks every ten days; and there, by the ordinary effect of the accumulation of interest, they saw it grow to the point where, by the age of retirement, they found themselves masters of a sure capital or a life annuity. Almost all the artisans would deposit a smaller or larger amount of their salary in the society; and instead of devoting

---

11 If the English support the burden of destructive wars better than we do, it is because they are advanced in political economy; and many times, before and since the revolution, France lost its immense resources because its leaders were ignorant of the elements of that science.

to their pleasures or to intemperance, three or four days in every ten, they would spend no more than one on their relaxation. The pleasures that one tastes within the family are the least expensive; therefore, they prefer them in order to add to their savings; and when the day of rest comes, one no longer sees as before in Olbie, cabarets full of brutish drunks, singing and swearing by turns: but, in the fields surrounding the city, one often meets a father, mother and their children all animated by a tranquil joy, that of happiness, walking towards some country rendezvous with other friends of the same trade as themselves.

The Olbians were not content to give themselves, relative to political economy, a legislation favourable to morality; they gradually eliminated from their legislation all that was contrary to political economy. They felt that it was in vain for the moralist to work to make men good, if one allowed laws to remain which had the effect of rendering them perverse (O). This is what made them suppress the lotteries (P), which attracted greed, laziness, and sometimes theft, and encouraged that belief, fatal to the prosperity of empires, which founded one's fortune on luck rather than on industry.[12] They are far, by consequence, from authorising and even further from encouraging the publication of books of magic, where one uses the interpretation of dreams and the calculations of necromancy, to encourage the poor man to part with the last écu that he possesses, the écu with which he could have retired a debt or perhaps bought dinner for his children. Deadly tax! supported by the dreams of the destitute, and not by wealth that has a thousand better ways to build its treasure.

Like lotteries, gaming houses disappeared; and when one walks through the neighbourhoods where they were formerly congregated, one no longer meets some wretched man, with wild-looking eyes, searching, with an uncertain step, a bridge from the height of which he might hurl his misfortune.

After having destroyed, as far as possible, the causes of corruption, the Olbians turned towards the encouragement of good conduct and fine actions. They anticipated and exceeded the counsel of the famous *Beccaria*, who wants to set up a prize for virtuous actions, just as one exacts a fine for misdemeanours. Everything became an instrument of compensation (Q). Functions to which were attached power or perquisites, permits for exemptions, honourable missions, became the prize for a brilliant act, for the exercise of sublime or sustained private virtue, for irreproachable conduct in sensitive circumstances, for the zeal which supported the founding or sustenance of an establishment of humanity, and even for a good book, the difficult fruit of long study and useful meditation. The word 'favour' was erased from the dictionaries. All nominations for public office carried notice of the titles that

---

12 The worker who deludes himself with the hope of winning 30 or 40 thousand francs in a few minutes, works with a poor attitude to earn 30 or 40 sols per day; and nevertheless, this latter work is the sole productive work, the sole that contributes to the wealth of the state.

the candidate had earned which qualified him for the position; they listed all functions that the candidate had previously undertaken; and, so that the public could judge the merit of the titles, each nomination was printed in a list of nominations, published by the Government, in which all of the articles could be reprinted and openly debated.

But in a Republic, many of the positions are determined directly by the people. How, one might ask, can these, which are the source of all the others, be an instrument of compensation for the most virtuous, if the people, destitute of wisdom and morality, give them to the most hypocritical and the most impudent?[13] This misfortune which, it is true, was cruelly felt in the infancy of the Olbian Republic diminished and finally disappeared as the people became more enlightened.

When the citizens of a state can meet, see each other and listen to each other freely, they discover soon enough those among themselves who deserve to be held in esteem; since it is in their interest to elect those persons incapable of abusing their positions to torment and rob the electorate, they set aside the schemer and choose the good.

In order that the citizens of a canton could learn to know one another, the Olbians set up in each neighbourhood, not political societies (R), but social clubs, where all citizens listed on the civic register met often in the evening, usually on holidays and days of rest. They could even bring their family. In these meetings, which were most often held in a location with an adjoining garden, one would see not general discussions, but individual conversations. Here, one might take refreshment, while others play ball, billiards, different games of skill; over there, someone is reading the news of the day. Soon enough, the inhabitants of the same neighbourhood knew the character, and even the habits of one another, and this resulted in enlightened elections, favourable to the general interest, which one could regard as true recognition of private virtue.

Moreover, people made good choices because good examples were set.

We would hardly have recognised the full extent of the power of example, when it is given by eminent people of dignity and merit, if it were not for China, where the emperor, on one certain day in the year, places his own hand on the plough. The power of example is so firmly in the hands of the government, that I do not believe one can cite a single nation which exhibited morality when its government was lacking it, nor a single nation which lacked morality when its government furnished a model of morality.

In Thomas More's *Utopia*, the Utopian government, the moment it is at war with another nation, sets a price on the head of the enemy prince, his ministers and his generals; they welcome and they give great lands and an honourable existence to the murderers; they spread invitations to treason throughout the country of the enemy; all, finally, to avoid battles and the

---

13 One must not lose sight of the fact that this book was written in Year VII. The constitution of Year VIII eliminated some of these worries.

shedding of human blood. It is not thus that Camillus conducted himself with the Faliscan schoolmaster. If Utopia were ever to exist, the people would use this beautiful system to great profit; and in particular, in lawsuits with one another, would seek to bribe the cook of their rivals, in order to avoid the scandal of a trial. Men who govern, beware: you speak and act in front of big children: not one of your gestures, not one of your words is lost (S).

When the people of Olbie saw positions occupied by men of probity and instruction who were devoted to the public good rather than a single party (T), they became accustomed to prize these qualities, and they were ashamed to make a poor choice.

The candidates, in their turn, saw that merit rather than gold was the means of advancement, and began little by little to value gold less than merit. This was a great accomplishment; because the more useful is gold, the more willing one is to sacrifice virtue to it. If it could protect against death, if it could buy power and beauty, good health, sincere friends, the love of our spouses, the respect of our children, independently of the other enjoyments that it can buy, I do not think anything could stop the most virtuous man from acquiring gold.

To diminish to an even greater extent the power of gold, the leaders among the Olbians declared a great disgust for the display of luxury. Simplicity of taste and manners became a preferred motive and a matter of honour. The leaders of the state adopted a general system of simplicity in their clothes, their pleasures and their social relations. Neither their domestic servants nor the soldiers in their guard bore witness to a stupid deference for luxurious livery.[14] Most of the people developed by degrees the same habit; and soon one would no longer see a troop of imbeciles stupefied at the sight of diamond jewellery or some other bauble of the same type (U). People were no longer held in esteem in proportion to their consumption: and what was the consequence? They consumed nothing beyond that which was necessary for their utility or their comfort. Luxury, attacked at its root which is opinion, gave way to a comfort more generally shared (V); and, as always happens, happiness grew at the same time that morals were reformed.

As the taste for luxurious display diminished, money which had been dedicated to it was turned to more praiseworthy and productive directions. It gave life to manufacturing, raised the value of industry and talent that were perishing in poverty without profit for society, without glory for the nation. Before long the wealth that was given to vain ostentation by grand people began to be less valued. Some decided to attach their name to a public edifice, or perhaps to make abundance flow in the canals dug at their expense; some turned to opening a great road, and others to constructing a new harbour;

---

14 I agree that a government cannot use this method, except when the economy and order in fiscal affairs ensures that it never needs to appeal for aid from the wealthy; aid even more ruinous for public morals than for the treasury.

finally, they pursued the glory of being called the benefactors of the country, and their wealth was pardoned.

The Olbians would have been but weak moralists if they had no appreciation of the extent to which women influence morals. We owe to women our first memories and our last consolations. As children, we are the work of their hands: we are that still when we reach adulthood. Their destiny is to dominate us without cessation, by the authority of their kindness, or by that of pleasure; and where women are not virtuous, it is vain for us to aspire to virtue. It is by the education of women that we begin that of men.

Happily, that nature which poured upon this half of our species charm and beauty, appeared to take pleasure in endowing them at the same time with the most lovable qualities of the heart; and perhaps the pride of men will be forced to acknowledge that, if we except justice which is the virtue that often orders us to overcome our tastes and affections and is the partner of strength, nature has generally given to women moral qualities in a higher degree than to us. They are more prone to pity, more disposed to kindness, more faithful to their promises, more devoted in their affections, more patient in misfortune. Precious qualities! There is not one whose gentle effects I have not felt. If some women do not possess all , there is not a single one who does not carry its seed in her heart; and, leaving aside exceptions, ignoring the ironies of frivolity, I dare affirm that the sex which has the most charm, is also that which has the most virtue.

The Olbians do not, as is done in some sects, attack the inclination which attracts men to women. It is an instrument as powerful as it is gentle: is it necessary to break it rather than to use it? Neither do they follow the counsel of Plato who, in his imaginary Republic, wanted a lottery to determine once and for all, in an entire class of citizens, an exchange that reduces us to the level of brutes when it is not ennobled by faithfulness and the delicate preferences of the soul. On the contrary, the Olbians blend honest love with all of their institutions that can admit it; and, if it is necessary to remark upon it, they have taken some advice from our centuries of chivalry.

They recognise the necessity of giving women the two virtues that become them more than any others, and without which the charm and the ascendancy of their sex will vanish soon enough: I mean to say gentleness and chastity. Among this people the gentleness of women emanates from a general morality which is itself the fruit of all the other institutions. Domestic and private virtues were esteemed and revered because they were useful, and poor management being an obstacle that repels equally esteem and fortune, much attention was given to those habitual considerations which civilise the morals and which, if I can express it thus, smooth the path of life.

Some professions, having the effect of hardening the heart or making bitter the character, were forbidden to women, and they enjoyed some privileges consistent with their tastes and their qualities. It was to them that the government ceded responsibility for national charity; it protected the associations that some women formed to aid girls to marry, and pregnant women; praiseworthy associations which present a touching scene of generous femininity, making common cause with their unfortunate sisters.

The sexes mixed less in society, even among the working class. Good principles of political economy having spread a little comfort in that class, the women were no longer forced by indigence to share with men those difficult and disgusting occupations which one cannot watch them undertake without shuddering. They were able to give their time and their effort to the care of their households and their family which were much better tended, and they lost those masculine aspects which, in their sex, are something hideous: woman and gentleness are two ideas that I do not know how to separate. The power of women is that of gentleness against strength: the moment that they try to obtain something by violence, they are no more than a monstrosity.[15]

Chastity is perhaps, for women, of even greater importance than gentleness. Those who are no longer pure lose, not only their most seductive attractions, but lose almost all the means of preserving the other qualities of their sex, and exercising those gentle functions which nature has given them. If she is not married, she repels all those among whom she may find a spouse; if she is a wife, she draws chaos into her household. If a man breaks the laws of chastity, he is guilty without doubt; but still he may be an upright lawyer, solid friend, good son, good brother, in all an esteemed and useful citizen; but a woman who is no longer chaste is nothi – what do I say! Nothing? She is a living cause of disorder.

The power of the senses and indigence are, for women, the two principal causes of libertinism. As for the first, a good legislation pertaining to marriage and divorce diminished by degrees this problem in Olbie. Tastes were consulted; differences in wealth posed few difficulties to legitimate unions; and these unions themselves underwent all the changes compatible with the maintenance of the social order. Let us make easy the path of virtue and not imitate those moralist–legislators who placed their temple at the peak of a high mountain that one can reach only by a narrow path. That condemns the entire world to the abyss!

The second cause of corruption among women, indigence, merits all of the attention of those who want to base morals on social institutions. Poverty, a cruel scourge for everyone, is frightful for the more interesting half of the human race. It not only deprives women of the common sweetness of life, it pushes them to the most shameful corruption, the most devoid of the charm that sometimes disguises the ugliness of vice. One must be hungry to sell her favours! What other motive than imperious need could make so many of the unfortunate overcome the disgust of prostitution? The unfortunate women! without choice, without desire, often the victim of grievous evils, almost always with shame in their souls, they solicit with the gracious smile of the rejected!

---

15 They are neither women nor men, these beings in petticoats, with wild eyes and raucous voices, who, among the population of our cities, resist men, either to insult them or to lead them by the hand. This is a third sex.

Who would not prefer to be other than this? Among the Olbians, they are offered a more desirable alternative: they grasp it with enthusiasm.

One day, walking in the streets of Olbie, I collided with an obstacle that I had not noticed. Some people gathered around and, because a little blood ran down my face, they took me into the closest house. I found myself soon enough alone with three properly and simply dressed women, who appeared to be the mistresses of the house. They gave me first aid; they wanted me to stay a while to recover my strength. Their house did not really have the air of a private home, and it piqued my curiosity. They noticed, and seeing that I was a foreigner, they answered my questions in these words:

'We are a large society of women. This house was given to us by the State, and the State continues to shelter us as it does many similar societies; but we are not a burden upon the State. The work that is done here is adequate to pay our expenses (which are modest), and to provide a small payment to those among us who do more work than our rules require. We have three matrons and three treasurers, a third of whom are replaced each month. We are not permitted to receive strangers except in this common room, and we can see no one except in the company of two of our sisters. We can leave in groups of three with the permission of at least two of the matrons.'

'Our number is limited by the size of the house. We choose our colleagues; but as long as there are applicants, we are obliged to keep our house full. When one enters the society, no vow is exacted, and no obligation is imposed except to follow the established rules. There are among us women who were married, and others who are not yet married. All can leave the house and establish themselves if the opportunity arises. When they leave, they can take their own savings but the savings of the community remain behind. The only burden that the State imposes upon us is the obligation to teach a certain number of students women's work, and to care for a certain number of old women.'

'If a student, an old woman or even a sister requires discipline, we have appeal to the administration which, ordinarily, expels her: this is almost the only direct act of authority which the government imposes upon us.'

'Our life is very pleasant: we enjoy the moral strength that pervades any type of association, and a liberty adequate to know the pleasures of society. We are loved, we are cared for; more of us leave the house for the arms of a husband, than the rest of the Eternal.'

I then learned that to qualify for entry into these civil societies, girls and women without means undertook an extremely regular lifestyle. One should not be surprised: comparing the rewards that they enjoy in these communities with those of libertinage, is it surprising that so many choose this life?

This induced me to learn a few other aspects of the legislation of Olbie with respect to women. All occupations that are exclusively related to women are reserved for them. No man is permitted to work in any industry that concerned the dress or hairdressing of women; and, among the arts and trades, there are some that are reserved solely for women, such as embroidery, the transcription of music, cooking, and many others; this allowed the poorest of women to earn an honest living. Are there not enough professions remaining for men, who have the whole world open to them, and who, in any case, can always find an honourable means of subsistence by serving the State in the navy or the army?

It has always been regarded as a tremendous problem to determine the extent to which public authority can enquire into the details of private life without violating natural liberty, without hindering mental development. Apart from degrading espionage, there exists, perhaps, a single method. Authority cannot, without tyranny, scrutinise motives: let it focus on outcomes. In Lacedaemon [Sparta], two brothers went to trial: the magistrates fined the father, who was punished for not having inspired in his sons more unselfishness and more mutual love.

But to exercise such authority, can we rely upon our modern tribunals, who recognise the crimes that the laws prohibit, but not the virtues that morality demands, and who never take a decision except on the basis of juridical proof? Might we not imitate, at least in some aspects, the Censure of the ancients?

We are too ready to believe that institutions, put into practice by the people of the ancient world, are no longer applicable to our morality. We believe that the people of that period were different than our contemporaries. Alas! it is sufficient to read history to realise that we do nothing but revive the stupidities and crimes of our predecessors. If some institution produced some good at one time, why should it not do so again? Does anyone believe there was a time without difficulties and antagonists? Aristotle complained bitterly about the Ephori of Lacedaemon; he declared that among them one could find unenlightened people who were as hard on others as they were indulgent of themselves.[16] In Rome, a few years after the establishment of Censors and in all the fervour of that wonderful institution, did we not see those magistrates who were thought to have so much integrity pour out all their resentment on the dictator Mamercus Emilius, an illustrious person in peace and war, because he reduced the tenure of their position from five years to a year and a half? As soon as his rule was over, they used their authority to deprive that respectable citizen of his right to vote, and raised his tax to eight times that which he had been accustomed to paying.

Indeed, if the detractors of the period used these abuses, as they undoubtedly did, to decry the Ephorate and the Censure, and had they been successful, they would not have been any less the institutions that maintained the purity

---

16 De Rep. lib. II, pag. 9.

of morals in Sparta, and to which must perhaps be attributed the three hundred years that the Roman Republic would yet endure.

If only we would turn our attention to fixing what experience has shown to be the vicious aspects of these institutions; if only we would take from them the political prerogatives that made them so dreadful;[17] but not prohibit them solely because they were born in Rome and in Sparta.

It was from this point of view that they were considered by the Olbians. The censors in Olbie were responsible for the inspection of morals and nothing more; and it is for this reason that they were called *Moral Guardians*. Their tribunal was composed of nine elders, chosen from among those citizens who had exercised honour in their private and public duties throughout their lives, but who were now completely retired from business and by consequence not susceptible to hopes or to fear. These elders could only impose a moderate fine, equal, more or less, to the sum of the taxes of the condemned; and, in very serious cases, public censure.

No job in the State, however eminent it may be, is outside the authority of the decrees of this tribunal, and no citizen is obscure enough to be beneath their applause, if they have earned it through uncommon virtue. Their judgements, like those of a jury, are the result of secret deliberation, and their decision is informed by all possible means: open depositions, secret information, public demands when these are of a certain intensity, voluntary interrogation, frank explanations, all serve to enlighten.

This tribunal never determines guilt in those cases it intends to criticise; that would require that it be established by juridical proof, and often the tribunal has only moral evidence. For the same reason, it never gives the motivation of its decisions, and is never held responsible; its members are inviolable. Here is the announcement of a public judgement that it once rendered against a dishonest judge:

PEOPLE OF OLBIE

HONOUR VIRTUE AND DETEST VICE[18]

[Name]…the Moral Guardians demand, before the eyes of
your fellow citizens, that you no longer accept gifts from your
clients, and listen to nothing but the voice of fairness when
making your judgements. Put in the poor box a fine equal to
the sum of your annual taxes.

---

17 The Ephori joined to their civil influence a very extensive political power, in that they called the assemblies of the people, received ambassadors, etc. The Censors, in Rome, could move a citizen from one tribus to another, exact rents and taxes, etc.

18 Why, in the modern world, are those phrases neglected which, like banners, rally the opinions of a people, and serve, at least, to show the contradiction between principles and actions?

When a bureaucrat had been the object of a similar judgement, he was obliged, as long as he held the same job, to add to all the other titles that accompanied his name in all public records, this: *censored by the Moral Guardians.* There were few who would not have preferred to submit their resignation.

The Moral Guardians declared national honours in public ceremonies. One time, a man came to recommend to them his benefactor: they praised at the same time the patron and the man who recommended him (X).

It is clear that functions so delicate demand that those chosen to exercise them be selected with special care. Each of these magistrates of morals was elected for two years and could be re-elected indefinitely, but not by the same electors; each province elected in its turn a Moral Guardian, and the term of the person elected never ended when that same province had another opportunity to choose. If he found himself replaced or re-elected, it was by another province.

When it is time to name a Guardian, this question is asked: 'Who is, among retired people, the most honest man in the province?' The citizens with the right to decide split into two juries. One of the two elected the candidate, but the decision that it made had to be sanctioned by the other. If the second refused to sanction the choice, they chose another and the first jury could, in its turn, choose to sanction or to refuse its assent.

I said that the Moral Guardians number nine; all nine investigate a case; when it comes time to decide, three of them are chosen by lot and only these three decide but they must be unanimous. Their judgements are listed in two series, one called the *Book of Merit*, and the other the *Book of Blame*. It was not the Olbians, but the Chinese who recognised the use that one might make of such books (Y).

We have seen that the Moral Guardians also bestow honours in public ceremonies; this induces me to discuss the sort of national festivals that exist in Olbie, and the role that they play in morality.

The talents of men are a burden when they are not used. Children only amuse themselves by destroying because they do not yet know how to use their energy constructively.[19] Similarly a man who does not do good, occupies himself by doing evil. It is therefore expedient to occupy him usefully; but one is never occupied usefully without directing towards a fixed goal a certain amount of constant moral or physical means: but, that concentration becomes tiring, and relaxation (that is occupations which, for the moment, do not demand the concentration of efforts towards the same goal) becomes necessary.

These recreations may be favourable or contrary to morality. They are contrary when they become harmful; such as the combat of the Roman gladiators; such as the diversions of a base people who do not know how to relax from work except by giving in to excesses of debauchery and all types of disorder, that is, in doing evil to oneself and others.

---

19 This, in part, is why the ignorant man, who is no more than a grown child, does more evil than good.

For recreation to be moral, it is sufficient that it not have harmful effects; it produces good by that alone, in that relaxation gives us the resources to continue our useful work. If to that advantage, it adds another by elevating our physical or moral talents and tastes, it is even better.

Nevertheless, it is necessary to be careful not to try so hard to make recreation useful that it is not relaxing. Let us not forget that here relaxation is the essential thing, and utility is nothing but an accessory.

It is from this perspective that the Olbians considered the fine arts, theatre, public festivals; and it is because of this principle that they preserved themselves from the austerity of the Spartans and early Christians. They believed that these must first please, touch, and seize the soul by honest means; and then (but only if it is possible without destroying these) direct them towards a moral and useful goal.

They thought very highly of stage plays (Z). Theatre gives us a more intense ability to sympathise with others; precious emotion, the opposite of selfishness, one of the most beautiful attributes of man, and which has something attractive even in its weakness! They had a theatre like the French, where in a series of engaging scenes, developed with art, there was not a guilty example nor a vicious idea, which was not presented with all the horror that it deserved and must inspire; and where models of humanity and greatness of soul were constantly offered, with the ornamentation necessary to make them enchanting.

With respect to national festivals, the Olbians sought the means to make them powerfully attractive; because one cannot direct hearts when one cannot capture them. Unless one attends a very curious spectacle, one never takes pleasure in these activities except by playing a role. The theatre is enjoyable even though the spectators are purely passive; but it requires the prestige born of the united efforts of the poet, the actor and the designer to sustain the attention of the public; as soon as one of these magicians does his trade badly, the play becomes boring and fails. But it is difficult to offer a great many people, assembled for a national ceremony, an amusement as vivid as that which results from the ensemble of talents of many artists who bring into play all the resources of their industry and all sorts of seduction. The magistrate who orders public festivals has recourse only to involving the spectators themselves in the scene, to arrange things so that each one of them sees himself as personally interested in the effectiveness of the affair; otherwise he would be arranging not a festival, but a more or less tedious stage play.

Therefore the Olbians, believing that people who are exposed to formless parades which they cannot see well and speeches that they cannot hear will not have much of a taste for public festivals, try to capture their interest in a more effective way. They put into practice this principle: That you put into your celebrations not what you would like to see, but what others want to find (AA).

The young woman who, by virtue of the instincts of her sex and the tastes of her age, desires homage, wants to find herself noticed and admired at these celebrations; there she will have this pleasure. From the era of chivalry, women enjoyed the tournaments where their lovers appeared ornamented with their colours, and were crowned by their hands: women do not even now lack the opportunity to enjoy the same pleasure. In Olbie, each village has its own miniature tournament during the days of celebration. In different locations they established archery contests, or perhaps target practise, or even water games; not where one jumps into the river, but rather sailing or rowing races which favour skill, bodily strength and well-constructed boats. The most skilled receive their prizes from the hands of young girls who would always sigh at the end of these festivals.

Mothers revel in their children: it was they who led their sons to the races by the hand, and who then accompanied them to the stage to await the prize. The Olbians encourage maternal pride: motherly love adorns their institutions.

The grown man is ambitious for power and prizes. This tendency, when it is unbridled, makes tyrants; well directed, it can make good citizens. Military ranks and jobs working for the festival police, were given to men who had distinguished themselves; but, at the same time, they must possess the other required talents and must be blameless of any moral weakness; and the desire to win prizes of pure skill must be accompanied by projects conducive to morals and education.

But what gives a great character to these festivals is the distribution of honours and prizes by the Moral Guardians, to citizens who had earned them by their virtues. This tribunal extends its reach to the depths of the furthest provinces; sometimes at the most unexpected time, it happens that the most obscure individual would earn an award from the nation which would be awarded at the very next festival. National recognition seeks out citizens who have been useful to the public, after the example of the Romans who were so careful after the calamities that befell their Republic to pile evidence of their gratitude on foreigners, slaves and even animals who, during their troubles, rendered them some important service.

But it is not always, not even often, a brilliant action that earns these awards. It is more often perseverance in admirable conduct; after all, brilliant actions are rarely good for society. What benefit came to the Romans from the conquest of the Gauls, if it was not the tyranny of Caesar (BB)? Good morals, eminently useful when met with in high places, are even more useful to the State, and more than one may believe, in a private situation. Every admirable citizen not only does no harm to the public or his fellow citizens in all his many interactions with them, not only never speculates on actions contrary to the general interest, but surrounds himself only with admirable people; he chooses from among honest people, his son-in-law, his associate, his servants, his apprentices; he is, more than he imagines and without the government noticing, an active instrument of compensation for good conduct, of shame and deprivation for vice. And I am not here speaking of the good example he creates for his family and neighbours and in his community; of the good education he gives to his children – no, I do not hesitate to say: if the majority of a nation is made up of such men, that nation would be the most happy in the world; it would not be difficult to prove that it would also be the richest and most powerful.

Until now, I have considered happiness as compensation: it should also be seen as a means. It sweetens the morals that misfortune has made bitter. But joy is not happiness, and fireworks do not the least good for morality. True happiness is made up, not of diversions, but of a constant and sustained satisfaction. The Olbians were convinced that they work for morals by multiplying the satisfactions and gentle pleasures of life.

Their cities and villages are pleasing, their houses commodious, clean and of a simple elegance.[20] There are many fountains and public gardens. Communication between different provinces is easy; the people have become more sociable and their consciousness has expanded. One can promenade along paths: a large, high path with benches and shelters at various places along it makes the walker fit and content. The simple citizen sees the country as a mother, since it is so kind to him; and he will rest there awhile to ponder the general good since the State has taken so much care of his particular wellbeing.

But if the attention of society towards its members is always present before their eyes, they are also always made aware of their duties towards society.

The language of public monuments makes itself understood by all men because they address the heart and the imagination. Olbian monuments rarely recall purely political exercises, because political duties are abstract, founded more on reason than emotion and, in the end, because their observation necessarily follows from the observation of private and social duties which, like the strands that constitute the largest cable, form in their entirety the strongest link in the political body. The Olbians have only one Pantheon for great men and many for virtues. They do not refrain from raising a temple to Friendship, and placing over its gate a wooden sign carrying the words: To Friendship. When one enters, everything reminds the soul of the gentle pleasures of this delicious emotion and the duties that it imposes. The eyes linger on statues of Orestes and Pylade, of Henri and Sully, of Mantaigne and Laboétie. Engraved on their pedestals are the principal events of their lives or their most memorable words. Among the inscriptions that decorate the walls of the temple, are these:

Love so that you may be loved.

One true friend is a wonderful thing.[21]

Love is not made for corrupt hearts.[22]

---

20 That requires comfort, always comfort, of a standard that implies it is useless to work for morality before having worked in political economy: otherwise, there will only be excellent speeches and wonderful spectacles, after which people remain quite as vicious as before because they will not be less impoverished.

21 La Fontaine.

22 Voltaire.

The friendship of a great man is a gift of the gods.[23]

Adversity is the crucible where friends are formed.[24]

Let your friend see into the innermost folds of your heart, and rest assured that sentiments you fear to show him will be driven out.[25]

The friend that we need is not the one who flatters us.[26]

One should expect everything except the ingratitude of a friend.[27]

A hundred other temples were raised to celebrate other virtues. It is not only in the cities that monuments speak to the people; it is also in other much frequented places, on boulevards, along great streets. Rock and bronze recall above all praiseworthy actions, or perhaps useful ideas. Statues, tombs teach the people to what they must aspire, what should excite their regret, what deserves homage.[28] It is thus that Plato claimed that one could study morality by crossing Attica.

The maxims are always chosen from among the most useful and the most common. We have seen the way in which true notions of political economy are favourable to morality: so be it! notions of this type mix with all the others; the farmer, the lawyer, the manufacturer, by walking, by travelling, becomes enlightened with respect to his true interests; the following maxims, for example, resound continually from the simple and yet striking tower:

Heaven helps those who help themselves.[29]

One pays heavily in the evening for the foolishness of the morning.[30]

If you love life, do not waste a moment, because life is made of these.[31]

Laziness moves so slowly that Poverty catches him in an instant.

---

23 Voltaire.
24 Isocrates [436–338 BCE; Isocrates was an Athenian orator].
25 Saint-Lambert.
26 Plutarch.
27 Saint-Lambert.
28 These monuments do not have the same effect in museums, where they are only visited by the curious, nor in the palace, where the people never go; rather, when they are met with along the path of walkers and travellers, they are noticed and spoken of: each day they reveal ideas to the minds of many thousands of people; education is spread at the same time that morals benefit.
29 La Fontaine.
30 Bacon.
31 This maxim and the next are Franklin's.

Do you have something to do tomorrow? Do it today.

It costs more to feed a vice than to raise two children.

Don't use your money to buy forgiveness.

If you don't want to listen to reason, it will not fail to make itself felt.

Modelled on these, one encounters yet more precepts applicable to different professions, and even to different jobs in society; but it is sufficient, I think, that I have listed the ones you just read.

The fathers of the families follow, little by little, the example offered by public authority; and the example that, in the beginning, is followed a little, is that which is unfailingly imitated more over time. In their houses one may read maxims applicable to order inside the family, and children nourished on these maxims, which experience shows them to be valid, regulate their conduct on the basis of them and transmit them to their children. One is happy because one is wise: men and nations will not be happy otherwise.

SAY'S NOTES

Note A

I cannot imagine that there can be duties perfectly useless for other creatures or for ourselves. All virtue which does not have utility as its immediate object appears to me futile, ridiculous, similar to that accomplishment of Talapoin, which consists of standing on one foot for years on end, or to some other humiliation harmful to ourselves, useless to others and which even God must regard with pity.

Note B

It may be believed that it is superfluous to search for ways to make man faithful to those responsibilities which have for a goal his own wellbeing, since self-interest must naturally lead him to fulfil them. That would be true if man always knew his true interests; but he often sacrifices them, either to passions, to false and even ridiculous opinions, like those Indians who, to reach paradise, throw themselves under the wheels of the chariot of the grand Lama; or those pious coenobites who, to attain the same goal, spend their days fasting and lacerating themselves.

And in the end, the man who sacrifices a solid and durable good to a passing pleasure, is not better enlightened with respect to his real interests. Montesquieu said: 'When the Canadian savages want the fruits of a tree, they cut the tree at the base and pull it down; such is despotism.' Montesquieu could have said equally justly: such is vice.

Note C

I believed I would stray too far from my subject if I attacked the truth of such and such a religion; I must prove only that they rarely make human morals better. I will consider in what follows whether they do not have a more harmful than favourable influence on men. This does not address true believers, but those unbelieving people, perhaps more numerous, who are nevertheless persuaded that it is dangerous to open the eyes of common people.

That religions have not made human morals better is a truth of which history, unfortunately, offers many proofs. The times of the greatest devotion have always been the times of the greatest ferocity, of the most profound barbarism; the eras that each nation would have wished the power to erase from its archives. Pagans only abandoned human sacrifice because the enlightenment of philosophy had shaken, among the most important, the faith of their fathers. It was necessary to destroy the religion of the druids to abolish this type of horror. The most humane people of the Orient are the Chinese people; but the power there is in the hands of the emperor and his mandarins, who are all enlightened and philosophical men. The Muslim people, who are without comparison the most religious in the world are, whatever their adherents say, the most immoral. All the vices of Europe are found among them; they give themselves up to barbarous sensuality which makes them shiver and shake: their manner of waging war is inhumane; among these people, treaties have no guarantee except self-interest. A pasha betrays the sultan and the sultan ignores the pasha, as soon as they believe that they can do so with impunity. Money is everything among these people; virtue nothing.

There is more: religions do not eliminate those vices and crimes to which they appear most opposed. What sect had a kinder founder and more gentle principles than the Christian religion? It is the only one that proclaimed humility a virtue. Forgetting injuries and pardoning offences are among the first rank of duties. *If someone strikes your face*, said its author, *offer him the other cheek.* The followers of that religion were imbued with these maxims from infancy; they were threatened with eternal damnation if they did not put them into practice: but what sect offers more examples of intolerance and ferocity? Which has had clergy more arrogant in power and more intractable in vengeance? The time when that religion burned with the greatest brightness, that is, between Constantine and Louis XIV, was a more fertile period for crimes than any other, and the discovery of a new world served only to extend further human horrors and the barbarism of the disciples of sweet Jesus. 'The bones of five million men,' it is said in one of the best books of the century, 'are buried in those unfortunate soils where the Portuguese and the Spanish carried their greed, their superstition and their fury. They give evidence to the end of time against that doctrine of the political utility of religions which still finds apologists among us.'[32]

---

32 A Historical Sketch of the Progress of the Human Mind, by Condorcet.

I am not arguing that religions caused all of the evils that followed in their wake. The defects of reason and institutions, of which these are but the consequences, were undoubtedly the principal cause of that great deterioration of morals; the evidence shows rather that religion did nothing to hinder it.

Present benefits, or at least very near and obvious benefits, are the only ones that have an impact on the human mind; for the same reason, close and painful evils are the only one that man truly fears. The effect of the one and the other is like an explosion of cannon powder, which causes a violent noise when it is near and can hardly be heard at a great distance. It is for the same reason that time heals unhappiness, however violent it may have been.

This tendency of the human mind is perhaps that which makes the rewards promised and chastisements threatened by religions so ineffective. Examine carefully the motives weighing against love in the heart of that woman whose lover has demanded a rendezvous: the fear of scandal that would result among her acquaintances and parents; the fear of an illicit pregnancy and illegitimate child would plunge her into an abyss of regret; these are what dissuade her, more than the boiling lakes of hell, which certainly ought to inspire much more terror. If on certain occasions that terror of hellfire was exalted by particular circumstances, such as a beautiful sermon or an imposing and solemn ritual, the effect did not endure but was erased by degrees, and the world went on as before.

It is the same with rewards. I can hardly believe that the happiness of seeing God, face to face, ever gave birth to a beautiful deed.

But not only does it appear to me proven that religious opinions do not hinder evil; they have, on the habits of men, influences I believe to be very grievous.

It is generally believed today by people who make some use of their reason, that threatening children with the wolf or the devil is a poor way to make them wise. They know that such a practice peoples the imagination with phantoms, that it clouds their judgement, makes the soul timid, and by consequence incapable of great and generous emotions, and finally that because that type of argument is not susceptible to demonstration, its authority will diminish rather than grow leaving the mind deprived of more solid motives for good conduct. So why use for the education of men, a method recognised as poor for that of children?

In the second place, man only gives so much attention to the things that preoccupy him; if the number of his duties is increased, this necessarily diminishes the care that he may focus on the accomplishment of each one; and so one sees ridiculous practices taking the place of essential obligations. 'Our predecessors,' said Voltaire with characteristic wit, 'proved by three points and counterpoints, that the women who spread a little crimson on their cheeks are doomed to Eternal damnation; that Polieucte and Athalie are works of the devil; that a man who has two hundred écus worth of sea fish served at his table one day in Lent has ensured his salvation, and that a poor man who eats mutton, for two and a half sous, spends eternity with all the demons.'[33]

One senses that people who make the execution of such grave duties the object of their studies, cannot direct the mass of their affections towards their real duties, which moreover are put in second place by religious people, as worldly duties. Man is always given to indulgence towards himself; once he has accomplished those duties that he sees as indispensable he rests, satisfied with his efforts. A religious person tacitly reasons thus: *It is not possible for a creature to be perfect; those who complain of me have not done so much; it is easy enough to satisfy the world after one has accomplished the rest to one's satisfaction, etc.* He uses these reasons and others like them, and too often lives badly with men, believing himself in good enough favour with God.

In the ancient papal states, the same man who rushed forward in good faith to receive the benedictions of the Holy Father would, for thirty-six francs, undertake to slay your enemy.

With respect to the economy, religious practices absorb time and talents that could be employed productively. At present, it is well known how religious orders, which in their sloth consume without replacing, impoverish a state. The same difficulty surrounds all ministers of cults; it is only less obvious in

---

33 [If Say is quoting Voltaire directly (and he uses quotation marks), I cannot find the source. Voltaire was always saying things like that and it could be anywhere from a *conte* to the *Correspondance*. *Polyeucte* (Corneille 1642) is a tragedy, in which the hero is converted to Christianity and suffers martyrdom in the third century of the Common Era. The play is loosely based on what was known about the historical St. Polyeucte. *Athalie* is a biblical tragedy by Racine, written late in his career, based on the story of the very nasty queen of Judah known as Athalia. The point is that both plays deal with subjects closely connected with the Christian faith or the Bible, yet during the time of Corneille and Racine, and even Voltaire, the theatre was still condemned as a work of the devil by the Church and actors risked being excommunicated and refused Christian burial even if they performed in such apparently 'moral' plays. The Lenten fish and meat reference is sprinkled all through Voltaire's work. An example:

'Pourquoi dans les jours d'abstinence l'Église romaine regarde-t-elle comme un crime de manger des animaux terrestres, et comme une bonne oeuvre de se faire servir des soles et des saumons? Les riche papiste qui aura eu sur sa table pour cinq cents francs de poisson sera sauvé, et le pauvre, mourant de faim, qui aura mangé pour quatre sous de petit salé sera damné!'
(Voltaire Dictionnaire philsophique, 'Carême')

This is an interesting example in which Say uses quotation marks to present a paraphrase, as he does with Adam Smith. One can neither assume that what is in quotation marks is a faithful reproduction, nor that what is unacknowledged is Say's original work.]

those countries where they are less numerous. Days of rest which are not absolutely necessary to recoup physical and moral strength, produce an evil of the same type.[34] Those people who study public economy understand well the value of this argument.

Other obligations are even more harmful to the public, and are even directly contrary to the duties of the citizen. One very sad example of this sort of danger can be found in Flavius Josephus.

> 'During the siege of Jerusalem,' said this historian, 'Pompey had constructed a terrace from the height of which the Romans battered the temple with their war machines. If the Jews had not been hindered by their belief of not doing anything on the day of the Sabbath, not even those acts necessary to defend themselves, the Romans could not have constructed that terrace. As soon as Pompey realised that, he only had his soldiers work on the Sabbath...The Romans chose for the assault a day of fasts and prayers; after having taken the temple, they killed all those they found therein. The Jews did not stop their prayers and sacrifices, swayed neither by fear of death nor by the desire to care for their brothers whom the Romans had slain, so great was their respect for divine institutions!'[35]

Now there was a useful devotion! And but think of the naiveté of that good Jewish historian, who regarded this circumstance as so honourable for his nation and his religion that, in the fear that the truth of his story would not be believed, he invoked the witness of Tite-Live [Livy] and Strabon.

The same thing almost happened in Rome during the reign of Aurelius. The barbarians were at the gates of the city and the emperor at the head of the army held them in check, but he needed reinforcements: the Senate offered sacrifices. He wrote to encourage them to speed up: *'One would imagine,'* he said, *'that you were assembled in a Christian church rather than the Roman Pantheon.'*

Not a single religion locates the supreme virtue in the good that one does for others; this is nothing but a secondary idea in all; the essential point is the attachment to dogma, to faith, that is to the sect and its rites. They all say to you, DO GOOD, right; but above all be faithful to our beliefs: whoever does not believe is a reprobate, a libertine, a villain whom it is dangerous to trust.[36]

---

34 One sees, in Crevecoeur, that the people of Connecticut observe so scrupulously the day of rest, that they do not brew their beer on Saturday, for fear it will work on Sunday.

35 Josephe, liv. xiv, chap. 8.

36 The reason for this is simple: the principal concern of each sect is and must be to preserve itself; no individual, no body can ever place its survival in second place. One sees in Saint Cyprien that during his time (and it was a good time for the Christian church) the disciples of Christ were much more praised by the chiefs

When dogma confirms obviously absurd ideas, the absurdity does not take long to be noticed by the enlightened people first, and then by everyone else. Then, minds fashioned from infancy to regard belief and morality as the same thing believe that the latter is just as vain as the former, and the neglect that they feel for dogma causes them to neglect the moral ideas, sometimes very laudable, which accompany dogma. It is perhaps to this cause that we must attribute in part the excesses with which the population, in some of our cities, tarnished themselves at different times since the revolution; they had no other morality than that of the priests: the shock of political events must, sooner or later, overturn the priests; but this reversal would not have had to destroy the morality of the people, if they had had a true morality: that which is in the heart and in the habits.

Further, and this is a very remarkable thing, the holy books, in almost all religions, exhibit a revolting immorality. Plato, in his Republic, did not want to raise young people on the genealogy of the Greek gods contained in the holy books of the time. He thought that these books were full of examples of dissension between men, vengeance on the part of the gods, and in general, poor models offered by important authorities. He added that it is a notorious misfortune to accustom people early to find nothing extraordinary in the most atrocious actions. Is it not shameful for us that, in that Greek mythology which excited such vivid indignation in the soul of a disciple of Socrates, we can, nevertheless, find neither a patriarch who lent his wife for money like Abraham, nor incest as disgusting as that of Lot, nor stories as scandalous as those of the Levite Ephraim, Onan, Jahel, Judith, David, and a thousand others?

In the end, cruel experience has proven that superstition, or fanaticism which is nothing but superstition in action, is of all the passions the most damaging and the most fertile for acts of cruelty. In seeking the cause of that disastrous characteristic, one finds that all the passions except that one come from a desire or an appetite which might incite violence, but in which the violence is not continual. Once the object of the passion is obtained, or when the opportunity is past, humanity and conscience again take their places. Fanaticism alone is not subject to these pauses; it causes evil without remorse. The fanatic does not believe himself to be supporting his own cause in defending his opinion; he believes, to the contrary, that he denies himself and deserves the greatest praise while he commits the greatest sacrifices; like the delusions of the inquisitors who called their butcheries *acts of faith*! But what crime is more dangerous than that which is mistaken for a virtue!

---

of their sect for their faith and their attachment to dogma, than for the morality of their behaviour: heresy, apostasy attract all the thunder of the church; the violation of simple rules of morality earn only reprimands and exhortations. This system survived until the middle of the eighteenth century, when dogma began to be ignored in favour of morality; but even this negligence was a blow against religion.

It might be said that these evils are beginning to cease, that the morals of Europe no longer allow the furies of fanaticism. Eh! that tendency is owed to the philosophical mind which weakened the influence of religious opinion, even among those who still profess to believe. Ideas have become so liberal among the people who believe themselves to be the most orthodox, that a hundred years ago they would have passed for heretics if they had professed the same opinions. Their spirit of tolerance, their incredulity on some points that they have rejected as too ridiculous, would have passed then for a libertinage of spirit and a slackening leading straight to perdition.

Another conviction that results from the contemplation of past events, is that religions destroy a part of the happiness of man on earth, the only one which the political moralist can worry about. In the Christian religion, for example, the terrors of the soul, the futile duties, the many penances, the useless defences, the length of the prayers, the severity of the practices, alter the character.

> The evangelical spirit is offered from all sides,
> But penance to do, and torments deserved,

said Boileau. In those periods and countries that it dominated completely, man was sad, gloomy, dazed: the past offered him only regret, the present nothing but shackles and the future only fear. Compare Greek statues with those of the medieval period: the beauty of the art aside, you will in general notice the serenity of contentment, the tranquillity of the soul in the former; and in the others, you will always see the sombre melancholy of cruel people dominated by terror and troubled by their conscience.

If one cites examples which prove that religion has produced some incontestable good, it proves nothing but that it is a poor method that may succeed sometimes, but is nevertheless accompanied by the gravest dangers.

If one takes refuge in a few religious principles and abandons the others, such as divine intervention, the priests and the rest, one limits oneself to embracing a philosophic system such as that of Socrates, concerning the existence of God and the immortality of the soul, or that of Zenon, or even that of Epicurus; but even that is philosophy.

But even if the danger of superstition were graver, one must never be tempted to crush it by intolerance or persecution. First, because persecution is itself an evil and a frightful one, and beyond that it attacks the most obvious and inviolable of all rights, that of all men to think as they like. Further, because the method is directly opposed to the goal: obstinacy is one of the defects of man, and the persecutions of some emperors served brilliantly to establish Christianity.

In matters of opinion, only the arms of persuasion ought to be employed, and the rest left to time and the natural progress of the human mind.

Note D

I must here deal with an objection that will surely be made: 'According to you,' someone will say, 'the enticement of happiness is necessary to make men virtuous, and virtue procures happiness; therefore it carries with it its own encouragement; and therefore all institutions that employ happiness as a means to virtue are superfluous.'

I ask that an important distinction be considered. The happiness that virtue brings to a nation, when it is generally or almost generally practised, is a happiness composed of all the pure and tranquil joys that follow the exercise of goodwill, whether one is the agent or the object. The nearest happiness that I claim here as a *means* and not as an *end*, is the immediate and personal reward which one pursues in corrupt societies, although it certainly does not promise an end to present remorse, nor future regret, nor the evil fruits of intemperance, nor the harm caused by the hatred and lack of trust of others. To the extent that political societies take steps towards virtue, this happiness used as a *means* will change into the happiness which is the result of virtue, the only goal that really deserves the ambition of men, and the only goal capable of producing a constant contentment to the extent that our nature permits.

Note E

The most important revolutions are not political. They simply pass political power from the hands of a single man or a small number of men to the multitude, which is then obliged to return it to a small number or even a single man, especially in large countries. What is the result when no moral revolution follows a political revolution? Nothing, or almost nothing. Power changes hands, but the nation remains unchanged. Opinions, passions, ignorance and by consequence misfortune, persist; the same faults of the governors renew themselves, etc.

> Quid leges sine moribus
> Vanoe procifiunt? – Hor.

Note F

It is expedient to treat immediately an objection that many people will certainly make against the assertion that the establishment of a republican government favours purity of morals. They will say that experience itself provides evidence against that claim, and they will enjoy finding examples of immorality in the period of the birth of the French Republic. To argue against them, I will borrow the tools furnished me by an author who published a work on the matter that occupies me, citizen de T...[sic], whose work and initials reveal a profound thinker and excellent writer. Here is what he said on the subject:[37]

> 'Unfortunately, no one can deny that for many years in France, crimes have been more numerous, passions more exasperating, personal unhappiness more apparent; in a phrase, that social disorder is greater than before. The best citizens are those who are the most afflicted.'

> 'What is the cause of that sad fact? Unreflective people, and that is the great majority, will respond that the revolution has *demoralised* the French nation: and they believe that they have explained everything. But what do they mean? [...] Do they want to suggest that the change of government has made our morals more depraved, our sentiments more perverse? They forget that morals and the sentiments of men do not change much from one day to the next, nor even over a few years. It is certain, by contrast, that the present time is always the disciple of the past, and that we are governed today by the habits, the passions and the ideas contracted or acquired under the previous social order. If these are the causes of our actual evils, one must not hesitate to attribute them all to that ancien régime so foolishly yearned for...'

> '[Do they want to imply] that the principles on which the new social order rests are destructive to morality? That claim would be unsupportable: because what especially characterises the new system and distinguishes it from the past, is that it professes more respect for the natural and original rights of men than for the arrogations of the past; that it consults the interests of the many more than those of the few; that it esteems personal qualities more than the advantages of fate; that it places reason above the prejudices of habit, submits all opinions to its consideration and obeys reason more than authority and precedent. Surely no one could deny that the adoption of each of these ideas is a step towards justice. Even the most violent opponents of this system have never attacked it on these bases. Everyone, even while declaring it impractical, is convinced that it is a sublime theory. Therefore it is not its principles that are opposed to moral health; to the contrary.'

> 'Nevertheless, by what calamity has the sum of moral evil grown larger under the reign of truth than under that of error? *It is because internal and external trouble accompanied that great and sudden reform, which again increased the needs of the state, and by consequence the disorder of the*

---

37 [The elipses and insertions in square brackets in Say's quotation of Tracy indicate places where Say omits sentences or changes wording. The sole adjustment he marks in the text is the omission of a significant statement, which is indicated without square brackets.]

administration, and undermined repressive laws the moment that they were most necessary. With these two circumstances, moral practice deteriorated, just as its theory was perfected. [...]'

'We should add, for our consolation, that if moral evil has grown, it can only be momentary. Not being a consequence of our political institutions, being even contrary to their spirit, it cannot long persist. Either it will undermine those institutions, or the institutions will subjugate it. And since the institutions could emerge at all, they must have deep roots. Evil is always evil; but it is quite different when it is the effect of the established order rather than the difficulty that surrounds the establishment of that social order. It is, it seems to me, a difference not enough recognised, whether because no one wants to recognise it or because no one is able to recognise it.'

Note G

A question that appears to me worth examining carefully, is to know whether, among the methods of encouraging moderate wealth, it is useful to employ a geometric progression in the tax tables rather than an arithmetic progression.

It is said that a tax which imposes more heavily on revenue as revenue increases, tends to discourage industry, because the burden is greater the more successful the individual. It is also said that by following an always increasing progression, the tax must end by taking the entire revenue; this would be equivalent to expropriation.

It seems to me that these two problems result solely from certain types of geometric progressions, but that there are others from which they do not follow at all. There are some that increase always in proportion to increases in revenue, which never take the entire increase as tax revenue, but only a part of the increase, just as certain geometric curves approach a straight line without joining it. For example, for each increase in revenue, the share of the State may take only a tenth of the increase above the last contribution; industry would not be discouraged, because the industrious individual would always profit from nine-tenths of the increase produced by his industry.

Once this distinction is made, this seems the only equitable approach; because the needs of man do not increase in proportion to his fortune, the surplus increases progressively as wealth grows. And the tax must be in direct proportion to the surplus only; the necessary income, that is that portion without which one cannot live, must never be taxed; otherwise the tax would end in death.

To achieve the same goal, it has been suggested that one should exempt a revenue that is believed to be *necessary* to live, and tax the rest without progression. But, in a state of civilisation, it is impossible to establish the level of the necessary. The necessary merges by imperceptible degrees into the surplus; and it is precisely this gradation which is equitably addressed by a well-conceived progressive tax, that is, a tax which never absorbs more than a moderate portion of the increase of revenue.

It is also equitable because, in a state of civilisation, increases in revenue are more difficult to attain at lower revenues. According to a popular saying, *the first hundred écus are harder to earn than the last hundred thousand francs*; that is, once one has achieved a certain degree of fortune, the ease of earning is increased in the proportion of 333 to 1. I am far from wanting the progression of taxes to increase in that proportion which, if the saying is correct, would be required by equity.

Note H

'In China, there are properly only three classes of men: the lettered, from among whom are chosen the mandarins, the farmers and the artisans, among which are included merchants. It is only in Peking that one finds the highest degree of the lettered men, those who, in a public examination, show that they have acquired much knowledge of moral science and government, such that they were taught by the ancient Chinese authors, and with which the history of the country is intimately bound. The emperor distributes among these graduates all the civil jobs in the State'

Macartney, vol. III, pag. 184.

Note I

In Olbie, pastures and in general all rural property, are fenced by hedgerows. One would not suspect that this was favourable to morals. Nevertheless, one who takes the trouble to observe how the people that are employed in the country to lead the animals to pasture (and they are ordinarily children) learn the habit of idleness, and often retain it all their lives, is often happy when they are not infected by that of thievery or other vices! But when the pastures are enclosed the animals can be left without guardians, and there are fewer lost hours and abilities, and fewer bad habits found. No law, no rule is without influence on morals. Formerly, in Olbie, no one appeared to realise that.

Insofar as the actual political system demands a permanent army, even in peace time, corruption that stems from the idleness of military men in the garrison must be avoided. The best method would be to imitate the Romans, who used the spare time of their troops to construct useful roads which extended to the extremes of the empire, those bridges, amphitheatres, and porticoes which still excite our admiration. Hanibal used the same system: it is reported that, in order to give his troops pursuits destructive to idleness, he forced them to plant olive trees along the coasts of Africa.[38] I know that we have entrenched ideas to conquer, but there are ways to do this. One can

---

38 Aurel, Victor, in the *Life of Probus*.

flatter the pride of the military bodies, by attaching their names to the works that they execute; one can give them higher pay, and count the years dedicated to these efforts as years of war, etc.

Note K

When the influence of money becomes very great in a nation, and the effort to earn it is considered the highest of all, the politics of that nation become narrow, exclusive and even barbarous and perfidious. It is the influence of merchants which determined and directed most of the wars that England fought since she became eminently commercial. 'The violence and injustice of human leaders,' said Smith,[39] 'is an ancient evil against which I fear there may be no remedy; but the capricious ambition of kings and ministers has not been, during the last century and this, more fatal to the peace of Europe than the jealous impertinence of merchants.' Because, if a nation is entirely composed of shopkeepers, how will they raise themselves to those liberal ideas which, alone, can ameliorate human faults?

Imagine for a moment that each of the communes, small and large, that make up France, instead of trying to increase their communication and extending the relations between themselves, surrounded their territory by an enclosure and, in order to encourage the sales of their own manufactures, prohibited the introduction of products from the neighbouring commune, or at least imposed huge duties; would these communes become happier, richer and well supplied? Hardly, you might say. Well then! these lines of strong fortresses, these customs, these commissions that ornament the borders of States, are just as harmful to each and every one. Under the pretext of keeping the money inside, one shuts abundance outside. The day the barriers between nations fall, would destroy the most important cause of wars, and usher in an era of general prosperity. But how can one make this understood by those who do nothing but construct price-currents?

Note L

Rich or dignified men often have so little consideration for men of talent, that it borders on disdain. The reason for this, I believe, is that since rich and important men can exercise a great influence in short order, they regard men of talent as persons whose influence is weaker and more distant, and believe that they have little to fear or hope from them. It is that which engenders contempt.

The more mediocre are men made powerful by their jobs or wealth, the more likely they are to believe that the influence of talent is weak and distant; they must as a consequence disdain talent more than others.

---

39 *Wealth of Nations.*

By contrast, if they have talent themselves, they recognise its value and attract and encourage talent; and an infallible proof of personal merit in a powerful man is to see him surrounded by men of merit. I have searched long in history, and I have not found many examples that contradict this principle.

But one feels that it cannot be justly applied except by absolutely objective spectators; because, if it is true, the fools in power and the fools who surround them are too ready to believe themselves both geniuses, to distinguish the one from the other.

Note M

The great veneration that I have for Rousseau, the certainty I possess that his works will be among those which contribute the most to the future perfection of the human race, have never shut my eyes to that which I believe to be erroneous in his writings. His enthusiasts do him wrong, as they always do. By admiring everything in his works, they have discredited that which is beautiful, sublime and admirable; they have encouraged detractors.

I would have liked it better if he had not written his diatribe against human knowledge. The principles appear false to me, the conclusions forced, and the examples not at all conclusive. Here is one of the most striking examples:

> 'What can I say of that metropolis of the orient that, by its position, seemed as if it should have been the creature of the entire world, of that asylum for the sciences and the arts banished from the rest of Europe, more perhaps by wisdom than barbary? All the most shameful debauchery and corruption; treason, assassins and the blackest poisons; the crossroads of all the most atrocious crimes: this is what forms the substance of the history of Constantinople.'

This is very true. The history of the Eastern Empire is one of the most disgusting that one can read. But is it not more because the Romans transported there all of their vices and corruption, than because they brought it their arts? Why seek out an indirect and disputable cause when there is a direct and natural one?

The same excesses that soiled the reigns of the Tiberiuses and Neros, were repeated in the Greek empire, with a more hideous and vile character if it is possible. But if the sciences and the arts had been the cause of that corruption, it would have diminished at the same time that the sciences and the arts degenerated there; but far from that, it increased.

Rousseau says that it was perhaps more by wisdom than barbary that the arts were banished from the rest of Europe. That is, that it was by wisdom that Attila sacked Italy, and the Vandals pillaged wealthy Spain and that African coast ornamented by such flourishing cities; it was by wisdom that the barbarous Christians of the west fought the crusades, etc. etc.

Let us be fair: it is civil and political institutions that encourage the corruption of morals. The morals of the Romans became abominable when the lottery of arms put the wealth of the world into their hands and overthrew the republic. The morals of the empire of Constantine did not become less corrupt by the same means, and they took on a more vile and ferocious character as the government, without ceasing to be absolute, became weaker and the people more superstitious.

Another error. In this discourse, Rousseau continually confuses virtue with the love of liberty and the courage to defend it; and, by this measure, he finds the Chinese the most vicious of people.

Note N

In our cities, there are actually a large number of professions in which the workers earn in six days their expenses for ten. They may, therefore, in saving for themselves one day for rest, put aside the value of three days each décade [revolutionary week]. In cities, each day may be worth two francs: therefore a worker can, with this behaviour, put six francs aside each ten days in the savings bank. A man who, from the age of twenty, puts aside six francs every ten days until the age of fifty-five, would have by that age, through the effect of interest accumulated at five per cent, a capital of nearly twenty thousand francs; but for the worker to have confidence in a savings bank, it is necessary that he not fear the fiscal ideas of a changeable government, which may be capable, in the following year, of suppressing or perverting the establishment.

Note O

'A person who violates the laws of his country, while certainly very deserving of blame, may be incapable of trespassing against the laws of natural justice. He could have been an excellent citizen, if the laws had not made a crime of that which is not one in the eyes of nature. One sees, for example, few people taking care to avoid smuggled goods, if they can get away with it. To show scruples against buying merchandise introduced fraudulently, would be considered in certain regions, a ridiculous delicacy; although one thereby protects against the theft of public revenue, as well as the perjury that it ordinarily accompanies; the indulgence of the public encourages the smuggler; and while public force troubles him in his operation, he is ready to employ open resistance to protect that which he is accustomed to see as a trade.'

'Under a corrupt government, where the people's money is used to fatten rascals or revenue-officers, or dissipated in foolish enterprises, individuals are very unlikely to hesitate to defraud the tax collector; from that, tricks, false declarations, etc. etc.'[40]

---

40 Smith, *Wealth of Nations*, vol. III, page 378 of the English edition. [Smith 1976: 429–30; this is a paraphrase rather than a precise quote, particularly towards the end.]

The result of all this, is that without morality in legislation, without morality in the administration, one must never count on the morality of the people.

Note P

When the question arose, in Olbie, of suppressing the lotteries, an official of the treasury claimed that a million pieces of gold would be lost annually to the public treasury; someone replied: 'If the lotteries bring you one million, the portion of morals that the lotteries destroy are worth ten.'

I remember, on this subject, what happened during a war in this same country of Olbie. An excessive tribute was imposed on a conquered people; it was believed that this measure was necessitated by the costs of the army. A sage stepped forward and said: 'If you are just and moderate, you will receive a little less in the way of tribute, but you will need fewer soldiers to make yourself obeyed. Justice and moderation will be worth one thousand men, and will cost less to feed, without mentioning the good reputation that you will leave behind.'

In all other countries, they would have turned their backs on this speaker: in Olbie, he was made collector of tributes, and he conducted himself according to his principles; which, by the way, does not happen every day.

Note Q

At first, it was objected that in the distribution of positions, one must above all consider the talents required by the job which were more important than using the position as a reward; but they found all types of positions for all types of talents; and besides, gold and positions are not all the encouragements at the disposition of the leaders of a nation. The smallest recognition often has more value than the largest benefit.

Some would claim that true patriotism must be disinterested, and that one must sacrifice himself for his country without expecting anything; they would argue the above in very beautiful phrases which would be applauded by the multitude even if this were all they would applaud. But leaving such an assembly, the philosopher will propose to the one who applauded most vigorously, what can I say? to the orator who, with the fire of persuasion and damp eyes, demonstrated such generous sentiments; he will propose to them, I say, the least sacrifice for the public good – and he will not obtain it. Reconsidering these reflections, and knowing better the means of moving the spirit of men, he will no longer let the public good depend on empty discourse; he will realise the necessity of resting it on a less brilliant and more solid base.

Why is it that from the time of the Roman republic, the Questors given the delicate task of following the armies and collecting the spoils of the conquered, were distinguished by their probity? It is that Questure was the first step towards becoming a chief magistrate. Among a people where one can gain everything without being honest, most will always believe it is not worth the trouble to bother.

Note R

It is not in political societies that one can make good choices for public offices: intrigue and cleverness are there too much on display and people have too great a care to tint their speech to the colour of the moment; whereas in habitual meetings and simple relaxation one learns to understand the sentiments and virtues of the private man. It is there that one knows if he is honest in commerce, if he cares for his father, his spouse, his son; if he has natural good sense and acquired learning. And it is these qualities that one must know to make a good choice. Therefore, if one wants meetings of citizens to be useful for public matters, it is necessary to ensure that they are not political meetings.

Note S

If the example of the leaders of a nation strongly encourages the spread of moral habits, it must be attributed not only to our penchant towards imitation, but also to a kind of envy which does not want to do less than eminent people. One says to oneself: so and so has done this, why should not I? Eraste, who plays such a great role, allows himself this action; why should I restrain myself? He is great and disdainful: if I were to be affable, people would think me humble; if I were to be a good man, they would think me of no consequence.

But, by contrast, as long as powerful men are sociable and virtuous, people are embarrassed to be different; one says to oneself: so and so who is very much above me, is simple and good; if I were to be arrogant and have bad morals, I would become odious and ridiculous. Even if one does not really reason thus, the sentiments of decency and personal interest ensure that one behaves as if one did.

In Olbie, it used to be that when a fire raged, it was up to those who could take themselves away from their work to bring aid. Many times the First Magistrates worked the pumps, and gave temporary shelter and clothing to the victims; since then, it has become the task of those who would gain distinction by the same good deeds.

Note T

The First Magistrates complain of the difficulty of finding men worthy of their confidence. In effect, the circle of people they know, however extended it may be, is always strongly limited relative to the great number of positions they have to fill. But, from their side, do they place a great enough importance on the exercise of this aspect of their jobs? and, understood rightly, is this not the most important part of what they do? Most of the actions, and even the decisions that emanate from a man in an important position, come not from him, but from his delegates. However extensive may be his power, the eminent Magistrate has only one head, two arms, and twenty-four hours in his day; he makes the important decisions, but the greater number, those that make up most of the contacts between the administration and the people, he leaves to others, even when they are made in his name; and if one considers the sum of the intentions of others, which are supposed to be the expression of his own, one will find that that sum exceeds by very much the influence of his own will.

It results that, whatever his personal morality and instruction, the morality and instruction of those he employs have an even greater influence, not only on the public fortune but also on his own security and his own glory. He profits from all the good they do, and suffers from all the bad; and if one has sometimes seen important men, because of stupid jealousy or to reserve to themselves more honour and power, surrounded by mediocre men and restricting the authority of meritorious people whom they have not replaced, one has also seen that they were always the dupes of this calculation, and that they bore the burden of the faults of their subordinates and the hate and contempt that their subordinates inspired.

For all kinds of reasons, the choice of employees is the most important of the functions of the chiefs of a state; and when they dedicate the major part of their time and effort to do it well, to gather information and memoranda, to go to look for hidden merit or to determine those who do not justify their confidence, they are only doing a very reasonable thing.

Let one judge by this how little deserving of their functions are men who consider their jobs as nothing but the opportunity to oblige their acquaintances or to take revenge on their enemies, those who place into positions all their parents, their neighbours, the companions of their pleasures, and the protégés of their people!

Note U

Philosophers have said: How can a man glorify himself with braided dress, a woman with lace, with jewels? Is there a single person who can confuse these toys with personal merit, the sole characteristic by means of which one might reasonably be praiseworthy? These philosophers, with estimable intent, have not realised that these advantages were of the same type as all those by means of which men glorify themselves; they are proud of all that augments their personal influence. Sometimes that influence is composed of the strength and beauty of the body (although to a small degree in policed societies), talents, positions, fortune; and since luxuries are the marks of a great fortune, braids and diamonds are worn with pride, luxurious teams are displayed, and splendid meals given, just as one takes pride in one's positions and talents; the more the power and talents are recognised as solid, the less the need for these external signs: often they are even disdained; but the mediocre have great need for them. This is in the nature of things.

The task of the legislator–moralist is not, therefore, to repress ostentation which will never be destroyed; but to arrange things in such a manner that wealth, of which pomp is the sign, will have less power than it has had; then there would be less temptation to display it.

This enterprise is difficult but it is not impossible, especially since it is not necessary to totally destroy the power of money but only to weaken it and to honour unselfishness. *Malè se res habet, cùm quod virtute effici debet, id tentatur pecuniá.* Cic.

Note V

'One will no longer respect people in proportion to their consumption: what will happen? They will consume nothing above what is truly necessary to their utility or to their comfort. Luxury, attacked at its root which is opinion, will give way to a comfort more generally shared.'

I have tried, in this sentence, to give a good idea of the word *luxury*, which would not have excited so much discussion if it had been better understood. In limiting it, as I believe must be done, to things which are not truly necessary to utility and comfort in life, one will call luxuries only those objects which have no value but that of opinion. Therefore some silver tableware which is more commodious and deteriorates less easily than that of pewter or iron, would not be a luxury; but a food out of season, a dish which costs six hundred francs two months before you can buy it for six sous, would be a luxury, because one would not serve it at table, except by ostentation, when a cheaper dish could give as much pleasure.

In criticising luxury, I would not insist on the foolish pretension of returning man to a savage state, where there are no utensils but fingers and teeth; no clothes but the skins of animals; no housing but caves. I would allow the use of all that leads to the wellbeing of citizens in rich and industrious nations, without for all that making apologies for the pursuit of sensuality which is condemned in other reports. After having limited the number of things which are pure luxuries, I do not hesitate to pronounce that luxury is harmful to states, large or small, and that the country where there is the least, would be the richest and most happy.

One of the falsest principles of political economy, or perhaps an assertion that is not a principle except in the eyes of those who do not have the simplest notions of what political economy is, is that which argues that a man is useful to the state in proportion to what he consumes. *According to this ranking,* responds J. J. Rousseau to a similar assertion, *a Sybarite would be worth thirty Lacedemonians.*

All countries, by their agriculture and their commerce, create some or many products, but these are never without limits; one cannot consume in a country more than is consistent with its soil and its industry; if one finds persons there who consume an abundance of the products of the soil and industry, there must also be others who endure proportional deprivation. This is the reason that luxury and poverty always go together.

Suppose, for example, that among a people a certain number commit themselves to one profession and others to another, but always to a useful profession; this country would be abundantly provided with useful things. But now the desire to show off is introduced, and the fashion of ornamenting clothing with braid spreads among the richest inhabitants. What will happen? a portion of each class of workers turns to making braid: then instead of one hundred thousand workers who make good fabric or linen, there will not be more than eighty thousand who follow that profession. Nevertheless, comfortable people do not desire to have one shirt or dress less; it is therefore necessary that a portion of the inhabitants be dressed in rags and forgo a shirt. This consequence is unavoidable.[41]

You will even see that people whose resources give them the possibility of being well dressed, will forgo a shirt to wear braid. If I may be permitted, I will cite here a quotation of Franklin, where one will find his usual originality.

> 'Almost all the parts of our bodies,' said he in a letter to Benjamin Vaughan, 'oblige us some expense: our feet need shoes, our legs hose, etc. Our stomach demands food. Even though tremendously useful, our eyes, when we reach the age of reason, demand assistance in the form of a small expense for glasses; but it is not these eyes that make chaos of our finances; the eyes of others are the eyes that ruin us.'

And that which ruins the individual ruins the state.

And yet some say: the workers who are occupied in creating luxuries would not be employed in another manner. They are in error; there are never fewer unemployed hands than in regions where morals are simple and where, by consequence, few luxuries are produced. You say that luxury keeps the workers alive: yes; but how do they live? Have you visited the city in France where luxury creates the most work, Lyon? Have you seen, during the times when work is best, these miserable workers, gaunt, thin, ragged, crammed into buildings of eight stories, pell-mell with their wives, their children, their apprentices, their sick parents? If, instead of making gold brocade, they made good fabric, they could have had good clothing. One can say the same for the mason, the carpenter, the cultivator; it is only in a country where there is no luxury, or very little, that one sees everyone well dressed, well housed, well nourished, and content.

A government that wants to enrich and make a nation moral must therefore avoid exhibiting luxury objects to the admiration of the people, and above all, they must not let it be believed that ostentation is necessary to be a person of consequence. Such a government would not recognise, as signs of authority,

---

41 In this case, the number of people employed in the manufacture of fabric diminishes as the price of manual labour increases. The products are by consequence more expensive. The poorest citizens are deprived of a part of these products. Instead of renewing their clothing, they wear it threadbare, they repair it, and one never meets any longer the artisan dressed in good clothing. This is what follows from the situation imagined.

gilt, velvet, lace, embroidery; the Consuls in Rome were noticeable only by the colour of their robe and by the emblems that were carried in front of them; and the Tribunes, whose power was so respected that the emperors themselves were jealous, were for three centuries endowed with no exterior markings.

We must be careful and make haste to reform that which, in our habits, tends to pervert our morals. It is, for us, to live or to perish; because a republic without republican morals, cannot survive.

Note X

I know well all the opposition that a similar institution would encounter among us. It would have for enemies, first the men to whom good morals are unimportant, and then all the mean spirits. But it is not these people that a government which strongly desires the public good must consult. They have, for a long time, known how to impose shackles. 'Your ideas,' says Saint Lambert who knows them, 'will be treated as chimerical, and your schemes as romantic, by weak and narrow men who believe insane everything that they do not understand, and impossible all that they cannot do.' It is because people of this stripe are extremely numerous that one generally needs more constancy and courage than one would believe to work for good. There is no crime that will not find a defender; there is not one benefit that could not bring us to the point of a sword. Sapere audete.

Note Y

'No method is neglected, in China, to encourage good actions and hinder evil; and hope of praise and fear of blame are equally employed. There is a public register called the *Book of Merit*, in which are inscribed all the striking examples of estimable conduct; and among the titles of a man, are mentioned especially the number of times that his name was inserted in this book. On the other side, he who commits faults is disgraced; and it is not sufficient that he limits himself to carrying a reduced title, he must also add to his name the fact for which he was disgraced.'

Voyage of Macartney, vol. iv, page 158.

Macartney speaks elsewhere of a tribunal of censors, whose goal is the preservation of public and private morality. The Europeans call it the *Ceremonial Tribunal*, because in effect it regulates them according to this principle unanimously received among the people, that the exterior forms, followed scrupulously and without relenting, always master opinions and habits. *The spirit of conformity* is the distinctive character of the Chinese; and it is necessary often to propose their example to a nation among whom the best regulations fall into disuse by the end of three months, and where even laws are a matter of fashion.

Note Z

The festivals and theatre have another good effect, in that they separate the mind from superstition and fanaticism, which are propagated primarily when the general spirit is sombre and melancholic,[42] and when the people do not know what to do with their leisure. We have never seen times when diversions, and above all theatre, were common, characterised by the furies of fanaticism. The excesses of this type, so common in modern history, mount, for each nation, in those periods when it does not any longer have much theatre, and that which remains is vulgar and imperfect. The more accessible are innocent pleasures, the less people are disposed to hate and destroy one another.

Note AA

If one absolutely insists upon giving theatre to the people in large cities, one must at least attract their attention by striking and sensitive allegories, which are above all clear to everyone. If these allegories are to be well understood, printed programmes describing all the parts of the play, with signals designed in advance and well executed marking the different periods are required. If a public festival is to capture people as a spectacle, the subject must be in direct rapport with the emotions and condition of the onlookers.

It is also necessary that the secondary features reinforce the effect of these large representations; that one use, for example, order and competence in their execution; that the location be commodious, and that nothing contradicts or destroys the impressions of pleasure that are acquired there; that no one be exposed to hazardous accidents, and that the tranquil pedestrian can attend without fear of being trampled by the horses or run over by the wheels of carriages; that the policing be done by solid barriers rather than sentinels which always extinguish enthusiasm and derail pleasure. The spectators believe in their own dignity, seeing it respected by others.

For man to be virtuous, it is necessary that he respect himself and that he have a high opinion of the dignity of his being: one must, therefore, carefully avoid all that may tend to lower the people in their own eyes, in the fear that they will conduct themselves according to the way they are treated. An insolent soldier, dignitaries who affect airs of grandeur or who demand humiliating respect, hinder morality for that reason.

Note BB

This judicious and spiritual saying of a woman is well known: Give us the currency of great actions. But some privileged men are called to give, at the same time, great actions and *their money*. We must be even more grateful to

---

42 The founders of all the religions and their successors, have, for this reason, a horror of all sorts of spectacles.

them, because up until now the people have had the stupidity to attach less glory to useful acts than to striking acts; but the people are learning: they are preparing for an era when things will not continue thus. The names of the peacemaker, the creator of public prosperity, will no longer be surrounded by less glory than that of the conqueror; and everything indicates that it is left to France to distribute at the same time these two types of glory.

18 Jean-Baptiste Say reconsiders *Olbie*

If I were to rewrite my *Olbie*, I would base it on an entirely different foundation. I would demonstrate that the morality of nations depends on the degree of their instruction.

Instruction consists in forming correct ideas about the nature of things, of not seeing in anything other than that which is really there. One is proportionately better instructed as there are more things that one understands well.

On the positive knowledge of the nature of things, depends knowledge of our true interests, and on the knowledge of our true interests the perfection of the social arts. If one wants to consider the social arts without overcoming these hurdles, one plants a tree without roots, one creates a utopia, a dream more or less chimerical.

I would show that eras one could call enlightened were exceedingly few. Brilliant yet imperfect ideas occupied a small number of heads, a Socrates, a Xenophon, a Cicero, and yet how many of these ideas were not incomplete, how many of these people had correct ideas in all areas, in geography, in physics, in political economy? All the rest were plunged in the crassest ignorance or what is worse, in the most dangerous prejudice. We should be ashamed to call these eras of enlightenment, and it is not surprising that morality is encountered in these eras only rarely.

It may be said that the enlightenment itself, if it were as I suppose, never attained this goal because one never supposed it to be general, and that enlightened people desiring to be virtuous would always be the victims of the wicked who would not be restrained by scruples. It requires only a tyrant to hold the most enlightened nation in abjection and despair.

I do not think so. I will not give men the honour of believing that they will ever see a time when there will not be tyrants among them; but I see that their work becomes more difficult in proportion as nations become more enlightened, and note that it is not necessary for a nation to be composed of scholars to be what I call enlightened; it is not that; it is sufficient that each person have a correct idea of the things which concern him, that which is good is not absolute and, as a consequence, chimerical but gradual and one necessarily approaches closer to the good social life as one is more certain to have correct ideas concerning those things which concern one. It is a gift of nature to feel oneself on the right path from the first step one takes. Tyrants feel, without demonstration, an instinct to destroy enlightenment, confuse ideas, darken minds by false instruction and prejudice. The unhappy do us evil without doing themselves any good.

[This handwritten note is in the possession of Professor A. Heertje, who kindly sent me a copy. It is also reprinted in Say's *Oeuvres Diverses* (1848: 581–2), with very minor stylistic variations which do not affect the translation. Professor Heertje's bound volume, to which this note is appended, appears to have been made in 1826. Therefore, it seems likely that this letter was not written before that date.]

19 A.-L.-C. Destutt de Tracy: 'What are the methods of founding morality among a people?' by Cit. D...

The *Institut National* first proposed the solution to this important question as the subject of a prize, but it later constrained the competition in order to focus on public ceremonies. I shall not discuss what motives may have led that learned company to narrow, at this time, such a good project. Although I do not intend to treat this topic in anything but a very concise way, I will adopt it in its most extensive form, fearing that I may fool myself about the importance of one aspect of the problem if I consider it out of context. I write only to clarify my ideas, and I want them to be well coordinated.

Chapter I   The punishment of crimes

The first step in morality is, without a doubt, to prevent large crimes; and the most effective method is to punish them. What is important is not that the penalty be stringent, but that it be inevitable. The most useful principle of morality that one may inscribe in the heads of sensate beings, is that all crime is a certain cause of suffering for whoever commits it. If the social organisation attained perfection such that this maxim were a fact without exception, by that alone the greatest evils of humanity would be annihilated. The true support of society, the solid foundations of morality are therefore the henchmen and executors of laws. It is these who are given the responsibility of arresting the guilty, guarding them, establishing their crimes and pronouncing the sentence which is to be imposed upon them. I will permit myself a few reflections on each of these.

Arresting wrongdoers is a worthy function, because it is useful, but there is nothing wonderful about it. One ought not to devote oneself to it through enthusiasm; it must be a profitable trade, it is vulnerable to the most dangerous of horrors, that of hidden evil; it is necessary that the profession be solid, and that evil not be able to destroy it easily. It is difficult, it is perilous; it is necessary that one be rewarded for doing it well, and that the gendarme be compensated in proportion to his convictions. But this situation of being always occupied in harming men, even though guilty, and basing one's profit on their unhappiness, cannot help but destroy in the long run sensitivity and pity, these two precious emotions of man which are the source of all his good impulses, and which are, so to speak, the instinct of virtue. The morality of the gendarme is therefore more exposed to corruption than that of many other citizens; it is necessary that he be contained by the office of his superiors, and sustained by their esteem; they must be of long service in order to be trusted, and they must have the need to be recognised favourably; it is necessary, in the end, that this great body, the national gendarmerie, have a constant organisation, with an invariable order of promotion, and that it be in the hands of a single permanent chief, who derives his fate and glory from the perfection of the service.

These observations are common to any large system of administration; and I think that they must be considered inviolable rules any time that a strong fear of the abuse of power and a justified concern for public liberty does not force their abrogation. Then, it is certainly true that it is necessary to sacrifice some part of present welfare to future concerns. But it remains always true that a public service is never so well run when it is directed by a collection of men named for a short term, than when it depends on a single and permanent chief who makes of it his personal affair; and it is even more certain that in all public establishments the passage from one manner of being to another, even when it is an improvement, is always a moment of crisis when one tests all the evils of both regimes, and that if the uncertainty of individuals concerning their own fate is prolonged, it results in disorder that becomes irremediable, except perhaps by time; proof that if one wants to make things better, one will be more successful by going slowly.

With respect to the guards of the *houses of detention*, I have only one thing to say: it is that they must be vigilant so that their prisoners do not escape. I think that they should be part of the gendarmerie, and report to the same chief. To arrest and guard are two services of the same type. They should be regulated by the same principle; that is, that the greatest interest of society is that no criminal should escape or evade the law.

With respect to juries, these are without a doubt wonderful institutions in that they are composed of independent men who are indifferent to the accused. As a consequence, neither prejudice nor authority can push them to injustice; and the most important thing is without doubt that those charged with the punishment of crimes not commit them themselves in the exercise of their duty. But this is not all; it is also necessary that they desire to fulfil their function according to the general interest of society. But in times of trouble, carried away or dominated by a faction, they agitate often as members of a party; and in calm times, when an excess of scruples and commiseration verge on weakness, they frequently conduct themselves as sensitive individuals. In both cases, it is not rare that they lack the objectivity that is the first quality of public men. It is therefore more under the banner of liberty than under that of practice that I admire this institution. It is always certain that, like any other institution, in the first moments of their establishment they will have almost all the trouble of which they are susceptible, and almost none of the benefits for which they were proposed. This does not mean to argue that they ought to be destroyed, but that, in case of need, they ought to be maintained so that they need not be established again.

When there are jurors, criminal judges are much less important. Nevertheless I believe it useful that they be, insofar as possible, independent of both governors and tribunals. I would like them, therefore, to be well paid, named for a long term and itinerant. But the public prosecutors should not be too active. They must answer to the government, and be dismissable by them for simple negligence.

If we make the executors of the laws subject to the laws themselves, I will repeat that I do not demand that the penalties be severe, but that they be graduated and proportional not only to the enormity of the crime, but to the temptation to commit it.

It is for the procedure that the legislator should reserve all his severity. It must certainly allow the just defence of the accused; but it must above all not lose a single opportunity for conviction. And, in this respect, I must repeat a maxim which applies more or less to all that I am about to say, and which, I believe, has been oddly abused. It is this: *It is better to let escape a hundred criminals than to condemn a single innocent.* Certainly there is no more atrocious crime than that of oppressing knowingly an innocent with the apparatus of the justice system: and of all the most abominable instruments of punishment, and the most capable of committing a great many more, is the public executioner. In this sense, the maxim is very true, without the least restriction. Without a doubt, it is a horrible misfortune that an unjust condemnation be pronounced in error. All humanity must tremble; but one need not fear consequences for public and private morality. On the contrary, a recognised error prevents ten others, and is not pardoned except by irreproachable conduct. And if, by an exaggerated fear of this assuredly frightening but always rare calamity, because all interests are united in preventing it; if, I say, by that fear we are led to argue that procedures be so favourable to the accused, that many guilty people can save themselves because of the fear that an innocent may succumb, I say that in the name of humanity, one is suggesting the cruellest of principles. If you think a moment with me of all the crimes which are born of that hope of impunity, and of all the innocent victims of these crimes, you will see that humanity itself leads to a diametrically opposed conclusion.

One may write volumes on each of the subjects that I am about to write of; but I want only to indicate my views. If they are just, whoever puts some into practice will have contributed powerfully to founding moral health in his country. All is in this principle by which I began, that what one might do most effectively to achieve morality is to render as inevitable as possible the punishment of crimes. Now let us move on to less important subjects.

Chapter II   Of the repression of less serious offences

After the punishment of crimes, nothing is so interesting as the repression of misdemeanours of all sorts. This chapter, which can occupy but little space here, must occupy a great space in the head of the man of State. Unfortunately, he cannot punish directly all that is blameworthy; but he can with art dispose of things in a manner such that bad conduct becomes materially prejudicial to its author, not to mention the punishment by means of public opinion which can never be avoided if institutions have shaped that opinion well.

The goodness of the organisation of civil tribunals, the simplicity and the celerity of the procedure, the severity of measures against fraudulent traders, the charging of costs against false witnesses, the care to exclude from nominations to all useful positions with the government men with a poor reputation, contribute powerfully to the achievement of this goal. The attention to not employ men, insofar as possible, except in the province where they were born, and in the career to which they were first destined, is again an active way of ensuring that they will be always under the eyes of those who know them; they cannot but obtain the fruits of their past conduct. One cannot think enough about how dangerous are men uprooted from their homes.

I feel that here would be the place to speak of the police; this power is the most difficult of all to organise because of all it is the most likely to become impotent or oppressive. But since the object of my work is to determine which impressions are the most influential on men, rather than developing the means of producing those impressions, I cannot present more than a few thoughts. I will limit myself therefore to say of the police that the rules that they enforce ought never be petty, but that the friends of liberty must guard themselves from taking umbrage too easily against their activity. Providing that they be required to bring promptly to the tribunals those whom they arrest, they cannot be dangerous, especially if the supreme authorities of the State are well constituted. With these safeguards, one can without inconvenience leave them much latitude to arrest. Faithful to my principles, I would prefer a little inconvenience to paralysis; because the second basis of morality is certainly to make as difficult as possible the success of misdemeanours.

Chapter III   Occasions of harm to others

If no crime can remain unpunished, and no misdemeanour may succeed, one can hardly conceive of that which remains to do to make men good, and encourage the happiness of a society. But unfortunately all blameworthy actions are not punishable by the law, and among those which may be expressly condemned, a large number always escape their just desserts. The laws of society are the work of men. They cannot help but express the weakness and imperfection of their authors. They cannot have, like those of nature, that certainty and continuity of action, that plenitude of power which always ensures that we cannot escape their empire, and that they will reach us in the least details of our existence. The effect of human laws can never be so certain, so complete as that of the laws of mechanics; because these are the expression of necessity itself, and the first are only convention.

This observation has not escaped those who have meditated on the happiness of their fellows. Strongly aware of the insufficiency of the means of repression, they tried to eliminate among men the possibility of reciprocal harm. They tried to pull up the root of all moral evil. They believed that they found it in property. In effect, they said, what injustice would be possible if nothing belonged to individuals? And all the old legislators or philosophers, were forced to found society on the absolute community of all goods; or, if they did not try to execute it, they believed that in theory it was the perfect society, and many moderns have imitated them in that error. They did not realise that for such a community to have its full effect, it was necessary that each man should totally abnegate his own person and join entirely and without restriction the common mass; because if he preserves only the property of his thought and his hands, it follows that he has that of the work of his hands; and by a necessary consequence, that the game he shoots, that the tool that he makes, that the harvest he seeds, in a word all the products of his work cannot belong to anyone but him. In the end, when man can trample all the laws of nature, even to renounce all their immediate consequences, he will not be more at peace with his fellow man; because all the individual interests will be born again when it comes time to share the pains and joys of the common mass: and they will not be less opposed in this sharing than they were in the direct and individual possession of goods that we know. Rousseau at least was more consistent than the ancients. When he announced that 'yours' and 'mine' were the cause of all crimes, he decided without hesitating that society was the source of all vice; and he found perfection in a state of isolation, of which, in reality, we cannot even conceive the possibility. But in the end, one cannot deny that there is no moral evil where there are no moral relations.

All the paradoxes that troubled so many heads and made villains of virtue, reduce to this insignificant truth. Instead of all this, it would have been better to say: Any time when two sentient beings exist, there exist two distinct interests which may become opposed. Let us consider how to conciliate and contain them. The idea of 'yours' and 'mine' derives inevitably from that of 'you' and 'I'; we cannot destroy that. Let us make it so that 'you' and 'I' are neither oppressive nor oppressed. Let us not hope for better. For a real and peaceful community to be possible, it is necessary that a man may enjoy and suffer through the organs of another as if they were his own. Then he will truly love his fellow man as himself, and moral evil will at last be banished from the earth.

That is a degree of perfection to which it is impossible for us to aspire. The legislator who wants us to love our neighbour precisely as ourselves, and he who wants us to live in total isolation, prescribe for us two things equally impossible, giving to our morality two foundations equally false. The nature of men is such that they cannot come together without having distinct and opposing interests, and yet they are forced to deal with one another to help themselves, and even to survive. What can they do? and, in effect, what do they do? They prescribe common rules to prevent each other from using those too frequent opportunities that they have to harm one another. These rules are the laws of which we have spoken, those which punish crimes and repress misdemeanours. They are the true support of morality. They cannot destroy occasions of evil, but they limit their pernicious effects. This is the effect of good laws.

But the misfortune is that in all our societies, begun before knowing the true interests of men, we have a crowd of laws which, far from diminishing the effects of harm to society and its members, create new opportunities.

All useless laws, for example, do not remedy a single evil, and have created more, by furnishing a new opportunity to ignore the respect due public authority.

All impractical laws are of the same type.

All those which create in classes of people interests opposed to those of other classes, giving citizens the opportunity to hate and attack one another.

All laws which prohibit things innocent in themselves, cause new mischief. They make of those who contravene them a new class of criminal; and of those who watch over them, another troop of beings living off the misfortune of their fellows; two great evils which did not exist without these laws.

All negligence in administration, all disorder in the finances of the State, open the door to fraudulent markets and perfidious combinations which are really new ways to harm the public.

All institutions that propagate or favour an error, a prejudice, a superstition, give arms to men to wound others.

All laws that want to reverse by violence the eternal nature of things, like that which tries to substitute paper for gold, work an abundant source of new crimes.

The obscurity alone of laws, their changeability, their lack of uniformity throughout the territory of the same society, furnish men with the means to trick one another.

By contrast, all decisions tending to found all interests in the general interest, to draw all opinions towards the reason that is their common centre, to allow all irrelevant things to take their natural course, to place again all citizens under the direction of nature inasmuch as it is innocent, to give them again full exercise of the individual liberty that is not harmful; and from another side, all that which encourages simplicity, clarity, regularity and constancy in the action of government, all these, I say, are effective means to diminish the number of occasions of harm. One might say that a good constitution is only a collection of measures well combined, in such a way that those responsible for repressing evil do not have the opportunity to commit it; and that is all it can do for the good of the people.

There is therefore almost no administrative or legislative act which has an insignificant moral influence if only on account of increasing or diminishing the opportunities for mischief. But it must not be forgotten that the perfection which men may attain in this respect consists in not creating a single new occasion to harm one another, and that all their social art cannot annihilate one of those unfortunate opportunities for crime which are inherent in their nature, and for that reason indestructible. That is what makes me say again that the most powerful of all the moral tools, after which the others are almost negligible, are repressive laws and their perfect and complete execution.

Chapter IV   On the disposition to harm society and its members, or vicious inclinations

Since it is a chimerical project to take from men all opportunities to harm one another, there is no other method to prevent harm than to take away the desire: and since the action of repressive laws cannot be complete enough, nor their execution infallible enough, to immediately annihilate the desire to commit a harmful action each time that it emerges in the mind of a man, it is therefore necessary to combat moral evil in a nation through recourse to all indirect means of fighting the inclinations of the members of a society. These are so many auxiliary methods of which each is very weak compared with those of which we have spoken until now, but which taken together have nevertheless a great power, and become an important supplement to the limitations of more powerful means.

It is here that our subject becomes immense, because there is nothing in the world which does not influence to a greater or lesser extent the penchants of men. Nevertheless if, as has been demonstrated, all the acts of their will are only the consequences of the acts of their judgement, it follows that to direct the one nothing is required but to direct the other, and that the sole manner of making one want to do a thing is to make one prefer it. Thus, all these diverse means of working good or evil on the inclinations of men reduce in the end to indoctrinating them well or badly. This vast system of encyclopaedic education is naturally divided into two very distinct parts, the education of men and that of children. Let us first consider the former, of which the latter will never be but a consequence.

§. I Of the moral education of men

Since we cannot enjoy and suffer except as a result of our faculties such as they are, since it is outside our power to make of ourselves other than that which we are, since we can know nothing of changing that which constitutes our nature and that of all the beings who surround us, since every time that we neglect this major force, we know nothing but impotence and defeat, it follows that our greatest interest is to study the laws of this invincible power, to know that which *is*, and that the *truth* is the sole path to *wellbeing*. But since all is bound together, all is enchained by an infinite multitude of relations, since not a single truth is isolated and foreign to the others, we must conclude that not a single idea is irrelevant to our happiness or really useless, and that all errors are harmful.

It is a very old and very absurd belief that moral principles are fixed in our minds, and that they are the same in all; and, following this dream, to imagine I don't know what origin more celestial than all the other ideas that exist in our understanding. I am always stunned that Voltaire who introduced us to Locke and made us appreciate him, Voltaire who fought and vanquished so many metaphysical prejudices, has continually proclaimed and propagated that idea. Religion, he says in twenty places, is a human creation; and also that it varies between times and places; but morality is entirely divine; it is imprinted in us by the hand of the Supreme Being: that is why moral principles are the same for all men. And the proof that he gives for this false assertion, is that everywhere murder and theft have been placed in the ranks of crimes, that everywhere violence and swindling are condemned. I would be as satisfied if it were said that physics is a divine creation and that men have never argued about its principles; because all agree that fire is hot, that the sun is bright, and that water is liquid.

Without doubt two men could not live together without feeling that if one of them killed or wounded the other, he would destroy or disrupt their society; and that if after having come to understand and agree to not harm one another they break their promises, all security would vanish, all happiness would be destroyed: just as they could not survive without perceiving that they would burn in fire and get wet in water. In all areas there are truths so striking that no one could have neglected them. But what does this prove? is there the least difference in their most important consequences, just because their links have become so subtle as to be unnoticed by all minds? and has morality been more exempt from this difficulty than the other sciences? That could not be sustained. Assuredly the error of morality which consists of thinking that all our vices come from the right of property, or that if the soul dies with the body we have no interest in being honest people, is absolutely of the same type as the error of physics which consists of believing that the earth is fixed in space, or that the air weighs nothing. It is one part and the other of not understanding the cause of observed events, and not following the chain of phenomena.

Let us therefore banish that old prejudice which is nothing but an offshoot of that which supposes all our ideas innate, that is that our perceptions exist before we perceive them, and recognise that morality is a science that we build like all the others out of our experiences and our reflections. Its first and simplest notions are evident by themselves. Everyone recognises them. But those of a more elevated order do not strike all minds equally and, as they become more complicated, extended and connected, they surpass the grasp of a greater number of men. You cannot make a savage better understand the sensitivity of our moral sentiments, or the ties of our social duties, than the most learned theories of physics: and many so-called civilised men are quite as incapable of the one as the other. I will go further. Morality being nothing but the knowledge of the effects of our inclinations and of our sentiments on our happiness, it is nothing but an application of the science of the generation of those sentiments and of the ideas derived from them. Its progress therefore cannot precede that of metaphysics: and that, as reason and experience prove,[1] is always subordinated to the state of physics of which it is only a part. It follows therefore that of all the sciences morality is always the last to be perfected, always the least advanced, always the one in which opinions must be most divided. As well, if we examine these matters carefully, our moral principles are so far from being uniform that there are as many manners of seeing and feeling as there are individuals; that it is this diversity that constitutes that of characters; and that without our noticing it, each man has his own system of morality, or better a confused heap of ideas without order which hardly deserves the name of system, but which takes its place for him.

According to this explanation, it would seem that all that could be done to render these opinions more similar and more just, to found a more certain and healthy morality, reduces to expanding and perfecting as far as possible, direct teaching. Nevertheless I am far from supporting that conclusion. I will observe:

1   That in the total mass of a people, very few men have the time and will to follow a long course of instruction.
2   There are even fewer who have the capacity to understand and retain a vast system of connected ideas.
3   Happily, in society there is hardly anyone but the legislator who is obliged to understand all parts of morality in such a systematic and rigorous way; all the other citizens need know only a few principal results of major importance, a little like artisans who are content to pursue their art with a few proven rules, and ignore most opportunities to learn more of the advanced theories on which it is based.
4   I will add that of all the truths which we know, those which we know least well are those which were taught to us directly; but those which we have deduced ourselves from observing our surroundings, those of which we are reminded daily by continual experience, it is these that

---

1   The reason for that dependence is not immediately apparent. It is not necessary to have a great knowledge of physics to observe well the manner in which our ideas are formed, and even the most admirable discoveries in physics are yet very inadequate to unveil the causes of the generation of ideas. It seems therefore that these two sciences being separated by impenetrable shades, are independent from one another. Nevertheless since the human mind is always impatient to connect its ideas, as Smith observed, its explanations are bolder the more it lacks facts capable of contradicting them. [I]t follows that a mania of hypotheses dominated physics in times of ignorance, and subjugates even more metaphysics since it is even less well understood. From that are born all the gratuitous suppositions of the spiritualists and all the dreams of platonic philosophy which still muddles many heads and transports them beyond the limits of the known to the very limits of the possible. And these fantasies disappear gradually as progress in physics augments the mass of what is known, giving us the courage to consent to ignore what is beyond and discouraging us from trying to guess.

we truly comprehend, which inform all our plans and which influence all our actions.[2]

Finally, it must not be forgotten that man has only three types of needs to satisfy: his physical needs, the need to regard himself well thought of by his fellows, and that of respecting his own being, of liking himself, and being content with himself. He has only three things to avoid to be happy: punishment, blame and remorse. He has therefore only three motives to conform his actions to moral precepts as he understands them, that is to conduct himself in the most virtuous manner which is the one most useful to his fellows. But, of these three motives the last is the only one that direct teaching can support and fortify. The first two, which are incomparably more powerful on almost all men, may be either favoured or annulled or even actively reversed by all the social institutions, insofar as they are good, imperfect or evil. One can see, therefore that even the best direct instruction cannot produce any other effect than to force into a small number of heads abstract truths of moral health, and that by consequence, far from being the unique or principal support of morality, its utility is limited to accelerating the success of investigations of this type and perfecting the theory of that science, but it cannot expand and propagate morality in practice. The teaching given to men may form in a country a few more enlightened speculative moralists; but this will never quickly renew the virtue of the largest part of the nation.

Legislators and governors, these are the true teachers of the mass of the human species, the only ones whose lessons will be effective. Moral instruction is above all, it cannot be too often repeated, entirely within the actions of legislation and administration. We have already seen how great is their power to augment or diminish the number of opportunities that men have to harm one another, and to punish and repress reprehensible actions; let us show by a few examples that they have at least as much power to choke the seeds of vicious inclinations.[3]

A moralist could easily demonstrate to his listeners or readers, that if they make vile, pecuniary interest the basis of their conduct within their family, they will deprive themselves of an interior happiness that would procure for them a thousand times more contentment than the wealth that they strive for. The legislator who establishes the equality of inheritances and the impossibility of contesting the will would abolish with one stroke of the pen the genesis of all sentiments of rivalry between relatives, and protect the attentions of love from any suspicion of being self-seeking.

---

2 This is what was said by an intelligent woman, *reason enlightens, but does not drive*; add when your decisions are not made on the basis of habits.

3 One ought not to be surprised to find reference here to institutions already mentioned in preceding chapters; repressing crime, minimising the opportunity to commit crimes, and fighting vicious inclinations, are effects which are often confused. It is often the same effect considered from three different aspects.

It could easily be proven that a man, to be happy, must try to have a companion who suits him and children who resemble him: but the law of divorce alone would destroy three-quarters of the marriages of convenience, maintain the union of the others by the possibility of rupture, and improve all educations by the good intelligence of parents.

An incompetent professor will repeat everyday that one should decide only on the basis of reason, that reason is the sole guide of man, that it alone is sufficient to make him understand that he has a true interest in being just; he will gain little. The legislator will stop paying priests, and stop permitting them to meddle in civil actions and teaching: at the end of ten years, everyone will think like the professor, without him having said a word.

Another will strive to make people see that virtues and talents are the sole precious qualities. After the law recognises or forbids the equality of ranks, the general opinion will be for or against him.

In vain will he show that success in the sciences is the most meritorious method of serving one's country, if it is apparent that a cunning scoundrel acquires in one year more recognition and credit than a great man by long work.

It is very easy to demonstrate that a man who earns a comfortable subsistence by honest industry which is useful to his country will taste more internal satisfaction than he who lives by shameful trickery or languishes in idleness. Nevertheless if a thousand paths are open to enrich oneself by extortion and fraud, or receiving from the state large benefits without having earned them, all will take them; whereas if all methods of too rapid enrichment are eliminated by an administration economical with the goods of the state, by a great security and an ease of lending which lowers the price of money, by a great freedom of exercising all types of industry, a freedom I understand to include exporting and importing, which diminishes profits by competition; if finally the prompt dispersion of acquired fortunes is favoured by the equality of inheritances and the impossibility of contesting, you will see soon enough everyone committing himself to useful work and undertaking the morals of an active life and a modest existence.

You may preach beautifully of loyalty and love and the respect for innocence; the law has only to encourage denunciations and permit confiscation and you will see betrayals and unjust condemnation multiply.

The multiplicity of seizures will make more administrators become knaves, and more knaves become administrators, than all the lessons in the world could prevent.

Too many sales and purchases in too short a time by public functionaries is sufficient to transform three-quarters of them into speculators on bribes and in the violation of their duties, despite all the philosophical and religious sermons, and, what is even stronger, despite all the surveillance of the law itself. As for that of public opinion, the great number of the guilty will render it soon enough ineffective.

It is useless to multiply these citations. I have accumulated such a great number, much less to prove a truth so obvious than to give examples of dispositions that I regard as having the most influence on the morality of men.

Founded on these reflections and on all those that they suggest, if I were called to respond to this question: What are the means of giving to grown men a good moral education? I would say without hesitating and with a profound feeling of absolute certainty:

> First and before everything else, *the complete, rapid and inevitable execution of repressive laws*.

Without this, nothing can stem the flow of vice.

I would then immediately add another as indispensable: *An exact balance between the receipts and the expenses of the state*.

As long as this does not exist, no order is possible in society. A thousand shameful paths lead rapidly to fortune. The honest professions cannot sustain this unequal struggle. Everyone is discontent with his position. All men are displaced. All ties are confused. The mass of the nation is impoverished and vexed and by consequence brutalised and degraded. Even the expenditure that one can make for his good is one more evil, because it augments ruin. And to heighten the desolation, the law often authorises and protects the things that probity condemns. If I had not considered anything but the filiation of evils, I would have placed this article ahead of that of repressive laws; because it is the disorder of finances that engenders the impotence of justice.

After these two capital points, of an importance to which no other is comparable, I will demand,

> 1 the proclamation of equality, the destruction of all privileged groups, of all hereditary power, and the exclusion of priests from all salary and all public functions, including that of teaching morality.

This is the only method of creating good national judgement; and good sense creates virtue. The uniformity of laws, customs, administration, habits, weights and measures would be one beneficial and necessary consequence of these dispositions.

> 2 Immediately after comes divorce, the equality of inheritances and the almost complete prohibition of the freedom to contest.

These are the eternal bases of domestic virtues, of the peace within families and of the good education of children: and what is more, they favour the dispersion of accumulated wealth, and destroy many methods of acquiring it quickly without praiseworthy industry. This consideration is not to be disdained.

3 I ask again the entire and absolute freedom to exercise all types of industry, that of interior and exterior commerce without interference or restriction, and that of lending at interest with easy terms and guarantees which can be given by a good legislation on mortgages.

These dispositions are not only precious as a complement to individual liberty, and as homage to the natural rights of man: they also have the effect of augmenting comforts and joys, of turning all minds towards honest industry, and of limiting excessive profit through competition. They inhibit, as far as possible, disorderly and sudden fortunes. I will add here the wish that the State never augment the interest on money and the number of idle rentiers by borrowing; but that is a necessary consequence of good financial management without which none of this is possible.

This small number of desires accomplished, crime is punished, reason invigorated, domestic happiness assured, equality maintained as far as it is possible and useful, economy rendered necessary and work honourable. I can hardly imagine what more one might desire to make men virtuous; and I have not yet said a word about public instruction itself.

The greatest claim for public instruction is that it is necessary to bring about so many good things. Nevertheless, after having indicated so hastily the methods of great effectiveness, I am a little ashamed to pause at the weak and distant utility that the morality of grown men may gain from direct lessons given in schools and public festivals. It seems to me that this neglects the artillery of an army to focus on its music. It is good nevertheless to speak of these establishments, if only to show, whatever the degree of importance attached to them, that their success and even their existence, is entirely subordinated to the institutions which I have traced.

First, when the finances of a State are disordered, when necessaries are lacking, when public promises are not fulfilled, I know of nothing useful or honest to do, as soon as these cost an *écu*. Next, as everyone knows, it is not the lessons given but those received which are valuable. When you would be lavish with teachers, preachers, lesson books, and moral catechisms, would you create the inclination? would you create the need? would you create the interest to listen to the one and study the other? is it not only in the circumstances of which I have spoken that the citizens can make use of these dispositions, without which all direct instruction is at best useless?

Imagine a nation agitated by the liveliest passions, pummelled by the most violent movements, where greedy men are without reins, where almost everyone is in difficulty, where fortunes are won or lost in a day, where no existence is assured, no reputation is intact, and where people do not live where they were born; and gain some idea, if you can, of the profound indifference that will greet your schools and your festivals, and of their complete uselessness.

Imagine, by contrast, a people in the circumstances that I have described above, who have been rendered laborious, modest, sensible, happy, comfortable, do you doubt that the need of instruction and common pleasures would be long to emerge? Public festivals will be established. They will desire schools. Esteemed individuals will open them; they will run them, pay for them, and profit from them. An unstressed public treasury will supplement in part the fees, either for the poorest cantons, or for the most expensive types of instruction. Anywhere the government is required to pay all the expenses, it is a certain proof that there is not enough financial comfort to profit from even free lessons. This would be lost expenditure, and the most effective help that the governors could give to the governed, is always the money that they do not take from them.

Nevertheless, if the laws make the citizens, it is the legislators who make the laws: and I have said that, to make good laws, it is necessary that they understand a methodical theory of domestic and social morality. It is therefore necessary to ensure that they have the means of acquiring that theory, of learning it in depth, and of eliminating the errors which obscure it and the prejudices which hide it. But that is not yet enough. I must not forget that I have also said, on the basis of reason and experience, that the progress of moral science can never precede and follows only distantly[4] that of the physical sciences and mathematics, and of their applications to the arts which extend from them. The art of navigation is perhaps that (after printing) which has contributed the most to the advancement of metaphysics, by making us familiar with people in all the different stages of the human mind. It is therefore necessary for the idea of the good institutions that I desire to originate in the head of a few men, that they have the opportunity and the methods of studying all aspects of human knowledge, and to extend its limits. Happily it is not difficult for the State to provide them with this valuable help. It would suffice for a few schools to enlighten the different public services, and a small number of others to perfect the learned theories and to form masters; and to allocate a small sum annually to encourage those who distinguish themselves, to compensate superior men, to have a few useful or curious books printed; to give machines and instruments, and to support experiments. These expenditures would be modest if they were made in recognition of merit, and would be very fruitful as soon as there are a few men capable of making them useful, and others disposed to profit from them.

That is all I have to say about the moral education of men. Let us move on to that of children.

§. II Of the moral education of children

This is already accomplished if their parents have good habits, and are, so to speak, moulded by wise institutions. It is impossible if society is riddled with

---

4 Is there need for more proof? There is almost no one who has not felt the necessity of a polytechnical school for physical sciences and mathematics. It is difficult to find a few thinkers who realise that it would be still more urgent to have a similar institution for moral and political sciences.

prejudice, vice and disorder. I appeal to the experience of all. Are the sentiments and inclinations of one's childhood ever formed on the basis of what one has heard in classes, in sermons, in public exhortations? Is it not rather more often on that which surrounds one, on that which one has seen, felt, experienced in all those instants when no one is trying to indoctrinate one? If the fathers are imbued with bad principles, either the teachers share them, which is most likely, and preach them with a new strength: or they fight against them and therefore will not be either heard, nor believed, nor followed; they will be completely useless. I have therefore had reason to argue that the moral education of children can never be other than the consequence of that of men. And whatever it is, it will soon enough be reformed or destroyed by the circumstances which surround them and the institutions which weigh upon them at the age when they take their places in society. Nevertheless one can certainly pervert by a thousand stupidities the natural good sense of a child; but it is physically impossible to give a single true principle of conduct other than habit to one who has not yet experienced a single passion nor a single event.

Independently of these considerations which are unique to the moral instruction of children, all the reflections which I have made on the education of men apply to the instruction of children. Do you wish to augment their knowledge? It is not only a profusion of lessons that one must offer them, but give to their parents the disposition, the methods and the interest to make use of them. This is true, above all of the least comfortable classes, that is those which compose nine-tenths of society. The least reduction of taxes will augment more the number of men knowing how to read and write, than a legion of schoolmasters. A degree more comfort among farmers will increase to a greater extent the products of the earth and national good sense, than all the societies of agriculture and all the professors of logic in Europe could do. It is not that I do not value all the prizes for research of the learned societies and the works of the teaching societies. I have made my profession of faith on that point, and I have said above what I believe useful to do in this area. But I regard these worthy establishments themselves as the necessary consequences of good social order, and as not helpful without it for creating public morality. When I compare their power in this regard to that of political institutions, I find the same proportions as between the forces of art and those of nature. The former cannot counteract the latter, and cannot modify them except by making themselves serve the designs of the latter. I am imbued, above all, with one principle, which is when there is a question of acting on animated beings, no attempt to work directly will succeed. *Set up favourable circumstances, and that which you desire will occur without your seeming to meddle.* I think that it is only thus that one can make men reasonable and virtuous.

Since I wanted to treat summarily the methods of founding morality among a people, I was forced to limit myself to indicating the most important. I believe above all to have accomplished my goal in assigning each the degree of importance that they appear to me to have.

Supplement

I cannot refrain, in finishing, from making a short application of these principles to the events of which we are witness. The principles must be drawn from facts; and if they are well deduced, they must in their turn succeed in explaining the facts themselves.

Unfortunately, no one can deny that for many years in France, crimes have been more numerous, passions more exasperating, personal unhappiness more apparent; in a phrase, that social disorder is greater than before. The best citizens are those who are the most afflicted.

What is the cause of that sad fact? Unreflective people, and that is the great majority, will respond that the revolution has *demoralised* the French nation: and they believe that they have explained everything. But what do they mean? Do they want to say that among us the sum of moral evil has grown? Then they have done nothing but repeat in other terms that which we just said; they simply announce the fact, and do not indicate the cause.

Do they want to suggest that the change of government has made our morals more depraved, our sentiments more perverse? They forget that morals and the sentiments of men do not change much from one day to the next, nor even over a few years. It is certain, by contrast, that the present time is always the disciple of the past, and that we are governed today by the habits, the passions and the ideas contracted or acquired under the previous social order. If these are the causes of our actual evils, one must not hesitate to attribute them all to that ancien régime so foolishly yearned for. But let us always be fair. This is outside the reproaches that are due to that régime, because as long as it survived, these habits and passions and ideas did not engender all the same consequences.

Finally, does the manifestation of which I seek the meaning imply that the principles on which the new social order rests are destructive to morality? That claim would be unsupportable: because what especially characterises the new system and distinguishes it from the past, is that it professes more respect for the natural and original rights of men than for the arrogations of the past; that it consults the interests of the many more than those of the few; that it esteems personal qualities more than the advantages of fate; that it places reason above the prejudices of habit, submits all opinions to its consideration and obeys reason more than authority and precedent. Surely no one could deny that the adoption of each of these ideas is a step towards justice. Even the most violent opponents of this system have never attacked it on these bases. Everyone, even while declaring it impractical, is convinced that it is a sublime theory. Therefore it is not its principles that are opposed to moral health; to the contrary. Nevertheless, by what calamity has the sum of moral evil grown larger under the reign of truth than under that of error? *It is because internal and external trouble accompanied that great and sudden reform, which again increased the needs of the state, and by consequence the disorder of the administration, and undermined repressive laws the moment that they were most necessary.* With these two circumstances, moral practice deteriorated, just as its theory was perfected. Nothing proves better the grave importance that I have given to these two great causes.

We should add, for our consolation, that if moral evil has grown, it can only be momentary. Not being a consequence of our political institutions, being even contrary to their spirit, it cannot long persist. Either it will undermine those institutions, or the institutions will subjugate it. And since the institutions could emerge at all, they must have deep roots. Evil is always evil; but it is quite different when it is the effect of the established order rather than the difficulty that surrounds the establishment of that social order. It is, it seems to me, a difference not enough recognised, whether because no one wants to recognise it or because no one is able to recognise it.

(le Cit. D...[Destutt de Tracy]. An VI. *Quels sont les Moyens de Fonder la Morale chez un Peuple?* Paris: Chez H. Agaisse, Imprimeur-Libraire, rue des Poitevins, no. 18.)

Notes

1 Introduction

1 Say published his reminiscences of that visit, during which he met with the most eminent philosophers and economists of Britain, in a small volume entitled *De l'Angleterre et des Anglais* (1815). He was charged with the task of reporting on the economic activity of England by the Restoration government in France.

2 Actually, Joanna Kitchin argues (1966: 35) that *La Décade* exhibited a moderate degree of collaboration with the Committee of Public Safety during the Terror. She claims that the editors apparently decided that only the Montagnards had the strength to defeat counter-revolutionaries.

3 The fleeting nature of fame and the vicissitudes of historical significance are well illustrated by the fate of Roederer. There is little question that Roederer was a more widely recognised economist in 1800 than was the young upstart Say. The importance attributed to Roederer is captured by his entry in the 'supplément' to *Biographie Universelle, Ancienne et Moderne*, published in 1846, in which Roederer 'l'un des personnages les plus célèbres de nos révolutions' (1846, 79: 294–316) gets twenty-three pages (in all fairness, not solely because of his economic analysis) relative to Say's much more modest entry (1827, 81: 224–34). And yet, it is the novelty of Say's economic writing that has stood the test of time. In contemporary encyclopaedias, Roederer merits hardly a mention.

4 The label *parti philosophique* is used by Moravia (1968: 7) to refer to the Auteuil circle. Roederer probably meant the term to refer to the group of moderate republicans associated with the *Institut National* during the Directory. There was some overlap, but the congruence was not perfect. During the 1750s and 1760s, *parti philosophique* referred to the *philosophes*.

5 The people who live in the far north are no longer called 'Eskimos' because that is a name imposed by a conquering people. We have decided to extend the courtesy of adopting 'Inuit', which is the name they gave themselves. Similarly, Lapps have become Sami, Bushmen San and Gypsies Roma. The parallel with 'idéologiste' and 'idéologue' seems too direct to require further comment. If we also remember that 'idéologue', unlike 'Eskimo', has developed a distinctly pejorative set of connotations, the case is strengthened. Whether the *idéologues* ever actually succeeded in constructing a science of ideas that met the criteria they established, the effort hardly seems worth denigrating at the outset. These individuals were idealists attempting to construct a better society, and that goal should be applauded whatever the shortcomings of the analysis and the methods proposed. They do not deserve the scorn they have received.

6 The word 'ideological' is used, throughout this book, as an adjective to refer to the *idéologues* and the social theory of *idéologie*. That is, 'ideological' should bring to mind Tracy rather than Marx; I do not ever use the word in its twentieth-century sense.

7   Hayek has argued that Hume studied Bernard Mandeville's *The Fable of the Bees*
    (Mandeville 1988 [1714, 1723]) and *The Origin of Honour* (1732) as he was
    planning the *Treatise* (Hayek 1978: 263). From this rich source, Hayek claims,
    emerged the first shoots of a new kind of social theory, to which he and others
    after him referred, following Mill, as the theory of spontaneous order (see
    Hamowy 1987). The message was quickly assimilated, and, by the end of the
    eighteenth century, Johnson, Smith, Tucker, Paley, Burke, Gibbon and Malthus,
    among many others, could all be found arguing that the various activities of any
    society, especially but certainly not exclusively its economic activities (Haakonssen
    1981: 12–35), arise in a gradual and unplanned manner in response to individual
    self-regarding behaviour in such a way that individuals are 'led by an invisible
    hand' to advance the social interest without knowing it or desiring it.
8   James (1977: 455–75) argues that the concept of *industrialisme* calls to mind the
    specifically French heritage of productive classes (which include workers,
    entrepreneurs and capitalists) and idle classes (specifically the landed aristocracy).
9   P. N. Furbank critically evaluates the idea of the Enlightenment as an identifiable
    period in intellectual history (Furbank 1992: 451–2). Despite the overuse of the
    term and an unfortunate tendency to use it to blur important distinctions between
    philosophers, it is a very useful concept that retains identifiable characteristics
    that will, I hope, become clear as the argument progresses.

2   A brief biography of Jean-Baptiste Say (1767–1832)

1   Biographical information on Say comes from a number of sources, but the most
    readily accessible are Palmer (1997) and the Michaud biographical dictionary. A
    death notice was published by de Candolle (1832), and a very useful *Eloge* by
    Blanqui (1841), which was read at the annual meeting of the Five Academies (3
    May 1841). Say's *Oeuvres Diverses* (1848), edited by Charles Comte, E. Daire
    and Horace Say, also contains a 'life and works' of Say that is probably the ultimate
    source of both Palmer and the Michaud.
2   Horace Say assisted Jean-Baptiste Say as editor of *La Décade* in 1797. He was
    also the author of 'Cours de fortifications', published in the first volume of the
    Journal de l'Ecole Polytechnique in 1794.
3   Louis Say's publications include:
    (1818) *Principales Causes de la Richesse ou de la Misère des Peuples et des Particuliers*,
    Paris.
    (1822) *Considérations sur l'Industrie et la Législation, sous le Rapport de leur
    Influence sur la Richesse des Etats, et Examen Critique des Principaux Ouvrages qui
    ont Paru sur l'Économie Politique*, Paris.
    (1827) *Traité Élémentaire de la Richesse Individuelle et de la Richesse Publique, et
    Éclaircissements sur les Principales Questions d'Économie Politique*, Paris. This
    volume was translated into English in 1829.
    (1836) *Etudes sur les Richesse des Nations et Réfutation des Principales Erreurs en
    Économie Politique*, Paris.
    (No date) *Influence de la Morale et des Dogmes Religieux sur la Richesse des Nations*,
    Nantes. Reprinted in *Traité Élémentaire*.
4   The political details recounted in this chapter and the next are well known. Doyle
    (1989) is a nice, concise source and an even shorter recitation of the key events
    can be found in Crystal (1994: C1065ff.).
5   Steiner (1997: n2) quotes what seems to be his first letter to Dupont, in which
    Say wrote (5 April 1814):

    During my period as Tribune, not wanting to deliver orations [pérorer] in
    favour of the usurper, and not having the permission to speak against him, I

drafted and published my *Traité d'Économie Politique*. Bonaparte commanded me to attend him and offered me 40 thousand francs a year to write in favour of his opinion; I refused, and was caught up in the purge of 1804.

I thank Philippe Steiner for bringing this passage to my attention.

6 Jefferson regularly advised his correspondents that they ought to read Smith's *Wealth of Nations* for the principles of political economy, unless a copy of Say's *Traité*, which treats the same material more concisely and lucidly, was available. See, for example, his letter to John Norvell of 11 June 1807 and that to Correa de Serra of 27 December 1814 (Jefferson 1903–4, XI: 223; XIX: 221ff.). In the latter, he wrote of the political economy developed by Smith and the Economists, which Say has given to us in a 'corrected, dense and lucid form' (224). A slightly less laudatory form of the same message was written on 31 January 1814, in which Jefferson claimed that he 'did not find in [Say] one new idea... nothing more than a succinct judicious digest of the tedious pages of Smith' (XIX: 82).

7 The dates of this lecture series are difficult to establish because, as Steiner notes, the archives of the *Athénée* have been destroyed (Steiner 1996: 38). Daire dates the series from 1815 (Say 1848: 12) as does Teilhac (1927: 33), although the latter was probably influenced by the former. Dejob (nd: 418–36) claims three series of lectures were delivered: 1816–7, 1818–9, and 1819–20. Steiner claims that the archives do not permit a definitive solution to the problem, but that Say's account book does note that he was paid by the *Athénée* in April 1816 (600 francs), in March and May 1817 (800 francs) and in March and April 1819 (800 francs). He concludes that the most likely dates are, therefore, 1815–6, 1816–7 and 1818–9 (Steiner 1996b: 38). He further notes that Say mentions his courses in the January 1816 introduction to the second edition of *Angleterre et les Anglais* (1816), but not in the edition of the *Catéchisme* published in July 1815. In 1820, he began to teach at the *Conservatoire*, which suggests that he would not have continued at the *Athénée*.

8 For a history of the various translations of Say's *Traité*, see the table constructed by Steiner and published in Say (1996: 14–21). The rapid diffusion of his work throughout Europe and the Americas attests to the usefulness of this particular book as a basic text of political economy, simpler and easier to read than Smith's *Wealth of Nations*.

3 Jean-Baptiste Say and the institutions of *idéologie*

1 As were his cofounders of *La Décade* Andrieux, Duval and Ginguené.
2 For details of the evolution of the academic institutions, see Kennedy (1989: 155f.) and especially Palmer (1985).
3 Gusdorf (1978: 358n) traces the word 'psychologie' to its introduction in France during the 1740s by popularisers of Christian Wolff. In 1754, Charles Bonnet published his *Essai de Psychologie*.
4 My summary draws heavily on Jacques Godechot's article on the revolutionary press in Bellanger *et al.* (1969–76).
5 Joanna Kitchin's masterful study of *La Décade* is the source of this information about the newspaper and the individuals involved with it.
6 The details of the political context of *idéologie* are drawn from a number of sources, including especially Kennedy (1989) and Doyle (1989). Brian Head's study of Destutt de Tracy, Joanna Kitchin's analysis of *La Décade* and Staum's *Minerva's Message* furnish details from which this summary is constructed. I have noted only those facts that are not generally known and do not regularly appear in histories of the period.
7 See the discussion of the evolution of Pierre Daunou's political thought in Welch (1984: 26–7).

8 See *La Décade* (18, 10 Germinal an VI [30 March 1798]: 63–4; 18, 20 Germinal VI [9 April 1798]: 127; 18, 30 Floréal an VI [19 May 1798]: 377). See Welch (1984: 37).

9 The intimate relationship between the *idéologues* and the government in this period (even as the former are plotting to transform the latter beyond recognition) is apparent in *Le Moniteur*. *Idéologie* and government announcements appear side-by-side, and there is little question that the government saw *Le Moniteur* as sympathetic to the point of being relied upon to publish planted articles. See Kennedy (1989: 323).

4 Towards a psychology of rational individuals

1 Newton's demonstration of the superior explanatory power of a physical theory based on gravitational force was seen as reason to reject the metaphysical nature of the Cartesian system (Ehrard 1963, I: 143; Kaiser 1976, 337). But, in fact, it was mechanicism itself that had come under attack. Newtonian mechanical philosophy fared little better. As early as 1717, S'Gravesende recognised that Newton's hypothesis of gravitation was quite as metaphysical as Descartes's systems (Cassirer 1955: 61), a point that Hume was to use in the *History of England* to argue that 'while Newton seemed to draw off the veil from some of the mysteries of nature, he shewed at the same time the imperfections of the mechanical philosophy; and thereby restored her ultimate secrets to that obscurity, in which they ever did and ever will remain' (Hume 1982 [1778], VI: 542). Hume recognised that this undermined any crudely mechanical account of the interaction of bodies, whether that mechanicism emerged from rationalist or empiricist approaches to knowledge.

2 Needless to say, the world of ideas is less tidy than this portrait suggests, and rarely submits itself to such a simple dichotomy. One of the very best expositors of such Toryism is Alexander Pope, whose intellectual background is claimed to be Newtonian rather than Cartesian (Willey 1961: 5):

> And, spite of pride, in erring reason's spite,
> One truth is clear. Whatever is, is right.
>
> (Alexander Pope, *An Essay on Man*. Epistle I)

The rationalist and mechanistic tradition in France was continued by Nicolas de Malebranche, whose *De la Recherche de la Vérité* (1674–5) and *Entretiens sur la Métaphysique et sur la Religion* (1688) sought to reconcile Cartesianism with the writings of St. Augustine and Neoplatonism. Central to Malebranche's system is the idea, sometimes apparent in Descartes's writing, that human knowledge about the internal and the external world is possible only as the result of the interaction between human beings and God. Changes in human thoughts or in the perception of external objects are not caused either by the individual or the object, but rather by God. What are commonly referred to as 'causes' are simply 'occasions' for God to produce particular effects, and hence the views of Malebranche became known as Occasionalism. Similarly, Cartesian mind–body dualism was considered by Malebranche to be simply a special case of the impossibility of direct interaction between created things. More specifically, sensory experiences are not the sole source of human knowledge because human thought processes can only contemplate ideas. God's mind contains all the 'intelligible extensions' or ideas that human beings can hope to discover, and of which human ideas are partial representations (Collins 1967: 85ff.). In the hands of Malebranche, the Cartesian system became a defence of religion and, more properly, of the Church.

3 Whatmore (1998) has, in an essay detailing Say's use of general and particular

facts, argued that the concept seems to derive from Scottish philosophy, although he notes that Hume does not use it. Coleman (1995: 150) argues that 'Stewart's advocacy of theory in the guise of empiricism is not merely the result of an exaggeration of some of David Hume's doctrines. Stewart's false empiricism is just one example of a general tendency of Enlightenment thought.'

4 One can hardly set aside the rationalists without acknowledging the contributions of Benedict de Spinoza, Gottfried Wilhelm von Leibniz and Immanuel Kant. But the debate, at least as far as the empiricists and especially the *idéologues* were concerned, had already been won. When Kant, Leibniz or Spinoza enter the rhetoric of the *idéologues*, it is usually as foils against which 'correct' philosophy can be demonstrated (see Tracy 1803: 544–606).

5 One can see the importance of this train of thought on Tracy's preoccupation with 'signs', and the general focus of the *idéologues* on developing a language more certain and precise and less likely to embroil scientists (and ordinary human beings) in mere semantic struggles and discussions of the meaningless.

6 The method has obvious shortcomings. The most apparent is that Bacon ignores the possible plurality and complexity of causes, instead implicitly assuming that every property has a necessary and sufficient condition. The second is that causes may be at a considerable distance, both geographically and temporally, from effects. The third is that this method cannot be applied to metaphysics. However flawed may have been the method, all these accomplishments, perhaps most important of which is the focus on observation and experiment, had a profound effect on ideological writing.

7 This is the same Louis-Sébastien Mercier who wrote *L'An 2440*.

8 Louis-Sébastien Mercier, quoted in *Décade Philosophique*, 20 Floréal VIII: 306–9.

9 For Locke, of course, perception has a richer meaning than it now has, involving as it does the activity of the 'inner eye'.

5 Physiology, order and chaos

1 As were Cabanis and Pinel, Bichat was influenced by Condillac's sensationalist philosophy and by the 'vitalism' of the Montpellier school associated most strongly with Bordeu and Barthez. His most important contributions were the elaboration of Barthez's concept of 'life' and the distinction between living and non-living objects.

2 Bichat's work was an important influence on the social analysis that would develop from *idéologie*. Tracy, for example, attempted to unite these ideas from the scientific writings of Bichat and Cabanis with the co-dependent 'sympathy' and 'self-interest' that appeared in the psychology of his *Elémens* under the influence of David Hume and Adam Smith (Tracy 1817: 491 and 502–16; Head 1985: 79–87). Tracy, like Cabanis, equated sympathy with the external 'animal life', and self-interest with the life-conserving, but essentially passive, internal organic life of living beings.

3 In all of this, Cabanis's position on the existence of the 'soul' has been absent. Helvétius, we have seen, would deny any difference between physical sensitivity of the nerves and sensation whereas Condillac denied the materialist implications of his empirical sensationalism, arguing that a soul is different from the body and that a 'self' is necessary to integrate the sensory data collected by the body. In most of his work, Cabanis does not address Condillac's concerns, but by the end of his life he did recognise an immaterial 'soul' separate from the body. Like Condillac, he saw no contradiction between the two.

4 Rousseau's appeal to Lycurgus and Solon is echoed in *Olbie*.

5 However, Rousseau, unlike Machiavelli, stopped short of calling for a revival of pagan cults designed to instil virtue in the people.

6 From physiology to social theory: the body politic, sympathy and moral education

1 It is important to distinguish between 'instruction', which referred to intellectual training, and 'education', which was a much more inclusive term. Education, for example, included the deliberate inculcation of morality through such means as public festivals and artistic displays, whereas instruction encompassed elaborate schemes, such as Tracy's, for the organisation of knowledge that, through its influence on Thomas Jefferson, motivated the organisation of disciplines at the University of Virginia and the ideological plans for the reorganisation of secondary education under the supervision of the *Écoles Normales* (Palmer 1985: 242f.). Say's *Catéchisme d'Économie Politique* (1815), unlike the moral catechisms that were so much a part of Revolutionary 'education', would be a contribution to the 'instruction' of the people.

2 Judith Schlanger's 1971 analysis (*Les Métaphores de l'Organisme*) is particularly good on the nineteenth century, and offers quite a distinct picture from that created by Mirowski (1989). Although the latter focuses on rational mechanics, Schlanger demonstrates the pervasiveness of 'body politic' imagery in continental economics.

3 An idea that, of course, also goes back to Plato's *Republic*, in which the state is likened to a physical body and health is the creation of a natural order and government in the parts of the body, and the creation of disease is the creation of a state of things in which they are at variance with the natural order.

4 This equation of social groups with natural organisms has taken a number of forms throughout history, and modernity is hardly exempt. One might point to Freud's *Civilization and its Discontents* (1962), in which the body politic is founded on individuals whose instincts must be conquered to make possible the cultural group. Norman O. Brown developed this analysis into a metaphorical discussion of the relationship between human and political bodies to show the patriarchal and authoritarian structures of both in *Love's Body* (1966). Shulamith Firestone, in the *Dialectic of Sex, the Case of Feminist Revolution* (1970), attempted to transform Freud's analysis into a feminist and a socialist theory. These organic analogies were pervasive throughout the eighteenth century.

5 Waterman takes issue with Smith's claim 'that Tories accepted subordination because they pretended that government was "of divine institution" ', arguing instead that Tories 'perceived social and political relations in terms of a sacramental unity in the Body of Christ and an earthly foreshadowing of the eternal city' implicitly based upon the theological organicism of pre-Reformation Christianity, which was transmitted through the 'language and idiom of the *Book of Common Prayer*' (Waterman 1994: 130). That is, he claims, it is not 'government' that is divinely ordained, but rather the organicism of human society. The Whig conception, by contrast, creates the social body, and the subordination that necessarily characterises it, through the decisions of individuals to subject themselves to the subordination required by membership in a society on the basis of the utility each anticipates.

6 See Leith (1965) for a short and readable analysis with a lengthy bibliography. Palmer (1985: 190–7) summarises the issue well.

7 Of which both Ginguené and Duval, co-owners of *La Décade*, were members.

8 'Of the 2,639 persons guillotined in Paris during the Revolution well over half were put to death in...June and July of 1794.' (Palmer 1985: 196)

9 This is an interesting difference from British social theory. Butler had argued, for example, that 'self-love' is not incompatible with 'love of one's neighbour', which allowed subsequent social theorists to go so far as to argue that self-love is, in fact, a Christian virtue. This idea had a powerful influence on social theorists, including Smith and Hume. See Waterman (1994).

10 Head claims that Tracy's unfortunate use of the term 'indoctrinate' (above, p. 258) is merely an 'illiberal enthusiasm for the correctness of his own "rational" morality' (Head 1985: 98).

7 The amelioration of poverty in *Olbie*: the roles of educators, administrators and legislators

1 Say uses the word 'fortunes'. It is not clear whether he distinguished between wealth and income.
2 See Palgrave (1906–9: 244ff.).
3 Carlo Antonio Broggia's *Trattato de' Tribute, delle Monete e del Governo Politico della Sanità* (1743) develops the analyses of Vauban, Verri and his contemporaries. These writers were part of the intellectual landscape with whom anybody in France concerned with public finance could be expected to be familiar. Say's *Cours Complet* cites the work of both Vauban and Verri.
4 The differential emphasis on prisons versus parades seems to depend on both the temperament and the age of the writer. Say liked parades in 1800, but he was thirty-three. Tracy, a generation older and imprisoned during the Terror, had an understandable (if perverse) belief in the efficacy and necessity of prisons.
5 Say does not always emphasise these distinctions consistently, often recognising that the great distinction is between 'workers' [industrieux], comprising entrepreneurs, savants and labourers, and those who live exclusively on the return to their property. The exclusivity in the latter distinction is important because Say vilified the 'idle', but noted that very often an entrepreneur and even a labourer will bring some capital to production (see Say 1803: 33). The commonality of interest between 'workers' seemed so apparent to Say that he began to call the returns to entrepreneurship, capital *and* to labour 'profit' (see Say 1843: 314).
6 Tracy, too, argued that basic economic wellbeing was necessary for a desire to profit by education:

> The least reduction of taxes will augment more the number of men knowing how to read and write, than a legion of schoolmasters. A degree more comfort among farmers will increase more the products of the earth and national good sense, than all the societies of agriculture and all the professors of logic in Europe could do.
>
> (above, p. 258)

And, of course, the consequences of economic wellbeing will work particularly on the education of children because 'it is not only a profusion of lessons that one must offer them, but give to their parents the disposition, the methods and the interest to make them profit by them. This is true, above all, of the least comfortable classes, that is those which compose nine-tenths of society.' (above, p. 258).
7 He does use the passive tense. It is not clear whether the state or the private sector ought to establish the savings banks but the general tenor of his argument is that the enlightened will establish institutions, to which the mass of citizens will become attached over time as they learn the benefits that accrue from them.
8 Pierre-Louis Roederer, 'Introduction', *Journal d'Economie publique, de Moral et de Politique* I (Year IV): 3, as quoted in Kaiser (1980: 147).

8 On domestic virtue

1 Some of the material in this chapter is a substantially modified version of Forget (1997).

2 'Féminisme', according to my *Petit Robert*, was first used in French in 1837 and its introduction is usually ascribed to Charles Fourier, a socialist who expanded his influence in the 1830s. Therefore, although it may be anachronistic to use the English word 'feminism' to describe the activities of the revolutionary decade, it cannot be so argued with respect to later periods. I use the word in the same sense that Fourier did, which is to label a political activism focused on extending the franchise and reforming social conditions to expand the social and economic roles allowed women. [Similarly, 'socialisme' was regularly used in 1831 and was derived from the earlier English (1822) or Italian (1803) usage.]

3 For a complete translation of *Declaration of the Rights of Women*, and an excellent (if now somewhat dated, but still very useful) bibliographical essay on the many roles of women in the Revolution, see Yves Bessières and Patricia Niedzwiecki (1991).

4 Wollstonecraft wrote for an English audience and her work was an explicit response to Burke.

5 Imbert, *La Décade philosophique*, 30 Pluvisôe 11, pp. 321–8; and 10 Ventôse 11, pp. 385–94; and Laya, *La Décade philosophique*, 10 Prairial 13, pp. 403–12; and 10 Messidor 13, pp. 11–26.

6 See the letter from Tracy to Jefferson, 22 February 1821 published in Tracy (1926: 208–11). Although Tracy did not publish *De l'Amour* in French, it was widely circulated and its influence has been tracked to Stendhal, for example (see Berrian 1954).

7 Tracy is referring to Condorcet and Sieyès (Welch 1984: 122).

8 And it is surely superfluous to note that one need not judge, but rather attempt to understand what may have induced an individual to develop his position and what may have been the consequences of that position.

9 'Let us make easy the path of virtue and not imitate those moralist–legislators who place their temple at the peak of a high mountain that one can reach only by a narrow path. That condemns the entire world to the abyss!' (above, p. 211).

10 Tracy's *De l'Amour* (1926) strongly supported the right to divorce on the grounds cited.

11 Actually, the organisation is more like the Béguine communities of the medieval period, in which middle class women chose to live in communities without permanent vows and support themselves by working in hospitals and asylums.

9 Natural order and spontaneous order

1 Hayek is often given credit for coining the phrase 'spontaneous order', but John Stuart Mill refers to 'the spontaneous order of nature' in 'Nature', the first of his *Three Essays on Religion*:

> The consciousness that whatever man does to improve his condition is in so much a censure and a thwarting of the spontaneous order of Nature, has in all ages caused new and unprecedented attempts at improvement to be generally at first under a shade of religious suspicion...
>
> (J. S. Mill 1969 [1873]: 381).

Moreover, he opens his 'Considerations on Representative Government' with a caricature. At one end of the intellectual spectrum, Mill claims, are those who believe that social order requires the self-conscious intervention of legislators and administrators, who are charged with the duty of creating social institutions according to the precepts of a rationally conceived plan. At the other extreme, are those who view government as a 'spontaneous product' of individuals pursuing their own interests. Mill is quite aware that this is a caricature, recognising that 'it would be difficult to determine which position is more absurd if either were held exclusively' (J. S. Mill 1977 [1861]: 374–5).

2 Recall the well-known passage from Adam Smith's *Theory of Moral Sentiments*, in which Smith refers to 'the man of system' who treats individuals as chess pieces to be moved around at will (Smith 1984 [1759]: 234). The editors note:

> It seems likely that Smith had the French Revolution in mind when writing this and succeeding paragraphs. His remarks in [paragraphs] 15 and 17 about a 'spirit of system' and 'the man of system' may refer to the constitution-makers of 1789, or perhaps to the rationalist philosopher Richard Price...especially if Smith is echoing d'Alembert's disparaging use of the phrase 'the spirit of system' to describe rationalism in the Preliminary Discourse of the *Encyclopédie*.
>
> (Smith 1984 [1759]: 231n6)

3 Among its more unexpected appearances is this passage from Sade's *La Nouvelle Justine, ou les Malheurs de la Vertu* (1797), the four volumes of which constitute the first part of the definitive edition of this work, of which the second part, in six volumes, bears the title: *La Nouvelle Justine, ou les Malheurs de la Vertu, suivie de l'Histoire de Juliette, sa soeur [ou les Prospérités du vice]*:

> A totally virtuous universe could not endure for a minute; the learned hand of Nature brings order to birth out of chaos, and wanting chaos, Nature must fail to attain anything: such is the profound equilibrium which holdeth the stars aright in their courses, which suspendeth them in these huge oceans of void, which maketh them to move periodically and by rule. She must have evil, 'tis from this stuff she creates good; upon crime her existence is seated, and all would be undone were the world to be inhabited by doers of good alone. [...] Why do we decline to acknowledge that she has done with men what she has done with beasts? are not all classes, like all species, in perpetual strife, do they not mutually batten one upon the another, does not one or the other weaken, wilt, perish away, depending upon the state or shape which Nature's laws must give to the natural order?
>
> (Sade 1988 [1797]: 172)

But I must concur with Octavio Paz, who notes that Sade's 'ideas have undoubted interest; nevertheless, Bataille and Blanchot exaggerate: he was not Hume' (Paz 1998: 81).

4 This reading of Hume has not gone unchallenged. There are many instances when he claims that ''twas therefore a concern for our own, and the public interest, which made us establish the laws of justice' (Hume 1978: 496). Haakonssen (1981: 26) claims that such passages 'are the result of carelessness', but Raphael and Macfie claim only that Hume 'did not agree that benevolence is the sole motive of virtuous action' (Smith 1984: 12–13). Hirschman, by contrast, recognises the evolution of Hume's thinking on such a complex topic but is prepared to agree that Hume ultimately acknowledged that the 'love of gain' would predominate over the less constant passions, including concern for the public interest and, more importantly, 'the love of pleasure', which was the source of most of the malignant and vicious passions of human nature (Hirschman 1977: 66).

5 The distinction between the legislator 'whose deliberations ought to be governed by general principles which are always the same', and 'that insidious and crafty animal, vulgarly called a statesman or politician, whose councils are directed by the momentary fluctuations of affairs' is also made by Smith (1976 [1776], IV, II: 490). For an insightful discussion of the role of the legislator, see Winch (1978: 159–60 and 170–3).

6 Elizabeth Fox-Genovese discusses the physiocratic conception of natural law and rights in *The Origins of Physiocracy: Economic Revolution and Social Order in Eighteenth Century France* (Ithaca: Cornell University Press, 1976).

7 The revolutionary pamphlets of Volney, Condorcet and Sieyès are the most well known.

8 The distinction between politics and political economy has been explored by Steiner in his 1997 article entitled 'Politique et économie politique chez Jean-Baptiste Say', by Forget (1993), by Kaiser (1980), by Whatmore (1998) and by Fontaine (1996).

9 The articles in *La Décade* to which I refer are: 'Boniface Veridick à Polyscope sur son projet de théâtre pour le peuple' (10 Germinal an IV: 38–44); and 'Sciences sociales: compte rendu de Cabanis "Quelques considérations sur l'organisation sociale en général et particulièrement sur la nouvelle constitution" ' (10 Nivôse an VIII: 9–17).

For a different interpretation of these articles, see Steiner (1997).

10 Note that Say consistently uses the word 'indépendance' rather than 'liberté' because he wants to refer to the freedom of citizens from the economic servitude of the *ancien régime*, rather than the political 'liberty' of the ancients. In Say's usage, it relies upon the establishment of a modern industrial state. Compare this usage to that of Tocqueville, who made the same distinction in the second part of *Démocratie en Amérique* (1951 [1840]), and Benjamin Constant *De la Liberté chez les Modernes* (1980 [1819]). See Steiner (1997: n16).

11 This particular passage was written as an aside in a bound volume of Say's writing that is now in the possession of Arnold Heertje, and was published by Say's literary executors (without a date of composition) in *Oeuvres Diverses* (1848). Heertje's volume appears to have been bound in 1826, so the comment was probably written after that date (see Schoorl 1980: 33n41).

10 Say's social economics as a contribution to the pedagogical programme of *idéologie*

1 Staum (1996: 233–4) lists members and associates of section 4 (Political Economy) of the class of Moral and Political Sciences, which was established in 1795:

Members: Emmanuel-Joseph Sieyès, Jacques-Antoine Creuzé-Latouche, Charles-Maurice de Talleyrand, Pierre-Louis Roederer, Jean-Gérard Lacuée, Pierre-Samuel Du Pont de Nemours, Charles-François Lebrun.

Associates: François Véron de Forbonnais, Jean-Antoine-Cauvin Gallois, Germain Garnier, Emmanuel-Étienne Duvillard de Durand, Antoine Diannyère, Philippe-Rose Roume de Saint-Laurent.

Of these, he identifies Sieyès, Roederer and Gallois as *idéologues* on the basis of their authorship of a major work in medical or philosophical *idéologie*, or a treatise on the elements of ethics, politics or economics, and having at least two of the following characteristics:

1 attendance at the salons of Mme Helvétius, Destutt de Tracy or Mme de Condorcet between 1794 and 1809;
2 on the staff of or a contributor to *La Décade*;
3 moderate republican after 1794, and opponent of Bonaparte after 1801.

Of course, membership in other sections did not preclude individuals contributing to political economy: for example, Destutt de Tracy was a member of the first section, and Jean-Jacques Garnier was an associate of the History section.

2 This intriguing work is, unfortunately, only available in Dutch.
3 See Whatmore (1998) for an analysis of the significance of 'general and particular facts' in Say's economics. He traces the distinction to Scottish philosophy, as did Coleman (1995).
4 I thank Evert Schoorl for drawing these to my attention.
5 Say's own boarding school anticipated a trend that was institutionalised after the Revolution. The reconstruction of the educational system in France that created the *Institut National* was part of the same programme. See Chapter three (above).
6 The distinction between 'general facts' and 'particular facts' was very widespread in France and Scotland by the mid-1790s. Hume, for example, claims:

> [I]t is certain that general principles, if just and sound, *must always prevail in the general course of things*, though they may fail in particular cases; and it is the chief business of philosophers to regard the general course of things. I may add, that it is also the chief business of politicians; especially in the domestic government of the state, where the public good, which ought to be their object, depends on the concurrence of a multitude of causes.
>
> (Hume 1985: 254)

7 See 'Rapport fait au nom de la section des finances sur le projet de loi qui tend à mettre à la disposition du Gouvernement 300 millions sur les produits de l'an XI' (Say 1848: 198–204). See especially footnote 1, which the editors note demonstrates how it was already difficult to publish dissenting ideas:

> The finance section of which I was a member, judging that it would be dangerous to make this report, replaced it by a few words to the tribune. The report seemed to find fault with the government for not justifying independently each type of expenditure.
>
> (Say 1848: 198n)

8 That 'the people' would read and learn from a treatise on political economy may seem a very idealistic goal, but it is important to remember that Paris had a reputation for literacy even during the period. Say noted in the first edition of his *Traité* (1803) that it was not uncommon to find ordinary workers in the better establishments with personal libraries of ten or twelve books. What immense progress could be achieved, he enthused, if only we could excise the bad and the useless books and replace them with one or two books of real merit (Say 1803, I, chapter 13: 82). Contrast this with the situation in England where Say found 'no reading and little philosophy', but noted that 'there are nevertheless two sorts of publications read, which are of primary importance: the Bible and newspapers. It remains to be seen what instruction can be derived from these.' (Say 1815: 21–2)

11 *Idéologie* and Say's theory of value

1 Therefore, it is not unreasonable when discussing the value theory to use citations drawn from throughout the body of Say's work. I've tried to match citations from the English translation of the fourth edition of the *Traité*, from which I've taken many of the translations, with similar passages in the first edition. Some of the examples change from edition to edition, but I maintain that there is little substantive change in the analysis.
2 Philip Mirowski documents the presence in Say's *Traité* of mechanical metaphors and claims that 'Say...derives his conservation rule from Descartes' (Mirowski 1989: 169); '...Say and Smith appeal [...] to the same structural metaphors...' (Mirowski 1989: 170); Say adopts 'another variant of the Cartesian reduction of

all phenomena to matter in motion...' (Mirowski 1989: 170), and concludes that 'since Say was apparently ill equipped to actually understand the rational mechanics of his time, he had no inkling of what was involved to render this metaphor determinate; therefore, he initiated a tradition in nineteenth-century France of mere polemical assertion of the market's efficacy based on little more than bravado' (Mirowski 1989: 170). Although Mirowski also recognises that Say occasionally 'compares the laws of the social body to those of the human body' (Mirowski 1989: 170), he rejects the importance of this insight. In fact, he suggests that Say is simply inconsistent in using the 'social body' metaphor when he 'cannot find a good word to say about physiocracy' (Mirowski 1989: 170). Judith Schlanger, however, has argued persuasively that the distinction between the organic metaphor and that of the machine is a false dichotomy (Schlanger 1971: 47–9). She demonstrates that eighteenth-century writers habitually move between the two systems of language, as Mirowski notices is typical of Say. Moreover, she challenges the simplistic assertion that there are distinctive characteristics clearly and exclusively attributed to one or the other metaphor. There is, she claims, no such stability as Mirowski posits for other authors, and the inconsistency he discovers in Say is, in fact, the general rule.

3 I am aware of the very large secondary literature that seeks to determine whether 'demand and supply analysis' can be attributed to one or another classical economist, most particularly Ricardo (see Hollander 1979). All Schumpeter means by this statement, and all I seek to claim, is that the demand and supply mechanism itself, without explicit and careful derivation from a notion of marginal utility, is useful for explaining the movement of market prices, but that it is consistent with attempts to locate the source of value in utility, in labour and in cost. It is not, that is, a mechanism that is unique to a marginalist worldview. This was a widely held notion in classical economics. John Stuart Mill, for example, claimed 'All influences upon price operated by way of demand and supply, and the cost theory was dependent thereupon' (J. S. Mill *Collected Works* [hereafter referred to as CW] IV: 33–4). Similarly, Ricardo wrote 'I do not say that the value of a commodity will always conform to its natural price without an additional supply, but I say that the cost of production regulates the supply and therefore regulates the price' (Ricardo *Works* II: 280). Only Malthus seemed to argue that Ricardo rejected demand and supply in determining the long-run cost of commodities (*Occasional Papers of T. R. Malthus*: 189), a position that has attracted a great deal of attention, positive and negative, over the years (cf. Hollander 1979: 668).

4 Say criticised Condillac (perhaps unfairly) for not recognising that value is not determined by the amount of utility that any particular consumer derives from a commodity purely according to his own needs, but rather by the amount of money (if that is the medium in which payment is made) that the public at large is willing to exchange for the utility created in a commodity by industry (Say 1843: 143).

5 This is so because Say has just claimed that production consists in the creation of utility rather than matter, and therefore if one intends to measure production it is useless to talk about pounds, lengths and so on (Say 1803: 24).

6 According to Say:

> The *current price* of a product always tends to the level of its *natural price*. If it exceeds the *natural price*, the production of this product, which pays better than others, will attract land, capital and industry; the quantity offered grows relative to the quantity demanded, and the price falls. Alternatively, when the *current price* falls below the *natural price*, the price necessary to pay for productive services, those services which find themselves inadequately paid will withdraw; production stops and the quantity offered falls relative to the quantity demanded, and price rises until it reaches a level where it can compensate productive services appropriately.
>
> (Say 1803, III: 60)

7 Blaug (1978: 316), much to Lutfalla's amusement (Lutfalla 1991: 25), wondered whether such an idea is of essentially Roman Catholic inspiration whereas a labour theory of value might be more congenial to Protestant visions of the world, which place labour and work at the centre of their theologies. But, of course, Say is (at most) Protestant, as Blaug recognises.

8 I am not suggesting that Smith had a labour theory of value, but rather that Say rejected those elements of the labour theory of value he purported to find in the *Wealth of Nations* (Forget 1993).

9 It certainly is a pervasive concern of Say's to overthrow the influence of Physiocracy in France. Many citations are possible, from the first edition of the *Traité* (see 1803: 26 and 27) to the *Cours Complet* (1843: 568ff.).

10 Part of this chapter originally appeared, in a significantly modified form, in Forget (1994).

11 Say's use of metaphorical reasoning maintains this same pattern throughout his economic work. His organisation of the book and his analysis of the law of markets changes dramatically from the first to the second edition of the *Traité*, his population analysis varies significantly over time as Malthus becomes an important influence on his economics, and other theoretical features of Say's economics change in important ways over the course of his lifetime (and especially between the first and second editions of the *Traité*). Nevertheless, the basic orientation he brings to an understanding of how markets work, as reflected in his use of language, does not change. For that reason, I blend examples taken from various editions of the *Traité* (including the American translation of the fourth edition) and the *Cours Complet* to illustrate particular points. When the same argument appears in the first and the fourth editions of the *Traité*, I have given dual references but used the language of the fourth edition.

12 There is no evidence that the illustration is inconsistent with the analysis in the first edition of the *Traité*, and it is such a nice statement of the problem that I will adopt it.

13 The evidence they cite is from the Prinsep edition, and the precise passage appears for the first time in the second edition:

> The price thus established helps to determine the extent of demand, which grows in proportion as the price of the product falls; because as the price is reduced, the product falls within the means of a greater number of consumers.
>
> (Say 1814, II: 5–6)

The first edition, though, is written as though he had the concept in mind:

> Consumption…resembles a pyramid, of which the width represents the number of consumers or the extent of demand, and the height represents the price…
>
> (Say 1803, III: 72)

14 Compare this passage from the first edition of the *Traité*, in which Say explicitly sets aside the uncertainty that individual behaviour in the markets can cause:

> I know well that expectations influence prices in advance. When the season suggests an abundant production of wine, wine falls in price. But variations of this type are founded on presumptions, on types of opinions, the incontestable influence of which can only be based upon other guesses. Hope, fear, malice, the desire to oblige, all the passions and all the virtues can influence the price that one offers or receives. It is only by a purely moral estimation that one can understand the deviations in the positive calculations that concern us now.
>
> (Say 1803, III: 66–7)

12 Class analysis and the distribution of income

1 Despite Cantillon's early conception of three social classes, the adoption of the capitalist, labourer, landlord class division in French economics was considerably slower than it was in England, owing perhaps to the influence of Jean-Baptiste Say. The idea played an important role only after Sismondi's contributions, and became politically important in the revolution of 1848 with Flora Tristan and Louis Blanc. Joan Scott has demonstrated how two very different visions of social structure came into intellectual combat in 1848 (Scott 1988: 113–38). Under the direction of Horace Say, Jean-Baptiste's son, the Chamber of Commerce commissioned a statistical representation of work in Paris. The report depicts a conflict-free world of *petite entreprises*, in which *industrie* denotes entrepreneurship as well as labour and in which the interests of all classes are in fundamental harmony. This was, Scott argues, a conscious attempt to dispute 'the radical claims of socialist revolutionaries, showing them to be misapprehensions, if not dangerous fantasies':

> The *Statistique* constructed and justified a model different from that offered by socialists and according to which economic, political, and moral order would be restored.
>
> (Scott 1988: 124)

The 'social harmony' analysis she explicitly attributes to Jean-Baptiste Say.

2 Blaug (1986: 212) claims that Say, relative to Cantillon for example, plays down the role of the entrepreneur in buying at certain spot prices and selling at uncertain forward prices. Steiner claims that this is an important aspect of Say's analysis and is, in fact, essential to make sense of his analysis (Steiner 1998a: 211).

3 This is a characteristic assumption and shows up in many places throughout the body of Say's work:

> Even though workmen attached to an industry may be better employed elsewhere...nevertheless, old workers and even farm entrepreneurs, manufacturers and merchants cannot change profession without suffering a considerable damage.
>
> (Say 1803, I: 291–2)

In this context, he distinguishes these factors from pure capital, which can easily be exported to animate foreign industry and 'in truth, the nation will lose nothing in interest, as long as the capitalist knows how to make it pay' (Say 1803, I: 291).

4 A considerably more difficult question emerges when we consider who creates the demand for entrepreneurs, as Steiner has recognised (Steiner 1998a: 211). It is the entrepreneur who channels the demand for the other productive services, but who, Steiner asks, creates a demand for entrepreneurship? Steiner correctly notes that Say's texts are largely silent on this point, but he addresses the question by distinguishing between the entrepreneur as a production manager, the role that Say emphasises when he attempts to explain the return to entrepreneurship in terms of market forces, and the entrepreneur as 'an agent...characterised by alertness in confrontation with uncertainty' (Steiner 1998a: 211) and on this distinction places Say's entrepreneur in the Cantillon–Knight tradition, which emphasises the role of uncertainty.

5 This accounts for the increasing animosity towards Ricardo and, especially, MacCulloch that Steiner finds in the fifth edition of the *Traité* (1826) and the *Cours Complet* (1928–9) compared with the fourth edition of the *Traité* (1819) (Steiner 1998a: 206). It is the simplistic corn model, much more apparent in

MacCulloch than Ricardo, that seems to suggest that returns to the different factors are determined by different laws, to which Say is reacting so vehemently.

6 Malthus was well aware of the distinction between Say's position on rent and his own. In the 1836 edition of his *Principles*, Malthus notes:

> In his 5th edition, vol. II, 346, he [i.e. Say] describes the subject anew, but he does not seize the right view of it. He still considers the price of the produce of land which occasions rent too much as the result of a common monopoly.
>
> (Malthus 1986 [1836]: 138)

By monopoly, Malthus apparently meant the excess of price over cost of production, or the upward slope of the supply curve, a characterisation with which Say would have agreed (Viner 1958: 360).

7 On this, see Marian Bowley (1973: 127 and 216), Larry Moss (1976: 110) and Samuel Hollander (1979: chapter 6 and p. 670).

8 I cannot find this passage in either the 1803 or 1814 editions.

9 'Until when must books on political economy contain chapters like this one?' (Say 1803, III: 249)

13 The ubiquitous law of markets

1 Depending on how you count. I can't find proposition five in Baumol's article.

2 The relevant passage from the fourth edition is translated by Prinsep as:

> It is worth while to remark, that a product is no sooner created, than it, from that instant, affords a market for other products to the full extent of its own value. When the producer has put the finishing hand to his product, he is most anxious to sell it immediately, lest its value should diminish in his hands. Nor is he less anxious to dispose of the money he may get for it; for the value of money is also perishable. But the only way of getting rid of money is in the purchase of some product or other. Thus, the mere circumstance of the creation of one product immediately opens a vent for other products.
>
> (Say 1821: 134–5)

3 In the second edition (Say 1814, II: 164), the mechanism of equilibration was still described as the loss of interest entailed in holding stocks of money. In the third edition, this mechanism was augmented by a feared loss of purchasing power in a period of rapid inflation and ongoing inflationary expectations (Say 1817, I: 145), a factor Say had already considered in a slightly different context in the first and second editions (Say 1803, I, 137; 1814, I: 165).

4 Consider Say's 'first letter to Malthus', in which he argues that the reason that English goods cannot find a market in Italy is because of the fact that punitive English trade laws mean that Italy cannot sell goods to England. If trade were liberalised, Italian production would increase, Italian sales to England would increase and English sales to Italy would increase (Say 1843: 617 'first letter to Malthus').

5 Note the similarity of this passage with Say (1880: 59).

14 *Idéologie* and the economics of J. B. Say

1 Even the popular press, in no less venerable a publication than *The New Yorker*, bears witness to our ancient and, presumably, human need to find meanings hidden to the unenlightened:

The news that the Bible encodes information about major events in world history…will have come as no surprise to people who spent much of 1969 listening to the Beatles' 'Abbey Road' played backward. These people learned long ago that if you are ingenious enough, patient enough, and perverse enough, texts will always reveal themselves to say what you want them to say. The sea of signs is without a bottom. There are no meanings so deep that deeper meanings cannot somehow be found.

(Menand 1997: 35)

15 An introduction to the translations: the public morality contest of Year VIII

1 In 'A study of the semantic field denoting happiness in ancient Greek to the end of the 5th century B.C.' (1969), C. de Heer claims that 'the sense of Ὄλβιος is more cognitive than emotive' (Heer 1969: 15), and that:

Ὄλβιος is applied to denote the possession of highly prized goods, material wealth, children, a wife who is singularly endowed, possessions which render a man's life complete or single him out as being above the ordinary. Applied to things it denotes possessions which render man Olbios and are given as a token of divine favour, or to which the gods attach their sanction in order to render them enduring.

(Heer 1969: 15)

The precision with which Say chose precisely the correct term to denote the sort of bourgeois happiness (or calm contentment and material ease), which he saw as the goal of good administration and political economy, demonstrates both that Say had attained at least an adequate classical knowledge notwithstanding the modern and scientific orientation of his boarding school and that *Olbie* was written with a care that justifies our attention. The style of this little book is beguilingly naive, but it contains a depth of analysis not dissimilar to the tracts of Rousseau upon which it was modelled.

2 The summary of the history of this particular prize contest is based on Staum's *Minerva's Message* (1996). See especially appendix 4, pp. 245–6.

3 Archives de l'Institut, Académie des Sciences morales et politiques, B4. See: Martin S. Staum (1996) *Minerva's Message. Stabilizing the French Revolution*. Montreal: McGill-Queen's University Press.

4 It is not entirely devoid of humour, although intentional humour is in short supply. I certainly laughed at the suggestion that one of the great achievements of the future Paris was to 'rationally plan' traffic circulation on the great innovation of having the traffic flowing in one direction confined to one side of the road. It brought to mind two pictures: one of imagined traffic circulation in 1770, and the other of the contemporary traffic flows I watched around L'Étoile. Rational traffic circulation is symbolic of the benefits to be derived from rational planning, according to Mercier. Because of the intervention of the state, there is no striving for precedence on the basis of competition and self-interest. This, of course, is a particularly striking example when we remember that our contemporary textbooks often point precisely to the problem of traffic circulation as an instance in which an implicit contract will emerge spontaneously without the necessary intervention of authority.

5 Sir Thomas More coined the word 'Utopia' from the Greek *ou* meaning 'not' and *topos* meaning 'place', which thus means 'nowhere'. During his embassy in Flanders in 1515, More wrote book II of *Utopia*, in which he described a communist and pagan nation entirely governed by reason; this was a significant contrast to the Christian Europe he described in book I written the next year, where self-interest

and greed for power and wealth governed political decisions. There are many sources on utopianism. Among the best are Manuel and Manuel (1979) and Baczko (1978). This latter discusses *L'An 2440* at length.

6　An alternative tradition, characterised by Swift's *Gulliver's Travels* (1726), is more directly satirical.

7　I cannot guess and I cannot find any references that speculate why the title may have been changed. Who knows?

8　The publishing history of this text is explored in Wilkie (1984).

9　This 'dream travel' is a device borrowed from medieval allegory. Mercier's protagonist falls asleep and awakens in a 'new world', which is explained to him by his philosopher guide, very much as Dante's 'pilgrim' is guided through *The Inferno* after a similar 'voyage'. It may seem clichéd today, but Mercier needed a device for time travel and there were not a lot of models from which to choose. Some utopias, such as Plato's *Republic* and indeed Say's *Olbie*, dispensed with the problem altogether by never having a narrator physically travel to a destination that actually existed. Had Mercier chosen the more conventional spatial distancing of the utopia from the everyday world, he could have relied upon ships to the South Pacific, or even the space travel that had begun to appear in contemporary literature such as Voltaire's *Micromégas* (1752).

10　There are many studies of the idea of progress. One that is still worth consulting is Bury (1932).

11　Note this passage from *De l'Angleterre et des Anglais*, in which Say contrasts England ('The English all work') and Paris:

> One is noticed there [i.e. in England] if one appears unoccupied and looking about. There are hardly any of these cafés full of idle people from morning to evening, and the walks there are deserted except on Sunday; there everyone is absorbed by business.
>
> (Say 1815: 19–20)

12　He was particularly critical of the alleged atheism of *idéologie*, and argued that social order could better be attained through an adherence to Kant's philosophy (Staum 1996: 54). As we have already seen, he lost no opportunity to deride the 'dolls' and 'men-machines' of Condillac.

13　According to Staum, 'Mercier...polished his reputation for originality with an anti-Newtonian flat earth theory and with a critique of the genius of French classical dramatists.' (Staum 1996: 54).

Bibliography

Manuscripts

Archives d'Autun
– papiers d'Amaury Duval

Archives de l'Institut, Académie des Sciences morales et politiques
– liste de mémoires à imprimer
– liste chronologique des mémoires lus par personne et par section
– concours sur la morale d'un peuple (2 concours, 15 et 8 mémoires)

Bibliothèque nationale
– manuscrits de J.-B. Say

British Museum
– Francis Place papers

University College (London)
– Bentham Collection

Books and articles

Albistur, M. and Armogathe, D. (1977) *Histoire du Féminisme Français: Du Moyen Âge à Nos Jours*, 2 vols, Paris: Edition des femmes.
Albury, W.R. (1986) 'The order of ideas: Condillac's method of analysis as a political instrument in the French Revolution', in J. Schuster and R. Yeo (eds) *The Politics and Rhetoric of Scientific Method: Historical Studies*, Dordrecht: Reidel.
Allix, E. (1910) 'J.-B. Say et les origines de l'industrialisme', *Revue d'Économie Politique* 24: 303–13, 341–63.
—(1911) 'La méthode et la conception de l'économie politique dans l'oeuvre de J.-B. Say', *Revue d'Histoire des Doctrines Économiques et Sociales* 4: 321–60.
—(1912) 'Destutt de Tracy, économiste', *Revue d'Économie Politique* 26: 425–30.
—(1912) 'L'Oeuvre économique de G. Garnier, traducteur d'Adam Smith et disciple de Cantillon', *Revue d'Histoire des Doctrines Économiques et Sociales* 5: 317–42.
—(1913) 'La rivalité entre la propriété foncière et la fortune mobilière sous la Révolution', *Revue d'Histoire des Doctrines Économique et Sociale* 6: 297–348.

Andrieux, F.-G.-J.-S. (1818–23) *Oeuvres de F.-G.-J.-S Andrieux*, 4 vols, Paris: Nepveu.

Augello, M.M. (1981) 'Il dibattito in Francia su economia e società e la soluzione "industralista" (1814–1830)', *Rassegna Economica*: 7–38.

Azouvi, F. (ed.) (1992) *L'Institution de la Raison: La Révolution Culturelle des Idéologues*, Paris: J. Vrin.

—(ed.) (1995) *La Science de l'Homme Selon Maine de Biran*, Paris: J. Vrin.

Bacon, F. (1878) *The Works of Francis Bacon*, Cambridge, MA: Hurd and Houghton.

Baczko, B. (1978) *Lumières et l'utopie*, Paris: Payot.

—(1988) 'The social contract of the French: Sieyès and Rousseau', *Journal of Modern History* 60, suppl.: 98–125.

Baecque, A.D. (1997) *The Body Politic, Corporeal Metaphor in Revolutionary France, 1770–1800*, trans. C. Mandell, Stanford, CA: Stanford University Press.

Baker, K.M. (1964) 'The early history of the term "Social Science" ', *Annals of Science* 20: 211–26.

—(1967) 'Scientism, élitism, and liberalism: the case of Condorcet', *Studies on Voltaire* 55: 129–65.

—(1973) 'Politics and social science in eighteenth-century France: the "Societe de 1789" ', in J.F. Bosher (ed.) *French Government and Society 1500–1850*, London: Athlone Press.

—(1975) *Condorcet: from Natural Philosophy to Social Mathematics*, Chicago: University of Chicago Press.

—(1982) 'On the problem of the ideological origins of the French Revolution', in D. LaCapra and S.L. Kaplan (eds) *Modern European Intellectual History: Reappraisals and New Perspectives*, Ithaca: Cornell University Press.

—(1989) 'Sieyès and revolutionary discourse', in L. Valtz (ed.) *The Languages of Revolution*, Milan.

—(1990) *Inventing the French Revolution*, Cambridge: Cambridge University Press.

Balassa, B.A. (1959) 'John Stuart Mill and the Law of Markets', *Quarterly Journal of Economics* 73: 263–74.

Baumol, W.J. (1977) 'Say's (at least) eight Laws, or what Say and James Mill may really have meant', *Economica* 44: 145–61.

Becker, G.S. and Baumol, W.J. (1952) 'The classical monetary theory: the outcome of the discussion', *Economica* 19: 355–76.

Bellanger, C. *et al.* (1969–76) *Histoire générale de la presse française*, 5 vols, Paris: Presses Universitaires de France.

Beraud, A. (1992) 'Ricardo, Malthus, Say et les controverses de la "seconde génération" ', in A. Beraud and G. Faccarello (eds) *Nouvelle Histoire de la Pensée Économique*, Paris: La Découverte.

Berman, L. (1968) 'The Marquis de Sade and his critics', *Mosaic* 1: 57–73.

Bernardin de Saint-Pierre, J. (1818) *Oeuvres complètes de Jacques-Henri Bernardin de Saint-Pierre*, L. Aimé-Martin (ed.), Paris: Méquignon-Marvis.

Berrian, A.H. (1954) *Stendhal and the Idéologues*, unpublished PhD thesis, New York University.

Bessières, P. and Niedzwiecki, Y. (1991) 'Women in the French Revolution (1789), bibliography', in *Women of Europe Supplements*, Brussels: Women's Information Service, Commission of the European Communities.

Bichat, F.-X. (1801) 'Anatomie générale appliquée à la physiologie et à la médecine', in Bichat (1852) *Recherches Physiologiques sur la Vie et la Mort*, Cerise (ed.), Paris: V. Masson.

—(1816) *Traité des membranes en général et de divers membranes en particulier*, Paris: Méquignon-Marvis.

—(1834) 'Anatomie générale', in M. Alibert *et al.* (eds) *Encyclopédie Médicale*, Paris: au Bureau de l'Encyclopédie.

—(1852) *Recherches Physiologiques sur la Vie et la Mort*, Cerise (ed.), Paris: V. Masson.

Biot J.-B. (1817) ' "Traité d'économie politique" par Jean-Baptiste Say', *Journal des Savans:* 396–400.

Biran, F.G. Maine de (1922–30) *Oeuvres Complètes*, P. Tisserand (ed.), Paris: Félix Allcan.

—(1987) 'Influence de l'habitude sur la faculté de penser', in G. Romeyer-Dherbey (ed.) *Oeuvres, tome 2*, Paris: J. Vrin.

—(1988) 'Mémoire sur la décomposition de la pensée', in F. Azouvi (ed.) *Oeuvres, tome 3*, Paris: J. Vrin.

Blaug, M. (1978) *Economic Theory in Retrospect*, 3rd edn, Cambridge: Cambridge University Press.

—(1986) *Great Economists Before Keynes*, Cambridge: Cambridge University Press.

—(1991) *Jean-Baptiste Say (1776 [sic] –1832)*, *Pioneers in Economics 15*, Aldershot: Edward Elgar Publishing.

Blum, C. (1986) *Rousseau and the Republic of Virtue, the Language of Politics in the French Revolution*, Ithaca: Cornell University Press.

Bowen, M. (1977) 'Introduction' in *L'An 2440, Rêve s'il en Fut Jamais* [1770], L.-S. Mercier (author), A. Pons (ed.), Paris: France Adel.

Bowley, M. (1973) *Studies in the History of Economic Theory Before 1870*, London: Macmillan.

Braudel, F. and Labrousse, E. (1975) *Histoire Économique et Sociale de la France*, Paris: Presses Universitaires de France.

Breton, Y. (1986) 'La place de la statistique et de l'arithmétique politique dans la méthodologie économique de Jean-Baptiste Say: Le temps des ruptures', *Revue Économique* 37: 1033–62.

—(1990) 'Germain Garnier, l'économiste et l'homme politique', in G. Faccarello and P. Steiner (eds) *La Pensée Économique Pendant la Révolution Française*, Grenoble: Presses Universitaires de Grenoble.

Breton, Y. and Lutfalla, M. (1991) *L'Économie Politique en France au XIXe Siècle*, Paris: Economica.

Bridenthal, R. and Koonz C. (1977) *Becoming Visible: Women in European History*, Boston: Houghton Mifflin Company.

Brinton, C. (1934) *A Decade of Revolution, 1789–1799*, New York: Harper.

Brodribb, S. (1992) 'Critical response to "Machiavelli's sisters" '. *Political Theory* 20: 332–6.

Brown, N.O. (1966) *Love's Body*, New York: Random House.

Buchanan, D. (1814) *Observations on the Subjects Treated in Dr. Smith's Inquiry into the Nature and Causes of the Wealth of Nations*, Edinburgh (vol. 4 of Buchanan's edition of the *Wealth of Nations*). Reprinted New York: A. M. Kelley, 1966.

Burrow, J.W. (1988) *Whigs and Liberals: Continuity and Change in English Political Thought*, Oxford: Oxford University Press.

Bury, J.B. (1932) *The Idea of Progress: an Inquiry into its Origin and Growth*, New York: Dover.

Busse, W. and Trabants, J. (eds) (1986) *Les Idéologues: Sémiotiques, Théories et Politiques Linguistiques Pendant la Révolution Française*, Amsterdam: J. Benjamins.

Butterfield, H. (1965) *The Origins of Modern Science*, revised edn, New York: Free Press.

Cabanis, A. (1975) *La Presse Sous le Consulat et l'Empire*, Paris: Société des Études Robespierristes.

Cabanis, P.-J.-G. (1823) *Oeuvres Complètes*, F. Thurot (ed.), Paris: Bossanges.

——(1867) *Rapports du Physique et du Moral de l'Homme* [1802], Paris: Victor Masson et fils.

——(1956) *Oeuvres Philosphiques*, C. Lehec and J. Cazeneuve (eds), Paris: Presses Universitaires de France.

Cahiers des Doléances des Femmes en 1789 et Autres Textes (1981) Paris: Editions des femmes.

Cameron, R.E. (1961) *France and the Economic Development of Europe 1800–1914*, Princeton: Princeton University Press.

Campbell, T.D. (1971) *Adam Smith's Science of Morals*, London: Allen and Unwin.

Canard, N. (1801) *Principes d'Économie Politique*, Paris: F. Buisson.

Cantillon, R. (1755) *Essai sur la Nature du Commerce en Général: Traduit de l'Anglais*, London: Gyles.

Carey, R.G. (1947) *The Liberals of France and Their Relation to the Development of Bonaparte's Dictatorship, 1799–1804*, Chicago: University of Chicago Press.

Cassirer, E. (1955) *The Philosophy of the Enlightenment*, trans. F.C.A. Koelln and J.P. Pettegrove, Boston: Houghton Mifflin.

Chartier, R. (1991) *The Cultural Origins of the French Revolution*, Durham, NC: Duke University Press.

Chipman, J.S. (1965) 'A survey of the theory of international trade: part 2, the neoclassical theory', *Econometrica* 33: 685–760.

Church, C.H. (1967) 'The social basis of the French central bureaucracy under the Directory', *Past and Present* 36: 59–72.

——(1973) 'In search of the Directory' in J.F. Bosher (ed.) *French Government and Society 1500–1850*, London: Athlone Press.

Cobban, A. (1964) *Rousseau and the Modern State*, Hamden: Archon.

Coleman, W.O. (1982) *Death is a Social Disease: Public Health and Political Economy in Early Industrial France*, Madison: University of Wisconsin Press.

——(1995) *Rationalism and Anti-rationalism in the Origins of Economics*, Cheltenham: Edward Elgar Publishing.

——(1996) 'How theory came to English classical economics', *Scottish Journal of Political Economy* 43: 207–28.

Collins, J. (1967) *God in Modern Philosophy*, Chicago: Gateway.

Colloque de la Pensée Économique Pendant la Révolution Française, Vizille (1989) 4 vols, Grenoble: Presses de l'Université de Grenoble.

Compte C. (1817) 'Le "Traité d'économie politique" par Jean-Baptiste Say', *Le Censeur Européen* 1: 159–227; 2: 169–221.

——(1828) 'Le "Cours complet d'économie politique pratique" de M. Say', *Le Moniteur Universel* 1761–2.

——(1833) 'Notice historique sur la vie et les ouvrages de J.-B. Say', in Say (1843).

Condillac, Etienne Bonnot de. (1776) *Le Commerce et le Gouvernement Considérés Relativement l'Un à l'Autre*, Paris: Jombert et Cellot.

——(1947–51) *Oeuvres Philosophiques*, G. Le Roy (ed.), Paris: Presses Universitaires de France.

—(1971) *An Essay on the Origin of Human Knowledge*, trans. T. Nugent, with an introduction by R.G. Weyant, Gainesville, FL: Scholars Facsimiles and Reprints.

—(1981) *Langue des Calculs* [1798], S. Auroux and A.-M. Chouillet (eds), Villeneuve-d'Ascq: Presses Universitaires de Lille.

Condorcet, M.-J.-A.N. Caritat, Marquis de (1785) *Essai sur l'Application de l'Analyse à la Probabilité des Décisions Rendues à la Pluralité des Voix*, Paris: Impr. royale.

—(1795) *Esquisse d'un Tableau Historique des Progès de l'Esprit Humain*, Paris.

—(1805) *Elémens du Calcul des Probabilités et son Application aux Jeux du Hasard à la Loterie, et aux Jugements des Hommes*, Paris: Royez.

—(1847–9) *Oeuvres de Condorcet*. A. Condorcet O'Connor and M.F. Arago (eds), Paris: Firmin Didot.

—(1988–9) *Cinq Mémoires sur l'Instruction Publique*. C. Coutel and C. Kintzler (introduction and eds), Paris: Edilig.

Constant B. (1957) *Oeuvres*, Paris: Gallimard.

—(1980 [1819]) 'De la liberté chez des anciens comparée à celle des modernes', in B. Constant, *De la Liberté Chez les Modernes: Écrits Politiques*, Paris: Hachette.

Coole, D. (1993) 'Constructing and deconstructing liberty: a feminist and poststructuralist analysis', *Political Studies* 41 (Mar): 83–95.

Crépel, P. and Gilain, C. (eds) (1989) *Condorcet Mathématicien, Économiste, Philosophe, Homme Politique*, Paris: Minerve.

Creuzé-Latouche, J. (an II [Year 2]) *Discours sur la Nécessité d'Ajouter à l'École Normale un Professeur d'Économie Politique*, Paris: Imprimerie nationale.

Crocker, L.G. (1963) *Nature and Culture, Ethical Thought in the French Enlightenment*, Baltimore: Johns Hopkins Press.

Crouzet, F. (1964) 'Wars, blockade, and economic change in Europe, 1792–1815', *Journal of Economic History* 24: 567–88.

Crystal, D. (1994) *The Cambridge Biographical Encyclopedia*, Cambridge: Cambridge University Press.

Daire, E. (ed.) (1846) *Les Physiocrates. Collection des principaux économistes II*, Paris: Guillaumin.

—(1848) 'Notice sur la vie et les ouvrages de J.-B. Say' in C. Comte, E. Daire and H. Say (eds) *Oeuvres Diverses de J.-B. Say*, Paris: Guillaumin.

Damamme, D. (1987) 'L'économie politique sous le Consulat et l'Empire, misère de l'économie, science de la richesse', *Oeconomia*: 49–62.

Darnton, R.C. (1968) 'The Grub Street style of revolution: J.-P. Brissot, police spy', *Journal of Modern History* 40: 301–27.

—(1971) 'The high Enlightenment and the low-life of literature', *Past and Present* 51: 81–115.

—(1971) 'In search of the Enlightenment: recent attempts to create a social history of ideas', *Journal of Modern History* 43: 113–32.

—(1971) 'Reading, writing and publishing in eighteenth-century France: a case study in the sociology of literature', *Daedalus* 100: 214–56.

—(1991) 'The literary revolution of 1789', *Studies in Eighteenth-Century Culture*: 3–26.

—(1992) *Gens de Lettres, Gens du Livre*, Paris: Odile Jacob.

—(1996) *The Forbidden Best-Sellers of Pre-Revolutionary France*, New York: Norton.

Daston, L. (1988) *Classical Probability in the Enlightenment*, Princeton: Princeton University Press.

—(1987a) 'Rational individuals versus laws of society: from probability to statistics', in L. Krüger, L.J. Daston, and M. Heidelberger (eds) *The Probabilistic Revolution*, Cambridge, MA: MIT Press.

—(1987b) 'The domestication of risk: mathematical probability and insurance 1650–1830', in L. Krüger, L.J. Daston, and M. Heidelberger (eds) *The Probabilistic Revolution*, Cambridge, MA: MIT Press.

Dautry, J. (1951) 'La révolution bourgeoise et l'Encyclopédie (1789–1814)', *La Pensée: Revue du Rationalisme Moderne* 38: 73–87; 39: 52–9.

Dawson, D. (1991–2) 'Teaching sensibility: Adam Smith, Rousseau, and the formation of the moral spectator', in *Études Écossaises Colloquium Proc.*, Grenoble: Presses de l'Université de Grenoble.

Degérando, J. (1800) *Des Signes, et le l'Art de Penser Considérés dans leurs Rapports Mutuels, 4 vols*, Paris: Goujon fils, Fuchs, Henrichs.

—(1802) *De la Génération des Connaissances Humaines*, Berlin: G. Decker.

Dejob, C. (No date) *L'Instruction Publique en France et en Italie au XIXe Siècle*, Paris: Colin.

Descartes, R. (1963) *Oeuvres Philosophiques*, F. Alquié (ed.), Paris: Garnier.

—(1968) *Discourse on Method and Other Writings*, Harmondsworth: Penguin.

Diderot, D. (1951) 'Sur les femmes', in A. Billy (ed.) *Oeuvres*. Paris: Gallimard, pp. 949–58.

Diderot, D. and d'Alembert, J. le Rond (eds) (1751–80) *Encyclopédie ou Dictionnaire Raisonné des Sciences, des Arts et Métiers*, Paris: Le Breton.

Dorigny, M. (1980–1) 'Les Girondins et la propriété', *Bulletin d'Histoire Économique et Sociale de la Révolution Française*: 15–31.

—(1988) 'La formation de la pensée économique de Sieyès d'après ses manuscrits (1770–1789)', *Annales Historiques de la Révolution Français*, 271: 17–34.

Dowd, D.L. (1969) *Pageant-Master of the Republic: Jacques-Louis David and the French Revolution*, New York: Books for Libraries Press.

Doyle, W. (1980) *Origins of the French Revolution*, Oxford: Oxford University Press.

—(1989) *The Oxford History of the French Revolution*, Oxford: Oxford University Press.

Drucker, P. (1985) *Innovation and Entrepreneurship*, New York: Harper and Row.

Dunoyer, C. (1827) 'Esquisse historique des doctrines auxquelles on a donné le nom d'industrialisme, c'est-à-dire des doctrines qui fondent la société sur l'industrie', *Revue Encyclopédique*: 368–94.

—(1827) 'Examen critique du "Traité d'économie politique" de M. Say', *Revue Encyclopédique*: 63–90.

—(1845) *De la Liberté du Travail ou Simple Exposé des Conditions dans Lesquelles les Forces Humaines s'Exercent avec le Plus de Puissance*, Paris: Guillaumin.

—(1853) 'Gouvernement', in C. Coquelin and C. Guillaumin (eds) *Dictionnaire de l'Économie Politique*, Paris: Guillaumin, pp. 835–41.

Du Pont de Nemours, P.-S. (1794) *Vues sur l'éducation nationale*, Paris: the author.

—(1955) *On Economic Curves*, H.W. Spiegel (ed.), Baltimore: The Johns Hopkins University Press.

—(1977) *The Economic Writings of Du Pont de Nemours*, J.J. McLain (ed.), Newark, DE: University of Delaware Press.

—(1979) *Oeuvres Politiques et Économiques*, Nendeln: KTO Press.

Durkheim, É. (1973) *Moral Education: A Study in the Theory and Application of the Sociology of Education*, E.K. Wilson (ed.), New York: The Free Press.

Duruy, A. (1882) *L'Instruction Publique et la Révolution*, Paris: Hachette.

Duvillard de Durand, E. (1787) *Recherches sur les Rentes, les Emprunts, et les Remboursements*, Paris: E. Duvillard de Durand.

Ehrard, J. (1963) *L'Idée de Nature en France dans la Première Moitié du XVIIIe Siècle*, Paris: Bibliothèque général de l'école pratique des hautes études. Section 6.

Ekelund, R.B. and Thornton, M. (1991) 'Geometrical analogies and market demand estimation: Dupuit and the French contribution', *History of Political Economy* 23: 397–418.

Eltis, S.M. and Eltis, W. (1998) *Condillac: Commerce and Government*, Cheltenham: Edward Elgar Publishing.

Euzent, P.J. and Martin, T.L. (1984) 'Classical roots of the emerging theory of rent-seeking – the contribution of Jean-Baptiste Say', *History of Political Economy* 16: 255–62.

Faccarello, G. (1998) *Studies in the History of French Political Economy*, London: Routledge.

Faccarello, G. and Steiner, P. (eds) (1991a) 'Une génération perdue?', in G. Faccarello and P. Steiner (eds) *La Pensée Économique Pendant la Révolution Française*, Grenoble: Presses Universitaires de Grenoble.

Faccarello, G. and Steiner, P. (eds) (1991b) *La Pensée Économique Pendant la Révolution Française*, Grenoble: Presses Universitaires de Grenoble.

Fargher, R. (1952) 'The retreat from Voltaireanism', in *The French Mind: Studies in Honour of Gustave Rudler*, Oxford: Clarendon Press.

Favre, P. (1983) 'La constitution d'une science du politique, le déplacement de ses objets, et l'irruption de l'histoire réelle', *Revue Française de Science Politique*: 181–219; 365–402.

Feller, É. and Goeury, J.-C. (1975) 'Les archives de l'Académie des Sciences morales et politiques, 1831–1848', *Annales Historiques de la Révolution Française* 47: 567–83.

Ferrier, F. (1805) *Du Gouvernement Considéré dans ses Rapports avec le Commerce*, Paris: Perlet.

—(1822) *Du Gouvernement Considéré dans ses Rapports avec le Commerce ou de l'Administration Commerciale Opposée aux Économistes du 19e Siècle*, 3ème edn, Paris: Pélicier.

Filmer, R. (1949) *Patriarcha and other Political Writings of Sir Robert Filmer*, P. Laslett (ed.), Oxford: Oxford University Press.

Firestone, S. (1970) *Dialectic of Sex, the Case for Feminist Revolution*, New York: Bantam.

Foley, V. (1976) *The Social Physics of Adam Smith*, West Lafayette, IN: Purdue University Press.

Fontaine, P. (1993) 'The concept of *Industrie* from the physiocrats to J.-B. Say', *Contributions to Political Economy* 12: 89–97.

—(1996) 'The French economists and politics, 1750–1850: the science and art of political economy', *Canadian Journal of Economics* 29: 379–93.

Forget, E.L. (1993) 'J.-B. Say on Adam Smith: an essay on the transmission of ideas', *Canadian Journal of Economics* 26: 121–33.

—(1994) 'Disequilibrium trade as a metaphor for social disorder in Say's *Traité d'Économie Politique*', *History of Political Economy*.

—(1997) 'The market for virtue: Jean-Baptiste Say on women and the family', *Feminist Economics* 3: 95–111.

Forrest, A. (1981) *The French Revolution and the Poor*, Oxford: Oxford University Press.

Foucault, M. (1965) *Madness and Civilization – a History of Insanity in the Age of Reason*, trans. R. Howard, New York: Vintage Books.

—(1972) *Naissance de la Clinique – Une Archéologie du Regard Médical*, Paris: Gallimard.

—(1994) *The Order of Things*, New York: Vintage Books.

—(1995) *Discipline and Punish*, New York: Vintage Books.

Fraisse, G. (1994) *Reason's Muse: Sexual Difference and the Birth of Democracy*, Chicago: University of Chicago Press.

Freud, S. (1962) *Civilization and its Discontents* [1930], New York: Norton.

Frick, J. (1987) 'Philosophie et économie politique chez J.-B. Say', *Histoire, Économie, et Société* 60: 51–66.

Furbank, P.N. (1992) 'Poverty and compassion', *Raritan* 12: 138–56.

Furet, F. (1981) *Interpreting the French Revolution* [1977], Cambridge: Cambridge University Press.

Gaffarel, P. (1889) 'L'opposition littéraire sous le Consulat', *La Révolution Française: Revue d'Histoire Contemporaine* 9: 307–26; 397–432.

Ganilh, C. (1806) *Essai Politique sur le Revenu Public*, Paris: Giguet et Michaud.

—(1809) *Des Systèmes d'Économie Politique, de Leurs Inconvénients, de Leurs Avantages et de la Doctrine la Plus Favorable aux Progrès de la Richesse des Nations*, Paris: Xhrouet.

—(1815) *La Théorie de l'Économie Politique, Fondée sur les Faits Résultant des Statistiques de la France et de l'Angleterre, sur l'Expérience de Tous les Peuples Célèbres par Leurs Richesses et sur les Lumières de la Raison*, Paris: Déterville.

—(1817) *De la Législation, de l'Administration et de la Comptabilité des Finances de la France, Depuis la Restauration*, Paris, Déterville.

—(1825) *De la Science des Finances et du Ministère de M. le Comte de Villèle*, Paris: Trouvé.

Garnier, G. (1796) *Abrégé Élémentaire des Principes Économiques*, Paris: H. Agasse.

—(1802) 'Préface et notes sur les "Recherches sur la nature et les causes de la richesse des nations" ', Paris: H. Agasse.

Garnier, J.-J. (1786) *Histoire de France Depuis l'Établissement de la Monarchie*, vol. 29, Paris: Saillant et Nyon, Veuve Desaint.

Gide, C. and Rist, C. (1947) *Histoire des Doctrines Économiques*, 7th edn, Paris; trans. E.F. Row, Boston, MA: Heath, 1948.

Gillispie, C.C. (1959) 'The Encyclopédie and the Jacobin philosophy of science – a study in ideas and consequences', in M. Clagett (ed.) *Critical Problems in the History of Science*, Madison: University of Wisconsin Press.

Ginguené, P. (1807–13) *Rapports lus à l'Assemblée Générale de l'Institut sur les Travaux de la Classe d'Histoire et Littérature ancienne Paris*.

Girarad, L. (1985) *Les Libéraux Français*, Paris: Aubier.

Gobert, A. (1925) *L'Opposition des Assemblées Pendant le Consulat*, Paris: E. Sagot.

Godechot, J. (1968) *Les Institutions de France Sous la Révolution et l'Empire*, 2nd edn, Paris: Presses Universitaires de France.

Godineau, D. (1998) *The Women of Paris and their French Revolution*, trans. K. Streip, Berkeley: University of California Press.

Goetz, R. (1993) *Destutt de Tracy, Philosphie du Langage et Science de l'Homme*, Geneva: Droz.

Goldstein, J. (1987) *Console and Classify: the French Psychiatric Profession in the Nineteenth Century*, Cambridge: Cambridge University Press.

Goodman, D. (1989) 'Enlightenment salons: the convergence of female and philosophic ambitions', *Eighteenth-Century Studies* 22 (3): 329–67.

—(1994) *The Republic of Letters: a Cultural History of the French Enlightenment*, Ithaca: Cornell University Press.

Goodwin, A. (1937) 'The French Directory – a revaluation', *History* 22: 201–18.

Gordon, B.J. (1965) 'Say's Law, effective demand, and the contemporary British periodicals, 1820–1850', *Economica* 32: 438–56.

Granger, G.-G. (1956) *La Mathématique Sociale du Marquis de Condorcet*, Paris: J. Vrin.

Grégoire, H. (1814) *De la Domesticité Chez les Peuples Anciens et Modernes*, Paris: A. Egron.

Greenleaf, W.H. (1964) *Order, Empiricism and Politics: Two Traditions of English Political Thought*, Oxford: Oxford University Press.

Grimsley, R. (1967) 'Some aspects of "nature" and "language" in the French Enlightenment', *Studies on Voltaire* 56: 659–77.

Guillois, A. (1894) *Le Salon de Mme Helvétius. Cabanis et les Idéologues*, Paris: Calmann Lévy.

Gusdorf, G. (1978) *La Conscience Révolutionnaire, les Idéologues*, Paris: Payot.

Haakonssen, K. (1981) *The Science of a Legislator, the Natural Jurisprudence of David Hume and Adam Smith*, Cambridge: Cambridge University Press.

—(1990) 'Natural Law and moral realism: the Scottish synthesis', in M.A. Stewart (ed.) *Studies in the Philosophy of the Scottish Enlightenment*, Oxford: Clarendon Press.

Hahn, R. (1971) *The Anatomy of a Scientific Instititution – the Paris Academy of Sciences, 1666–1803*, Berkeley: University of California Press.

Haines, B. (1988) 'The Athénée de Paris and the Bourbon Restoration', *History and Technology* 5: 249–71.

Halévy, E. (1955) *The Growth of Philosophical Radicalism*, Boston: The Beacon Press.

Hamowy, R. (1987) *The Scottish Enlightenment and the Theory of Spontaneous Order*, Carbondale, IL: Southern Illinois University Press.

Hampson, N. (1974) *The Life and Opinions of Maximilien Robespierre*, Oxford: Basil Blackwell.

—(1983) *Will and Circumstance: Montesquieu, Rousseau and the French Revolution*, Norman, OK: University of Oklahoma Press.

—(1988) *Prelude to Terror, the Constituent Assembly and the Failure of Consensus, 1789–1791*, Oxford: Basil Blackwell.

Haraway, D.J. (1991) *Simians, Cyborgs and Women, the Reinvention of Nature*, London: Routledge.

Harth, E. (1992) *Cartesian Women: Versions and Subversions of Rational Discourse in the Old Regime*, Ithaca: Cornell University Press.

Hashimoto, H. (1980) 'Notes inédites de J.-B. Say qui couvrent les marges de la *Richesse des Nations* et qui la critiquent: rédigées avec une introduction', *KSU [Kyoto Sangyo University] Economic and Business Review* 7: 53–81.

—(1982) 'Notes inédites de J.-B. Say qui couvrent les marges de la *Richesse des Nations* et qui la resument: rédigées avec une introduction', *KSU Economic and Business Review* 9: 31–133.

Hayek, F.A. (1949) *Individualism and Economic Order*, London: Routledge and Kegan Paul.

—(1955) *The Counter-Revolution of Science*, New York: The Free Press.

—(1967) 'The results of human action but not of human design', in Hayek *Studies in Philosophy, Politics and Economics*, Chicago: The University of Chicago Press.

—(1973) *Law, Legislation and Liberty. Rules and Order*, London: Routledge and Kegan Paul.

—(1978) *New Studies in Philosophy, Politics, Economics and the History of Ideas*, London: Routledge and Kegan Paul.

—(1988) *The Fatal Conceit. The Errors of Socialism*, Chicago: University of Chicago Press.

Hazard, P. (1963a) *The European Mind 1680–1715*, trans. J.L. May, Cleveland: World Publishing Co.

—(1963b) *European Thought in the Eighteenth Century from Montesquieu to Lessing*, trans. J. L. May, Cleveland: World Publishing Co.

Head, B.W. (1982) 'Origins of "La Science Sociale" in France, 1770–1800', *Australian Journal of French Studies* 19: 115–32.

—(1985) *Ideology and Social Science. Destutt de Tracy and French liberalism*, Dordrecht: Martinus Nijhoff.

Hébert, R.F. and Link, A.N. (1982) *The Entrepreneur*, New York: Oxford University Press.

Hecht, J. (1986) 'Une héritière des Lumières, de la physiocratie et de l'idéologie: la première chaire française d'économie politique (1795)', *Economies et Sociétés, Cahiers de l'I.S.M.E.A., série P.E.* 6: 5–48.

Heer, C. de (1969) *Makar, Eudaimon, Olbios, Eutyches*, Amsterdam: Adolf M. Kakkert.

Heertje, A. (1971) 'Two letters from James Mill to Jean-Baptiste Say', *History of Political Economy* 3: 415–18.

Helvétius, C.-A. (1794) *Oeuvres Complètes*, 4 vols, Paris: P. Didot l'ainé.

Hesse, C. (1991) *Publishing and Cultural Politics in Revolutionary Paris 1789–1810*, Berkeley: University of California Press.

Hill, M.J. (1973) 'The French perception of and reaction to early nineteenth century industrialization', *Proceedings of the Annual Meeting of the Western Society for French History* I: 199–213.

Hirsch, J.P. (1975) 'Commercial ambience, spirit of system and power on the eve of the French Revolution', *Annales – Economies, Sociétés et Civilisations* 30: 1337–70.

Hirschman, A.O. (1977) *The Passions and the Interests*, Princeton: Princeton University Press.

Hoffmann, P. (1977) *La Femme dans la Pensée des Lumières*, Paris: Éditions Ophrys.

[Holbach, P.T. Baron de] (1774) *Système de la Nature, par Mirabaud*, 2 vols. London [Paris].

Hollander, J. and Gregory, T.E. (eds) (1928) *Notes on Malthus' 'Principles of Political Economy'*, Baltimore: Johns Hopkins.

Hollander, S. (1973) *The Economics of Adam Smith*, Toronto: University of Toronto Press.

—(1979) *The Economics of David Ricardo*, Toronto: University of Toronto Press.

—(1985) *The Economics of John Stuart Mill*, Toronto: University of Toronto Press.

—(1997) *The Economics of Thomas Robert Malthus*, Toronto: University of Toronto Press.

Hont, I. and Ignatieff, M. (1983) 'Needs and justice in the *Wealth of Nations*: an introductory essay', in Hont and Ignatieff (eds) *Wealth and Virtue, The Shaping of Political Economy in the Scottish Enlightenment*, Cambridge: Cambridge University Press.

Hooper (1772) *Memoirs of the Year Two Thousand Five hundred*, London:Horner, F.

(1853) *Memoirs and Correspondence of Francis Horner*, L. Horner (ed.), London.

Hume, D. (1978) *A Treatise of Human Nature* [1739–40], L.A. Selby-Bigge and P.H. Nidditch (eds), Oxford: Oxford University Press.

—(1982) *The Philosophical Works of David Hume*, T.H. Green and T.H. Grose (eds), London: Longmans, Green.

—(1985) *Essays Moral Political and Literary*, E.F. Miller (ed.), Indianapolis: Liberty Press.

Hunt, L. (1984) *Politics, Culture, and Class in the French Revolution*, Berkeley: University of California Press.

—(1992) *The Family Romance of the French Revolution*, Berkeley: University of California Press.

Hunt, L., Lansky, D. and Hanson, P. (1979) 'The failure of the liberal republic in France, 1795–1799: the road to Brumaire', *Journal of Modern History* 51: 734–59.

Jacyna, L.S. (1987) 'Medical science and moral science: the cultural relations of physiology in Restoration France', *History of Science* 25: 111–46.

James, M. (1977) 'Pierre-Louis Roederer, Jean-Baptiste Say and the concept of "industrie" ', *History of Political Economy* 9: 455–75.

Jardin, A. (1985) *Histoire du Libéralisme Politique*, Paris: Hachette.

Jefferson, T. (1903–4) *The Writings of Thomas Jefferson*, A. Lipscomb and A.E. Bergh (eds), Washington: The Thomas Jefferson Foundation.

Jennings, J. (1992) 'The déclaration des droits de l'homme et du citoyen and its critics in France: reaction and "idéologie" ', *Historical Journal* 35: 839–59.

Jenyns, S. (1790) 'A free inquiry into the nature and origin of evil [1787]', in *The Works of Soame Jenyns, Esq.*, London.

Johnson, S. (1787) 'Review of a free inquiry into the nature and origin of evil', in *The Works of Samuel Johnson, LL.D.*, London.

Jones, J.F. (1978) *La Nouvelle Héloïse, Rousseau and Utopia*, Geneva: Droz.

Jones, R. (1992) 'Philosophical time travellers', *Antiquity* 66: 744–57.

Kadish, D.Y. (1991) *Politicizing Gender: Narrative Strategies in the Aftermath of the French Revolution*, New Brunswick, NJ: Rutgers University Press.

Kafker, F.A. (1967) 'Les encyclopédistes et la Terreur', *Revue l'Histoire Moderne et Contemporaine* 14: 284–95.

Kaiser, T.E. (1976) 'The idéologues: from enlightenment to positivism', unpublished PhD thesis, Harvard University.

—(1980) 'Politics and political economy in the thought of the ideologues', *History of Political Economy* 12: 141–60.

Kaplan, S.L. (1982) 'The famine plot persuasion in eighteenth-century France', *Transactions of the American Philosophical Society* 72, Philadelphia: American Philosophical Society

—(1984) *Provisioning Paris, Merchants and Millers in the Grain and Flour Trade During the Eighteenth Century*, Ithaca: Cornell University Press.

Kates, G. (1985) *The Cercle Social, the Girondins, and the French Revolution*, Princeton: Princeton University Press.

Kates, S. (1998) *Say's Law and the Keynesian Revolution: How Macroeconomic Theory Lost Its Way*, Aldershot: Edward Elgar Publishing.

Kennedy, E. (1973) 'Destutt de Tracy and the origins of ideology', unpublished PhD dissertation, Brandeis University.

——(1978) *A 'Philosophe' in the Age of Revolution: Destutt de Tracy and the Origins of 'Ideology'*, Philadelphia: American Philosophical Society.

——(1989) *A Cultural History of the French Revolution*, New Haven: Yale University Press.

Keohane, N.I. (1980) *Philosophy and the State in France: the Rennaissance to the Enlightenment*, Princeton: Princeton University Press.

Keynes, J.M. (1973) *The General Theory of Employment, Interest and Money* [1936], London: Macmillan.

Kitchin, J. (1966) *Un Journal 'Philosophique': La Décade (1794–1807)*, Paris: M.J. Minard.

Klein, D. (1985) 'Deductive economic methodology in the French Enlightenment: Condillac and Destutt de Tracy', *History of Political Economy* 17: 51–71.

Knight, I. (1968) *The Geometric Spirit: the Abbé de Condillac and the French Enlightenment*, New Haven: Yale University Press.

Koolman, G. (1971) 'Say's conception of the role of the entrepreneur', *Economica* 38: 269–86.

Koyré, A. (1948) 'Condorcet', *Journal of the History of Ideas* 9: 131–52.

Krüger, L., Daston, L.J. and Heidelberger, M. (eds) (1987) *The Probabilistic Revolution*, Cambridge, MA: MIT Press.

Kula, W. (1986) *Measures and Men*, Princeton: Princeton University Press.

Laboulle, M.J. (1939) 'La mathématique sociale: Condorcet et ses prédécesseurs', *Revue d'Histoire Littéraire de la France* 46: 33–5.

Ladd, E.C. (1962) 'Helvetius and d'Holbach – La moralisation de la politique', *Journal of the History of Ideas* 23: 221–38.

Lambert, P. (1952) 'La loi des débouchés avant J.B. Say et la polémique Say-Malthus', *Revue d'Économie Politique*: 5–26.

Lameth A. de (1819) 'Economie politique', *La Minerve*: 164–71.

Landes, J.B. (1988) *Women and the Public Sphere in the Age of the French Revolution*, Ithaca: Cornell University Press.

La Revellière-Lépeaux, L.-M. (1796) *Réflexions sur le Culte, sur les Cérémonies Civiles, et sur les Fêtes Nationales*, Paris: H.J. Jansen.

Larrère, C. (1992) *L'Invention de l'Économie au XVIIIe siècle: Du Droit Naturel à la Physiocratie*, Paris: Presses Universitaires de France.

Lavoisier, A. (1789) *Traité Élémentaire de Chimie*, 2 vols, Paris: Cuchet.

Lawrence, C. and Shapin, S. (1998) *Science Incarnate: Historical Embodiments of Natural Knowledge*, Chicago: University of Chicago Press.

Leary, D.E. (1990) *Metaphors in the History of Psychology*, Cambridge: Cambridge University Press.

Lebeau, A. (1903) *Condillac, Économiste*, Paris.

Lebrun, R.A. (1988) *Joseph de Maistre: an Intellectual Militant*, Montreal: McGill-Queen's University Press.

Le Roy, G. (1937) *La Psychologie de Condillac*, Paris: Boivin.

Leroy, M. (1962) *Histoire des Idées Sociales en France*, Paris: Gallimard.

Le Roy Ladurie, E. and Goy, J. (1981) *Tithe and Agrarian History from the 14th to the 19th Century*, Cambridge: Cambridge University Press.

Lee, V. (1975) *The Reign of Women in Eighteenth-Century France*, Cambridge, MA: Schenkman.

Lefebvre, G. (1962) *The French Revolution*, vol. I, trans. E. Moss Evanson; vol. II, trans. J. Hall Stewart and J. Friugliettei, New York: Routledge and Kegan Paul.

—(1964) *The French Revolution from 1793 to 1799*, New York: Columbia University Press.

—(1966) *The Thermidorians*, trans. R. Baldick, New York: Routledge and Kegan Paul.

—(1967) *The Directory*, trans. R. Baldick, New York: Routledge and Kegan Paul.

Leith, J.A. (1965) *The Idea of Art as Propaganda in France, 1750–1799: a Study in the History of Ideas*, Toronto: University of Toronto Press.

—(1968) *Media and Revolution*, Toronto: CBC Publications.

—(1991) *Space and Revolution: Projects for Monuments, Squares, and Public Buildings in France, 1789–1799*, Montreal: McGill-Queen's University Press.

Levan-Lemesle, L. (1980) 'La promotion de l'économie politique en France au XIXe siècle jusqu'à son introduction dans les facultés (1815–1881)', *Revue d'Histoire Moderne et Contemporaine*: 270–94.

Levasseur, E. (1905–6) 'L'économie politique au Conservatoire des Arts et Métiers', *Revue d'Économie Politique*.

Levi, A. (1964) *French Moralists: the Theory of the Passions 1585–1689*, Oxford: Oxford University Press.

Levy, D.G., Applewhite, H.B. and Johnson, M.D. (eds and trans.) (1979) *Women in Revolutionary Paris, 1789–1795: Selected Documents*, Urbana: University of Illinois Press.

Lichtheim, G. (1967) 'The concept of ideology', in Lichtheim (ed.) *The Concept of Ideology and Other Essays*, New York: Random House.

Liesse A. (1901) 'Un professeur d'économie politique sous la Restauration', *Journal des Économistes*: 3–22; 161–174.

—(1932) 'La loi des débouchés, conditions suivant lesquelles elle s'exerce', *Journal des Économistes*.

Liggio, L.P. (1985) 'Richard Cantillon and the French economists: distinctive French contributions of Richard Cantillon and J.B. Say', *Journal of Libertarian Studies* 7: 295–304.

Lindgren, J.R. (1973) *The Social Philosophy of Adam Smith*, The Hague: Martinus Nijhoff.

Locke, J. (1954) *Essays on the Law of Nature*, W. Von Leyden (ed.), Oxford: Clarendon Press.

—(1956) *An Essay Concerning Human Understanding*, Chicago: Henry Regnery.

Lough, J. (1982) *The Philosophes and Post-Revolutionary France*. Oxford: Oxford University Press.

Lovejoy, A.O. (1948) *Essays in the History of Ideas*, Baltimore: Johns Hopkins University Press.

—(1936, 1960) *The Great Chain of Being – a Study of the History of an Idea*, New York: University of Chicago Press.

Lutfalla, M. (1979) 'Jean-Baptiste Say et les siens: une famille d'économistes – trois générations des Lumières à la IIIe. République', *Revue d'Économie Politique* 3: 389–407.

—(1986) '19th Century enlightenment: French economic liberals 1789–1851', *Economia delle scelte publiche*.

—(1991) 'Jean-Baptiste Say, le fondateur' in Y. Breton and M. Lutfalla *L'Économie Politique en France au XIXe Siècle,* Paris: Economica.

Mably, G. Bonnot de (1797) 'Doutes proposés aux philosophes économistes, sur l'ordre naturel et essentiel des sociétés politiques' [1768], in *Oeuvres Complètes de Mably,* vol. 21, Paris: Bosange, Masson and Besson.

MacIntyre, A. (1981) *After Virtue: a Study in Moral Theory,* London: Duckworth.

Malthus, T.R. (1986) 'Principles of political economy [1836]', in E.A. Wrigley and D. Souden (eds) *The Works of Thomas Robert Malthus,* vols 5 and 6, London.

Mandler, P. (1990) *Aristocratic Government in the Age of Reform,* Oxford: Oxford University Press.

Manuel, F.E. (1956) 'From equality to organicism', *Journal of the History of Ideas* 17: 54–69.

Manuel, F.E. and Manuel, F.P. (1979) *Utopian Thought in the Western World,* Cambridge, MA: Belknap Press.

Margerison, K. (1978) 'P.-L. Roederer, the industrial capitalist as revolutionary', *Eighteenth-Century Studies* 2: 473–88.

—(1983) *P.-L. Roederer: Political Thought and Practice in the French Revolution,* Philadelphia: American Philosophical Society.

Martin, K. (1980) *The Rise of French Liberal Thought, a Study of Political Ideas from Bayle to Condorcet,* 2nd edn, Westport, CN: Greenwood Press.

Marx, K. (1954) *Capital,* Moscow: Progress Publishers.

Matucci, M. (ed.) (1991) *Gli 'Idéologues' e la Rivoluzione,* Pisa: Pacini.

Mauzi, R. (1960) *L'Idée du Bonheur dans la Littérature et la Pensée Françaises au XVIIIe Siècle,* Paris: Albin Michel.

Meek, R.L. (1967) 'The Scottish contribution to Marxist sociology', in *Economics and Ideology,* London: Chapman & Hall.

—(1973) *Precursors of Adam Smith,* London: Macmillan.

—(1976) 'New light on Adam Smith's Glasgow lectures on jurisprudence', *History of Political Economy* 8: 439–77.

—(1976) *Social Science and the Ignoble Savage,* Cambridge: Cambridge University Press.

Mellon S. (1958) *The Political Uses of History, a Study of the Historians of the French Restoration,* Stanford: Stanford University Press.

Melzer, S. and Rabine, L. (eds) (1992) *Rebel Daughters: Women and the French Revolution,* New York: Oxford University Press.

Mémoires de l'Institut National des Sciences et Arts. Sciences Morales et Politiques, (an IV–an XI [1796–1803]), Paris: Baudouin.

Menand, L. (1997) 'Is "The Bible Code" this year's highbrow Ouija board?', *The New Yorker* (June 16): 35.

Ménard, C. (1978) *La Formation d'une Rationalité Économique: A.A. Cournot,* Paris.

—(1980) 'Three forms of resistance to statistics', *History of Political Economy* 12: 524–41.

Mercer, P. (1972) *Sympathy and Ethics: a Study of the Relationship Between Sympathy and Morality, with Special Reference to Hume's Treatise,* Oxford: Clarendon.

[Mercier, L.-S.] (1771) *Memoires de l'An 2440: Rêve s'il en Fût Jamais.* Amsterdam.

—(1781) *Tableau de Paris,* Neufchatel: S. Fauche.

—(1789–98) *Paris Pendant la Révolution, ou la Nouveau Paris,* Paris: Poulet-Malassis.

—(1799) *L'An 2440: Rêve s'il en Fût Jamais,* Bresson et Carteret.

—(1977) *L'An 2440, Rêve s'il en Fût Jamais* [1770], A. Pons (ed.), Paris: France Adel.

Mercier de la Rivière, Paul Pierre Le (1910) *L'Ordre Naturel et Essentiel des Sociétés Politiques* [1767], E. Depître (ed.), Paris. Reprinted in Daire (1846)

Meunier, C.E. (1942) *Essai sur la Théorie des Débouchés de J.B. Say*, unpublished PhD thesis, University of Toulouse.

Michel, G. (1898) 'Une dynastie d'économistes: Jean-Etienne, Jean-Baptise et Horace Say', *Journal des Économistes*.

Mill, A.J. (1960) *John Mill's Boyhood Visit to France*, Toronto: University of Toronto Press.

Mill, J. (1804) 'Lord Lauderdale on public wealth', *Literary Journal* 4: 1–18.

—(1805) 'Traité d'économie politique', *Literary Journal* 5: 412–25.

—(1806) 'Sir James Steuart's Works', *Literary Journal* 1 (2nd series): 225–35.

—(1807) *Commerce Defended*, London: C. and B. Baldwin.

[—] (1808) 'Mill's commerce defended', *Eclectic Review*, 4: 554–9.

Mill, J.S. (1923) *Principles of Political Economy, With Some of their Applications to Social Philosophy* [1848], W.J. Ashley (ed.), New York: Longmans, Green and Co.

—(1961 onwards) *Collected Works of John Stuart Mill*, J. Robson (ed.), Toronto: University of Toronto Press (referred to as CW).

—(1969) 'Three essays on religion', in CW.

—(1977) 'Considerations on representative government', in CW.

—(1981) 'Autobiography', in CW.

Minowitz, P. (1993) *Profits, Priests, and Princes: Adam Smith's Emancipation of Economics from Politics and Religion*, Stanford: Stanford University Press.

Mirabeau, Honoré de Riqueti Comte de (1791) *Travail sur l'Éducation Publique, Trouvé dans les Papiers de Mirabeau l'Aîné par P.-J.-G. Cabanis*, Paris: Imprimerie nationale.

Mirowski, P. (1989) *More Heat Than Light*, Cambridge: Cambridge University Press.

Montesquieu, C.-L. de Secondat, Baron (1961) *De l'Esprit des Lois*, 2 vols, Paris: Le Seuil.

Moore, F.C.T. (1970) *The Psychology of Maine de Biran*, Oxford: Oxford University Press.

Moravia, S. (1968) *Il Tramonto dell'Illuminismo – Filosofia e Politica Nella Società Francese (1770–1810)*. Bari: Laterza.

—(1972) 'Philosophie et médecine en France à la fin du XVIIIe. siècle', in *Studies on Voltaire and the Eighteenth Century* 89: 1089–151.

—(1974) *Il Pensiero Degli Idéologues: Scienza e Filosofia in Francia, 1780–1815*, Florence: La Nuova Italia.

—(1976) 'Les idéologues et l'âge des lumières', *Studies on Voltaire and the Eighteenth Century*: 1465–86.

Mornet, D. (1933) *Les Origines Intellectuelles de la Révolution Française: 1715–1787*, Paris: Colin.

Moses, C.G. (1984) *French Feminism in the 19th Century*, Albany: State University of New York.

Moss, L. (1976) *Mountifort Longfield: Ireland's First Professor of Political Economy*, Ottawa, IL.

Murphy, A.E. (1987) *Richard Cantillon: Entrepreneur and Economist*, Oxford: Clarendon.

O'Brien, D.P. (1975) *The Classical Economists*, Oxford: Oxford University Press.

Okin, S.M. (1994) 'Political liberalism, justice and gender (review article)', *Ethics* 105: 23–43.

Olsen, M. (1992) 'A failure of enlightened politics in the French Revolution: The Société de 1789', *French History* 6: 303–34.

—(1993) *The Emergence of the Social Sciences, 1642–1792*, New York: Twayne.

Outram, D. (1989) *The Body and the French Revolution: Sex, Class, and Political Culture*, New Haven: Yale University Press.

Ozouf, M. (1988) *Festivals in the French Revolution*, Cambridge MA: Harvard University Press.

Paganini, G. (1992) 'Psychologie et physiologie de l'entendement chez Condillac', *Dix-huitième Siècle* 24: 165–78.

Palgrave, Sir Robert Harry Inglis (1906–9) *The Dictionary of Political Economy*, London: Macmillan.

Palmer, R.R. (1985) *The Improvement of Humanity: Education and the French Revolution*, Princeton: Princeton University Press.

—(1997) *An Economist in Troubled Times*, Princeton: Princeton University Press.

Paz, O. (1998) *An Erotic Beyond: Sade*, trans. E. Weinberger, New York: Harcourt Brace.

Perrot, J. (1988) 'Condorcet: de l'économie politique aux sciences de la société', *Revue de Synthèse*, IVe série, vol. I: 13–37.

—(1992a) *Une Histoire Intellectuelle de l'Économie Politique (XVIIe–XVIIIe Siècle)*, Paris: Éditions de l'École des hautes Études en Sciences sociales.

—(1992b) 'La main invisible et le Dieu caché' in *Une Histoire Intellectuelle de l'Économie Politique*, Paris: Editions des Hautes Etudes en Sciences Sociales, pp. 333–54.

Perrot, J. and Woolf, S.J. (1984) *State and Statistics in France 1789–1815*, Chur: Harwood Academic Publishers.

Petitain, G. (1801) *Question proposée...L'Émulation...*, Paris: Renouard.

Petty, W. (1986) *The Economic Writings of Sir William Petty*, C. Hull (ed.), Fairfield NJ: A. M. Kelley.

Piau-Gilot, C. (1981) 'Le discours de Jean-Jacques Rousseau sur les femmes, et sa réception critique', *Dix-huitième Siècle* 13: 317–37.

Picavet, F. (1891) *Les Idéologues – Essai sur l'Histoire des Idées et des Théories Scientifiques, Philosophiques, Religieuses, etc. en France Dupuis 1789*, Paris: F. Alcan.

Pinel, P. (1787) 'Extrait d'un mémoire lu à l'Académie des sciences en 1785 sur l'application des mathématiques sur le mécanisme des luxations en général', *Journal de Physique* 31, part II: 350–562.

—(1788) 'Extrait d'un mémoire lu a l'Académie des sciences en 1786 sur le mécanisme des luxations de l'humerus', *Journal de Physique* 33, part II: 12–24.

—(1792) 'Recherches sur une nouvelle mode de classification des quadrupèdes, fondée sur la structure méchanique des parties osseuses qui servent à l'articulation de la mâchoire inférieure', *Actes de la Société d'Histoire Naturelle de Paris*: 50–60.

—(1797) 'Mémoire sur la manie périodique ou intermittente', *Mém. de la Soc. Méd. d'Emulat. de Paris* 1.

—(1799) 'Observations sur les aliénés et leur division en espèces distinctes', *Mém. de la Soc. Méd. d'Emulat. de Paris* 3.

—(1801) *Traité Médico-Philosophique sur l'Alienation Mentale ou la Manie*, Paris: J.A. Brosson.

—(1804) *La Médecine Clinique Rendue plus Précise et Plus Exacte Par l'Application de l'Analyse, ou Recueil et Résultat d'Observations sur les Maladies Aigues Faites à la Salpétrière*, Paris: J.A. Brosson. [3rd edn, Paris: 1815]

—(1809) *Traité Médico-Philosophique sur l'Alienation Mentale ou la Manie*, 2nd edn, Paris: J.A. Brosson.

—(1812) 'Analyse', in *Dictionnaire des Sciences Médicales*, Paris: Crapart et Pancoucke.

—(1813) *Nosographie Philosophique, ou la Méthode de l'Analyse Appliquée à la Médecine*, 5th edn [1st edn 1798], Paris: J. A. Brosson.

—(1859) *Lettres de Pinel*. Paris: Maradin.

Pocock, J.G.A. (1985) *Virtue, Commerce, and History*, Cambridge: Cambridge University Press.

Polkinghorn, B. (1985) 'A Communication: an unpublished letter of J.B. Say', *Eastern Economic Journal*: 167–70.

Polowertzky, M. (1993) *A Bond Never Broken: the Relations Between Napoleon and the Authors of France*, Rutherford: Fairleigh Dickinson University Press.

Popkin, J. (1990) 'The press and the French Revoluton after two hundred years', *French Historical Studies* 16: 664–83.

—(1990) *Revolutionary News: the Press in France, 1789–1799*, Durham, NC: Duke University Press.

Pranchère, J.-Y. (1996) 'L'autorité contre les lumières: la philosophie de Joseph de Maistre', unpublished thesis, Université de Lille.

Pribram, K. (1983) *A History of Economic Reasoning*, Baltimore: Johns Hopkins Press.

Quantin, P. (1987) *Les Origines de l'Idéologie*, Paris: Oeconomia.

Ramsey, M. (1988) *Professional and Popular Medicine in France, 1770–1830*, Cambridge: Cambridge University Press.

Raymond, G.M. (1802) *Essai sur l'Émulation dans l'Order Social*, Geneva: J.J. Paschoud.

Régaldo, M. (1976) *Un Milieu Intellectuel: La Décade Philosophique (1794–1807)*, PhD thesis Paris IV, Paris and Lille: Atelier Reproduction des thèses, Université de Lille III.

Rendall, J. (1984) *The Origins of Modern Feminism: Women in Britain, France and the United States, 1780–1860*, New York: Schocken Books.

Resnick, D.P. (1973) 'Political economy and French anti-slavery: the case of J.-B. Say', in *The Proceedings of the Annual Meeting of the Western Society for French History* I: 199–213.

Reynaud, P.-L. (1953) 'Préface', in Say (1953).

Ricardo D. (1819) *Des Principes de l'Économie Politique et de l'Impôt* …, with notes by J.-B. Say, Paris.

—(1952 onwards) *The Works and Correspondance of David Ricardo*, P. Sraffa (ed.), Cambridge: Cambridge University Press.

Riese, W. (1969) *The Legacy of Philippe Pinel*, New York: Springer.

Robert, A. (ed.) (1989–90) *Dictionnaire de Parlementaires Français* , Paris: Bourloton.

Robespierre, M. (1965a) *Discours et Rapports à la Convention*, Paris: Union Générale d'Editions.

—(1965b) 'Sur les rapports des idées religieuses et morales avec les principes républicains, et sur les fêtes nationales. Rapport présenté au nom du Comité de Salut public' (18 Floréal an II [7 May 1794]), in M. Robespierre (ed.), *Discours et Rapports à la Convention*, Paris, Union Générale d'Editions: 270.

Robinson, D.N. (1981) *An Intellectual History of Psychology*, New York: Macmillan.

Robinson, J.A.T. (1957) *The Body: a Study in Pauline Theology*, London.

Roederer, P. (1853–9) *Oeuvres du Comte P.-L. Roederer*, A.-M. Roederer (ed.), Paris: Firmin Didot frères.

Roger, J. (1963) *Les Sciences de la Vie dans la Pensée Française du XVIIIe Siècle: la Génération des Animaux de Descartes à l'Encyclopédie*, Paris: A. Colin.

Roggi P. (1972) 'Sette lettere di J-B Say à J.C.L. Sismondi', *Rivista di politica economica* 963–79.

Roll, E. (1978) *A History of Economic Thought*, New York: Prentice-Hall.

Rosen, G. (1946) 'The philosophy of ideology and the emergence of modern medicine in France', *Bulletin of the History of Medicine*, 20: 328–39.

Rosenfield, L.C. (1968) *From Beast-Machine to Man-Machine – Animal Soul in French Letters from Descartes to La Mettrie*, 2nd edn, New York: Oxford University Press.

Ross, I. (1995) *The Life of Adam Smith*, Oxford: Clarendon.

Roussel, J. (ed.) (1988) *L'Héritage des Lumières: Volney et les Idéologues*, Angers: Presses Universitaires d'Angers.

Rousseau, J.J. (1964) *The First and Second Discourses*, trans. R.D. Masters and J.R. Masters, New York: St. Martin's Press.

—(1969) 'Julie, ou la nouvelle Héloïse [1762]', in *Oeuvres Complètes*, B. Gagnebin and M. Raymond (eds), Paris: Gallimard.

—(1973) *The Social Contract and Discourses* [1758], London: J.M. Dent and Sons.

—(1978) *On the Social Contract* [1762], trans. J.R. Masters, New York: St. Martin's Press.

—(1979) *Emile*, trans. A. Bloom, New York: Basic Books.

Rousseau, N. (1986) *Connaissance et Langage chez Condillac*, Geneva: Droz.

Roussel, P. (1775) *Système Physique et Morale de la Femme, ou Tableau Philosophique de la Constitution, de l'État Organique, du Tempérament, des Moeurs, et des Fonctions Propres au Sexe*, Paris: Vincent.

Rudé, G. (1959) *The Crowd in the French Revolution*, New York: Oxford University Press.

Sack, J.J. (1993) *From Jacobite to Conservative*, Cambridge: Cambridge University Press.

Sade, D.A.F. Marquis de (1988) *Juliette* [1797], trans. A. Wainhouse, New York: Grove Press.

Salerno, J.T. (1985) 'The influence of Cantillon's *Essai* on the methodology of J.B. Say: a comment on Liggio, Richard Cantillon and J.B. Say', *Journal of Libertarian Studies* 7: 305–16.

Say, Jean-Baptiste (1789) *De la Liberté de la Presse*, Paris.

—(1795) 'Quelques idées sur le projet de constitution de la commission des onze', *La Décade* [20 Messidor an III]: 79–90.

—(1796) 'Boniface Veridick à polyscope sur son projet de théatre pour le peuple' *La Décade* [10 Germinal an IV]: 38–44.

—(1800a) *Olbie, ou Essai sur les Moyens de Réformer les Moeurs d'une Nation*, Paris: Déterville.

—(1800b) 'Sciences sociales: compte rendu de Cabanis "quelques considérations sur l'organisation sociale en général et particulièrement sur la nouvelle constitution" ', *La Décade* [10 Nivôse an VIII]: 9–17.

—(1803) *Traité d'Économie Politique ou Simple Exposition de la Manière Dont se Forment, se Distribuent et se Consomment les Richesses*, 1st edn, Paris: Crapelet.

—(1814) *Traité d'Économie Politique*, 2nd edn, Paris: Déterville.

—(1815) *De l'Angleterre et des Anglais*, Paris: Arthus Bertrand.

—(1815) *Catéchisme d'Économie Politique ou Instruction Familière qui Montre de Quelle Façon les Richesses sont Produites, Distribuées et Consommées dans la Société; Ouvrage Fondé sur les Faits, et Utile aux Différents Classes d'Hommes, en ce qu'il Indique les Avantages que Chacun Peut Retirer de sa Position et de ses Talents*, 1st edn, Paris: Crapelet.

—(1817) *Petit Volume Contenant Quelques Aperçus des Hommes et de la Société*, Paris: Déterville.

—(1817) *Traité d'Économie Politique*, 3rd edn, Paris: Déterville.

—(1818) 'Lettre à Ternaux aîné', in Baron G.L. Ternaux *Mémoires sur les Moyens d'Assurer la Subsistance de la Ville de Paris par l'Établissement d'une Compagnie de Prévoyance*, Paris: Ballard.

—(1818) *Des Canaux de Navigation dans l'État Actuel de la France*, Paris: Déterville.

—(1818) *De l'Importance du Port de la Villette*, Paris: Déterville.

—(1819) *Traité d'Économie Politique*, 4th edn, Paris: Déterville.

—(1820) *Lettres à M Malthus sur Différents Sujets d'Économie Politique, Notamment sur les Causes de la Stagnation Générale du Commerce*, Paris: Bossange.

—(1821) *Catéchisme*, 2nd edn, Paris: Bossange.

—(1822) 'Compte rendu de brochures de la Society of the Friends of Peace', *Revue Encyclopédique*: 316–18.

—(1824) 'De la balance des consommations avec les productions', in Say (1848).

—(1824) 'De la première colonie formée par les américains en Afrique', *Revue Encyclopédique* 24: 5–18.

—(1824) 'Notions sur le Grèce pour l'intelligence des événements qui se préparent dans cette portion de l'Europe', *Revue Encyclopédique* 24.

—(1824) 'Essai historique sur l'origine, les progrès et les resultats probables de la souveraineté des Anglais aux Indes', *Revue Encyclopédique* 24.

—(1825) 'Examen critique du discours de M MacCulloch sur l'économie politique', in C. Comte, E. Daire and H. Say (eds) (1848), *Oeuvres Diverses de J.-B. Say*, Paris: Guillaumin.

—(1825) 'Compte rendu de C. Ganilh "De la science des finances et du ministère de M. de Villèle" ', *Revue Encyclopèdique*: 641–48.

—(1826) *Catéchisme*, 3rd edn, Paris: Aimé André.

—(1826) 'De l'économie politique moderne, esquisse générale de cette science, de sa nomenclature, de son histoire et de sa bibliographie', *Encyclopédie Progressive* I: 217–304.

—(1826) *Traité d'Économie Politique*, 5th edn, Paris: Calmann-Lévy.

—(1826) 'De la crise commerciale', *Revue Encyclopédique* 32: 40–5.

—(1827) 'Compte rendu de Malthus "Definitions in Political Economy" ', *Revue Encyclopédique* 33: 494–6.

—(1827) 'Réclamation à la "Revue Encyclopédique" ', *Revue Encyclopédique* 33: 559–60.

—(1827) *De l'Objet et d'Utilité des Statistiques*, Paris: Rignoux.

—(1828) 'Discours d'ouverture au cours d'économie industrielle', in C. Comte, E. Daire and H. Say (eds) (1848), *Oeuvres Diverses de J.-B. Say*, Paris: Guillaumin.

—(1828-9) *Cours Complet d'Économie Politique Pratique, Ouvrage Destiné à Mettre Sous les Yeux des Hommes d'Etat, des Propriétaires Fonciers et des Capitalistes, des Savants, des Agriculteurs, des Manufacturiers, des Négociants et en Général de Tous les Citoyens l'Économie des Sociétés*, Paris: Rapilly.

—(1843) *Cours Complet d'Économie Politique Pratique* [1822], 'entirely reviewed by the author and augmented with notes, edited by Horace Say, his son' and *Mélanges et Correspondance d'Économie Politique*, C. Comte (ed.), Brussels: Société typographique Belge.

—(1848) *Oeuvres Diverses de J.-B. Say*, C. Comte, E. Daire and H. Say (eds), Paris: Guillaumin.

—(1880) *A Treatise on Political Economy* [Philadelphia, 1880, based on Paris 1826], New York: Augustus M. Kelley, reprinted 1971.

—(1953) *Textes Choisis*, P.-L. Reynaud (ed.), Paris: Dalloz.

—(1992) 'Notes sur les principes de l'économie politique et de l'impôt de David Ricardo [1919]', in D. Ricardo *Principes de l'Économie Politique et de l'impôt*, Paris: Flammarion.

—(1996) *Cours d'Économie Politique et Autres Essais*, P. Steiner (ed.), Paris: Flammarion.

Sayers, J. (1982) *Biological Politics*, London: Tavistock.

Schlanger, J. (1971) *Les Métaphores de l'Organisme*, Paris: Vrin.

Schoorl, E. (1980) *J.B. Say*, Amsterdam: Coöp. Drukkerij PET u.a.

—(1982) 'Bentham, Say and continental utilitarianism', *The Bentham Newsletter*, 6: 8–18.

Schumpeter, J.A. (1954) *History of Economic Analysis*, E. Boody Schumpeter (ed.), New York: Harvard University Press.

Scott, J.W. (1988) *Gender and the Politics of History*, New York: Columbia University Press.

Servet, J.M. (ed.) (1989) *Idées Économiques sous la Révolution, 1789–1794*, Lyon: Presses Universitaires de Lyon.

Sèze, P.-V. de (1786) *Recherches Physiologiques et Philosophiques sur la Sensibilité ou la Vie Animale*, Paris: Prault.

Shapin, S. (1994) *A Social History of Truth: Gentility, Credibility and Scientific Knowledge in Seventeenth-Century England*, Chicago: University of Chicago Press.

—(1996) *The Scientific Revolution*, Chicago: University of Chicago Press.

Shattuck, R. (1996) *Forbidden Knowledge from Prometheus to Pornography*, New York: St. Martin's Press.

Shklar, J.N. (1969) *Men and Citizens: a Study of Rousseau's Social Theory*, Cambridge: Cambridge University Press.

Sieyès, E. (1985) *Écrits Politiques*, R. Zapperi (ed.), Paris: Éditions des Archives contemporaines.

Simon, J. (1885) *Une Académie sous le Directoire*, Paris: Calmann Lévy.

Simon, W.M. (ed.) (1972) *French Liberalism, 1789–1848*, New York: John Wiley & Sons.

Sismondi, J.C.L. Simonde de (1820) 'Examen de cette question: le pouvoir de consommer s'accroît-il dans la société avec le pouvoir de produire', in *Annales de Législation et de Jurisprudence*: 111–44.

—(1824) 'Sur la balance des consommations avec les productions', in Sismondi (1971) *Nouveaux Principes d'Économie Politique*, 2nd edn [1827], Paris: Calman-Lévy, pp. 343–69.

—(1837) *Études sur l'Économie Politique*, Paris: Treuttel et Wurtz.

—(1971) *Nouveaux Principes d'Économie Politique*, 2nd edn [1827], Paris: Calman-Lévy.

Skinner, A.S. (1967) 'Say's Law: origins and content', *Economica* 34: 153–66.

—(1979) *A System of Social Science: Papers Relating to Adam Smith*, Oxford: Oxford University Press.

Smith, A. (1798) *Théorie des Sentiments Moraux;* traduite de l'édition 7ième [1792] par Sophie de Grouchy, Marquise de Condorcet, avec *Considérations sur la Première Formation des Langues,* et un appendice 'huit lettres à Cabanis sur la sympathie', Paris: F. Buisson.

——(1802) *Recherches sur la Nature et les Causes de la Richesse des Nations,* trans. G. Garnier, Paris: H. Agasse.

——(1843) *Recherches sur la Nature et les Causes de la Richesse des Nations,* trans. G. Garnier, reviewed and corrected, with a bibliographic note by J.A. Blanqui and commentaries by Buchanan, G. Garnier, Macculloch, Malthus, J. Mill, Ricardo, Sismondi, augmented by notes of J.-B. Say, Paris: Guillaumin.

——(1976) *An Inquiry into the Nature and Causes of the Wealth of Nations* [1776], R.H. Campbell and A.S. Skinner (eds), Oxford: Oxford University Press.

——(1982) *Lectures on Jurisprudence,* R.L. Meek, D.D. Raphael and P.G. Stein (eds), Indianapolis: Liberty Fund. A reprint of the 1978 Glasgow edition, Oxford University Press.

——(1984) *The Theory of Moral Sentiments* [1759], D.D. Raphael and A.L. Macfie (eds), Indianapolis: Liberty Fund. A reprint of the 1976 Glasgow edition, Oxford University Press.

Solomon, J.R. (1997) *Objectivity in the Making, Francis Bacon and the Politics of Inquiry,* Baltimore: Johns Hopkins.

Sowell, T. (1972) *Say's Law: an Historical Analysis,* Princeton: Princeton University Press.

Spengler, J.J. (1945) 'The physiocrats and Say's law of markets', *Journal of Political Economy* 53: 193–211; 317–47.

——(1960) 'Richard Cantillon: first of the moderns', in J.J. Spengler and W.R. Allen (eds), *Essays in Economic Thought: Aristotle to Marshall,* Chicago: University of Chicago Press.

Starobinski, J. (1988) *Jean-Jacques Rousseau, Transparency and Obstruction,* trans. Goldhammer, Chicago: University of Chicago Press.

Staum, M.S. (1980a) *Cabanis: Enlightenment and Medical Philosophy in the French Revolution,* Princeton: Princeton University Press.

——(1980b) 'The class of Moral and Political Sciences, 1795–1803', *French Historical Studies* 2: 371–97.

——(1982) 'Images of paternal power: intellectuals and social change in the French National Institute', *Canadian Journal of History* 17: 425–45.

——(1985) 'The Enlightenment transformed: the Institute prize contests', *Eighteenth-Century Studies*: 153–79.

——(1985) 'Human, not secular Sciences: ideology in the Central Schools', *Historical Reflections/Réflexions Historiques* 12: 49–76.

——(1987) 'The Institute economists – from physiocracy to entrepreneurial capitalism', *History of Political Economy* 19: 525–50.

——(1996) *Minerva's Message, Stabilizing the French Revolution,* Montreal: McGill-Queen's University Press.

——(1998) 'French lecturers in political economy, 1815–1848: varieties of liberalism', *History of Political Economy* 30: 95–120.

Steinbrügge, L. (1995) *The Moral Sex, Woman's Nature in the French Enlightenment,* trans. P.E. Selwyn, New York: Oxford University Press.

Steiner P. (1987) 'J.-B. Say et l'enseignement de l'économie politique en France (1815–1832)', *Oeconomia*: 153–79.

—(1989) 'Intérêts sinistres et intérêts éclairés: problèmes du libéralisme chez J.-B. Say', *Cahiers d'Économie Politique*: 21–41.

—(1990) 'L'économie politique pratique contre les systèmes: quelques remarques sur la mèthode chez J.-B. Say', *Revue d'Économie Politique*: 664–87.

—(1991) 'Comment stabiliser l'ordre social moderne? J.-B. Say, l'économie politique et la Révolution', in G. Faccarello and P. Steiner (eds) *La Pensée Économique Pendant la Révolution Française*, Grenoble: Presses Universitaires de Grenoble.

—(1995) 'Quels principes pour l'économie politique? Charles Ganilh, Germain Garnier, Jean-Baptiste Say et la critique de la physiocratie', in B. Delmas, T. Demals and P. Steiner (eds) *La Diffusion Internationale de la Physiocratie (XVIIIe et XIXe siècles)*, Grenoble: Presses Universitaires de Grenoble.

—(1996a) 'L'économie politique comme science de la modernité', in Say *Cours d'Économie Politique et Autres Essais*, P. Steiner (ed.), Paris: Flammarion, pp. 9–35.

—(1996b) 'J.-B. Say et les colonies, ou comment se débarrasser d'un héritage intempestif?', in R. Demier and E. Diatkine (eds), *Le Libéralisme à l'Épreuve: Smith et l'Économie Coloniale*, Paris: Maison des Sciences de l'Homme.

—(1997) 'Politique et économie politique chez J.-B. Say', in *Revue Française d'Histoire des Idées Politiques*: 23–58.

—(1998a) 'Jean-Baptiste Say: the entrepreneur, the free trade doctrine and the theory of income distribution', in G. Faccarello (ed.) *Studies in the History of French Political Economy*, London: Routledge.

—(1998b) 'The structure of Say's economic writings', *European Journal of the History of Economic Thought*, 2: 227–49.

Stephens, W. (1922) *Women of the French Revolution*, New York: E.P. Dutton.

Stewart, D. (1858) *Biographical Memoir of Adam Smith* [1793], Edinburgh.

Stigler, G. (1965) *Essays in the History of Economics*, Chicago: University of Chicago Press.

Stimson, S.C. (1989) 'Republicanism and the recovery of the political', *Critical Issues in Social Thought*: 91–112.

Talleyrand-Périgord, C.-M. de (1791) *Rapport sur l'Instruction Publique*, Paris: Imprimerie nationale.

Talmon, J.L. (1960) *The Origins of Totalitarian Democracy*, New York: Praeger.

Taylor, W.L. (1965) *Francis Hutcheson and David Hume as Predecessors of Adam Smith*, North Carolina: Duke University Press.

Teilhac, E. (1927) *L'Oeuvre Économique de Jean-Baptiste Say*, Paris: Alcan.

Teysseire, D. (1989) 'Lien social et order politique chez Cabanis', *Studies on Voltaire and the Eighteenth Century* 267: 353–400.

Theocharis, R.D. (1983) *Early Developments in Mathematical Economics*, Philadelphia: Porcupine Press.

Thweatt, W.O. (1979) 'Early formulators of Say's Law', *Quarterly Review of Economics and Business* 19: 79–96.

—(1980) 'Baumol and James Mill on "Say's" Law of Markets', *Economica* 47: 467–9.

—(1980) 'Say's Law of Markets – comment', *Economica* 47: 467–9.

Tiran, A. (1993) 'Pietro Verri, aux origines de la théorie de la valeur et de la loi des débouchés de Jean-Baptiste Say', *Revue d'Économie Politique*: 445–71.

—(1995) 'Jean-Baptiste Say, manuscrits sur la monnaie, la banque et la finance (1767–1832)', *Cahiers Monnaie et Financement*: 1–229.

Tocqueville, A. de (1951) *Oeuvres Complètes*, Paris: Gallimard.

Tracy, A.L.-C. Destutt de (1790) *Translation of a Letter from Monsieur de Tracy, Member of the French National Assembly, to Mr. Burke, in Answer to his Remarks on the French Revolution*, London: J. Johnson.

—(1798a) 'Mémoire sur la faculté de penser', *Mémoires de l'Institut National des Sciences et Arts – Sciences Morales et Politiques*: 283–450.

—(1798b) 'Sur un système méthodique de bibliographie', *Gazette National, ou Moniteur* 8,9 (Brumaire): 151–2; 155–6.

—(1798c) *Quels sont les moyens de fonder la morale chez un peuple?*, Paris: H. Agasse.

—(1801a) *Projets d'Éléments d'Idéologie*, Paris: Didot.

—(1801b) Dissertation sur quelques questions d'idéologie. *Mémoires de l'Institut National des Sciences et Arts – Sciences Morales et politiques*: 491–514.

—(1801c) Dissertation sur l'existence, et sur les hypothèses de Mallebranche et de Berkeley à ce sujet. *Mémoires de l'Institut National des Sciences et Arts – Sciences Morales et Politiques*: 515–34.

—(1801d) 'Réflexions sur les projets de pasigraphie', *Mémoires de l'Institut National des Sciences et Arts – Sciences Morales et Politiques*: 535–51.

—(1803) 'De la métaphysique de Kant, ou observations sur un ouvrage intitulé "Essai d'exposition succinte de la critique de la raison pur" ', *Mémoires de l'Institute National des Sciences et Arts – Sciences Morales et Politiques:* 544–606.

—(1804) *Analyse Raisonné de l'Origine de Tous les Cultes ou Religion Universelle; Ouvrage Publié en l'An III par Dupuis, Citoyen Français*, Paris: Courcier.

—(1817) *A Treatise on Political Economy; to Which is Prefixed a Supplement to a Preceding Work on the Understanding, or Elements of Ideology, with an Analytical Table, and an Introduction on the Faculty of the Will*, trans. T. Jefferson, Georgetown, Washington DC: Joseph Milligan.

—(1817–18) *Elémens d'Idéologie*, Paris: Courcier [reprinted 1970, Paris: J. Vrin].

—(1819) *Commentaire sur 'l'Esprit des Lois' de Montesquieu*, Paris: Desoer.

—(1825) 'Observations sur le système actuel d'instruction publique' [an IX], in *Elémens d'Idéologie*, vol. II, Paris: Veuve Courcier, pp. 325–95.

—(1825) 'Pièces relatives à l'instruction publique', in *Elémens d'Idéologie*, vol. II, Paris: Veuve Courcier, pp. 261–324.

—(1825) *Élémens d'Idéologie*, 4 vols, Paris: Veuve Courcier.

—(1826) *Élémens d'Idéologie*, 5 vols, Brussels: A Wahlen.

—(1926) *De l'Amour*, G. Chinard (ed.), Paris: Les Belles Lettres.

—(1970) *Élémens d'Idéologie. I. Idéologie Proprement Dite* [1817], Paris: Vrin.

—(1970) *Élémens d'Idéologie. II. Grammaire* [1817], Paris: Vrin.

—(1970) *A Treatise on Political Economy* [Georgetown, 1917], New York: Augustus M. Kelley.

—(1984) *Traité de la Volonté et de ses Effets* [2nd edn 1818], Geneva: Slatkine. Also in Deneys and Deneys-Tunney (eds), *Corpus No. 26–27: A.-L.-C. Destutt de Tracy*.

Tucker, J. (1931) *A Selection from his Economic and Political Writings* [1756], New York: Columbia University Press.

Van Duzer, C.H. (1935) *Contribution of the Ideologues to French Revolutionary Thought*, Baltimore: Johns Hopkins University Press.

Van Kley, D.K. (1991) 'New wine in old wineskins: continuity and rupture in the pamphlet debate of the French prerevolution, 1787–1789', *French Historical Studies* 17: 447–65.

Venturi, F. (1971) *Utopia and Reform in the Enlightenment*, Cambridge: Cambridge University Press.

Vernon, R. (1986) *Citizenship and Order*, Toronto: University of Toronto Press.

Véron de Forbonnais, F. (1767) *Principes et Observations Économiques*, Amsterdam: M.M. Rey.

Vicq d'Azyr, F. (1805) *Oeuvres de Vicq d'Azyr*, J.L. Moreau (ed.), Paris: L. Dupont-Duverger.

Vignery, R.J. (1965) *The French Revolution and the Schools – Educational Policies of the Mountain 1792–1794*. Madison: University of Wisconsin Press.

Vila, A. (1997) *Enlightenment and Pathology, Sensibility in the Literature and Medicine of 18th Century France*. Baltimore: Johns Hopkins Press.

Viner, J. (1958) *The Long View and the Short*, Glencoe, IL: The Free Press.

Volney, C.-F. (1791) *Les Ruines, ou Méditation sur les Révolutions des Empires*, in Volney (1820) *Oeuvres Complètes*, A. Bossange (ed.), Paris: Bossange frères.

—(1820) *Oeuvres Complètes*, A. Bossange (ed.), Paris: Bossange frères.

—(1980) *La Loi Naturelle/Leçons d'Histoire* [1793, 1795], J. Gaulmier (ed.), Paris: Garnier Frères.

Voutsinas, D. (1964) *La Psychologie de Maine de Biran*, Paris: SIPE.

Vyverberg, H. (1989) *Human Nature, Cultural Diversity and the French Enlightenment*, New York: Oxford University Press.

Walras, L. (1952) *Eléments d'Économie Politique Pure*, 4th edn, trans. W. Jaffé, Homewood, IL: R. D. Irwin.

Waterman, A.M.C. (1994) ' "The grand scheme of subordination": the intellectual foundations of the Tory Doctrine', *The Australian Journal of Politics and History*, 40: 121–33.

—(1996) 'The nexus between theology and political doctrine in church and dissent', in K. Haakonssen (ed.) *Enlightenment and Rational Dissent*, Cambridge: Cambridge University Press.

Weintraub, K.J. (1966) *Visions of Culture*, Chicago: University of Chicago Press.

Welch, C. (1984) *Liberty and Utility: the French Idéologues and the Transformation of Liberalism*, New York: Columbia University Press.

Whatmore, R. (1998) 'Everybody's business: Jean-Baptiste Say's "general fact" conception of political economy', *History of Political Economy* 30: 430–68.

Wilkie, E.C. Jr (1984) 'Mercier's *L'An 2440*: its publishing history during the author's lifetime', *Harvard Library Bulletin* 32: 5–31; 348–400.

Willey, B. (1961) *The Eighteenth Century Background – Studies on the Idea of Nature in the Thought of the Period*, Cambridge, MA: Harvard University Press.

Williams, D. (1935) 'The influence of Rousseau on political opinion, 1760–1795', *English Historical Review* 48: 414–30.

Williams, E.A. (1994) *The Physical and the Moral: Anthropology, Physiology, and Philosophical Medicine in France, 1750–1850*, Cambridge: Cambridge University Press.

Williams, L.P. (1953) 'Science, education and the French Revolution', *Isis* 44: 311–30.

—(1956) 'Science, education, and Napoleon I', *Isis* 47: 369–82.

—(1959) 'The politics of science in the French Revolution', in M. Clagett (ed.) *Critical Problems in the History of Science*, Madison: University of Wisconsin Press.

Winch, D. (ed.) (1966) *James Mill: Selected Economic Writings*, Edinburgh: Oliver and Boyd.

—(1978) *Adam Smith's Politics*, Cambridge: Cambridge University Press.

—(1983) 'Science and the legislator: Adam Smith and after', *Economic Journal* 93: 501–20.

—(1991) 'Adam Smith's politics revisited', *Quaderni di Storia dell'Economia Politica* 9: 3–27.

—(1996) *Riches and Poverty*, Cambridge: Cambridge University Press.

Wollstonecraft, M. (1792) *A Vindication of the Rights of Woman*, London: J.J. Johnson.

Wrigley, E.A. (1987) 'The classical economists and the industrial revolution', in *People, Cities and Wealth*, Oxford: Oxford University Press.

—(1988) *Continuity, Chance and Change*, Cambridge: Cambridge University Press.

Zerilli, L.M.G. (1991) 'Machiavelli's sisters: women and "the conversation" of political theory', *Political Theory* 19: 252–76.

—(1994) *Signifying Woman: Culture and Chaos in Rousseau, Burke and Mill*, Ithaca: Cornell University Press.

Index

Some titles of works are abbreviated. References to notes are not indexed.

For Product Safety Concerns and Information please contact our EU
representative GPSR@taylorandfrancis.com Taylor & Francis Verlag GmbH,
Kaufingerstraße 24, 80331 München, Germany

Printed and bound by CPI Group (UK) Ltd, Croydon, CR0 4YY
08/05/2025
01864502-0001